ReFocus: The Films of Xavier Dolan

ReFocus

ReFocus: The International Directors Series

Series Editors: Robert Singer, Stefanie Van de Peer and Gary D. Rhodes

ReFocus is a series of contemporary methodological and theoretical approaches to the interdisciplinary analyses and interpretations of international film directors, from the celebrated to the ignored, in direct relationship to their respective culture—its myths, values, and historical precepts—and the broader parameters of international film history and theory. The series provides a forum for introducing a broad spectrum of directors, working in and establishing movements, trends, cycles and genres including those historical, currently popular, or emergent, and in need of critical assessment or reassessment. It ignores no director who created a historical space—either in or outside of the studio system—beginning with the origins of cinema and up to the present. *ReFocus* brings these film directors to a new audience of scholars and general readers of Film Studies.

Titles in the series include:

ReFocus: The Films of Susanne Bier
Edited by Missy Molloy, Mimi Nielsen, and Meryl Shriver-Rice

ReFocus: The Films of Corneliu Porumboiu
Monica Filimon

ReFocus: The Films of Francis Veber
Keith Corson

ReFocus: The Films of Andrei Tarkovsky
Sergei Toymentsev

ReFocus: The Films of Jia Zhangke
Maureen Turim and Ying Xiao

ReFocus: The Films of Xavier Dolan
Edited by Andrée Lafontaine

edinburghuniversitypress.com/series/refocint

ReFocus:
The Films of Xavier Dolan

Edited by Andrée Lafontaine

EDINBURGH
University Press

Edinburgh University Press is one of the leading university presses in the UK. We publish
academic books and journals in our selected subject areas across the humanities and social
sciences, combining cutting-edge scholarship with high editorial and production values
to produce academic works of lasting importance. For more information visit our website:
edinburghuniversitypress.com

Edinburgh University Press Ltd
The Tun—Holyrood Road
12(2f) Jackson's Entry
Edinburgh EH8 8PJ

First published in hardback by Edinburgh University Press 2019

Typeset in 11/13 Ehrhardt MT by
IDSUK (DataConnection) Ltd, and
printed and bound by CPI Group (UK) Ltd,
Croydon, CR0 4YY

A CIP record for this book is available from the British Library

ISBN 978 1 4744 4457 6 (hardback)
ISBN 978 1 4744 4458 3 (paperback)
ISBN 978 1 4744 4459 0 (webready PDF)
ISBN 978 1 4744 4460 6 (epub)

Contents

Figures

Notes on Contributors

Mercédès Baillargeon is assistant professor of French and Francophone Studies in the School of Languages, Literatures, and Cultures at the University of Maryland. Her book, *Le Personnel est politique: Médias, esthétique et politique de l'autofiction chez Christine Angot, Chloé Delaume et Nelly Arcan*, was published in 2019 by Purdue University Press. She has published several articles on third-wave feminism, contemporary women's writing and first-person narrative, and Québec cinema, including a special issue of the journal *Contemporary French Civilization*, co-edited with Karine Bertrand (Queen's University, Kingston) on the transnationalism of Québec cinema and (new) media. Her current research explores the question of (post)nationalism in Québec cinema of the new millennium.

Liz Czach is associate professor in the Department of English and Film Studies at the University of Alberta (Edmonton, Canada). She researches and publishes in the areas of film festivals, home movies, and amateur film, and Québec and Canadian film. She was a programmer of Canadian film at the Toronto International Film Festival from 1995 to 2005. She is currently co-editing, with André Loiselle, *Cinema of Pain: On Quebec's Nostalgic Screen*.

Pascal Gagné is a doctoral candidate at the Institute of Feminist and Gender Studies, University of Ottawa (Canada). Pascal's research and publications focus on queer theory, collective memory, and affect. He has previously worked for associations promoting LGBTQ rights, HIV/AIDS awareness, and agencies supporting people with developmental disabilities to live in the community. His doctoral studies are funded by the Social Science and Humanities Research Council.

Florian Grandena is associate professor in the Department of Communication at the University of Ottawa (Canada). He has published numerous
articles on contemporary queer-themed French feature films, and is preparing
a book on the films of Olivier Ducastel and Jacques Martineau. Together with
Cristina Johnston (University of Stirling, UK), he is the co-editor of *New Queer
Images: Representations of Homosexualities in Francophone Visual Cultures*, and
*Cinematic Queerness: Gay and Lesbian Hypervisibility in Contemporary Franco-
phone Feature Films* (Peter Lang, 2011).

Andrée Lafontaine is Assistant Professor of Anglophone Literature and
Culture at the University of Tsukuba (Japan). She received a PhD in Film
and Moving Image Studies from Concordia University (Montréal, Québec),
and has previously worked at Aichi University. She was Managing Editor of
Synoptique—An Online Journal of Film and Moving Image Studies, and has
published in the *International Journal of Applied Psychoanalytic Studies*, and
the *Canadian Journal of Film Studies*.

Bill Marshall has held posts in French Studies at the Universities of South-
ampton, Glasgow, and Stirling, and was Director of the Institute of Modern
Languages Research in the School of Advanced Study, University of London,
2011–14. Professor Marshall's published works include *Quebec National Cinema* (McGill-Queen's University Press, 2001), *André Téchiné* (Manchester
University Press, 2007), and *The French Atlantic: Travels in Culture and History* (2009).

Fulvia Massimi holds a PhD in Film and Moving Image Studies from Concordia University (Montréal, Québec) and was a member of the editorial board
of *Synoptique: An Online Journal of Film and Moving Image Studies*. Her research
focuses on local and global understandings of gender and nationhood in the cinemas of Québec, Flanders, and Scotland. Under the supervision of Tom Waugh,
her dissertation examines the renegotiation of male representations and national
identities in current subnational film industries and imaginaries, notably in the
films of Xavier Dolan. Her entry on Queer Canadian cinema, co-authored with
Tom Waugh, is forthcoming in *The Oxford Handbook of Canadian Cinema* (2019).

Navaneetha Mokkil is assistant professor at the Centre for Women's Studies,
Jawaharlal Nehru University, New Delhi. Her areas of research include print
and visual cultures in India, public formations of sexuality, and transnational
circuits of world cinema. She completed her PhD in English and Women's
Studies from the University of Michigan (Ann Arbor) in 2010. She is the author
of *Unruly Figures: Queerness, Sex Work and the Politics of Sexuality in Kerala*
(2019). Her articles on the non-linear imaginations of sexuality in Indian

cinema have appeared in the journals *Inter Asia Cultural Studies* and *South Asian Popular Culture*.

Marie Pascal holds a PhD in Québec Literature and Film from the University of Toronto (Canada), where she wrote a dissertation titled "Les figures du paria et du marginal dans la transcréation québécoise." Her research focuses on transmedia analysis and narrativity in film and literature, and figures of negative alterity in francophone literature and film. She has recently contributed entries for the *Literary Encyclopedia* (on Anne Hébert's *Les Fous de Bassan* and *Kamouraska* and G. Bessette's *Le Libraire*), and published in *Contact, Classiques Garnier, Les Cahiers du GRELCEF*, and *Études françaises*.

Julianne Pidduck is associate professor at the Department of Communication, Université de Montréal. She has published widely on topics related to gender, sexuality, and the moving image. Author of *Contemporary Costume Film* (2004) and a short monograph on Patrice Chéreau's *La Reine Margot* (2005), her essays have appeared in scholarly journals including *Camera Obscura, Screen, GLQ, Studies in French Cinema, Jump Cut, Media Culture and Society*, and the *Canadian Journal of Film Studies*. Her current research explores the conditions of LGBTQ visibility in Québec film and video from the Quiet Revolution to the present.

Nick Rees-Roberts is Professor of Media and Cultural Studies at the Sorbonne Nouvelle Université—Paris 3. He is the author of *French Queer Cinema* (2008/2014) and *Fashion Film: Art and Advertising in the Digital Age* (2018), co-author of *Homo exoticus: race, classe et critique queer* (2010), and co-editor of *Alain Delon: Style, Stardom, and Masculinity* (2015).

Acknowledgments

I would like to offer my thanks to the series editors, Gary D. Rhodes and Robert Singer, for wholeheartedly embracing the project and for offering precious advice, and to the authors of this volume, whose insights and passion have pushed the book to completion. This project emerged from the immense pleasure and emotional impact provided by Dolan's films and a keen desire to delve deeper into Dolanian cinema's appeal to a vast audience. Dolan's cinema is solidly anchored in local specificity and yet, despite this (or more precisely *because* of this) it has resonated deeply across the globe. Since one of my aims has been to highlight Dolan's international appeal, I am particularly pleased to have received proposals from several countries, and from scholars working with various methodological approaches and frameworks.

I also wish to thank a number of people who have contributed their time, acumen, and energy: Julianne Pidduck, Antoine Damiens, Laurent Mellet, and Ger Zielinski. I would like to thank *Nottingham French Studies* for allowing us to reprint Bill Marshall's chapter, "Spaces and Times of Québec in Films by Xavier Dolan," and various permission holders for letting us reprint film stills and publicity pictures. My work on Dolan began some five years ago, when I co-edited with Kester Dyer and Fulvia Massimi a special issue of *Synoptique* on the Québécois filmmaker, while we were pursuing our PhDs. In many ways, this book is a continuation of that initial work and I am therefore indebted to both.

Finally, my deepest gratitude goes to my partner Ondrej Hlavacek for his indefatigable work copy-editing and proofreading the final manuscript. Without his moral and administrative support, and his command of the *Chicago Manual of Style*, this book might not have seen the light of day.

Film and Video Work by Xavier Dolan

J'ai tué ma mère/I Killed My Mother, 2009
Les Amours imaginaires/Heartbeats, 2010
Laurence Anyways, 2012
Indochine: College Boy, music video, 2013
Tom à la ferme/Tom at the Farm, 2013
Mommy, 2014
Adele: Hello, music video, 2015
Juste la fin du monde/It's Only the End of the World, 2016
The Death and Life of John F. Donovan, 2018
Matthias et Maxime/Matthias & Maxime, 2019

Introduction

Andrée Lafontaine

His name is Xavier Dolan; he's showing his first feature film, shot when he was 19, written when he was 17, and he stars in it. He financed the film himself, and fought like the devil to give birth to it.[1]

I come from a big place where people dream small.[2]

You don't have your whole life ahead of you. That's just an excuse to procrastinate.[3]

"Wunderkind," boy wonder," "young prodigy," "*enfant terrible*." From his very first directorial attempt (he had not even made a short yet!), the press struggled to conjure up enough laudatory words to shower over the young director hailing from Québec. Soon, however, hints of back-handedness and condescension began to appear in many of these compliments: "*notre surdoué*" (our overachiever), "Sun King," "darling child," "*notre génie du 7ᵉ art*" (our genius of the seventh art), "our little national genius." It was not long before the first use of the inevitable slur "spoiled child"—a typical recrimination directed at the "selfie generation." Within a few years, the director of complicated love/hate relationships, who claims to have never known love as something tender, had managed to foster a similar kind of relationship with the media.[4]

While some applauded the fact that Dolan was "*décomplexé*"—how he represented a generation that had finally rid itself of its inferiority complex—others read it as arrogance and entitlement. In a society where the Catholic Church extolled virtues of humility and poverty, celebrating someone's success has never been an easy affair. Though critics were quick to add that his talents as a filmmaker were undeniable, what unsettled them was not his films but his personality. First, there was the hair (Figure I.1), which, because it was

Figure I.1 Xavier Dolan, early promotional portrait. Courtesy of Ixion Communications.

"released" to public scrutiny weeks before his first film, ended up taking center stage, prompting archaic calls to "just cut it already." Then, it was his supposed narcissism (he made biographical films in which he starred), arrogance (he credited his success to his hard work and determination), and emotionality. Finally, it was his politics: never shy of speaking out, Dolan's public stances and numerous feuds ignited the columnists' fires and generated negative press. From his early support of the 2012 Québec student strike to marriage equality in France, Dolan developed a reputation for not only eloquently speaking his mind, but, more importantly, for generating a great deal of publicity for and attention to the issues at hand. Needless to say, not everyone was a fan. How dare he use his platform to express views outside his realm of expertise? How dare he talk back? How dare he speak in English at Cannes? How dare he talk about the working class? How dare he accept a modeling contract for a luxury brand? How dare he?

Dolan became, in fact, an early casualty of nascent "millennial bashing"— blaming the millennial generation for everything that is wrong with society, from falling sales of diamonds, mayonnaise, and designer handbags to killing the paper napkin and fabric softener industries.[5] In the face of such accusations, Dolan certainly did not turn the other cheek, and instead engaged in public epistolary exchanges, which only further enflamed those who believed the director should be seen and not heard. Despite his young age, however, there is little doubt that Dolan has a recognizable signature, earning him the undisputed (and somewhat slippery) moniker of *auteur*.

"NEVER A DULL MOMENT" WITH XAVIER

The use of the term "auteur" to designate certain film directors emerged in France with the *ciné-fils* of the *Cahiers du Cinéma* in the late 1940s and early 50s, and was later popularized in the UK through the periodical *Movie* and Peter Wollen's *Signs and Meaning in the Cinema* (1969), and in the United States with Andrew Sarris's essay "Notes on the auteur theory" (1962) and subsequent *American Cinema* (1968). Auteur theory was originally meant to have two chief functions. First, it served to distinguish great film directors (auteurs) from mediocre craftsmen (*metteurs en scène* or contract directors) of commercial cinema. Not all film directors are true auteurs. To qualify, one must display recurring themes or visual tropes, specific elements that make the viewer say, for instance, "this is a Spike Lee movie" or a "Woody Allen movie." Alfred Hitchcock is a classic example, as the director's obsessions (cold blondes, strangulation, guilt) and fears (falling, police officers) span his entire career. Similarly, Pedro Almodóvar's maximalist esthetic and vibrant colors make him a good candidate for auteur status. The second function, then, was to elevate these great auteur directors to the status of "artist," on a par with great writers, painters, and sculptors, thereby justifying the serious study of film.

Within the discipline of film studies, the exact meaning of auteur theory, and the importance it should have in the study of film, has shifted through the years. At its most over-deterministic point, auteur theory turned film studies into auteur studies, with films not exhibiting the auteur's idiosyncrasies taking a back seat. At its most romantic, auteurists elevated a handful of directors to the realm of high art geniuses. At its most inquisitive, auteur theory turned the critic into a detective with propensities toward psychoanalysis, approaching each film as a Rorschachian window into the director's soul. And at its most unreflective, auteur theory resulted in, to quote Pauline Kael, "glorifying trash." Detractors of auteurism have pointed out that to treat films as the product of a sole creator, when so many minds, eyes, and hands, not to mention wallets, contribute to the final product, seems misguided and overly simplistic.[6] Additionally, as Gerstner and Staiger have argued, auteurist approaches rob filmmakers—the makers of the film—of credit due.[7] A case often cited to show how auteurism attributes too great an artistic contribution to the director is Frank Capra. Capra championed what he called the "one man, one film" approach, a proto-auteurist approach where a single creative vision oversaw all aspects of the film. Among the many attributes of the Capra signature are his small town optimism and idealistic common-man-turned-hero, best exemplified in *Mr. Smith Goes to Washington* (1939), *Meet John Doe* (1941), and *Mr. Deeds Goes to Town* (1936). The heroes of these films, in fact, became widely known as "Capra-heroes" and "Capraesque." However, Joseph McBride points out in his 1992 biography of the film director that it is Robert Riskin—Capra's screenwriter and close collaborator—who should largely be credited for the development of this "Capra hero." Not only did the Capraesque hero align more closely with Riskin's politics (Riskin was a liberal Democrat, Capra a conservative Republican) but he disappeared from Capra's oeuvre after their falling out in 1939.[8]

As Tom Gunning notes, in the early years of cinema, "the concept of the director as a unifying force was not a factor."[9] During the following years of the studio era, as Jerome Christensen has argued, it in fact makes more sense to speak of studio authorship, since directors were, more often than not, hired hands, and filmmaking was a "corporate" art. To this day, many (some would say most) working directors succeed by being good workhorses, not by articulating a unique, personal vision, to create *profitable*, not memorable, films.

If anyone fits the auctorial bill today, however, it certainly is Xavier Dolan. From his very first film, *J'ai tué ma mère* (2009), critics noted the burgeoning filmmaker's signature. *J'ai tué* was a product of sheer stubborn determination, conceived outside the film industry and produced on its margins. As a result, it was largely undisturbed by external meddling and displayed a vast array of "imperfections" and authorial idiosyncrasies. Watching the final credits of any Dolan film, one quickly notices the extent of his involvement in each film, as his name is likely to appear under any heading: wardrobe department and costume design, art department, editing and montage, but also subtitling—he wrote the English subtitles for *Tom à la ferme* (2013), *Mommy* (2014), and *Juste la fin du monde* (2016)—and dubbing.

To approach Xavier Dolan as an auteur and to approach his films through auteur theory is in no way meant to deny the contribution of other collaborators. Among them, cinematographer André Turpin has no doubt played a significant role in the development of a Dolanian signature aesthetic. In addition to Turpin, a coterie of recurring actresses and actors has now become associated with Dolan's filmic universe, Anne Dorval and Suzanne Clément being the most memorable (see Julianne Pidduck's chapter in this volume). Rather than a signature, however, it may be more productive to speak of a "Dolanian sensibility."

DOLANIAN SENSIBILITY

Dolan's sensibility can perhaps be best summed up with one word: intimacy. Both in terms of thematic concerns and aesthetics, Dolan creates an intimate cinema. His films often concern the intricacies of human relations and close family relationships—often too close in fact—with significant screen time devoted to scenes occurring inside family homes. To emphasize the feeling of intimacy and closeness, Dolan favors tight framing and extreme close-ups, too close and too tight for some. *Mommy*'s much talked about 1:1 aspect ratio encased the mother-son duo in unyielding claustrophobia. Similarly, *Juste la fin du monde*'s extreme close-ups effectively recreate the family reunion from hell that many of us have had the displeasure to experience at one point or another.

At the center of Dolan's cinematic families are fascinating, complex, strong, and vulnerable mothers and their sons. From the flawed and emotionally bruised Chantale (Anne Dorval; *J'ai tué ma mère*) to the indomitable force of nature that is Die (also Dorval; *Mommy*), to the emotionally detached Julienne (Nathalie Baye; *Laurence Anyways*, 2012), to the raw lover-turned-stalker (Anne-Élizabeth Bossé; *Les Amours imaginaires*, 2010), Dolan excels in creating larger than life female characters. The director has often repeated that he feels close to women and their struggle, and that their struggle and refusal to back down, to keep fighting, is a source of inspiration.[10]

Mimicking the intensity and irrational aspects of these relationships, Dolan's approach seeks to create emotionally powerful, rather than cerebral, films. True to the melodramatic mode, all components of the film—music, lighting, performance, etc.—are directed at augmenting the film's emotional charge. In this sense, his films reflect his own tastes in cinema: he likes to be taken for a ride, and he likes to take his viewers on emotional rides. This penchant for high drama has certainly also been the director's Achilles heel, with *Juste la fin du monde* being widely criticized for its screeching "shoutyness." For Dolan, the shouting matches that abound in his films work hand in hand with other components of the films to serve a cathartic, therapeutic, purpose:

> Movies are about what I'm missing. Not what's missing from my life— what I'm missing in a nostalgic way, what I miss from when I was a kid. The textures, the colors, they're all things that I miss. All these movies are poured out of nostalgia, and so are these songs. They send us back to the precise moments where we first heard that song, where we made out to that song, where we had a breakup to that song. You soak it in and you never forget these things and suddenly you're in a dark theater room with all these people and you have nothing to do with this film, you didn't write this film. But here's our chance as the creators of the film to have you contribute to the story that we're telling because suddenly when you hear this song, it's your emotions, it's your sensibility, it's your memory of when your dad was rough, it's the pleasure you have when you think of the aunt who would always give you candies and that song would be playing in the background. It's all of these things and suddenly, you become a writer of the film and we're writing it together . . . The beautiful thing about directing films is that people take the work and insert it into their own lives in a moment of need, or in a moment of growth. The movie does not belong to you anymore—it become[s] their property.[11]

Along with color, music in Dolan's films serves to heighten emotions as well as propel the story. Unbothered by the tireless, and repetitive criticism, Dolan cuts through the politics of taste to showcase songs with high emotional impact and imbued with memories of a not-so-distant past. Once in their new context, these "tacky," "unrefined" songs take on a new life outside of social judgments of taste (Céline Dion's "On ne change pas" being the best example for most Québécois viewers, but Dido's "White Flag" also being a good example). In his own way, Dolan thereby embraces a camp aesthetic by recovering the pleasure of these "tacky," popular objects. Defying commonly accepted hierarchies of taste, Dolan's music-driven cinema uses all elements of mise-en-scène to intensify emotions, and create in viewers a visceral, cathartic experience. Dolan's is an explosive, raw cinema with few dull moments, much like the filmmaker himself.

BIRTHED AT CANNES: *J'AI TUÉ MA MÈRE*

A talented, if not avid, self-promoter, Dolan has excelled at disseminating a coherent life narrative. Born on March 20, 1989 in Montréal—Québec's largest city and the world's second largest primarily francophone (French-speaking) metropolis after Paris—Dolan-Tadros (as he was known back then) was raised in suburban Longueuil (on the south shore of the St Lawrence river, across from the Island of Montreal) by his mother from the age of two, after his parents divorced. While his father, Egyptian-born Manuel Tadros, was a successful singer (in the late 1970s), songwriter (in the 1980s and 1990s), voice actor, and actor (still working today), Geneviève Dolan worked as a school administrator. Of his father, Dolan has almost nothing to say. Talk about his youth inevitably circles back to his mother, aunts, grandmother, and, later, his numerous "surrogate mothers." By his accounts, Dolan was raised by women—solely women. Even the teacher, who played a crucial role in his life by encouraging and supporting his writing, was a woman. And yet, Dolan's father remains a constant figure in the background. Dolan's production company, "Sons of Manuel," was named as a nod to his father. He has also cast him in four brief yet memorable roles: a landlord in *J'ai tué ma mère* and *Laurence Anyways*, a bartender in *Tom à la ferme* and Salim in *The Death and Life of John F. Donovan*. He might be Dolan's father, but he systematically gets cast as non-family members, and characters associated with work and the outside world.

Although his father was involved in Montréal's entertainment industry, Dolan credits his aunt—who also worked in film—for casting him, at the age of four, in his first role in the miniseries *Miséricorde* (Jean Beaudin, 1994). From then on, Dolan appeared in a number of secondary roles in film and television as well as local and national commercials—notably a multi-commercial campaign for national pharmacy giant Jean Coutu. Of these early days on set,

Dolan reports asking many questions, learning the craft of filmmaking, one director even predicting that one day he'd be sitting in the director's chair.[12]

From the age of seven, Dolan was sent to two boarding schools, in an attempt by his mother to deal with his erratic and violent behavior. While his writing skills were nurtured under the tutelage of a devoted teacher, who encouraged him to turn his autobiographic novel, *Le Matricide*, into a film (it would later serve as the basis for *J'ai tué ma mère*), Dolan appears to have little else positive to say about his education. In fact, he has been a vocal critic of Québec's education system, reports having been bullied in school, and calls himself a dropout, "ashamed of his lack of education."

Aged seventeen, Dolan decided to leave college, where, after a week of attendance, he felt he was wasting his time. His mind was on making *J'ai tué ma mère*, and he needed to make it right away. Thanks to numerous interviews and press junkets, the production details of *J'ai tué* are well known. Undeterred by the funding agencies' rejections (partly because he had little to show them, having no formal training or experience) and unwilling to wait, Dolan decided to self-finance the film by investing his acting earnings. He approached Anne Dorval (Chantale Lemming) on a set, gave her the script, and began courting her. Dorval initially refused the role, telling Dolan the script needed work. Undeterred, Dolan diligently followed her advice and fixed the script. According to Dorval, it is precisely this dogged determination and hard work that won her over. The film would end up being produced on a meager $800,000 budget, some of which was eventually contributed by the SODEC, Québec's film funding agency, after shooting was interrupted for lack of money.

J'ai tué tells the universal story of teenage rebellion, of the highly volatile relationship between an immature son who believes himself an adult and his exasperated, often unbearable mother. The film opens with Hubert (Dolan) stating bluntly that he no longer loves his mother, follows their constant bickering, and ends with Hubert being sent to boarding school. Despite this rather depressing premise, the film is anything but. Instead, the filmmaker pokes fun at Chantale (chiefly, at her tastes and fashion; see Liz Czach's chapter), but also at Hubert, whose histrionics end up exasperating even his boyfriend. For most of the film, Hubert and Chantale are involved in a no holds barred verbal boxing match. Dolan may be punishing his mother with this film, but the cruelty of Hubert's tirades, coupled with Chantale's stoicism and painfully wounded facial expressions, brings us back into her corner. The film seesaws viewer sympathy away from Hubert in scenes of unbearable childishness, only to follow up with Chantale's blatant forgetfulness and questionable tastes, moving us back into Hubert's corner. Throughout the film, the spectator is cast in the role of referee, continually called upon to take sides, shifting allegiances, and ultimately declaring a tie between two sympathetic yet deeply flawed individuals.

Having been selected for the Quinzaine des réalisateurs—alongside *Poly-technique* and *Carcasses*, by fellow Québec filmmakers Denis Villeneuve and Denis Côté, all initially made without money from the Canadian government—*J'ai tué ma mère* premiered at Cannes to much media fanfare in Québec and in France, where major publications such as *Libération* and *Le Figaro* seemed to trip over themselves in their eagerness for a chance to interview the newcomer. Afterward, the federal funding agency, Telefilm Canada, came under fire for its lack of flair in privileging a series of commercial films that turned out to be monumental flops and rejecting celebrated and successful auteur productions. Dolan quickly became the face—and the voice—of a type of auteur cinema neglected by profit-seeking funding agencies. Using his new platform Dolan thanked moviegoers and chastised funding agencies, declaring "a public has confirmed the possibility of an independent Québec cinema, a cinema that survives well-intentioned but mercantile institutions. These institutions impose, to the public and to filmmakers, standards which underestimate people's intelligence and erase our identity." With these words, Dolan—a director unknown to everyone only a few weeks earlier, and the author of a film which had not even screened in Québec yet—opened a dialogue of sorts on the mandate of government funding agencies.[13]

Prior to the film's premiere, Québec media were peppered with snippets introducing the public to the young unknown. Published in the daily *Le Devoir*, a series of columns by film critic Odile Tremblay were instrumental in establishing Dolan's media presence and getting the early word out on the director's debut oeuvre. Tremblay was perhaps the first to introduce Dolan to the world with an article published in late 2008 documenting *J'ai tué ma mère*'s shoot.[14] By April, when Cannes announced the film's selection, Tremblay jubilantly profiled Dolan as a character in a fairy tale (see the first epithet above), but also invoked the tropes that would become constituent of his public persona: Tremblay likens Dolan's film to a birth, emphasizes his youth, vulnerability, but also his stubborn, dogged ambition, and confides that Dolan dreamed about accompanying his film to Cannes before having even shot it. Tremblay also presents herself as a protective friend, revealing that Dolan is in fact her nephew by marriage, thereby positioning herself as yet another female influence on the director's life. Her columns, a mixture of intimate proximity with the filmmaker and professional assessment, would significantly shape the initial reception of Dolan and his public image.

Shortly after *J'ai tué*'s opening, a huge sigh of relief could be felt in several film critics' and early supporters' accounts: thank God it wasn't just hype! Within the span of a few days, Dolan went from complete unknown to household name. And yet, only a handful of people had actually seen the film. Punctuated by laughter and impromptu bouts of applause, the film's opening screening was crowned by an eight-minute standing ovation, which saw Dolan tearfully embrace Dorval. Prizes were soon awarded by jury members who applauded his courage, determination, sincerity, and, of course, youth.

Despite *J'ai tué*'s unmitigated success at Cannes, and early international distribution deals for eleven countries, the film opened domestically on only twelve screens, ten of which were in Montréal—a result of both exhibition trends and local popular tastes. While film festivals used to launch a film's run into commercial theaters, they have increasingly become places to see the films one will *not* be able to see in the theater.[15] The types of films screened on the festival circuit and in commercial theaters have become increasingly dissimilar, with festivals favoring "auteur," art house films, and commercial screens limiting their offer to a handful of mainstream, mostly American, productions perceived as sure moneymakers. In this context, the number of venues willing to show domestic films (Québec and Canadian) has shrunk, a result of exhibitors' prerogatives and consumer tastes and habits. Regardless of the quality of Québec films, most cinemagoers prefer Hollywood to domestic productions.

Despite all this, *J'ai tué* had a spectacular opening weekend thanks to the generous publicity generated by Cannes, garnering an impressive $87,000. Three screens were added in smaller markets, then six. In the first ten days following its domestic premiere, the film had been seen by nearly 250,000 people. In Québec, the film remained in theaters throughout the summer, fall, and parts of winter, garnering $975,000, at which point it opened in English on a few screens in the rest of Canada. Given the French media blitz, the film opened in France to an astonishing fifty-eight screens, garnering a disappointing 18,000 filmgoers. For now, Dolan's popularity as a filmmaker would remain limited to the French-speaking world, largely within Québec's borders. The Canadian film industry seemed barely aware of Dolan's existence, the film failing to receive a single nomination at the Genie Awards (now the Canadian Screen Awards), and it would take four years for it to be shown in the United States, the initial distributor having folded shortly after acquiring the film.

LES AMOURS IMAGINAIRES AND *LAURENCE ANYWAYS*

The hunger and urgency that had fueled *J'ai tué ma mère* did not make way for what could have been a well-deserved respite. At Cannes, Dolan already had his next project, *Laurence Anyways*, ready for discussion with various partners and actors. *Laurence* was to be a much bigger project, both in scope and in budget, requiring some wait time for all elements to fall into place. With his first film still in theaters and amassing awards on the international film circuit, Dolan decided to use the momentum to make a "small," transitional feature, *Les Amours imaginaires*. Written in a whirlwind only a few weeks prior, the film would once again have to be funded privately, the hyperactive Dolan moving much faster than funding bureaucracies.

With a $600,000 budget and shot in 35mm in Montréal's hip(ster) Mile End neighborhood, the film features close friends and acquaintances of Dolan's. *Les Amours*, also written by and starring Dolan (alongside Monia Chokri and Niels Schneider, both beautifully photographed), once again alternates between mock documentary confessionals of failed love, and over-saturated, colorful narrative. A doomed love triangle, *Les Amours* multiplies references to the Nouvelle Vague, Godard, and, thematically, François Truffaut's *Jules et Jim* (1962). The film follows a complicated dance, wherein best frenemies Marie (Chokri) and Francis (Dolan) battle to win the heart of Nicolas (Schneider), a vapid beautiful blank slate on which the two infatuated lovers project their own desires. Nicolas is a tease, Marie is glassy, and Francis is disingenuous. They are thoroughly unsympathetic characters, so self-absorbed as to be blind to their surroundings. And yet, with near complete absence of insight into the three characters, Dolan perfectly captures the psychology of perversely obsessive romantic pursuits.

Despite its limited budget and lightning quick production, *Les Amours* proved to be a confident, breezy, and visually exciting film. Attentive to their adopted son's progress, Cannes selected the film in its *Un Certain Regard* category. It wasn't the main competition, but this category, rewarding young, innovative filmmakers who demonstrate a unique vision, brought Dolan a step closer to it. It had been seven years since a film hailing from Québec had made Cannes' Official Selection, twelve since a Québec film had made the *Un Certain Regard* selection, and Dolan was the only filmmaker from Québec competing in any category at Cannes that year.

Dolan's second trip to Cannes was greeted with much anticipation and enthusiasm, fans welcoming him like a hybrid rock star/long lost son. Critics who had championed him were relieved that Dolan was no one-hit wonder, but they were still not sure he would not turn out to be a one-trick pony. Amidst a reputedly weak and bleak year, the film received a ten-minute-long standing ovation on opening night, *Le Point* calling it one of the year's few pleasures.

Les Amours is all style, surface, and superficiality, its form perfectly matching its subject matter. Consequently, reviewers collectively noted the flimsiness of the screenplay, the vacuity of the trio of characters, the numerous slow motion scenes, the repetitiveness of Dalida's *Bang Bang*, Wong Kar-waiesque framing, Almodóvarian cinematography and numerous other borrowings. Noting these, however, *Sight & Sound* asked, in the end, "does it matter?" And that indeed summed up the gist of the divide: critics were either irritated by this exercise in style, or they were willing to accept it and enjoy the ride.

Undeterred by *J'ai tué ma mère*'s poor returns the year before (only 58,000 people had seen it), *Les Amours* opened in France in twice as many screens in September of 2010, preceded by a colossal marketing campaign unusual for such a small-budget film. "A delicious pop piece of jewelry," declared *Le Monde*, "an exciting film for those who haven't forgotten their youth," added *Le Figaro*. France was smitten not only with Dolan's film, but with the director himself, who charmed magazine editors as well as radio and television hosts, the first to note his acute fashion sense (see Nick Rees-Roberts's chapter in this volume). The legendary—and normally very European-centric—*Cahiers du Cinéma* featured an interview with Dolan alongside profiles of other Québec filmmakers. The *Cahiers*' early adoption, and continued support, of Dolan was not entirely surprising, however, given his "European" cinematic sensibility and aesthetic.

This time, the wide French opening paid off. On its first day, nearly 9000 people went to see the film, making it the most profitable film of the day (beating Oliver Stone's *Wall Street—Money Never Sleeps*). Some 45,000 French filmgoers saw the film on opening weekend, 61,000 in its first week, prompting the distributor to add screens outside large city centers, and holding it for a second week on all its fourteen Parisian screens. Within only a few days, Dolan's *Les Amours imaginaires* had garnered more money in France than it had during its entire run in Québec (a disappointing $502,300). Québec viewers, originally enthralled and curious with the young phenomenon, had rapidly gone back to Hollywood fare where they normally spend over 80 percent of their film-going budget: supporting local film talents, especially auteur films, does not come naturally to Québec filmgoers (that same year, Denis Côté's *Curling*, also praised by critics and rewarded on the international circuit, only managed $11,500). In 2010, Québec films made for only 9 percent of the domestic box office. Meanwhile 150,000 people saw *Les Amours* in France, twice as many (66,134) as in its home country.[16]

While promoting *Les Amours*, Dolan performed double duty and began working on *Laurence Anyways*, a much riskier project due to its $9 million budget. Going three for three on the theme of impossible love, the film would feature a much meatier and more complex story. Spanning over a decade, *Laurence* centers on a couple, whose love is put to the test when Laurence (Melvil Poupaud substituting Louis Garrel, who left the project two weeks before the start of shooting) decides to transition, and start living as a woman. Dolan had been toying with *Laurence*'s screenplay for four years, wanting to tell the story of a great love unfolding over a decade in which one partner assumes a different gender identity. Over the course of this period, they must face their own prejudice, ostracism, and, Dolan's perennial theme, the look of others which *others* us. This time, Dolan makes otherness, difference, and marginality central to his film, exploring marginality's multiple declinations.

Dolan's third film, his first made with public funds—having been financed by both SODEC and Telefilm Canada—would be a Québec-France co-production, with important implications for casting. Given the scope of the film, Dolan could afford a much-needed longer shooting schedule, from February to April, with an additional month in the fall. The final running time—168 minutes—was risky, yet necessary to depict events unfolding over a twelve-year period. A much more mature work, dealing with complex issues but still possessing Dolan's youthful passion, and now signature colors and composition, *Laurence* once again exploited a fruitful relationship with music, featuring numerous (too numerous for some) musical breaks. The stakes were high for Dolan, as this first "big budget" production would confirm the presence of a vision and mastery of the craft that his initial, smaller productions could only hint at. Already predicted to open at Cannes before filming even began, Thierry Frémaux—Cannes Film Festival Director—went so far as to express the hope Dolan would this time be competing in a more prestigious category.

On April 19, 2012, news broke that *Laurence Anyways* had been selected by Cannes, once again in its *Un Certain Regard* category. The twenty-three-year-old director welcomed the news with mixed feelings: his love affair with Cannes continued, but it was now clearly stagnating. The announcement was all the more disappointing in that a list of films in competition confirming Dolan's film among the chosen few had been leaked a few days earlier. The list turned out to be a hoax.

In the media, however, one could hardly tell that *Laurence* was in a non-competing category. Critics and lay filmgoers showed up in droves, hustling their way for tickets. Despite not being booed (part of Cannes' nastier side), *Laurence*, like its predecessor, would divide its audience; too many artistic flourishes, too many *tableaux*, not enough meat (*Le Figaro*, *L'Express*). Once again, critics saw the film's chief weakness in its writing, focusing too much on the visual composition and giving the viewer little insight into Laurence's motivations and desires. Despite Poupaud's strong performance, much acclaimed in the French media, it is Suzanne Clément (Fred) who would be recognized with one of the two Best Actress awards handed out that year, the *Un Certain Regard* jury opting to reward two women instead of the usual gender parity. Dolan greeted this award with tears of joy, showing no sign of disappointment that his own work went unrewarded. *Laurence* did, however, receive a second award, the now infamous *Queer Palm*, recognizing work that helps combat LGBTQ prejudice and homophobia. The announcement of the peripheral *Queer Palm* might have gone by without much fuss had it not been for Dolan's blunt refusal of the prize: "the very idea that such ghettoizing awards exist is disgusting," Dolan contentiously concluded (see Florian Grandena and Pascal Gagné's contribution to this volume).

As part of *Laurence*'s promotional efforts, Dolan toured Québec's main media outlets, visiting the prime time television show *Tout le monde en parle*. What turned out to be the focus of the show, however, was Dolan's blushing interaction

with Gabriel Nadeau-Dubois—the leader of the most activist student organization then on national strike—and his vocal support for the strike against tuition
fee increases. It was not so much Dolan's infatuation with Nadeau-Dubois, generally seen as a cute college-boy crush, but his strong support for the student
movement, an area some judged was outside of his realm of expertise. To add
insult to injury, Dolan and his crew later showed up at the Cannes red carpet
opening night wearing red squares, the student movement's insignia. One could
hear the fuming from all corners of the province ("How dare he air Québec's
dirty laundry in France?") giving the impression that Cannes was a pageant from
which Québec was seeking approval, as from an estranged parent. "By God," a
popular columnist implored, "don't embarrass us in front of people!"[7] Cannes,
however, was not so squeamish and before long, several other people were photographed wearing the red square, not the least of whom was the festival's director,
Thierry Frémaux. *Malaise*, as the Québécois would say.

With larger budgets comes increased pressure to find an audience. Soon,
it became clear that *Laurence* had not. Once the novelty had gone, people in
Québec had no intention of supporting their filmmakers by seeing their films;
taking pride in a young filmmaker's career abroad was enough. In the United
States, LGBT-friendly distributor Breaking Glass Pictures gave *Laurence* a
very limited release. In Québec, the film opened on twenty-five screens, but
only managed 20,000 entries in its first month, totaling a meager $493,064
for its entire run. The year 2012 was an abysmal one for the Québec film
industry: domestic filmgoing dipped under 5 percent of the market—a twelve-
year low—with 80 percent of moviegoers choosing Hollywood instead, and
6 percent favoring French films.[18] Dolan was far from the only director to do
poorly at home despite international acclaim: Kim Nguyen's highly praised
Rebelle was likewise snubbed, making just over $100,000. "Quebec films are
just too depressing, it's always about complaining," claimed Québec's largest
cinema operator Vincent Guzzo. "Depressing miserabilism," opined the province's most widely read daily newspaper.[19] Given the ever-declining audience,
what was the point of publicly funding films no one wanted to see? Despite his
unquestionable success abroad, Xavier Dolan became, in right-leaning circles,
the face of an unprofitable cinema and wasteful government spending.[20]

TOM À LA FERME AND *COLLEGE BOY*

A few days before *Laurence* opened, it was announced that Dolan's next film
project had received SODEC's green light. *Tom à la ferme* would be Dolan's
first attempt at adapting someone else's work, Michel Marc Bouchard's
2011 play *Tom à la ferme* (see Marie Pascal's chapter). While campaigning to
raise money for his fourth film, *Laurence Anyways* was awarded the Toronto

International Film Festival (TIFF)'s best Canadian feature award, an award accompanied by a $30,000 bursary. The timing could hardly have been better. This recognition also saw the beginning of a friendship with TIFF for a director who had until now only had eyes for Cannes.

With *Tom*, Dolan went back to a starring role and a much smaller production, with fewer sets, actors, and shooting days. He also went back to a style of filmmaking that had proven itself in the past: urgency—striking while the iron is hot. Described as a stripped down Hitchcockian thriller (although Dolan claims Jonathan Demme's *Silence of the Lambs* to be the chief influence), *Tom* promised to be unlike anything he had made so far. Évelyne Brochu (Sarah) and Lise Roy (the mother) reprised their theater roles, and Dolan gave himself, in addition to the title role, a much talked about retro blond haircut. *Tom* follows a young urbanite as he attends his boyfriend's funeral in rural Québec. There, he meets his in-laws for the first time, discovering they knew nothing of him. What is more, his boyfriend's mother is unaware of his homosexuality, having been convinced that her son was in a heterosexual relationship with a certain Sara. This elaborate lie was conceived by her eldest son, Francis, who goes on to manipulate a grieving *Tom* to join in the lie, and to convince him to produce a girlfriend and to stay over to help with farm work. Though both *Tom* and *J'ai tué* deal with issues of gay sons, their mothers, and the difficulty of coming out, the former tackles homosexuality in a much more mature, direct, and complex fashion

While *Tom* could not be finished in time for Cannes, Dolan was nevertheless present, perhaps like never before, in the French media. Cult French band Indochine asked Dolan to direct the music video for their new song "College Boy," giving him full liberty to develop the concept. The video, starring Antoine Olivier Pilon (who had a small part in *Laurence* and whom we go on to see in *Mommy*), details the daily violence suffered by a boy at the hands of his classmates. While meant to address all acts of school bullying of those who are different, acts ignored by classmates and adults alike, the video has been widely interpreted as a condemnation of homophobia, in part because Indochine has fervently denounced all forms of intolerance and celebrated sexual and gender diversity throughout their three-decade career. The root of the controversy, which ultimately resulted in the video being censored from all French television channels, lay in the graphic images of Pilon being crucified, shot, and tasered, all the while being filmed (for social media streaming?) by blindfolded passers-by. While *Le Point* judged the video's representation of violence to be a powerful, authentic representation of recent cases of bullying that ended in suicides, *Le Figaro* wondered whether Indochine wasn't simply going for shock value and polemic to boost album and ticket sales. Shot in Montréal in black and white (to make the violence more bearable, but also for financial reasons), *Indochine: College Boy* contrasts the ugliness of the violence perpetrated with the beauty of its form. After the video appeared online, the Conseil supérieur de l'audiovisuel (CSA), the French body charged with monitoring television content, said it would impose sanctions on any distributors showing the clip in order to "protect young viewers and human dignity" against images of unbearable violence.[21]

College Boy is in no way more graphic than the average action film. On the contrary, one could even argue, as Dolan did, that unlike many action flicks, his video shows no sympathy whatsoever for the perpetrators. What seemed to be at issue, in fact, was Dolan's perceived intrusion into France's heated debate on marriage equality. Interpreted as a denunciation of homophobic violence, the video was read as a critique of the rise of the political right, and an attack on France's defense of its Catholic heritage (the mass movement against equal marriage rights was largely led by Catholics or, rather, those opposing gay marriage presented it as a *defense* of France's Catholic roots and heritage).

From a Quebecer's perspective, where gay marriage has been widely accepted for years, France's hesitations appeared archaic and intolerant, and Dolan did not hesitate to say so, happily engaging with the media, denouncing the cowardliness at the heart of the CSA's decision, and publishing a widely circulated open letter to Françoise Laborde, the CSA's head. In the end, as is usually the case in such situations, the row resulted in mass interest in the video, with 2 million views in a matter of days.

Shortly after the *College Boy* controversy, Dolan accompanied his new film, *Tom à la ferme*, to the Mostra, where it became the first Québec film in official competition in twenty-five years. Venice gave what Cannes had denied. Whether the film could have been ready on time for Cannes or not, exploring other venues had proven judicious; *Tom* received a twelve-minute ovation from a reputedly restrained crowd. Critics were struck by the director's complete mastery of his craft and precision of vision. They were also glad that Dolan had let go of old habits, tics, and gratuitous effects. Except for some camera framing and compositions, one could hardly tell this was a Dolanian film. Gone were the excessive lengths and aesthetic flourishes. With *Tom*, Dolan refrained from imposing his style and aesthetic, instead letting the play take the lead in determining the form. Once again, however, Dolan had a hard time charming American critics. While *Variety* declared it his strongest and most commercial film, David Rooney, writing for *The Hollywood Reporter*, described it as an "egomaniacal exercise" and accused Dolan of narcissistically "fetishizing his own image."[22] A case of millennial bashing? Perhaps. Would he also accuse Charlie Chaplin, Woody Allen, or Orson Welles in the same manner? True to form, Dolan replied instantaneously and succinctly: "You can kiss my narcissistic ass."

Despite this new, sober approach, *Tom* turned out to be a very proficient thriller with strong, memorable scenes, which also revealed a restrained side to Dolan's acting. Incidentally, Dolan, who had pursued voice acting throughout his filmmaking career (being the voice, most notably, for Taylor Lautner and Rupert Grint in the *Twilight* and *Harry Potter* franchises respectively), went back to acting for other Québec directors, appearing in *Miraculum* (Daniel Grou, 2014) and the English-language film *Elephant Song* (Charles Binamé, 2014). Dolan has indicated on numerous occasions his preference for acting over directing, explaining that acting responds to a need to express himself, while directing is purely a means to orchestrate the type of films he wants to be involved in. "Acting is liberating," Dolan explains, directing is not: "it drains a lot out of you and it's fulfilling only temporarily."[23]

Tom was crowned with the International Federation of Film Critics (FIPRESCI) award, which commended Dolan for his "energetic, tense and sensual filmmaking," and *Tom* for "the rare example of convincing narrative disorientation on the winding road between genders and genres."[24] It would be six months before the film was released in Québec and in the UK, where Peter Bradshaw, writing for *The Guardian*, declared the "disorienting, strange, suspense drama . . . the one film to see" that week.[25] This was quite something, given Bradshaw's lukewarm reviews of Dolan's previous work, which he considered "self-indulgent." *Tom à la ferme* garnered an honorable $331,000 at the Québec box office, but wouldn't be released in the United States until two years later when it was acquired by Amplify for theater and VOD release.

MOMMY AND *HELLO*

Tom à la ferme had been made swiftly, with a sense of urgency, which suited both Dolan's personality and the tone of the film. It was also made with a low budget and while Dolan was multi-tasking various projects and creative endeavors. One of these was the preparation for his fifth feature, *Mommy*, which would signal a return to his preferred theme of mother-son relationships. Of *Mommy*, very little information circulated while in production, aside from perennial Cannes rumors. *Variety* was first to publish a list on which Dolan figured in competition, sending the Québec media into a frenzy. Another Québec director, veteran Denys Arcand, was hoping to make the list though it was unlikely that both would be selected.

Finally, on April 17, 2014, Cannes announced its selection: *Mommy* was among the eighteen films in competition. It had been eleven years since a film hailing from Québec had taken part in the competition section, Denys Arcand's *Les invasions barbares/The Barbarian Invasions* (2003) being the last. In addition to procuring the obvious honor, the official competition ensures, first and foremost, visibility. Film critics from all corners of the world—around 4000 each year—see and review all films in competition, and distributors pay particular attention. Making the selection therefore has very concrete, immediate effects.[26]

Inspired by a true event and by British filmmaker Ken Loach's aesthetic, *Mommy* presents a combative working-class family determined to overcome the difficulties of their situation.[27] The film concerns the emotional triangle between Steve, a charming and volatile adolescent suffering from ADHD, hyperactivity and various other emotional troubles, Diane "Die" Després, a mother in constant precarious unemployment, and their shy neighbor Kyla, a former teacher who takes over Steve's homeschooling. Bringing back familiar faces (Anne Dorval, who played the mother in *J'ai tué ma mère* and *Les Amours imaginaires*, Suzanne Clément, Hubert's teacher in *J'ai tué ma mère* and Fred in *Laurence Anyways*, and Antoine Olivier Pilon, the bullying victim of the *College Boy* video), and knee-deep in local cultural references, *Mommy* was by far Dolan's most "Québécois" film to date. Originally envisioned as his foray into American film, Dolan opted instead to anchor the tale of troubled adolescence in his childhood neighborhood, filming in Longueuil. The dialogues brilliantly shift back and forth from standard French to colloquial Québec French, high-lighting the musicality of spoken Québec vernacular. Upon the film's release, several Québec commentators criticized Dolan's use of language, some calling it nefarious defilement, others claiming it would project a poor image of Québec abroad, and some believing it would hurt the film's ability to be understood by French-speaking people outside of Québec (see Chapter 9 in this volume).

Despite its characters' bleak reality, and even bleaker future, the film was received at Cannes as a breath of fresh air, thanks to Dolan's decision to con-struct characters animated by indefatigable hope and to bathe them in light. The film's unrestrained emotions, meant to shock the system, emphasize the tragedy of motherhood and the violence of adolescence. In a rare moment of accord, French critics unanimously praised the film, *Libération* declaring it "THE film to see."[28] Dolan had emerged in France as a boy wonder, who had produced through sheer determination and genius an imperfect but sincere and touching film in *J'ai tué ma mère*. *Mommy* left the French press in collective awe for its maturity and intelligence, Dolan's precociousness no longer a factor.

Mommy, Dolan's most successful film to date, is perceptively discussed in this volume. Although it did not win the coveted Palme d'Or, it received a thirteen-minute standing ovation and was awarded, *ex aequo* with Jean-Luc Godard's *Adieu au langage/Goodbye to Language*, the Jury Prize. The jury was simultaneously rewarding the festival's youngest and its oldest filmmaker. While some thought splitting the prize was a mistake ("couldn't they have given the whole thing to Dolan"[29]), especially since Godard clearly did not want it, others saw in this move a nice touch, as if passing the torch from the innovator of the older to the new generation.

Watching Dolan's emotional acceptance speech, one could hardly tell that he had ever wanted anything else. The speech surprised many by its intelli-gence, eloquence, and heartfelt authenticity. His touching, personal homage to

Jane Campion (the head of the jury with whom he was sharing the stage) and their subsequent embrace, remains one of Cannes' most memorable moments. Sections of the speech circulated widely in the traditional and online media, especially the director's appeal to "his generation" to dream big, work hard, and dare to change the world. Acutely aware of how "tacky" and risible this can sound, Dolan refuses the cynicism of older, "wiser," generations, and persists in preaching the virtue of believing in dreams to anyone who will listen.[30]

Ironically (perhaps), Dolan's increased international success generated greater scrutiny at home. Among conservative critics, Dolan was accused, among other things, of presenting a lousy portrayal of men and absentee fathers in his films. Dolan was the symptom of a declining, crumbling society; "a weak, flabby society where revolt and tragedy have become impossible because everything is acceptable."[31]

In Québec, *Mommy* was released on sixty-four screens, a true rarity for a domestic film. The popular demand was so strong that small exhibitors outside major urban centers publicly denounced the limited number of copies in circulation. Perhaps thanks to its visceral local attachment and multi-generational appeal, this time, Québec spectators went to see Dolan's film in droves, garnering $466,776 on its opening weekend, with the film reaching the $1 million mark in less than two weeks, at which point twenty additional copies of the film were put into circulation. In France, on the back of the unmitigated enthusiasm of several media outlets and a strong marketing campaign, the film opened on 315 screens, drawing 50,000 viewers on opening day and beating Ben Affleck's *Gone Girl*. Distributor Didier Lacourt commented on this, calling it an "American blockbuster start"[32]—a pretty ironic statement given Dolan's notorious inability to break into the American market. Within five days, 273,000 people had seen the film in France, surpassing Denys Arcand's *Les invasions barbares* for the biggest Québec film to open in Europe, prompting the addition of seventy-five more copies of the film. Overall, *Mommy* would draw just over 1 million spectators in France. Not only had the French been untroubled by the language of *Mommy*—as the Québec columnists and funding agencies reviewers had predicted—but many were in fact charmed, noting how it contributes to the film's musicality and authenticity.[33]

After being nominated three times for *Laurence Anyways*, *Les Amours imaginaires*, and *J'ai tué ma mère*, Dolan won the César (the French equivalent of an Academy Award) for Best Foreign Film. At home, with 363,000 entries, *Mommy* was the tenth most widely seen film in 2014.[34] A rarity in Québec, Dolan had managed to create a film successful both locally and on the festival circuit, applauded by both film critics and moviegoers; an auteur film that made money. Despite its incredible success (over $3 million dollars in Québec alone), in the United States, the Academy of Motion Picture Arts and Sciences once again did not retain *Mommy* on its short list for Best Foreign Film.

In late summer of 2015, rumors began circulating that British singer Adele was in Québec, in the Eastern Townships village of Dunham, to shoot a music video with Dolan. The hitmaker had contacted Dolan, asking whether he would be interested in directing the video for her first single in three years ("Hello"). While many would have jumped at the offer, Dolan, who is used to working on material that evolves organically and to which he feels an emotional connection, flew to London to have a listen before accepting. With its sepia tones and shot in IMAX (the first music video to be shot in that format) the video quickly became the most viewed on YouTube upon its release on October 22, 2015. Within twenty-four hours, the video had reached an unprecedented 27.7 million views, continuing at a speed of 1 million views per hour, becoming the fastest video to reach 100 million views in five days. It currently has had well over 2 billion views.

Melding the spirit of Adele's song with his own sensibility and aesthetic—down to the use of extreme close-ups, mascara-tainted tears, dainty tea cups, and time defying bric-a-brac fashions—*Hello* adeptly captures Adele's beauty, strength, and vulnerability, as well as the pain and loneliness of failed relationships. The success of this video no doubt helped Dolan make Forbes' *30 Under 30* Hollywood and Entertainment list.

"A FASCINATING, SUSTAINED ASSAULT": *JUSTE LA FIN DU MONDE*

While Dolan did not have a film ready in time to show at Cannes in 2015, he certainly did not miss the festival. This time, he became the first Québécois to attend as a member of the main competition's jury, which had the Coen brothers as joint president. As everyone had their eyes turned toward Dolan's anticipated American debut (the anticipation would build for a few more years), it was announced that he would first shoot a film in Québec (Laval), with a group of A-list French actors: Marion Cotillard, Nathalie Baye, Vincent Cassel, Léa Seydoux, and Gaspard Ulliel. Based on Jean-Luc Lagarce's play about a famous writer going back to his family after a twelve-year absence to tell them he is dying, the film would again focus on a family and its struggle to communicate. Principal photography for *Juste la fin du monde* would start the day following the Cannes award ceremony. No time to waste. Much like *Tom à la ferme*, this second adaptation would center on a gay character's reticent return to the country. It would also be completed rapidly, assembling these in-demand actors in the same room being a challenge in itself. Dolan described the film both as "transitory" and as closing a chapter in his life, wanting from now on to invest himself in genre cinema and projects that emerge from outside of himself, projects that are "still personal, but less private."[35]

Given Dolan's close relationship with the festival (and the festival's history of supporting selected auteurs through thick and thin) and the film's powerhouse cast, everyone had already predicted *Juste la fin du monde* would be shortlisted for Cannes' main competition before shooting even began. As soon as the film screened for the press, however, rumors began circulating that Dolan's film had missed the mark, that it stood no chance of winning high honors there and that Dolan's honeymoon with Cannes had perhaps ended.

Mommy had been described in France as an emotional punch in the face, leaving viewers shaken. *Juste la fin du monde* went further in the same vein, using extreme close-ups to build tension and with characters shouting rather than talking to build up a maximum of intensity. This time, it would appear that Dolan had gone too far. Viewers who saw the film on a small screen might not grasp the extent to which people who saw the film in the theater felt assaulted. The relentless, claustrophobically tight close-ups were described as "insufferable"—no one, no matter how beautiful they are, should ever be seen from this close up.[36] Nevertheless, and despite early indications to the contrary, a twenty-minute ovation concluded the red-carpet screening.

Cannes 2016 was a destabilizing experience for Dolan. He arrived at the festival fully preoccupied with his next film, *The Death and Life of John F. Donovan*, set to begin production two months later. A massive production, the film gave a lot to think about for a director used to overseeing most aspects of his film. Dolan was thinking not only about camera angles, music, and editing, but about costumes (even selecting fabrics), make-up, and poster design. He also remained extremely proud of his latest film, declaring *Juste la fin* his best so far, and his first "adult" film (his "first as a man," he explained).[37] He never saw what was coming.

The year 2016 was also the year that cemented the increasing role of social media in the life of the film festival. Reactions to films by a handful of film critics were instantly shared with the rest of the world who, for months, would be unable to see the film for themselves but would be inundated by tweets. While his films had often divided, this time the critics were much more unanimous, and vocal, in their criticism. To a certain extent, that has always been the case. Film reviews precede most films' release and often constitute the viewer's first contact with a film, a contact that is filtered through the judgment, subjectivity, and tastes of the particular reviewer. What changed with social media was the tone in which critics felt they could express their opinions, unfiltered by the proprieties, journalistic rules, and editors of traditional media. And of course, the rapid-fire speed at which filmmakers could respond to those critics, engaging in twitter wars for all to see. That is essentially what happened with *Juste la fin du monde*, which, according to Dolan, required some time to digest. Writing for the *LA Times*, Justin Chang called it a "badly shot, shrilly performed and all-around excruciatingly misjudged dysfunctional-family torture session." Reviewers lined up, as if competing in their attempts to find the most outrageous "*bon mot*," resulting in dubious character assassination ("the work of a sulking self-conscious teenager, locked in his bedroom with his music blaring, feeling like the most misunderstood genius who never asked to be born").[38] The mercurial director felt personally attacked and was deeply wounded. He would later claim the experience had had an effect similar to the trauma of a car accident.

The film was far from terrible, and many critics did like it, praising its actors and its intensity. While calling it "exasperating," "excruciating," and "agonizing," *Variety* also declared it a cathartic experience.[39] Others were less charitable. *Vanity Fair's* Richard Lawson repeated accusations of narcissism, concluding that Dolan "still has trouble seeing past his own nose," and Jessica Kiang, of *Playlist*, added her opinion, calling Dolan a "petulant teenager" wallowing in "self-pity . . . and martyred self-involvement . . . tantamount to a persecution complex."[40] Taking issue with the quality of the English subtitles, and noting that Dolan had shot his film "in actual French, rather than his usual Canadian accents," a reviewer further lamented about the complexity of the French language, calling the characters' switching between the informal *tu* and formal *vous* problematic because it "doesn't have an English equivalent." These rather nonsensical remarks were not coming from some obscure blog: it was *Variety's* Peter Debruge.[41]

There was in fact a geographic cleavage in the critics' appraisals, with the Americans overwhelmingly disliking (at best) the film, and the Europeans loving it (it would later receive three Césars, two for Dolan for Best Director and Best Editing). In the moment, however, Dolan appeared to focus solely on the negative reviews. More familiar with the source material, the French press appreciated Dolan's adaptation, which beautifully transcreates Lagarce's tricky text into a cinematic context (see Marie Pascal's chapter in this volume). Ever the loving, protective, mother, Cannes rewarded her prodigal son not with one prize, but two. Dolan received the Ecumenical Award, an award given by an independent jury to humanitarian movies, "which touch the spiritual dimension of our existence," and the Grand Prix—the second most prestigious award at Cannes. With this award, Dolan wrote another first into Québec's film history book, no Québécois having ever received such high acclaim at Cannes before. Despite the high honor, however, this last Cannes left a bad taste in Dolan's mouth.

No doubt thanks to its high "French content," the film fared much better in France than in Québec. On opening weekend, the film garnered $222,684 in Québec but drew in an impressive 329,770 moviegoers in France, where it opened simultaneously (*Mommy* had opened to 50,000). Despite its success in the French-speaking world, *Juste la fin* would confirm once more Dolan's difficulty in breaking into the American market, unable to find a distributor south of the border. Upon his return home, his success was saluted at the National Assembly, he was invited to join the Academy, and he received an honorary doctorate conferred by Sherbrooke's Bishop's University. Not bad for a college dropout.

THE DEATH AND LIFE OF JOHN F. DONOVAN AND *MATTHIAS ET MAXIME*

News of an entry into American cinema began circulating in late 2014, when actors and actresses were signed on for a project titled *The Death and Life of John F. Donovan*. Negotiations to co-produce the film with the United States fell through, and in the end, the movie would be a Canada/UK coproduction. Co-written by Dolan and Jacob Tierney (who directed *Good Neighbors*, 2010, and *The Trotsky*, 2009), *Donovan* would be a significant departure for the actor who seemed more at home with smaller projects—smaller budgets, few actors, shot rapidly. Considering Dolan's usual speed (one movie per year), production of *Death* seemed interminable. With a $38 million USD budget, this was by far Dolan's biggest project.

Donovan fulfilled a creative dream for Dolan. Inspired by Paul Thomas Anderson's *Magnolia* (1999), the film has a complex structure involving various narratives. This complexity, added to a short shooting schedule and a lack of pre-production preparation, did not suit Dolan's omnipotent control and perfectionist personality. *Donovan* was shot in Montréal, Prague, and London in 35mm and 65mm.

Early news emerging from the production bore a note of concern, all the more so when it was announced that Jessica Chastain had been cut. Early production images that circulated online were beautiful, but the stakes were high for a director who had thus far been unable to break into the American market. Contrary to his other films, however, *Donovan* depended on finding a larger audience if it hoped to recoup its costs.

News broke that *Donovan* would not be opening at Cannes, where everyone was expecting it, but at the Toronto International Film Festival (TIFF) instead. For a director who had been "born" at and had been nurtured by Cannes, this was concerning and sent social media into a frenzy. The Cannes Festival itself seemed surprised, even hurt, by this decision, since the festival had shown interest in featuring the film as part of its official selection. Dolan and his producer justified their decision by arguing that TIFF was a better choice for their marketing vision. Despite its status, Cannes is first and foremost associated with auteur, European cinema. If Dolan is to break into the American market, all of Cannes' prestige will do little to help. But Dolan also claimed, in an Instagram post, that he wanted to avoid the "culture of trolling, bullying and unwarranted hatred" that had wounded him in the past. And since the movie itself is dealing with similar issues, Dolan wanted to avoid appearing as though he was taking a jab at Cannes.[42] This would be the second year in a row without Québec films competing in any category at Cannes.

A book on a hyperactive millennial director will necessarily be different from most filmmaker studies, as it involves dealing with an ever changing corpus including, in addition to the films, a plethora of tweets, Instagram posts, blog posts, and a myriad other media interventions. As I was writing this introduction, Dolan announced on twitter that Jessica Chastain had been cut from *The Death and Life of John F. Donovan* (*How dare he?*); shut down his twitter account (too many wasteful "hateful debates"), which made national news; announced that *John F. Donovan* would not open at Cannes as predicted but instead at the Toronto International Film Festival (*He must be retaliating for* Juste la fin du monde*'s tepid reception!*); declared his return to Montréal to shoot his next film project; made his American debut as an actor; released his biggest production to date, *John F. Donovan*; and announced he would appear in the much-anticipated *It* sequel, in addition to wrapping *Matthias et Maxime*'s shoot after "48 days of pure joy."[43] An effort has been made to include as many of these elements when pertinent, but the focus of the book remains centered on Dolan's work as a filmmaker. As the first book-length anthology on Xavier Dolan, this volume makes an intervention on the global reach of small national and subnational cinemas, and uses Dolan's cinema as a departure point to reconsider the position of Québec film and cultural imaginary within a global cinematic culture, as well as the intersections between national, millennial, and queer filmmaking.

The book is divided into three parts, each of which explores a significant thread of the director's work. Part 1, "Queer Universalism," examines Dolan's relationship with queer representations and LGBTQ politics. Fulvia Massimi's chapter explores the non-traditional and queer kinships found in Dolan's films, as well as his complex representations of motherhood and deeply complicated mother-son love. The filmmaker, Massimi maintains, develops an alternative, non-heteronormative and non-patriarchal national narrative through his staging of queer, alternative family structures. Through the concept of "*Dolandrama*," Julianne Pidduck critically examines Dolan's queer authorship in relationship with the tropes of melodrama and with his female leads. Finally, Florian Grandena and Pascal Gagné turn to *Tom à la ferme* and *Juste la fin du monde* to explore the queerness of time at play in films where gay characters are transported into straight spaces.

Part 2, "Local Auteur," approaches Dolan as a "deeply Québécois" filmmaker. Bill Marshall's chapter draws links between geography and queer politics and aesthetics through a close analysis of two of Dolan's films featuring central queer characters: *Laurence Anyways* (2012) and *Tom à la ferme* (2013). Situating Dolan within the context of Québec's contemporary national cinema, Liz Czach explores the class politics at play in the filmmaker's use of mise-en-scène. Looking closely at Dolan's two films based on stage plays, *Tom à la ferme* and *Juste la fin du monde*, Marie Pascal highlights the filmmaker's work as *transcreator*, that is, how the filmmaker conveyed through cinematic means literary elements present in the plays. Finally, Navaneetha Mokkil's takes a closer look at Dolan's resonance across cultural borders, as she maps the presence and reception of *Laurence Anyways* in India. Her chapter emphasizes the book's aim of showing how the universal is not produced by an erasure of local contexts, but rather through an exploration of specificities such as queer subjectivities, non-traditional family structures, and stigmatized vernaculars.

Lastly, Part 3, "Millennial Auteur," approaches Dolan as a millennial filmmaker. Self-taught and accomplished from a young age, Dolan's films can legitimately be considered exemplars of millennial filmmaking. This part explores the influence of nostalgia and music, as well as Dolan's forays into music video and fashion. Mercédès Baillargeon looks at the melancholic aesthetic of *Mommy* as a millennial aesthetic of failure, a reaction to the failed promises of late neo-liberal societies. Andrée Lafontaine's chapter turns attention to the language politics in Dolan's films, seeing in his use of *joual*—the Québec vernacular—and Franglais—the mixture of French and English spoken mostly by younger people in Montréal—a creative and affective strategy. Finally, focusing on fashion, Nick Rees-Roberts explores Dolan's brand across various media platforms, paying particular attention to the melodramatic tropes of exaggeration, failure, and vulgarity.

While Québec has a strong cinematic tradition, its cinema remains that of a "small nation" with specific challenges.[44] Dolan's films do not wholly escape these challenges, and yet, the filmmaker has undoubtedly been a crucial player in the film festival circuit of the past seven years, and has been an eloquent spokesperson for Québec's national cinema on the global stage. Meanwhile, his "very Québécois" profile, combined with the wide circulation of his films in foreign markets, continues to enhance the relevance of Québec's cultural specificity in wider frameworks of film reception. Despite his firm anchoring in Québec national cinema, this book delves into the filmmaker's universal appeal to interrogate how cinema achieves universality *through* specificity.

NOTES

1. Odile Tremblay, "Le p'tit à Cannes," *Le Devoir* (Montréal), April 25, 2009. My translation.
2. Xavier Dolan's press conference after winning the Jury Prize at Cannes for *Mommy*. My translation.
3. Xavier Dolan quoted in Emily Barnett, "'J'ai tué ma mère': plongée dans la violence d'une relation mère-fils," *Les Inrockuptibles*, July 10, 2009. Available at <https://www.lesinrocks.com/cinema/films-a-l-affiche/jai-tue-ma-mere/> (accessed March 1, 2019). My translation.
4. Sophie Monks Kaufman, "Xavier Dolan: 'I've never experienced love as something calm and tender,'" *Little White Lies*. Available at <http://lwlies.com/interviews/xavier-dolan-mommy/> (accessed November 16, 2017).
5. Kate Taylor, "'Psychologically scarred' millennials are killing countless industries from napkins to Applebee's—here are the businesses they like the least," *Business Insider*, October 31, 2017. Available at <https://www.businessinsider.com/millennials-are-killing-list-2017-8> (accessed October 31, 2018).
6. Pauline Kael, "Raising Kane," *New Yorker*, February 20, 1971.

7. David A. Gerstner and Janet Staiger (eds), *Authorship and Film* (New York: Routledge, 2003).

8. Joseph McBride, *Frank Capra: The Catastrophe of Success* (New York: Simon & Schuster, 1992).

9. Tom Gunning, *D. W. Griffith and the Origins of American Narrative Film: The Early Years at Biograph* (Urbana: University of Illinois Press, 1994), p. 46.

10. Noémi Mercier, "Xavier Dolan: 'Tout est possible,'" *L'Actualité*, September 15, 2017; Brandon Judell, "Mommy's boy: Xavier Dolan explains why women are like gay men," *HuffPost*, February 20, 2015. Available at <https://www.huffingtonpost.com/brandon-judell/mommys-boy-xavier-dolan-e_b_6590548.html>.

11. Kyle Buchanan, "Xavier Dolan on Blink-182, bottoming, and being the world's biggest Kate Winslet fan," *Vulture*, December 8, 2016. Available at <http://www.vulture.com/2016/12/xavier-dolan-on-his-new-film-critics-and-more.html>.

12. Tara Brady, "Xavier Dolan: 'I'm not an enfant terrible. I'm a human being reacting,'" *Irish Times* (Dublin), February 24, 2017. Available at <https://www.irishtimes.com/culture/film/xavier-dolan-i-m-not-an-enfant-terrible-i-m-a-human-being-reacting-1.2982538>.

13. See Mario Roy, "Cinoche et fric," *La Presse* (Montréal), March 30, 2010; Manon Dumais, "Xavier Dolan répond à Mario Roy," *Voir* (Montréal), April 2, 2010. Available at <https://voir.ca/manon-dumais/2010/04/02/xavier-dolan-repond-a-mario-roy-ajout/>; Odile Tremblay, "Entre Cannes et blogues," *Le Devoir* (Montréal), April 10, 2010; Isabelle Paré, "Cinéma et télévision: Ignatieff souhaite donner plus de moyens aux producteurs indépendants," *Le Devoir* (Montréal), April 29, 2010. The exchange between Roy and Dolan was later used in a pedagogical document to be used in high school French classes titled "Défendre ses idées/Supporting your ideas." Available at <https://www.sofad.qc.ca/media/doc/cours/457_X-5111.pdf>. No doubt influenced by these discussions, Telefilm Canada would in fact change its financing structure to reward not only profits, but also quality, the following year.

14. Odile Tremblay, "Cinéaste à 19 ans," *Le Devoir* (Montréal), October 31, 2008.

15. Martin Bilodeau, "Le Parallèle sur la voie du milieu," *Le Devoir* (Montréal), May 1, 2009.

16. Martin Tétu, "L'assistance aux films québécois sous la barre des 10%," *Optique culture*, no. 1, Institut de la statistique du Québec, Observatoire de la culture et des communications du Québec, February 2011, <http://www.stat.gouv.qc.ca/observatoire>.

17. Isabelle Maréchal pleaded "by God, don't embarrass us in front of people!" in "Le carré de la honte," *Journal de Montréal*, May 20, 2012. Available at <https://www.journaldemontreal.com/2012/05/20/le-carre-de-la-honte>. My translation.

18. Odile Tremblay, "Cinéma québécois—Le plus lent démarrage aux guichets en 11 ans," *Le Devoir* (Montréal), June 12, 2012; Odile Tremblay, "Baisse dramatique du cinéma québécois en salles," *Le Devoir* (Montréal), September 13, 2012.

19. Christian Dufour, "La langue de *Mommy*," *Journal de Montréal*, October 1, 2014, p. 35.

20. See Éric Duhaime, "Lettre à Xavier Dolan," *Journal de Montréal*, July 1, 2012. Available at <https://www.journaldequebec.com/2012/07/01/lettre-a-xavier-dolan>.

21. Hermance Murgue, "Clip d'Indochine: Françoise Laborde (CSA) pour une interdiction aux moins de 16 ou 18 ans," *L'Express*, May 2, 2013. Available at <https://www.lexpress.fr/actualite/medias/clip-d-indochine-francoise-laborde-csa-pour-une-interdiction-aux-moins-de-16-ou-18-ans_1245833.html> (accessed November 19, 2018).

22. David Rooney, "Tom at the Farm: Venice review," *Hollywood Reporter*, September 2, 2013. Available at <https://www.hollywoodreporter.com/review/tom-at-farm-venice-review-619296> (accessed July 6, 2018).

23. Nigel M. Smith, "Xavier Dolan: 'Film-making is not liberating,'" *The Guardian*, August 11, 2015.

24. Yael Shuv, "70th Venice Film Festival," Festival report. Available at <http://www.fipresci. org/festival-reports/2013/venice-film-festival>.

25. Peter Bradshaw, "Why *Tom at the Farm* is the one film you should see this week," *The Guardian*, April 3, 2014. Available at <https://www.theguardian.com/film/video/2014/ apr/03/tom-at-the-farm-film-you-should-watch-video> (accessed August 15, 2018).

26. And indeed, Dolan would leave Cannes with over $1.5 million in sales.

27. Dolan explains that he admires Ken Loach's effort to film people from the ground level, never from above. He attempts the same in *Mommy* by having the characters' tastes (in music, notably) determine the overall aesthetic of the film. See Pierre Foglia, "Xavier Dolan: la personnalité de l'année," *La Presse* (Montréal), January 1, 2015. Available at <http://www.lapresse.ca/actualites/dossiers/inspiration-2014/201501/01/01-4831978-xavier-dolan-la-personnalite-de-lannee.php>.

28. Gérard Lefort, "'Mommy', de cris et de grandeur," *Libération*, October 7, 2014.

29. Christian Viviani, "Mai en cinéma: morose mois de mai," *Positif*, 641/642, July/August 2014, p. 136; Michel Ciment, "Cannes 2014, 67ᵉ édition," *Positif*, 641/642, July/August 2014, pp. 68–70.

30. See his interview with Catherine Pogonat for "Mange ta ville," host Catherine Pogonat, directed by Éric Morin (Radio-Canada, ARTV). Available at <https://www.youtube. com/watch?v=AmIkDVHzvmY>.

31. Mathieu Bock-Côté, "Voyage sur la planète Dolan," *Journal de Montréal*, May 25, 2016; Christian Rioux, "La révolte impossible," *Le Devoir* (Montréal), July 24, 2009; Christian Rioux, "Anyway!," *Le Devoir* (Montréal), July 20, 2012; Christian Rioux, "L'enfant roi," *Le Devoir* (Montréal), October 10, 2014.

32. Michel Dolbec, "Mommy connaît un départ spectaculaire en France," *Le Soleil*, October 9, 2014. Available at <https://www.lesoleil.com/archives/mommy-connait-un-depart-spectaculaire-en-france-4ddaab982b9967fe3d427445f63d5d5a> (accessed August 18, 2018).

33. Jacques Rancière, "It's up to you to invent the rest," in Emiliano Battista (ed. and trans.), *Dissenting Words: Interviews with Jacques Rancière* (London: Bloomsbury, 2017), p. 298; "La rage au cœur," *La Croix*, October 8, 2014; Marc-Olivier Bherer, "Au Québec, Xavier Dolan ravive le débat linguistique," *Le Monde*, November 11, 2014; Louis Guichard, "'Mommy' Xavier Dolan," *Télérama*, 3378, October 11, 2014.

34. La Presse Canadienne, "Les Québécois ont vu moins de films américains," *Le Devoir* (Montréal), February 20, 2015.

35. Odile Tremblay, "*Juste la fin du monde* en compétition à Cannes," *Le Devoir* (Montréal), April 14, 2016.

36. Peter Bradshaw, "It's Only the End of the World review: Xavier Dolan's nightmarish homecoming is a dream," *The Guardian*, May 19, 2016. Available at <https://www. theguardian.com/film/2016/may/19/its-only-the-end-of-the-world-review-xavier-dolans-nightmarish-homecoming-is-a-dream> (accessed August 5, 2018).

37. Olivier Bombarda, "La fièvre insolente," *Bande à Part*, September 21, 2016. Available at <http://www.bande-a-part.fr/cinema/critique/juste-la-fin-du-monde-de-xavier-dolan-magazine-de-cinema/> (accessed July 20, 2018).

38. Justin Chang, "Cannes: how George Miller's jury got it wrong," *Los Angeles Times*, May 22, 2016. Available at <http://www.latimes.com/entertainment/movies/la-et-mn-cannes-film-festival-1463952778-htmlstory.html>; Jessica Kiang, "Cannes review: Xavier Dolan's shrill, shrieking drama 'It's Only the End of the World,'" *Playlist*, May 18, 2016. Available at <https://theplaylist.net/cannes-review-xavier-dolans-end-world-lea-seydoux-marion-cotillard-vincent-cassel-20160518/>.

39. Peter Debruge, "Cannes film review: 'It's Only the End of the World,'" *Variety*, May 18, 2016. Available at <https://variety.com/2016/film/festivals/its-only-the-end-of-the-world-review-xavier-dolan-1201777980/> (accessed June 24, 2018).

40. Richard Lawson, "Xavier Dolan's *It's Only the End of the World* is the most disappointing film at Cannes," *Vanity Fair*, May 19, 2016. Available at <https://www.vanityfair.com/hollywood/2016/05/xavier-dolan-its-only-the-end-of-the-world-review>; Jessica Kiang, "Cannes review: Xavier Dolan's shrill, shrieking drama."

41. Peter Debruge, "Cannes film review: 'It's Only the End of the World.'"

42. Catherine Shoard, "Xavier Dolan snubs Cannes over trolling and bullying," *The Guardian*, September 20, 2016. Available at <https://www.theguardian.com/film/2016/sep/20/xavier-dolan-snubs-cannes-film-festival-over-trolling-and-bullying> (accessed November 29, 2018).

43. Xavier Dolan (@xavierdolan), "We wrapped on *Matthias and Maxime* last night after 48 days of pure joy, and passionate creation. I'm grateful to have found a family of artists and friends with whom I get to make movies, and find escape," Instagram photo, November 16, 2018. Available at <https://www.instagram.com/p/BqORJGRA-eU/>.

44. See Mette Hjort and Duncan Petrie (eds), *The Cinema of Small Nations* (Edinburgh: Edinburgh University Press, 2007).

PART I

Queer Universalism

CHAPTER 1

The Transgressive Cinema of Xavier Dolan

Fulvia Massimi

In a 2015 interview following the success of his fourth feature, *Mommy* (2014), and discussing the upcoming shooting of his first Hollywood film, *The Death and Life of John F. Donovan* (2018), Xavier Dolan was asked to describe his relationship with his home country of Québec, as well as with his own family. The answers to both questions display a certain degree of similarity in their choice of words and in their conceptual formulation. In regard to his ties of national belonging, Dolan proclaims a "love–hate relationship" with Québec, underlining proximity to, but also critical distance from, his own national culture:

> I feel at the same time very close to Québec and then sometimes also very far. I feel very close to Québec in terms of language, identity struggles, quest for survival, quest of culture, modernity, urban planning, multi-ethnicity, and at the same time very distant in terms of exactly the opposite, sometimes its racism, Anglophobia, Francophobia . . . because Québec is a place where mostly Francophones and Anglophones cohabit, and there are old conflicts between them that do not concern me at all and leave people of my generation greatly indifferent.[1]

In response to the question "What's family to you?" Dolan articulates his answer in spatial terms, addressing a similar tension of contiguity and separation in the relationship with his mother. Despite the difficulties entailed by physical and geographical distance, the filmmaker expresses a feeling of reassurance in relation to the maternal household concluding that "family to me is like a lighthouse in the sea [a play on the French homophones "*mer*," sea, and "*mère*," mother]."

Emerging as a central preoccupation in Dolan's personal life and his cinematic production, the relationship of the Québécois subject with their own national identity is formulated in conjunction with, as well as in tension with, a familial microcosm that has surged as a cinematic repository for Québec's nationhood at large. In Dolan's films, the narrative progression and emotional evolution of the main character—mostly biologically male and queer—cannot be disconnected from their conflicted inclusion within a family unit they belong to either in terms of blood kinship (*J'ai tué ma mère*, 2009; *Laurence Anyways*, 2012; *Mommy*, 2014, *Juste la fin du monde*, 2016) or surrogacy (*Les Amours imaginaires*, 2010; *Tom à la ferme*, 2013). The transgressions operated by Dolan's cinema and discussed in this chapter thus stem from a reinterpretation of such a family-nation allegory, and deal more specifically with the relocation of motherhood and queerness at the core of Québec's cinematic and familiar master narrative. Whereas a large corpus of post-revolutionary and post-referendary Québécois films[2] have extensively reflected on tropes of struggling virility and future male legacy in Québec, Dolan has purposely refused to leave fatherhood and heterosexual masculinity at the center of his cinema. As I argued in a previous examination of Dolan's oeuvre,[3] paternal figures and heteronormative male subjects have been dislocated at the periphery of Dolan's work, allowing a revisiting of the hierarchy of gender power structures and the agency of female and queer subjects in Québec's nation-building processes not only in the cultural imaginary, but also in the societal structures of contemporary Québec.

In this chapter, I will expand on this framework of analysis to unpack the transgressive nature of Dolan's cinematic imaginaries and trajectories. In the spirit of Thomas Waugh's *The Romance of Transgression in Canada* (2006) and his understanding of transgression as a *queering* gesture at the core of Canadian cinemas, sexualities, and nations,[4] I will employ the concept of transgression to read Dolan's work as a system that engages with Québec's interlaced histories, geographies, and sexualities in a way that subverts their linear understanding within a heteronormative framework of thinking. This methodological approach is, however, challenging in itself. As the work of a white, cisgender, openly gay auteur deeply embedded in the structures of international film circuits and arthouse cinema, Dolan's films reinforce a series of formal and representational norms that contradict the notion of transgression as a re-centering of the marginal—namely through the absence of non-white characters, the privileging of middle-upper class settings (with the notable exceptions of *Tom à la ferme* and *Mommy*),[5] and a tendency to place queer subjects within a universalizing framework. The filmmaker's refusal of "queer" as a ghettoizing label on the occasion of the Queer Palm awarded to *Laurence Anyways* in 2012, and his insistence on referring to his films as narratives of "universal love," diverts in fact from Waugh's use of transgression as a way to reflect on how "peripheries define the centre" of Canadian cinemas as predominantly queer.[6]

Dolan's overarching intention to distance himself from the political implications of queer activism as an oppositional practice ("us" versus "them") thus falls under the conditions of a post-gay sensibility, wherein principles of acceptance and inclusion are predicated upon sameness ("us" *and* "them"). In this scenario, as Amin Ghaziani suggests, "boundaries between themselves [the queer subjects] and external audiences—and even among themselves internally" have to be profoundly renegotiated in order to allow for LGBTQ+ communities and identities to be formed.[7] In his article "Post-gay collective identity construction," Ghaziani argues indeed that post-gay practices exist along the tense lines of assimilation and diversity: "a post-gay society (1998 to the present) is distinguished by an increasing assimilation of gays into the mainstream alongside rapid internal diversification."[8] Such practices are, however, problematically linked to "politics of normalization," which entail the risk of valorizing subjects who conform to gender norms palatable to heterosexuals, to the detriment of those bodies and individuals who do not. In this light, how can the argument of transgression be sustained in relation to Dolan's work? As I will discuss in this chapter, Dolan's cinema presents an articulation of nonnormative subjects, spaces, and temporalities that lends itself to a queer revision of historical and geographical trajectories in Québec's contemporaneity. My co-option of the term "transgression" in relation to Dolan's work is therefore to be understood in the way his films champion maternal and non-normative male subjects over the centrality of fatherhood and straight masculinity as the privileged repositories of national traumas, thus *transgressing* the norm of the Québec family-nation as it has been presented on the national screen in the post-revolutionary and post-referendary moments of its film history.

The chapter can be divided into two main sections. First, I will define and contextualize the family-nation trope by building upon two canonical texts of Québec's film studies scholarship on the subject: Christiane Tremblay-Daviault's *Un cinéma orphelin* and Heinz Weinmann's *Cinéma de l'imaginaire québécois*. As both texts discuss the allegory of the national family in relation to popular Québec films from the 1940s to the 1980s, I will situate Dolan's work in relation to them, underlining how it functions as a revived landmark for the family-nation allegory in the globalized era of Québec cinema. Second, I will employ queer and feminist contributions in order to examine the transgressive trajectories traced by Dolan's films in narrative, audiovisual, gendered, and cultural terms. In particular, I will refer to Elizabeth Freeman, Jack Halberstam, and Michel Foucault's interventions on queer temporalities and geographies so as to understand how Dolan's cinema performs a counter-reading of normalized and normative conceptions of Québec's masculine national narrative through a revival of the national family theme.

The transgressive qualities of Dolan's body of work will not be solely understood within the limited scope of thematic and representational aspects. I will extend my line of inquiry to questions of queer aesthetics, spaces, temporalities, and glocal film imaginaries, and the way in which they allow an alternative futurity for Québec's national narratives and realities to be formulated. On the one hand, Dolan's work with formats, vernaculars, postmodern heterotopic spaces, and slippages of chronological and linear time, will provide an audiovisual and narrative counterpart to his alternative take on Québec's national and gendered historiography. On the other hand, the successful circulation of his films outside Québec's domestic market and within the international film festival circuit will offer an opportunity to investigate how the representation of national matters is affected by, and renegotiated through, cinematic tensions of local and global nature. Reviving its past, narrating its present, and envisioning its future, Dolan has been rethinking Québec's histories and geographies in light of the mutating position of Québec's nationhood, its cinema, and the allegory of its national family in a globalized era. Looking closely at his Québec-based films, I aim to assess how Dolan's work contributes to a crucial reimagining and rebuilding of Québec's intertwined gendered and national histories, using family as its neuralgic center.

TRANSGRESSIVE IMAGINARIES: THE FAMILY-NATION ALLEGORY

Despite several attempts to configure Québec as a "matriarchal society,"[9] feminist scholars such as Chantal Nadeau,[10] Diane Lamoureux,[11] and Mary Jean Green[12] have heavily questioned the "mythological" take on gendered nationhood in Québec. The political program of the Quiet Revolution (the period of modernization and secularization in 1960s Québec) as a masculinized and heterosexualized project rendered it indeed difficult for women to find their place within nation-building discourses and national narratives, if not through their reproductive functions as a matter of national survival and continuity. Canadian historian Jeffery Vacante has written extensively on such a connection between Québec's political history and its history of sexuality within the framework of men and masculinities studies. In his articles "Writing the history of sexuality and 'national' history in Quebec"[13] and "Liberal nationalism and the challenge of masculinity studies in Quebec,"[14] Vacante specifically locates in the Quiet Revolution the point of origin for the configuration of Québec's nationhood as a heteronormative, androcentric project. The promotion of male heterosexual power was conceived as a tool to overcome the myth of Québec's "homosexual" nation—since historically emasculated by the Church and subjugated by the anglophone colonizer.[15]

Such an equation of colonization and emasculation also appears at length in earlier writings on the metaphorization of female and queer subjects in Québec's national narratives.[16] In her 1999 piece "Bloody metaphors" Elspeth Probyn investigates the ways in which Québec is represented onscreen as a "normal" nation through the staging of gendered and sexualized metaphors, that is, how the otherwise extraordinary display of female sexuality and queer inclusion in Québec cinema, television, and literature is the symptom of homophobic and misogynistic panic, camouflaged and "normalized" to reinforce the actual norm of heterosexual masculinity. In his volume *Nationalism and the Politics of Culture in Quebec* (1988), Richard Handler as well points toward strategies of normalization of otherness in Québec's nationalist agenda, both within and beyond the revolutionary period, particularly in the assimilation of ethnic minorities. In a chapter aptly titled "A normal society," the author explains how the issues of immigration in Québec have been central to the province's nationalist discourses since the 1960s, and particularly in the late 1970s, when the "white paper on cultural development" introduced in 1978 by the sovereigntist Parti Québécois attempted to promote the integration of minorities without sacrificing the ambition of a homogeneous, monolingual nation.[17] As Handler rightly asks, however, "how can the desire for a homogeneous nation be reconciled with fair treatment of those elements in the nation that make for diversity?"[18] My intention to rethink familial dynamics in Québec via the work of Xavier Dolan thus stems from such a provocative interrogative. My focus on the gendered structures of the familial microcosm rather than on those of individual subjectivity is in fact substantiated by the very structures of Québec cinema as an Oedipal one, wherein the family acts as a synecdoche of nationhood at large—that is what I define in this chapter as the "family-nation allegory."

Tremblay-Daviault's *Un cinéma orphelin* and Weinmann's *Cinéma de l'imaginaire québécois* are foundational contributions in this sense. Tremblay-Daviault employs the notion of a "cinéma orphelin" to interrogate the troubled relationship of Québec's pre-revolutionary popular cinema (1940s to 1950s) with its Catholic legacy and French-Canadian roots.[19] Looking at feature films produced in the midst of the Duplessis era as her privileged corpus,[20] Tremblay-Daviault intends to detect and examine the relationship of homology between Québec's collective ideology at the time and the image of the world constructed by popular films as representatives of a given socio-cultural reality. Understanding films as objects produced under certain economic and cultural conditions rather than as mere spectacles, Tremblay-Daviault's book attempts to understand why popular cinema emerged at such a specific moment in Québec's history, and what functions it played in representing it. Although the author agrees to locate in the Quiet Revolution the emergence of an "authentically Québécois" cinema, the popular films analyzed in her volume are equally crucial to affect and determine the collective ideology imbued in the cinematic depiction of Québec's societal structures. As depictions of a traditional society entrenched in religious and family values, Tremblay-Daviault's examined texts are particularly concerned with the societal role played by the family unit and its relationship with both the individual (the film's protagonist) and the collective. Rural Québec in the 1940s and 1950s operates as a system based on kinship and familial legacy, wherein the soil passes from fathers to children to ensure the survival of nationhood itself. As Tremblay-Daviault notices, however, the very structures of this society—and consequently of its cinematic representation and imaginary—are deeply affected by the advent of modernization and the influence of the "money society" of 1950s North America over Québec's traditional one. The idea of Québec's national identity as utterly different from that of other North American contexts, and especially of other English Canadian provinces, hence strengthens between 1945 and 1960 as a site of contention of previous traditional ways of life, triggering a necessary revision and rethinking of the trope of the family-nation in Québec cinema as well.

Analogous concerns appear in Weinmann's *Cinéma de l'imaginaire québécois*.[21] The author recurs to the Freudian notion of "roman familial" to understand how Québec cinema from the 1950s onward has engaged with the complexity of its postcolonial struggle, as well as with the unresolved feelings of attachment to the Catholic Church as a surrogate family/motherland.[22] Weinmann locates in the aftermath of the first referendum defeat of 1980 the peak of Québec's difficulty in cutting the last ties with its literal and figurative motherlands.[23] This crucial moment of shift is defined as an "age of silence," marked by the regression of Québec to a state of infancy and inability to talk about the failure of sovereignty. As a result of this silent moment, representations of monoparental families wherein the child takes over the responsibilities of inadequate single parents start proliferating in Québec cinema. The concept of "roman familial" invoked by Weinmann as the privileged mode of expression of Québec's cinematic imaginary thus points toward the centrality of parental issues at play in Québec's master narrative as a way to engage with the disillusions of the post-revolutionary and post-referendary eras. That of the family-nation is, therefore, a pivotal trope enrooted in the history of Québec cinema as well as of its scholarly interpretations, to the extent that in more recent times Bill Marshall defined Québec cinema's specificity precisely as a "conjunction of Oedipus, the family romance, and nationhood."[24] In his chapter "Sex and nation," Marshall particularly reflects on the unbalanced nature of the gendered narratives based on family dynamics and brought onto the Québécois screen from the 1970s onward, and claimed that "one obvious complexity lies in the centrality of sexual difference to the scenario, and the way in which women (in the form of the mother) not only represent the ground on which father-son conflict is

played out, but in addition play a silenced role in which the politically specific positions of gender assignment are neglected."[25]

Dolan's films represent an anomaly in this sense. Not only do they disrupt
the primacy of father-son relationships in the national narrative of Québec's
post-revolutionary and post-referendary cinema by erasing the paternal figure
from their fabric, they also revisit Québec's cinematic and socio-political history by giving voice and presence back to those subjects lying at its margins.
The five features made by the filmmaker between his debut in 2009 (*J'ai tué
ma mère*) and the peak of his popularity in 2014 (*Mommy*)—which I will refer
to as the "Québec corpus"—constitute a pentalogy on gender and sexuality set
across and beyond the last two decades of Québec's post-referendary era.[26] In
J'ai tué ma mère, rebellious teenager Hubert (Xavier Dolan) struggles with the
acceptance of his own homosexuality and the tumultuous relationship with his
flamboyant mother Chantale (Anne Dorval). In *Les Amours imaginaires*, the
irruption of Nicolas (Niels Schneider) into the life of two young Montrealers,
Francis (Dolan) and Marie (Monia Chokri), threatens to disrupt their friendship. In *Laurence Anyways*, thirty-five-year-old teacher and aspiring writer
Laurence Alia (Melvil Poupaud) decides to undergo a desired sex change at the
risk of jeopardizing the relationship with his family and his long-time partner
Fred (Suzanne Clément). In *Tom à la ferme*—the adaptation of Michel Marc
Bouchard's homonymous play—advertising copywriter Tom (Dolan) embarks
on a journey in the outskirts of rural Québec to attend the funeral of his dead
lover and meet his partner's mother and brother for the first time. Finally, in
Mommy, problematic teenager Steve (Antoine Olivier Pilon) is released from
juvenile detention and taken under the care of his mother Diane "Die" Déprés
(Anne Dorval) and her neighbor Kyla (Suzanne Clément), in a near-future
Québec wherein the fictional law S-14 allows parents of troubled children to
hospitalize them without any due process. Comprising a circular structure that
opens with *J'ai tué ma mère* and ends with the reprisal of similar issues of
mother-son conflict in *Mommy*, Dolan's "Québec corpus" can be approached
as an intertextual system that engages with the intertwined trajectories of
Québec's histories, geographies, and sexualities in disruptive terms. In the following section of the chapter, I will examine how temporal and spatial strategies are employed in Dolan's work to (re)construct these trajectories.

TRANSGRESSIVE TRAJECTORIES: QUEERING TIMES
AND REMAPPING DESIRES

Moving backward and forward on Québec's historical timeline, Dolan's cinema
reflects the desire to revise crucial discourses of identity politics and national
models of subjectivity in the filmmaker's contemporaneity, with an eye turned

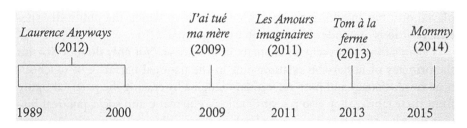

Figure 1.1 The "queer chronology" of Dolan's films.

to the past and one geared toward the future. The discrepancy between the chronological progression of the five abovementioned features, their actual historical setting, and the conscious anachronism of their mise-en-scène allows speculating on how Dolan's films operate within the discontinuities and ruptures of queer temporalities, both systemically and individually. The linear progression of his "Québec corpus" can indeed be deconstructed and reassembled in accordance with the historical period depicted within each film's narrative. This reconstructed "queer chronology" situates *Laurence Anyways* at the beginning of the timeline, and *Mommy* at the end of it—the former covering the decade from 1989 to 2000, and the latter the slightly futuristic moment of 2015 (Figure 1.1). Whereas it can be argued that film time and historical time coincide in *J'ai tué ma mère*, *Les Amours imaginaires*, and *Tom à la ferme*, since no explicit narrative marker seems to hint to a different time-setting, the anachronism of decors and costumes as a recurrent feature in Dolan's work can be read as a strategy of queer historiography reminiscent of Elizabeth Freeman's "temporal drag."

In her article "Packing history, count(er)ing generations" (2000), Freeman introduces the notion of "temporal drag" to discuss the incongruities and temporal disruptions of gender-crossing practices that function "in the mode of stubborn identification with a set of social coordinates that exceeded [one's] own historical moment."[27] Establishing a critical dialogue with Judith Butler's seminal work on gender performativity,[28] Freeman argues for the recuperation of the past as a strategy to rethink queer and especially lesbian identification outside the parameters of drag as a sequence of "future-oriented and transformative repetitions."[29] Whereas for Butler drag functioned as a re-enactment of the past along progressive lines of forwarding time (because everything that looks backward is a copy without originals), Freeman champions the anachronism and dissonance of one's performance of gender over the exact correspondence of gender identity to the criteria of one's contemporary socio-historical conditions. The shift promoted by Freeman's "temporal drag" thus suggests that the re-enactment of the past does not have to be limited to linear and conventionally generational understandings of time.

Figure 1.2 Outdated style in *Tom à la ferme.*

Processes of queer identification should not be subsumed into straight temporal trajectories, but should rather constitute a movement backward, forward, and across time. Not "how" but "when" queer performativity takes place hence becomes a key question in regard to Dolan's oeuvre. Herein, the transgressive use of formal and narrative devices allows the filmmaker to resume and revisit past national and gendered histories in order to meditate on the state of queer and female subjectivities in Québec's present. The kitsch extravaganza of Anne Dorval's clothing in *J'ai tué ma mère*, the vintage rebound of 1950s fashion in *Les Amours imaginaires*, and the outdated excesses of the characters' wardrobe in *Tom à la ferme* (Figure 1.2) are the most evident signs of temporal drag on display in Dolan's film, as they generate inconsistencies between the characters' identities and the time of their narratives. Although most explicit, the consciously anachronistic use of fashion is, however, not the only marker of temporal and queer transgression emerging from Dolan's cinema making consistent use of postmodern means of expression at the level of narrative, audiovisual, temporal and spatial organization.

In Dolan's work, narrative linearity is indeed often abandoned in favor of erratic reconstructions of the film's storyline as filtered through the characters' subjectivity and punctuated by moments of imaginative suspension. In this sense, the insisted use of slow motion, intertitles, breaks of the fourth wall, and montage sequences in a music video fashion translate on screen the emotional turmoil and identity struggles of the films' characters. These formal and narrative expedients are therefore not just self-reflexive signs of citational authoriality.[30] Rather, they work in tandem with Dolan's exploration and subversion of patriarchal and masculine lineages in Québec's contemporaneity, immediate future, and near past, as they are not only often associated with the characters' complex and negotiated understanding of their own sexuality and gender, but also of the times and places they inhabit in the world. In this sense, then, my use of the "queer" terminology in relation to these subjectivities aims to define a larger spectrum of non-normativity that encompasses the fluidity of sexual orientations and gender self-identification practices, as well as the non-conformity to social norms of mental health and psychophysical behavior (i.e. Steve in *Mommy*).

In his debut film, *J'ai tué ma mère*, the titular tale of matricidal rebellion and queer teenagehood is interpolated by segments of black and white in-video confessionality, recorded by the filmmaker/protagonist as the privileged format to frame his own subjectivity. Following an epigraphic quote from Guy de Maupassant's novel *Fort comme la mort* (1889),[31] the film opens on a close-up of Hubert talking about the impossibility of being a son for his mother. Details of the character's eyes and fingers are juxtaposed to the full close-up of his face, anticipating the sense of fragmentation further augmented by the following scene, a brief montage sequence of kitsch paraphernalia and grotesque slow motion details of Chantale eating her breakfast. Bits and pieces of Hubert's video-diary punctuate the narrative up to Chantale's discovery of the recordings toward the end of the film, when the two layers of diegetic narrative eventually collide. Along with these direct interpellations of the audience, the protagonist's subjective point of view is conveyed in the film through fantasy scenes that stage Hubert's mother as a dead body, a Carmen Miranda-like figure, and a blood-crying saint. At the peak of Hubert and Chantale's emotional and physical detachment from one another, a dreamlike sequence occurs in which Hubert imagines himself desperately chasing his mother in a wedding gown, without ever reaching her. Such an allegory of impossible mother-son bonding is supplanted at the end of the film by glimpses of found footage capturing Chantale and Hubert's blissful relationship at the time of the young man's childhood. This further interruption in narrative continuity suggests a renewed sense of affection between the two characters, which is achieved in the film through their eventual reconciliation in the intimate space of Hubert's "kingdom": a chalet in Montmagny (a city in the Appalachian region of Québec).

The insisted recurrence of breaches in the narrative texture of the film—often accompanied by formal choices that underline their oneiric and subjective nature—thus intervenes to resituate the main character in a time and space that does not obey conventional logics of linear progression, either cinematically or socially. Hubert's caustic and at times desperate escapism (a reaction to the homophobic society he is clustered into, as well as to the incomprehension of his putative family) generates pockets of queer temporality in which traditional gendered and family dynamics can be provoked and subverted. The character's final relocation into the safety of his childhood space also complements the non-linear nature of the film's temporality with an abrupt but motivated alteration of the film's geography. Almost entirely shot in Longueuil (Dolan's native town), *J'ai tué ma mère* in fact ends on a potentially hopeful note that opposes the lacustrine landscape of Montmagny to the suburban alienation of Montréal's south shore region. Shifting the film's closing location to a "place of the mind," and superimposing fragments of childhood memories on the present state of Chantale and Hubert's relationship, the two levels of the film's transgressive trajectory (non-linear time, non-coherent geography) collide into a moment that redefines and liberates both characters by resituating them into an alternative spatio-temporal dimension.

Similar to *J'ai tué ma mère* in its treatment of space and time from a queer angle, Dolan's second feature, *Les Amours imaginaires*, presents a triangulated friendship as the alternative to the traditional family unit by returning once again to strategies of narrative and visual discrepancy. In-camera testimonies of over-romanticized or unfortunate love narrated by unknown characters/interviewees punctuate the film, functioning as interruptions to, but also commentaries on, the main storyline, which witnesses the annihilation of male-to-female friendship at the hand of an angelic intruder and romantic contender. The characters' self-destructive longing is epitomized in the film by a music video-inspired sequence that presents Francis and Marie looking at Nicolas dancing with his mother Désirée (Anne Dorval) to the notes of The Knife's 2003 hit song "Pass This On." Devoured by reciprocal jealousy, the protagonists exchange a series of passive aggressive remarks, with Francis particularly endorsing Désirée's observations on Marie's outfit: "It's true that your dress is slightly anachronistic."

Functioning as a meta-textual commentary, Francis's words underline how both characters are actually out of place in their own time and space. Whereas they both offer a representative sample of the hipster demographics and culture of Montréal's artsy Mile End neighborhood, the two exist in a bubble of temporal suspension, dominated by subjective logics of over-fantasized but unrequited romance. This last point is particularly evident in the very same scene, as the characters look at Nicolas through the transfigurative lenses of their respective erotic fantasies—Jean Cocteau's homoerotic drawings for Francis, and Michelangelo's *David* for Marie—thus zooming out of their here-and-now existence to project their romance into the realm of the fantasmatic. Such an escapist, and ultimately delusional, attitude of the film's protagonists is replicated at the spatial level as well. Both in the urban setting of Montréal and within the natural landscape that frames the friends' escapade in the Québec woods (the sequences are shot between Pontneuf and Sainte-Croix), Francis and Marie appear disconnected from reality, constantly caught between their own romantic obsessions and the destructive game that opposes one another in the quest for Nicolas's love. Whereas in *J'ai tué ma mère*, nature functioned as a liberating space for the queer character in search of himself and for the mother in search of her lost son, in *Les Amours imaginaires*, personal and mutual annihilation intervenes to destroy the cathartic and sexually freeing forces of the non-urban location, ultimately offering to Montréal the possibility to redeem itself as the locus of queer-to-female solidarity. The film's bitter ending shot, which hints at the revival of Marie and Francis' threesome-like obsession toward a flirty Louis Garrel (in a brief cameo) suggests, however, the potential spiraling of the characters down the same rabbit hole that triggered their self-destructive journey at the beginning of the film. Regardless of their physical setting, this closing scene seems therefore to indicate that the only space for Francis and Marie to actually exist and love is the realm of fantasy rather than that of tangible reality—a form of spatio-temporal marginalization generated by the repression and rejection of their desires in the caustic confrontation with the only male heterosexual character in the film.

The *queering* of time and space in Dolan's cinema thus attempts to carve out a parallel dimension for subjects whose impulses and desires, as both individuals and parts of unconventional family/pseudo-family units, cannot be normalized and integrated within the same rationale of heteronormative thinking and practices. In the introductory chapter to her volume *In a Queer Time and Place: Transgender Bodies, Subcultural Lives* (2005), J. Halberstam embarks on the "perhaps overly ambitious" task of defining queer times and spaces as indicators of intersectional practices of postmodern living.[32] Moving away from the mere association of queerness and sexual identity, Halberstam theorizes unorthodox temporalities and geographies that can function as times and spaces of contention for queer subjects existing outside the heteronormative logics of spatio-temporal and (re)productive progression. As he argues, "queer subcultures produce alternative temporalities by allowing their participants to believe that their future can be imagined according to logics that lie outside of those pragmatic markers of life experience—namely birth, marriage, reproduction, and death."[33] Halberstam's rethinking of Western, white, middle-class, capitalist notions of reproductive time as the norm echoes Lee Edelman's claims on queer futurism outlined in his 1998 piece "The future is kid stuff: queer theory, disidentification, and the death drive." Therein, Edelman champions the non-reproductive nature of queer pleasure as the oppositional strategy to the "temporalization of desire" embedded in conservative politics that conceive child-making practices as the only teleological option:

> The consequences of such a compulsory identification both of and with the child as the culturally pervasive emblem of the motivating end, albeit endlessly postponed, of every political vision as a vision of futurity, must

weigh upon the consideration of a queer oppositional politics. For the only queerness that queer sexualities could ever hope to claim would spring from their determined opposition to this underlying structure of the political, their opposition, that is, to the fantasmatic ambition of achieving symbolic closure through the marriage of identity to futurity in order to reproduce the social subject.[34]

By opposing queer sexualities to the child figure as the embodiment of the future, Edelman urges for a paradox: how can there be a future without reproduction? And how can there be a *queer* future when the very notion of queerness is antithetic to the survival of the child and therefore of the human subject as a whole? In her 2009 volume *The Queer Child, or Growing Sideways in the Twentieth Century*, Kathryn Bond Stockton expands even further on this point, looking at different embodiments of the queer child figure in twentieth-century fiction. The author champions the queer child as the epitome of queer time precisely because its existence as a gay/homosexual child is denied by traditional historical narratives due to the taboos surrounding children's sexuality and childhood as an allegedly non-sexualized or straight moment in life. Employing the notion of "growing sideways" in opposition to that of "growing up," Bond Stockton proposes to re-position the queer child on a non-linear, non-vertical, diachronic, and horizontal history, which attempts to document the existence of a subject otherwise absent from historical accounts.[35]

The transgressive reprisal of the family-nation allegory as employed in Dolan's work can be read as an example of queer temporality and queer futurism precisely for its disjunction of the family microcosm from reproductive outcomes/purposes that extend to the national macrocosm as well. Mothers exist in Dolan's cinematic universe as no-longer-generational entities and male queer subjects as transformative rather than generative ones: the matrilineal quality of his cinema works paradoxically both in accordance and in discordance with queer logics of non-procreative times and futures. Several of Dolan's narratives are indeed punctuated by the actual and/or metaphorical death of a child. The loss of a son is the starting point for *Tom à la ferme* as well as the implied trauma of Kyla in *Mommy*; the metamorphosis of Laurence in *Laurence Anyways* allows for the replacement of an unloved son with a loved daughter, albeit also occurring to the detriment of Laurence and Fred's unborn baby, and Steve's suggested suicide attempt in the very last shot of *Mommy* hints at yet another instance of a queer child's death. This "vision of futurity" that passes through the family and at the same time *by*passes the very concept of family as a reproductive unit lies at the core of Dolan's work. It also deconstructs the family-nation allegory by offering a privileged position to the interaction between female and queer subjects, and by deflecting the centrality of male heterosexual subjects from Québec's national narrative. As mentioned above, such a double bind of de-construction and re-construction operates in Dolan's cinema through a series of choices that affect narrative and formal cohesiveness as well as temporal and spatial stability, resulting in the creation of those very times (but also spaces) of queer struggle investigated by Halberstam.

After defining queer temporality and counter-reproductive logics of time, Halberstam proceeds indeed to argue that a "'queer' adjustment in the way we think about time . . . requires and produces new conceptions of space."[36] As queer spaces are a direct consequence of queer understandings of time and history, Halberstam revisits key writings in postmodern geography—such as those by Edward Soja, Fredric Jameson, and David Harvey—to expose the absence of sexuality from their analysis as a result of neo-Marxist biases toward sex as a counter-activist "part of a ludic body politics."[37] Conversely, Halberstam champions gender and sexuality, alongside race and ethnicity, as pivotal categories of inquiry for the creation of "geographies of resistance," that is, subversive spaces of non-normative power where queer subcultures can survive and thrive.[38] The queer reconfiguration of geographical and formal spaces in concomitance with the sexual, gendered, and familiar development of Dolan's characters establishes yet another liaison with Halberstam's theoretical framework, reorganizing not only the temporal existence of queer and female subjects, but also their spatial relocation in the contemporary grand narrative of urban and suburban Québec.

Following *J'ai tué ma mère* and *Les Amours imaginaires*, ruptures in narrative linearity, temporal, and spatial coherence consolidate as a staple feature in Dolan's work, recurring whenever the main characters are undergoing moments of distress or psycho-physical evolution in conjunction with their own sexuality, their gender identity, and their relationship with significant others or loved ones—the latter most exclusively in the form of the maternal figure. Almost completely erased from the films' narrative, fathers appear only sporadically, either as pathetic imitations of patriarchal authority (*J'ai tué ma mère*), out-of-frame figures (*Les Amours imaginaires*), passive and silent presences (*Laurence Anyways*), or melancholic absences (*Mommy*), ultimately affecting the legacy of their sons only post-mortem, or not at all. As the use of narrative and aesthetic disruptions becomes even more ambitious and explicit in Dolan's following films, *Laurence Anyways*, *Tom à la ferme*, and *Mommy*—functioning as visual displays of Laurence's transformation into a woman, Tom's abusive relationship with his homophobic "brother-in-law" Francis, and Steve's mental illness—their complicity in the creation of queer forms of time and spaces of resistance continues to be linked to the way Dolan's characters come to terms with their gender and psychological troubles in unconventional family-nation microcosms.

Narrated in a somewhat chronological manner from 1989 to the verge of 2000, *Laurence Anyways* features several interruptions of linear storytelling from its very opening scene, which stages the eponymous protagonist exposed to the intrusive and scrutinizing in-camera gaze of a multicultural pool of Montréal-based observers. Caught on her way to the interview that functions as the background to the film's narrative, Laurence, her face hidden by an overly cinematic haze, is presented from an external point of view and through the judgmental look of others—of *all* others. The trespassing of the private space, the domestic safety of Laurence's apartment, into the dangers of the street, and therefore of public and transphobic contempt,[39] is the very first instance of geographical determination *Laurence Anyways* is setting up for the viewer. The dichotomy of the private and the public acts as a refrain throughout the film, granting Laurence the possibility to exist as her real self only within liminal spaces such as the cemetery or the Five Roses club, where old chanteuses and drag queens accept her as part of their, once again, alternative family.

The transgressive nature of Dolan's spatial mise-en-scène is epitomized to the fullest by an iconic sequence occurring later in the film and showing Laurence and Fred reunited after years of separation. The couple walks down the deserted, icy streets of the fictional location of the Île-au-Noir under a cascade of colorful clothes, accompanied by the upbeat of Moderat's electronic song "A New Error." The imaginary space fabricated by the characters' fantasy and patch-worked out of a series of different Québécois locations—both Bill Marshall and Valérie Mandia contend it might refer to the Île aux Noix on the Richelieu River[40] and L'Isle-aux-Coudres on the St Lawrence River[41]—serves as the setting for Laurence and Fred's impossible reconciliation, but also as a heterotopic moment in which several layers of subjective times and personal geographies collide and superimpose on one another.

In his seminal article "Of other spaces," Michel Foucault locates in utopias and heterotopias the representative spaces of postmodernity, or rather of what he defines as "the epoch of simultaneity [and] juxtaposition."[42] As the hierarchical nature of medieval spaces (the sacred above the profane) is supplanted by spatial coexistence and heterogeneity—a result of globalization and demographic "displacement" of people and goods[43]—utopias and heterotopias surge to embody the intersectional qualities of postmodern spatiality. Whereas utopian spaces do not exist in real life but entertain a relationship of analogy with society as "perfected forms" of it, heterotopias are actual spaces in which "real sites, all the other sites that can be found within the culture, are simultaneously represented, contested, and inverted."[44] The emphasis on simultaneity as the defining feature of a postmodern sense of space recurs in Foucault's further theorization of the six principles of heterotopias: they exist in every world culture, they develop in different ways according to the society they belong to, they juxtapose several spaces into one (i.e. the cinema), they are "heterochronical" in that they break with traditional notions of time (i.e. the cemetery), they are at the same time open and close, penetrable and impenetrable (i.e. the motel room), and finally, they create illusory spaces superimposed on real ones (i.e. the brothel).

The superimposition of the Île au Noir's fictional setting on Laurence and Fred's previous romantic routine (the cascade of clothes as a reminder of Laurence's habit of tossing a load of fresh laundry on Fred's head as she wakes up in the morning) thus evokes the simultaneity of the heterotopic space as well as its "relation to all the space that remains."[45] The illusory nature of the geographical location, augmented by the oneiric detail of clothing falling from the sky and by the pretense of sexual and gendered freedom, points indeed toward the illusory nature of Laurence and Fred's romantic reunion as well as to the ineluctability of their break-up. The characters' existence as a couple rests only on the fragile spatiality of an island cut off from the harsh socio-cultural conditions of the real; a place where transgender subjects are resisting the rules of heteronormativity while at the same time sheltering themselves from the risks entailed by their own visibility.

Dolan's sense for diachronic detours, heterotopic and ultimately "queer" spaces goes hand in hand with his interest in the manipulation of time and narrative continuity, but is not limited to the characters' sexuality, their storylines, or representational unfolding. It extends also to the very form of the film itself. In both *Tom à la ferme* and *Mommy*, explicit breaches in the storyline are indeed substituted by an unconventional use of film format(s). Shot in common US widescreen 1.85:1, *Tom à la ferme* witnesses a fluctuation in aspect ratios, with the screen letterboxing to the 2.35:1 format in conjunction with the protagonist's peaks of emotional distress and (homo)erotic tension. In *Mommy* the introduction of the 1:1 format as an allegory of the characters' imprisonment, as well as a hint to millennial practices of social media expression such as Instagram and Snapchat, is equally but even more explicitly prone to flexibility. The frame is literally opened by the direct intervention of the male protagonist halfway through the film, and again toward the end as a way to visualize the fantasy scene of Diane imagining an impossible happy-ending future for her son. Oscillating between hopeful opening and inexorable confinement, these variations in the film's aspect ratios add an extra layer of complexity to the transgressive architecture of Dolan's cinema, as they carve out of the screen itself several dimensions of temporal and spatial existence for female and queer characters to occupy.

Despite Dolan's international profile and his own detachment from specific issues of national identity—in a way that could be read as "post-national" inasmuch as his attitude toward queerness can be interpreted as "post-gay"—the formal, temporal, and spatial transgressions of his cinema lend themselves to be interpreted as signs of Québec's shifting stances in regard to the national question. As Bill Marshall argues,[46] Dolan's queer treatment of temporal and spatial trajectories—particularly in *Laurence Anyways* and *Tom à la ferme*—is not simply contingent on the filmmaker's engagement with issues of transgender awakening and homosexual-homophobic tension, but also establishes a clear link between his work and the "re-shapings in [the] risky category [of] a Québec national narrative, or more specifically, in shifts in perceptions of self and the world among (largely white) Francophone Québécois audiences."[47] Marshall situates Dolan's films within the broader history of queer cinema in Québec, from the pre-Omnibus confrontation with threatened masculinities in the 1960s to current narratives of queer coming out epitomized by Jean-Marc Vallée's *C.R.A.Z.Y.* (2005). Despite the filmmaker's own rejection of the "queer label" on the occasion of the Queer Palm Award at Cannes 2012, Marshall underlines how Dolan's work promotes a more encompassing understanding and employment of queerness as a way to problematize identity rather than enclosing it in the limitations of identity politics discourses. This is achieved, as above analyzed, by bending time and space to counter-heteronormative logics that mirror the sexual and gendered transgressions of Dolan's characters as well. What is especially resonant in Marshall's contribution is the way it revisits (via Dolan's work) the very national paradigm that informed his earlier volume, *Quebec National Cinema*. Rather than seeing in Dolan's cinema, its use of space, time, and language, a sign of post-national shift—that is the possibility to move beyond a national framework of inquiry—Marshall identifies in Dolan's transgressive trajectory and imaginary the epitome of a modernized, millennial understanding of the relationships between the local and the global, the national and the world, the anglophone and francophone souls in Québec's cinema and current society:

> The national "we" now so at home (in diverse, contradictory and even conflictual ways) in the suburbs is located in a space which, thanks to audio-visual media, internet networks, and a *décrispation* [thawing] of relations with the English language, is in a position to relay the multiple surfaces of belonging which constitute the new horizons of "Québecness."[48]

Instead of presenting a series of national allegories in the limited sense of the term, Dolan's work thus comes to symbolize nationhood in its most current complexity as a concept in flux; a construct that opens up and becomes malleable, no longer confined within univocal and modern conceptions of linear time, enclosed space, and gender binaries. The insistence on the notion of "allegory" in Marshall's piece as well as in this chapter as a whole is therefore not reliant on the processes of metaphorization and "normalization" of female and queer subjects as scrutinized by Robert Schwartzwald and Elspeth Probyn in "Fear of federasty: Québec's inverted fictions" and "Bloody metaphors and other allegories of the ordinary" respectively. Both Probyn and Schwartzwald point out how Québec's post-referendary fiction (be it in the form of television, cinema, or literature) endorsed the reduction of female and queer characters to scapegoats for the failure of Québec's sovereigntist project—or, as Probyn defines it, the achievement of "national normalcy." As a defining trope of the colonial relationship between Québec and Canada in the province's fictional imaginary, the feminization and homosexualization of the Québécois nation versus the heterosexist, hyper-masculinization of the anglophone colonizer perpetuated the construction of a national narrative that sees in women and queer subjects "wounds" and threats to the achievement of national sovereignty and self-determination. Dolan's cinema, on the contrary, works critically against such narrative paradigms by removing heterosexual masculinity from its framework and by giving material and discursive presence to queer subjects and maternal/female figures as agents of community building. Women and queer subjects are no longer synonymous with the failures and lacks of Québec's re-masculinizing project, but rather step out of the dark and into the core of a revisited family-nation allegory—a vehicle toward the reimagining and reconstruction of Québec's present and future history.

NOTES

1. Xavier Dolan, "Interview with Xavier Dolan on *Mommy*, family and *John F. Donovan*," by Alessia Gargiulo, *YouTube*, last modified January 22, 2015. Available at <https://www.youtube.com/watch?v=bNWxa3qsMqU> (accessed October 18, 2016).
2. I use the terms "post-revolutionary" and "post-referendary" to define films made in Québec after the Quiet Revolution of the 1960s and the two sovereignty referenda in 1980 and 1995.
3. Fulvia Massimi, "'A boy's best friend is his mother': Quebec's matriarchy and queer nationalism in the cinema of Xavier Dolan," *Synoptique*, 4/2, 2016, pp. 8–31.
4. Thomas Waugh, *The Romance of Transgression in Canada* (Montréal: McGill-Queen's University Press, 2006), p. 7.
5. Discussing his visual influences in an interview for French magazine *Premiere*, Dolan provocatively stated: "I quickly realized, for example, that I hate the 'aesthetics of poverty' in films. I dislike the way some directors approach the subject of lower social classes through a 'grey' way of shooting their films. I always found that disgusting. It is for this reason that in *Mommy* I used the square format. The real subject of the film is, in fact, the way working-class characters try to live the American dream, and how the American dream forcefully rejects them"; Xavier Dolan, "'C'est hyper important pour moi de sentir que Mommy est aimé,'" *Premiere*, October 7, 2014. Available at <http://www.premiere.fr/Cinema/News-Cinema/Xavier-Dolan-Cest-hyper-important-pour-moi-de-sentir-que-Mommy-est-aime> (accessed December 18, 2017). My translation.
6. Waugh, *The Romance of Transgression in Canada*, p. 8.
7. Amin Ghaziani, "Post-gay collective identity construction," *Social Problems*, 58/1, February 2011, p. 104.

8. Ibid. p. 103.
9. Matthew Evangelista, *Gender, Nationalism, and War: Conflict on the Movie Screen* (Cambridge, UK, and New York: Cambridge University Press, 2011); Aleksandar Dundjerovic, *The Cinema of Robert Lepage: The Poetics of Memory* (London: Wallflower Press, 2003), pp. 147–57.
10. Chantal Nadeau, "*Barbaras en Québec*: variations on identity," in Kay Armatage, Kass Banning, Brenda Longfellow, and Janine Marchessault (eds), *Gendering the Nation: Canadian Women's Cinema* (Toronto: University of Toronto Press, 1999), pp. 197–211.
11. Diane Lamoureux, *L'Amère patrie: féminisme et nationalisme* (Montréal: Éditions Remue-ménage, 2001).
12. Mary Jean Green, *Women and Narrative Identity: Rewriting the Quebec National Text* (Montréal: McGill-Queen's University Press, 2001).
13. Jeffery Vacante, "Writing the history of sexuality and 'national' history in Quebec," *Journal of Canadian Studies*, 39/2, 2005, pp. 31–55.
14. Jeffery Vacante, "Liberal nationalism and the challenge of masculinity studies in Quebec," *Left History*, 11/2, 2006, pp. 96–117.
15. As Vacante acknowledges, the call for secularization of the Quiet Revolution was supported by a strong reassertion of heterosexual masculinity based on two main arguments. On the one side, the rejection of the Church's educational system as an environment accused of instilling feminine values in boys and therefore preventing the production of "strong and virile leaders" for an independent nation. On the other, the homophobic dismantlement of colonial discourses based on the homosexualized, feminized metaphor of Québec as the passive partner of the anglophone colonizer. National independence thus became, for the leaders and theorists of the Quiet Revolution, an instrument to allow both the men and the (white, francophone) nation in Québec to emerge from a state of weakness and dependence. Vacante, "Writing the history of sexuality," pp. 36–7.
16. Elspeth Probyn, "Bloody metaphors and other allegories of the ordinary," in Caren Kaplan, Norma Alarcón, and Minoo Moallem (eds), *Between Woman and Nation: Nationalisms, Transnational Feminisms, and the State* (Durham, NC: Duke University Press, 1999), pp. 47–62; Robert Schwartzwald, "Fear of federasty: Québec's inverted fictions," in Hortense J. Spillers (ed.), *Comparative American Identities: Race Sex, and Nationality in the Modern Context* (New York: Routledge, 1991), pp. 175–95.
17. Richard Handler, *Nationalism and the Politics of Culture in Quebec* (Madison: University of Wisconsin Press, 1988), pp. 175–6.
18. Ibid. p. 176.
19. Christiane Tremblay-Daviault, *Un cinéma orphelin: structures mentales et sociales du cinéma québécois, 1942–1953* (Montréal: Éditions Québec/Amérique, 1981).
20. Maurice Duplessis (1890–1959) was Premier of Québec from 1936 to 1939 and again from 1944 to 1959. Due to the conservative policies of his government, his mandate as Premier went down in history as *La Grande Noirceur* (the Great Darkness).
21. Heinz Weinmann, *Cinéma de l'imaginaire québécois* (Montréal: Éditions de l'Hexagone, 1990).
22. In his 1909 "Le roman familial des névrosés," Freud discusses the "roman familial" as a fantasmatic and subconscious practice through which the pre-adolescent child imagines that it is part of a different family unit (often more powerful and richer), either by abduction, adoption, or simply by substituting alternative parental figures to their actual ones. This activity constitutes a necessary stage in the construction of one's identity, as it allows the subject to emancipate from parental influence and escape Oedipal dynamics. In Weinmann's allegorical use of the term, Québec represents the pre-adolescent subject and the province's motherlands its putative parents.

23. Working on a film corpus that spans only until 1989, Weinmann's volume ends its inquiry before the second referendary defeat of 1995, which I will take into consideration in my analysis of Dolan's films.
24. Bill Marshall, *Quebec National Cinema* (Montréal: McGill-Queen's University Press, 2001), p. 105.
25. Ibid. p. 104.
26. For coherence, I will not include Dolan's sixth feature and French-Canadian co-production *Juste la fin du monde* (2016) in the "Québec corpus" discussed here. Although arguably shot in Québec and displaying formal and thematic similarities with his previous films, the atemporal and aspatial nature of *Juste la fin du monde* does not entertain as clear a relationship with the histories and geographies of Québec I am interested in examining in this chapter. On the contrary, the removal of any reference to HIV seems to endorse the filmmaker's intention to de-historicize the socio-political implications of the 1990 play by Jean-Luc Lagarce that inspired the film.
27. Elizabeth Freeman, "Packing history, count(er)ing generations," *New Literary History*, 31/4, 2000, p. 728.
28. Judith Butler, *Gender Trouble* (New York: Routledge, 1990).
29. Freeman, "Packing history," p. 728.
30. In *The Seventh Art*'s video-essay on Dolan's style presented at TIFF 2015 and narrated in voice-over by Canadian filmmaker Patricia Rozema, the formal architecture of the filmmaker's oeuvre is conceived as a set of coherent tools to translate on screen the identity, gendered, and familial endeavors of "characters in transition." Rather than being dismissed as "mercurial," Dolan's style is read in close relationship to the subjectivities his films explore, as it is deemed "uniformly in service of establishing the portrait of these characters." The Seventh Art, "Xavier Dolan video essay: TIFF 2015," *YouTube*, January 5, 2015. Available at <https://www.youtube.com/watch?v=SaMzmQoMz_Y> (accessed December 29, 2016).
31. "On aime sa mère presque sans le savoir, et on ne s'aperçoit de toute la profondeur des racines de cet amour qu'au moment de la séparation dernière." (We love our mother almost unknowingly, and we don't realize how deep the roots of this love are until we part from her forever.) My translation.
32. J. Halberstam, *In a Queer Time and Place* (New York: New York University Press, 2005), p. 1.
33. Ibid. p. 2.
34. Lee Edelman, "The future is kid stuff: queer theory, disidentification, and the death drive," *Narrative*, 6/1, January 1998, p. 23.
35. Kathryn Bond Stockton, *The Queer Child, or Growing Sideways in the Twentieth Century*, Series Q (Durham, NC: Duke University Press, 2009).
36. Halberstam, *In a Queer Time and Place*, p. 6.
37. Ibid. p. 5.
38. Ibid. p. 13.
39. It is, however, necessary to mention that the scholarly reception of *Laurence Anyways* has been particularly ambivalent toward the transphobic critique embedded in its opening scene, as well as in its narrative as a whole. Despite positive critiques of the film as a "transgender love epic" in the online press, transgender researcher and advocate Karine Espineira has argued that the film contains several instances of banalization and stereotyping of the transgender figure that do not reflect the lived experience of transgender subjects nor allow their identification with the film's main character. Karine Espineira, *Médiacultures: la transidentité en télévision. Une recherche menée sur un corpus à l'INA (1946–2010)*, Collection Logiques Sociales: Série Sociologie du genre (Paris: Éditions L'Harmattan, 2015).

40. Bill Marshall, "Spaces and times of Québec in two films by Xavier Dolan," *Nottingham French Studies*, 55/2, 2016, p. 202; Valérie Mandia, "Le septième art hors des frontières nationales: le pouvoir de la langue et de l'imaginaire culturel dans les films du cinéaste québécois Xavier Dolan," *Francophonies d'Amérique*, 37, 2014, p. 110.
41. Marshall, "Spaces and times of Québec," p. 202.
42. Michel Foucault, "Of other spaces," trans. Jay Miskowiec, *Diacritics*, 16/1, Spring 1986 (March 1967), p. 22.
43. Ibid. p. 23.
44. Ibid. p. 24.
45. Ibid. p. 27.
46. Marshall, "Spaces and times of Québec," p. 190.
47. Ibid. p. 190.
48. Ibid. p. 201.

CHAPTER 2

The Dolandrama: Queer Male Authorship and the Fabulous Leading Lady

Julianne Pidduck

In 2014, the French magazine *Télérama* described Anne Dorval and Suzanne Clément as Dolan's "actresses-muses": "They inspire him, he brings out the best in them."[1] Dolan's pithy roles for women and his high esteem for his leading actresses are often seen as a proto-feminist gesture. Consider for instance Dolan's acceptance speech for the Jury Prize at Cannes for *Mommy* in 2014 that he prefaces with an homage to Jane Campion: "*The Piano* made me want to write roles for women, beautiful women with soul and will and strength. Not victims, not objects." In an era where the Québec film industry and even Cannes are pressed to account for a political and cultural economy of cinema that continues to situate women as objects and not as subjects or directors, the young director's passionate homage to Campion touched a nerve both in Québec and in transnational art cinema. If Dolan's fabulous female leads are neither victims nor objects—two terms that all-too-rapidly exhaust most women's roles in popular fiction—what is the nature of the bond between the (queer) male director and (his) actress-muse?

Part of the response to this question lies in Dolan's public persona as a young queer director. From his spectacular debut with *J'ai tué ma mère* at Cannes in 2009 at the tender age of twenty, Xavier Dolan made his mark in seven years as a multi-talented upstart filmmaker, an "enfant terrible" who revels in the limelight of European art cinema and Québec popular and not-so-popular culture alike. Publicly "out" from the beginning of his career yet highly ambivalent about gay or queer labels, Dolan's "self-fashioning" as a filmmaker and public persona, I argue, is imbricated with his passionate attachments to his fabulous leading ladies, and with his penchant for high-octane family dramas and impossible love stories. This chapter explores how Dolan's public persona as an artist and celebrity and his complex bonds with women, particularly mother figures, are staged both on-screen and in extra-filmic media coverage.

As a bridge between a study of Dolan's author persona and his penchant for high drama, I suggest that Dolan is developing his own brand of "Dolandrama." With a nod to gay-identified Spanish filmmaker Pedro Almodóvar's "Almodrama," this term evokes Dolan's cinema of stylistic and affective saturation crossed with a keen business sense.[2] Through the Dolandrama, I situate the young Québec filmmaker within a genealogy of melodramas and women's films directed by "queer" filmmakers—think Haynes, Cukor, Minnelli, Demy, Sirk, Pasolini, and Fassbinder. Like the Almodrama, the Dolandrama evokes melodrama not as a genre but in a broader sense as an "expressive code," and as a mode that has historically highlighted "female protagonists, the domestic sphere and socially mandated 'feminine' concerns."[3] Queer-authored melodramas focalizing women's experience touch on a special, sometime affinity between gay men and women. Jack Babuscio points to the trope of "woman as sign" in gay cultural projection that runs the risk of "using" women to their own advantage.[4] Yet Babuscio goes on to argue that gay men's experience of oppression can lead to a "heightened awareness of certain complications of human feeling," including insights into women's experience.[5] In a related account Stephen Maddison suggests that idealized representations of straight women by gay men are "markers of affiliations which resist heterosexualized manhood."[6]

Like the Almodrama, the Dolandrama is a cinema of aesthetic and affective saturation. These directors incorporate diverse cultural references that enable a reconciliation of the local and the global.[7] In this chapter, I explore Dolan's queer author persona and the recurring figure of mothers in his films in relation to Québécois and international discourses of gender, sexuality, and authorship. These intimate melodramas mine the widely intelligible dramatic possibilities of the family romance or star-crossed lovers, alongside the expressive capacities of music and mise-en-scène. In a perceptive 2013 profile, Gérard Grugeau describes Dolan as a young man of the millennial generation,

> steeped in literary, visual and musical references who lives on films, music videos, advertising images and Internet culture. He is a brilliant nerd, falsely superficial, breathing the exaggerated narcissism of a society turned in on itself, a society shaken by the messiness of contemporary forms of love and intimacy. Above all, Dolan is a versatile artist . . . who loves to see himself in the limelight.[8]

A prolific young director with a flair for marketing who released six features in seven years, Dolan went from cute new kid on the block to established *auteur* in a few short years. His meteoric success propelled by an ability to orchestrate continuous media visibility, Dolan now embodies like no other Québec film-maker the auteur-as-celebrity on a transnational stage. Author and films alike are branded with qualities of affective and stylistic intensity. I read Dolan's "performance" of authorship—strongly inflected by his close relations with women on-screen and off—as a production of *meaning, affect and value* in a global market. This essay opens with a reading of Dolan's "self-fashioning" as a filmmaker and public figure. Referring to selected and staged elements of his career and personal life, I explore Dolan's author persona as a perfor-mative practice that both *situates* and *distinguishes* him in relation to cultural discourses of gender, authorship, taste and class. In the second section, I inves-tigate Dolan's "bonds" with his actresses, concluding with close readings of *J'ai tué ma mère* and *Mommy.*

DOLAN'S "SELF-FASHIONING": AN *AUTEUR* IS BORN

For Claire Moran, "self-fashioning" has become central to the status of the modern artist from the nineteenth century. This process involves the inter-related practices of "self-fictionalizing" as a portrait or performance of the artist that is embedded in the works, and "self-posturing" where the artist's public self-presentation enables a "specific way of occupying a position" in the art world.[9] As an auto-fiction that "stages the artist," Dolan's first film *J'ai tué ma mère* exemplifies self-fictionalizing as "constructing a character, set-ting a scene, and 'modeling' a story."[10] Meanwhile, as a young filmmaker who consistently seeks media visibility, Dolan's "self-posturing" unfolds through interviews, photo shoots, and social media.

Developed by Moran in relation to modern art, the notion of self-fashioning has also been taken up in relation to film authorship. In her reading of Gus Van Sant, Janet Staiger argues, for instance, that this partly deliberate practice is a key force in the ongoing and often unstable production of mean-ing around the director and her works.[11] Meanwhile, Timothy Corrigan evokes the historical adaptability of the cinematic *auteur* as a *"commercial* strategy for organizing audience reception, as a critical concept bound to distribu-tion and marketing aims that identify and address the potential cult status of the author."[12] While discourses of authorship foreground the problem of individual cinematic enunciation or expression, Corrigan articulates perfor-mative and economic logics. I am particularly interested here in how Dolan's self-fashioning unfolds as a dialogic production of meaning and value, fore-grounding questions of gender, sexuality, and taste.

Dolan's first feature and the media buzz surrounding it encapsulate the complementarity of self-fictionalizing and self-posturing in a contemporary transnational film industry. *J'ai tué ma mère* attracted media coverage because of its audacious style, emotional intensity, and autobiographical narrative—in particular the director's youth. The film dramatizes a volatile and emotionally charged mother-son relationship set in a modest Montréal suburban neighborhood. Dolan plays the teenaged Hubert opposite Anne Dorval as Hubert's long-suffering mother, Chantale Lemming. Alternately sensitive and eager to please, sullen and abusive, the unmanageable Hubert is sent to boarding school (as was Dolan himself at the age of nine), runs away from home, and experiments with drugs. As I explore below in the close reading of the film, *J'ai tué ma mère* is a tale of broken communication between a teenaged son and his mother. Punctuated with confessional video diary sequences shot in grainy black and white, *J'ai tué ma mère* projects Dolan's face, his performance of an autobiographical character, and his relation with his mother in the spotlight, warts and all. Bringing together a stylized aesthetic with affective intensity, the film was a critical and box office success in Québec and in France.

The première of *J'ai tué ma mère* at Cannes in 2009 as part of *la Quinzaine des réalisateurs* launched Dolan's career. With this risky debut, Dolan "performs" his intertwined personal and filmic lives in the public eye, often in the company of women. Produced as part of this initial episode of self-posturing, Mert Tezer's video "Cannes 2009" chronicles Dolan's initial pilgrimage to Cannes, beginning with Dolan's arrival at the airport in Mickey Mouse ears. An articulate yet nervous young man with a lock of dark curly hair cascading over his eyes, and fingernails bitten to the quick, Dolan is accompanied for the most part by women (Dorval, executive producer Carole Mondello, supporting actor Suzanne Clément, and his mother Geneviève Dolan). The video culminates with the première of *J'ai tué ma mère*. Anxiously awaiting Dorval behind the scenes before making his entrance, Dolan addresses the camera: "I'm nervous, my heart is beating too fast." When Dorval arrives, she puts a reassuring arm around his shoulders and the cohort sets out with Dolan in the lead, closely followed by Dorval and Geneviève Dolan, hand in hand; Clément, Mondello, and supporting actor Niels Schneider bring up the rear. The video cuts to black during the screening, fading up on thunderous applause as the credits roll. Illuminated by a spotlight, the film's cohort is framed in their seats, with Dolan flanked by fictional and real-life mothers Dorval and Clément. The young filmmaker stands up to acknowledge the applause, then gently takes Dorval's hand, inviting her to stand beside him; he puts his arms around her in a long, tight embrace, burying his face in her shoulder, like a child.

Included as an extra on the K-Films Amérique DVD edition of *J'ai tué ma mère* (2009) and streamable on Vimeo, "Cannes 2009" complements the film's self-fictionalizing with a public "pose," as an artist as a young man making a fairy tale transition from out-of-control suburban delinquent to a young (prince) director full of potential under the bright lights of Cannes. The "behind the scenes" video promises a crafted realness, an affectively charged eventfulness: a nervous young man's dream realized against all odds; a feel-good moment staging the young man surrounded by older women and mother figures. And yet, Dolan's gentle and passionate homage to Dorval contrasts sharply with the brutality of his on-screen performance of Hubert who spews hatred at his mother. After Dolan and Dorval sit down, and Clément congratu-lates the young director, Geneviève Dolan (the director's actual mother) leans across Clément to kiss her son on the cheek, the last of the three women to congratulate him.

Widely disseminated in Québec media at the time, this moment encapsu-lates recurring themes in Dolan's self-fashioning and self-fictionalizing. Here and five years later with *Mommy*, Dolan's films emphatically foreground a pro-liferation of mothers and actresses; this articulation of queer authorship with a certain mode of resilient, poignantly suffering and fabulous women and moth-ers calls to mind Almodóvar's dedication of *All About My Mother* (1999): "To all actresses who have played actresses. To all women who act. To men who act and become women. To all the people who want to be mothers. To my mother." Diane Taylor's broad and suggestive concept of "performance" articulates self-fictionalizing and self-posturing: scripted and spontaneous, corporeal and ephemeral yet operating in complex relations to power and meaning, for Taylor, the term performance is "sometimes 'art,'" sometimes political 'actions,' sometimes business management, sometimes military prowess, performance aims to create effects and affects."[13] Whether embedded within theatrical or fictional works or unfolding in the public eye, the "performances" of Dolan and the women surrounding him here are calibrated to the Cannes stage, and projected toward multiple participants and audiences.

Richard Dyer's foundational work on stars turns on the paradox that stars are at once ordinary and extraordinary. Stars represent socially constructed "typical ways of behaving, feeling and thinking in contemporary society," and they also embody "the social categories in which people are placed and through which they have to make sense of their lives, and indeed through which we make our lives—categories of class, gender, ethnicity, religion, sexual orienta-tion, and so on."[14] At the same time, Dyer argues that stars are extraordinary, possessing a special quality that sets them apart; they are gifted, talented, pas-sionate, beautiful, sexy, troubled, or tragic. This paradox offers a strong point of departure for thinking about Dolan's "star-image." In his Cannes debut, he appeared as an ordinary teenager, a high school dropout without any particular cultural background—a claim to modest beginnings that paradoxically ampli-fies discourses of "innate genius," "wunderkind," or "enfant terrible" com-monly used to describe him.

Dolan's high-profile debut prompted media interest in his family back-ground. Raised by college administrator Geneviève Dolan in a modest Mon-tréal suburb, Dolan's father is Manuel Tadros, an Egyptian-born singer, songwriter, and actor. Brought up as Xavier Dolan-Tadros, the director now goes by the more common Franco-Québécois name Dolan. As a child actor, Dolan benefitted from his father's connections to work in Québec advertising (in well-known television publicity for the pharmacy chain Jean Coutu), and in film and television. In his frequent media appearances, Dolan talks a lot about the women in his life, but rarely mentions his father (who played minor roles in *J'ai tué ma mère* and *Tom à la ferme*) and paternal Egyptian family background. Social identities in general and author personas in particular are unstable, contradictory, strategic, and changing constructs, and Dolan no doubt has his reasons for adhering publicly to a white European francophone identity. Notably, when addressing Québécois audiences and media, Dolan often insists: "I write, I think, I dream in Québécois language and culture" (J'écris, je pense, je rêve en québécois). Also, Dolan's author persona is closely bound up with taste, and he deploys a contradictory set of cultural references in his self-fashioning and his films: North American and European high and popular culture, queerness and universality, and finally an insistence on a lower middle-class background alongside affinities with a cultural elite. Emphasizing that he is first and foremost an actor, Dolan nimbly navigates the relative categories of "ordinariness" and "extraordinariness" across global and local media contexts.

Dolan's complex negotiation of social categories is most evident in relation to his sexuality. "Out" in public since the beginning of his career, Dolan's original screenplays focalize queer, transsexual, and female characters and experience, while *Tom à la ferme* and *Juste la fin du monde* adapt works by queer playwrights Michel Marc Bouchard and Jean-Luc Lagarce respectively. And yet, like many francophone auteurs, Dolan vehemently refuses the categorization of gay or queer filmmaker. His refusal of the Queer Palme d'Or for *Laurence Anyways* was widely reported in the press, and this film's depiction of transsexual experience has been widely critiqued. Dolan moreover erases any mention of AIDS in his adaptation of *Juste la fin du monde*, a play that dramatizes the HIV+ playwright's last visit to his family. I would argue that Dolan's performance of queerness *matters* given the ways that "highly visible and successful lesbian or gay celebrities are subcultural myths, in that they actually structure iconographies of queerness."[15] That is to say that as an influential public figure, Dolan's mediated self-fashioning contributes to social discourses of queerness.

Interestingly, Dolan's self-fashioning and self-fictionalizing deploy numerous intertextual references to queer authors and icons, particularly in his early films. For instance, Dolan has two tattoos of quotes from Cocteau— "*À l'impossible je suis tenu*" (I am held to the impossible) on his left arm, "*L'oeuvre est une sueur*" (Work is sweat) on his right leg. Also, posters of River Phoenix and Émile Nelligan decorate the bedroom of the semi-autobiographical character Hubert in *J'ai tué ma mère*, and Hubert's boyfriend is named "Antonin Rimbaud." Further, Dolan's framing of Niels Schneider as the obscure object of desire in *Les amours imaginaires* recalls the beautiful boy in Visconti's *Death in Venice* (1971). More generally, Dolan's singular cinematic aesthetic and carefully groomed self-presentation can be read as an ostentatious performance of "taste": in 2015, Dolan became the male face of Louis Vuitton in a series of advertising campaigns, and he has appeared on the covers of fashion magazines such as *Essential Homme*, *Men's Fashion*, and *L'Express Styles*. Dolan's public persona and his films project idiosyncratic taste that in some ways corresponds with a discourse that "the homosexuality of an individual will be revealed primarily through matters of taste—not good or bad taste but a particular taste, a fondness for certain cultural artifacts over others."[16] And yet, Dolan complicates this performance of taste by insisting on popular cultural influences including *The Silence of the Lambs*, *Magnolia*, *The Lord of the Rings*, and *Batman Returns*.[17] He also cites James Cameron as one of his heroes, claiming *Titanic* as the main inspiration for *Laurence Anyways*. As I discuss below, Dolan's self-conscious negotiation of taste and distinction articulates interestingly with his performances of social class as a public figure and in his films.

This contradictory performance of taste and cultural capital shores up Dolan's public image as a youthful prodigy who sprang from the uncultured suburban hordes. As the "darling of Cannes" who became the prestigious festival's youngest jury member in 2015, Dolan has been described as the consummate *auteur* figure: not only a screenwriter, actor, director and producer, he also attends to editing, music, costumes, trailers, film posters, subtitling, and press kits. Dolan has been compared with Rimbaud, Woody Allen, and with Truffaut and Godard. While Corrigan points to the economic inflections of auteurism, Geneviève Sellier traces how the male auteur figure of the French New Wave rearticulated a longstanding romantic discourse of male artistic genius in the post-war period. For Sellier, the aspirations of French, Western, and international art cinema are strongly attached to an intrinsically masculine auteur figure "who masters the whole of the creative process, whose genius can be traced from film to film, and whose works have the legitimate right to state financing."[18]

Dolan's success in France boosts his profile in his home province, yet the filmmaker has been routinely critiqued as arrogant and narcissistic in Québec. A 2010 blog posting entitled "J'ai tué Xavier Dolan" ("I killed Xavier Dolan") proclaims: "He's not a great filmmaker, he's a little prick with a pair of Ray Bans and well-connected parents."[19] The outspoken Dolan does not hesitate to defend himself, particularly when the attacks become personal, as with "tête à claques" (assclown), "pédant" (arrogant), or "pédé" (faggot).[20] In response to a *Hollywood Reporter* critique of *Tom à la ferme* as "narcissistic," the film-maker tweeted "You can kiss my narcissistic ass."[21] This attack was taken up in the Québec film magazine *24 images* in 2015, where Rousseau skeptically takes apart the Dolan "myth" piece by piece: "This persona of a gifted so-called prodigy, ready to conquer the world . . . critics have always approached him as the savior of Québec cinema, famous for his 'refreshing' audacity, for his rebellious temperament, and for his ambition that comes very close to arrogance. However . . ."[22] In a 2014 interview with the French cultural magazine *Les Inrockuptibles*, Dolan responds to this critique that he equates with Québec cultural logic of humility and low expectations crystallized in the expression "être né pour un petit pain" (born for a small loaf).[23] In this same article, French journalist Romain Blondeau celebrates the filmmaker as a "symbol of youth that takes things on, makes demands and, as Dolan says, 'dreams in color.'" Dolan takes up these themes in his 2014 speech at Cannes to address "his generation": "There are no limits to our ambitions except for the ones we build for ourselves. I believe that everything is possible for those who dream, dare, work, and never give up."

Journalistic profiles of Dolan commonly mention his determination, focus, and a relentless work ethic. Grugeau's romantic account frames a young director "taken up in the euphoric urgency of creation."[24] This romantic intensity is seemingly coupled with a keen business sense. Dolan often mentions in interviews investing his earnings from his career as a child actor to finance *J'ai tué ma mère*, and Anne Dorval frequently describes a nervous but determined sixteen-year-old Dolan bringing his first screenplay to her in a dubbing studio. In 2016, Dolan described his remarkable success in this way: "I imagined myself on all of the sets and podiums until it happened."[25] Dorval also points to Dolan's control of the creative process, and his flair for marketing: "When he writes a script, he already has the final scene in mind, and is thinking about the trailer." The young director recounts aggressively promoting *J'ai tué ma mère* on the phone with a member of the pre-selection team the day before the Cannes selection meeting: "'It was midnight and I told him: 'I'm the youngest in the Festival, the journalists will be talking about me.' I sold my film and I sold myself, I wore him down."[26]

Dolan is openly gay and makes public his passionate relationships with women, while remaining discreet about his sexual and intimate relations with men. Dolan's performances of masculinity and sexual orientation are inflected through media discourse. For instance, a 2010 profile of *L'Actualité* foregrounds Dolan's "queer" qualities as the folly of youth: "We might call him a dandy, or precious, but always allowing for the excesses of youth." Meanwhile, the *Australian* frames Dolan with the headline "Mommy's Boy," suggesting the immaturity or "queerness" of a boy who hangs on his mother's apron strings. Meanwhile, the headlines "Xavier Dolan: tout sur la mère" (*La Presse*, Montréal) and "All about my mother" (*Sight & Sound*) reference Almodóvar's 1998 film, highlighting the leitmotif of emotionally charged relationships between mothers and their queer sons.[27]

A slight young man with "naughty-cherub good looks,"[28] Dolan presents himself on the cusp of boy and man, confounding norms of adult heterosexual masculinity. I have recently argued that the romantic figure of the gifted and sensitive young man who is too close to his mother is familiar in Québec with the figures of Émile Nelligan and Claude Jutra.[29] These queer figures are often understood through the prism of arrested development and "failed" romantic masculinity as indicative of failed heterosexual masculinity and the "arrested development" of the Québec nation.[30] Like Jutra and Nelligan, Dolan cuts a figure of queer male genius, a romantic myth that aligns nicely in a contemporary moment with what I would call the "queer art of success." Dressed to the nines, basking in the limelight, releasing a new film practically every year, raking in countless awards, Dolan is the model neoliberal queer subject.

MOTHERS, ACTRESSES, AND THEIR QUEER *AUTEUR*

Returning to my core question, what is the nature of the bond between the (queer) male director and (his) actress-muse? Anne Dorval offers one response:

> There aren't many auteurs who defend women like he does, who puts them on stage as he does. There are few roles for women like me, who are getting older and are no longer 18 . . . I think it's brave, I think it's audacious, I think it's marvelous that he writes women's roles . . . with so much dignity, so as to say "here is an ageing woman, she's beautiful, she's radiant, love her like I love her," I find that wonderful and unusual![31]

Dorval praises Dolan as a woman-friendly exception that proves the rule. Meanwhile, film theorist Fulvia Massimi cites Dolan's Cannes statement as a "call for a more profound and concrete engagement with the representation of femininity and queerness, in Québécois cinema and beyond."[32] On another reading, however, Dorval's gratitude for having good roles as a middle-aged woman could be seen as evidence of some women's depressingly low expectations of an industry still largely controlled by white men, both queer and straight. Led by Cate Blanchett, the 2018 March for Women on the Red Carpet included eighty-two women, representing the mere eighty-two female directors who have been featured at Cannes in its seventy-one-year history. Similarly, the marginal position of women in the Québec film industry has come under fire in recent years.[33]

Dolan's 2014 speech can be understood as an episode of "self-posturing" that positions him strategically as a young director and screenwriter committed to supporting women in the film industry. With an emotional warble in his voice, Dolan's passionate proclamation brings to light gendered power relations that have for the most part remained unspoken in the Cannes environment.

However, rather than taking Dolan's and Dorval's public statements at face value, I underscore Staiger's and Corrigan's cautionary note that such "postures" are contingent and contradictory as part of the ongoing performance of public personas in negotiation with a myriad of public discourses and relations of power. Critical readings of gender and sexuality need to consider the structural power relations that inform dialogic productions of meaning, value, and affect. Here, I reiterate a classic feminist dilemma that distinguishes between appearances and enunciation: to what degree do Dolan's films enable "truer" roles for women within an industry still largely dominated by white men? Or to put it differently, with a nod to Gayatri Spivak, can Dolan's working-class white female characters speak?

In his study of how gay male directors negotiate gender difference, Maddison comments on Almodóvar's "possessive intimacies with his muse-like female actresses."[34] These actresses, the author remarks, rely on Almodóvar as a powerful cultural producer for their livelihood. While Dolan has not achieved the status of the Spanish director, the success of *Mommy* enabled him great latitude in casting his subsequent works. With *Juste la fin du monde*, an adaptation of a play suggested to him by his "muse" Dorval, Dolan worked with an A-list French cast including Léa Seydoux, Marion Cotillard, and Nathalie Baye; *The Death and Life of John F. Donovan* features an all-star roster of Anglo-American actors including Natalie Portman, Kit Harington, and Susan Sarandon. Some Québec commentators have noted that Dorval has been sidelined as Dolan gains greater status in France and in Hollywood. Rather than engage this type of argument, I would like to underscore the striking exchangeability of leading ladies in a transnational film industry. Maddison likens this industry to a "homosocial network" where "women are exchanged as tokens of social desire between men."[35] In this context, leading ladies often rely on powerful male producers and directors for choice roles. As a case in point, Dolan's intimate public relationship with Chastain unfolded through social media and in the traditional press—including Chastain's familiar 2015 interview with the director for *Interview* where she addresses him as "sweetheart" and "babe." Three years later, Dolan announced in an Instagram post in February 2018 that he had decided to cut Chastain from *The Death and Life of John F. Donovan*.

What is the "added value" of the fabulous female star on the arm of the slight, boyish, and openly gay director? Dolan appears publicly in a series of "odd couples" with his leading ladies who are often, but not always, considerably older than he: Dorval, Clément, Baye, Seydoux, and most recently Portman and Chastain. While the couple of convenience pairing powerful older men with young beautiful women is a staple of the film industry, in what ways do Dolan's youth, sexuality, and sensitivity to gender relations reinflect this gendered power relationship? Interrogating the ambivalent relationships between the male auteurs of the French New Wave and their leading ladies, including Anna Karina and Jeanne Moreau, Sellier perceives these roles as inventions and fantasies of young wolves like Godard and Truffaut. Despite the actresses' top billing, Sellier argues that these directors "affirmed their creative power and invented new images of women whose seduction seems to emanate from the capacity that the men behind the camera have to reveal their secret charms."[36]

References to Dolan's conjuring power to "shape" his actresses' characters and their performances often arise in media coverage. For instance, the director is known for constantly "interrupting his actors' performances during takes, improvising directions ('Cough!' 'Shake your head!'), and even lines at the last minute!" According to Louis Guichard, this method has "destabilized" more than one of his actors, including Nathalie Baye on the set of *Laurence Anyways*.[37] Dolan is also known for personally handling costume design to shape characters. Baye wryly evokes Dolan's forceful insistence on the "colorful" allure of her mother character in *Juste la fin du monde*: "It didn't come from me, it was the boss. Xavier Dolan wanted the mother like that and I followed his direction, I obeyed. He wanted a colorful mother . . . He oversaw the make-up, hair, costume, fingernails . . . Nothing was left to chance."[38] In another example of Dolan's careful attention to costume design, Dolan describes the wardrobe for Dorval's mother character "Die" in *Mommy*: "She dresses like a 16-year-old teenager with a certain style, but with strange taste. She wants to be sexy, but also be comfortable because she works long hours."[39] In a close reading of media discourses surrounding Dolan, there is no clear consensus among his leading ladies concerning his demanding direction and close control of characterization. In contrast with Baye's wry account, Suzanne Clément describes how she and Dolan "constructed the character [of Kyla] together" for *Mommy*: "Xavier wanted a third role. He knew that Kyla stuttered, but he hadn't yet worked out her past."[40] She goes on to say: "I was able to reveal myself to him in a way that I've rarely done in my life. He allowed me to go to places in my life where I had never gone before as a woman and as an actress."[41]

Dolan insists on the mother figure as key to his films, even in works where she is not the central character; apparently Lise Roy's stage performance of Agathe, the mother figure in *Tom à la ferme*, moved him to adapt the play.[42] In a 2016 interview, he elaborates: "The mother is a bottomless well of possibilities, roles, and performances. First of all, each actress can renew the mother genre, even if she plays the same character again, it will never be exactly the same performance."[43] Dorval's two very different performances in *J'ai tué ma mère* and *Mommy*, and Baye's mother roles in *Laurence Anyways* and *Juste la fin du monde*, encapsulate Dolan's iterative account of the cinematic mother. In the Dolandrama, mother-son relationships generate contradictory intensities and affects—sensuality and weird desires, romantic love and screaming hatred, hope against all odds and crushing disappointment and betrayal.

If Dolan's leading ladies are neither objects nor victims, these relations of power, desire, complicity and identification confound standard conceptual frameworks for understanding cinematic articulations of gender and sexuality, including models of political economy, the heterosexual male gaze, or Sellier's account of the all-powerful male auteur. In his analysis of queer directors and their female stars, Maddison suggests that "women who bond with gay men do so as a form of political resistance" with idealized representations of straight women by gay men operating as "markers of affiliations which resist heterosexualized manhood."[44] Extending Eve Kosofsky Sedgwick's notion of the "homosocial," Maddison writes of "heterosocial bonds," where relations between women and gay men can contribute to renegotiating relations of difference. For this author, the term heterosocial "enables a differentiation between the role of women in the arrangement of hetero-normative male bonds"[45] grounded in the exchange of women, or in their objectification. Maddison posits that gay male–female identification potentially opens the possibility of a wide array of other relations. Drawing on these accounts, I conclude with a close reading of *J'ai tué ma mère* and *Mommy* situated within Québec discourses of gay authorship and motherhood.

MATRIARCHY AND MATRICIDE: ITERATIONS OF QUÉBEC'S MYTHIC MOTHERS IN *J'AI TUÉ MA MÈRE*

Dolan's films revisit the Québec cultural terrain of the family drama, a cinematic imaginary of orphans and lost children with strong mothers and absent fathers.[46] This familial configuration has often been construed as an allegorical expression of a "matriarchal" society, where "castrated" French Canadian men fail to take their rightful place at the head of the family in order to ensure the proper upbringing of sons, and by extension, the future of the nation.[47] In Dolan's intimate cinematic worlds, however, the intense mother-son dynamics confound a psychoanalytic allegory of the missing father, the "immature" queer son, or the arrested development of the nation. The Dolandrama focalizes strong mothers, mother-like characters, and sons in *Laurence Anyways*, *Tom à la ferme*, and *Juste la fin du monde*. In the film analysis that follows, I excavate the mother-son dyads in *J'ai tué ma mère* and *Mommy*.

The mythic mother figure is also a staple in Québec socio-cultural discourse. For Lori Saint-Martin, "in the country of the survival and the revenge of the cradle, the mother myth has reached a pinnacle. Given the importance of the mother in the Québec family circle, we thought that we were living in a matriarchy."[48] For Patricia Smart, "this solitary and powerful mother figure is an ideological construction created by a male hierarchy associated with the Catholic Church and modeled on pre-revolutionary France";[49] at times this strong mother figure can become the "monstrous mother" against whom the son must struggle to exorcise his demons[50]—a scenario that partly encapsulates the mother-son dynamic in *J'ai tué ma mère*. If the powerful mother figure is an ideological construct, what can we make of the mothers and strong female characters in the films of Dolan, a contemporary queer author conscious of gender dynamics?

J'ai tué ma mère probes Hubert's strange bond with his mother; the long-suffering, saint-like Chantale Lemming recalls the Québec mythic mother figure. At the heart of this film is the impossibility of communication between a mother and a teenaged son. The autobiographical character Hubert, played by Dolan himself, explains to his sympathetic teacher (Clément) that he and his mother "have nothing in common," that they are "completely incompatible." In its dramatization of domestic experience and complex attachments that the characters struggle to voice, *J'ai tué ma mère* treads the affective terrain of the melodrama, described by Thomas Elsaesser as a cinema of sublimation, where difficult or unspeakable emotions are expressed through music and mise-en-scène: "Dramatic situations are given an orchestration," with the "spoken word as a melodic dimension rather than an autonomous semantic discourse"; furthermore, diction is essential to "emotional resonance and dramatic continuity."[51] The Dolandrama is often a cinema of incessant talking and yelling in Québec's *joual* sociolect; however, it is often through evocative silences, music or corporeal performance that these relationships and emotions are expressed.

The Dolandrama stages intense attachments, ambivalence, misrecognition, power, and violence in family relationships. On a feminist reading, *J'ai tué ma mère* is troubling for its explicit dramatization of the protagonist's disdain or even hatred for his mother. In what follows, I foreground diegetic and non-diegetic gender dynamics surrounding narration and point of view, as well as the performative power of words to wound.[52] With the 2009 release of *J'ai tué ma mère*, based on a story he wrote in high school entitled *Le Matricide* (*Matricide*), Dolan did some fancy footwork in publicly "performing" his relationship with his mother. He claimed that the film was highly autobiographical and that Hubert was closely modeled on his own experience, but it was unclear to what degree Chantale Lemming (Dorval) resembled his mother. Continually asked in interviews if his mother had seen the film, Dolan's carefully composed response is published in the 2009 DVD booklet: "Yes, she has seen it. We haven't talked that much about it . . . She told me that it made her laugh and cry. That she liked it a lot . . . I know that she was hurt by certain crude and brutal elements." Dolan goes on to acknowledge his mother's support: "She even opened the doors of her home so that we could film there, accepting some . . . exaggerations of the interior décor." It is significant that *J'ai tué ma mère*, as a self-fictionalizing venture, was shot in the house where Dolan spent most of his adolescence. His mother's modest suburban home, cluttered with tacky ornaments, houses the mother-son drama. In a narrative privileging Hubert's point of view, the decor, and indeed everything about his mother, gets on the teenager's nerves.

J'ai tué ma mère is for the most part focalized through Hubert's perspective, punctuated with intimate, grainy, black and white video diary sequences. Shot in close-up and extreme close-up, the camera caressing Hubert's eyes, mouth, and face, these sequences delineate a highly subjective narrative space where the teenager confesses his wildly ambivalent feelings toward his mother. The film opens with one such sequence where Hubert confides to the camera: "I don't know what happened. When I was small we loved each other. I love her, I can look at her, say 'hello', sit beside her. But . . . I can't be her son. I could be anyone else's son but not hers." From this confessional, the film cuts to a montage of small ornaments and butterflies pinned to the wall. Next, a series of close-ups of Hubert's watchful eyes are intercut with a close-up of his mother Chantale eating an orange (juice dripping down her chin), and next, a bagel with cream cheese (cream cheese smeared around her mouth). Hubert sighs loudly in disgust, rolls his eyes, and brusquely orders his mother to clean her face. In the next scene, Chantale drives her son to school on a rainy day. Framed in a tight two-shot, mother and son squabble over the choice of radio station, and Chantale insists on listening to the news. In protest, Hubert puts on his headphones. Chantale, annoyed, insists that he talk to her: "I'm not your chauffeur." Next she runs a red light, at least according to Hubert who berates her: "You don't know how to drive." In exasperation, she abruptly leaves him by the side of the road. These sequences establish key themes and stylistic elements that will recur in Dolan's subsequent films.

J'ai tué ma mère is a coming of age tale that probes a teenaged boy's intense and often violent feelings about his mother, a film about taste and social class. Laced with well-observed everyday dynamics and pithy dialogues at once funny and cruel, at the heart of the film is a profound miscommunication between mother and son. Despite incessant terse exchanges and outright screaming matches, Dolan evokes "talking past each other": "'I grew up in an Egyptian family where everyone talks at once, or all by themselves. Talking all the time and not communicating is what I know . . . Shouting is a way of life.'"[53] As part of a cutting, condescending, and hateful barrage of words directed at his mother, Hubert "kills" Chantale with words, telling his teacher that his mother is dead.

J'ai tué ma mère follows a rhythm where scenes of affective intensity alternate with interludes of seething resentment or appeasement. Mother and son alternate in their efforts to make peace: Hubert cleans the house, does the laundry, and makes breakfast to please his mother, while Chantale suggests watching a film together and plans a special meal. Even so, Hubert's disdain and hatred for his mother escalates, along with Chantale's exasperation with her son. In a suburb where a teenager is stranded without a car, Chantale uses her power of mobility to leave Hubert by the side of the road in retaliation for his aggressive behavior. These episodes of abandonment culminate when Chantale drops Hubert off at the bus that will take him to boarding school.

> HUBERT (*walking away*): The last minute before I turn 18, I'll call you and that'll be the last time we'll ever talk. And those crumbs around your face when you eat like a pig, your fucking Alzheimer's, your revolting clothes that make me want to barf, your ignorant suburbanite expressions, your manipulation, you can shove it up your ass!
> CHANTALE: (*self-contained but visibly devastated, turns on her heel and walks back to the car*).
> HUBERT (*desperate*): What would you do if I died today? *He turns to walk away.*
> CHANTALE (*watching him walk away, responds almost inaudibly*): I'd die tomorrow.

This breathtaking scene dramatizes the hurtful power of words and the sometimes viciousness of parent-child power struggles. It also encapsulates the film's affective dynamic of language and silence and the struggle for expression in the melodrama. At the end of Hubert's tirade, Chantale's quiet avowal of her love for her son hangs in the air unheard.

Given the importance of diction and silence to the melodrama's "emotional resonance and dramatic continuity,"[54] it is important to consider the performative power of injurious speech in Dolan's inaugural film. On my first viewing, I was viscerally appalled by the tirade of insults scripted and uttered by Dolan as the film's screenwriter, director, and lead actor. Within the diegesis, Dorval's Chantale remains for the most part unresponsive to Hubert's injurious speech, countering his aggressivity with silence, distraction, and the power of mobility (access to a car in the suburbs, leaving him with his father, or sending him to boarding school). Weighing Chantale's mythic maternal powers of enduring, suffering, even sainthood (in one brief image amidst a stream-of-consciousness montage Dolan frames her as a saint) in relation to the violence of Hubert's words, let me consider the performative power of words to wound. Judith Butler evokes the body as the "blindspot of speech, that which acts in excess of what is said, but which also acts in and through what is said . . . There is what is said, and there is a kind of saying that the bodily 'instrument' of utterance performs."[55] Butler's account of the *speaking body* foregrounds the discursive force of the utterance, breaking down the opposition between body and spirit, matter and language. This said, it is especially difficult to assess the ethical consequences of diegetic speech in a fictional representation. As Butler argues, the insult "assumes its specific proportion in time."[56] The teenaged son's explosion of rage fleetingly materializes as physical violence in *J'ai tué ma mère* when Hubert pushes Chantale against the kitchen counter (and again, in Steve's destructive outburst in *Mommy*). It is important, however, to underscore the nuance of Butler's account where, in being called a name, one is "given a certain possibility for social existence . . . in the temporal life of language."[57] In other words, the insult can interpellate one as a subject and as *a body*, as intelligible, human, and hence potentially vulnerable. If the figure of the mother is interpellated here through language and image both as saint and abject body (the "other" of language and culture), she is also constituted as a vulnerable, suffering, and ultimately resourceful, subject in the cultural and formal codes of melodrama.

Hubert uses his power with words, a cultural capital that his mother does not possess, to humiliate and hurt her (Figure 2.1). His disdain and disavowal of his mother's taste, and the class position that it represents, is central to the film from the opening montage isolating butterflies and ornaments on the wall. The framing of Chantale's interior decor invites both humor and a judgment of taste on the part of the spectator. Pierre Bourdieu argues that while qualifiers of taste are specific to particular "fields of practice," they are ultimately subject to "a system of cognitive evaluative structures of a determinate state of the social world."[58] *J'ai tué ma mère* addresses what Bourdieu calls the "socially informed body" when, in a moment of truce, Hubert politely compliments Chantale on her tiger-striped lampshades that bring out the stripes of the tiger painting in

Figure 2.1 Cultural capital: Chantale's interior decor.

pride of place above the sofa. Later, he berates her for her ignorance of Jackson Pollock, and sarcastically recommends de Sade's *Philosophy in the Bedroom* as bedtime reading. Returning to Dolan's contradictory performance of taste and class in his public persona, the deployment of humor and qualifiers of taste in *J'ai tué ma mère* articulate dynamics of class and gender with the fictional (and, ostensibly, real) mother as the butt of both joke and judgment.

Does the over-presence of Dolan's own subjectivity, style, fictionalized experience, and point of view in this auto-fiction leave any space for the subjectivity of the fictionalized mother figure and the actress who portrays her? Or, does she operate as a cypher, a sounding board for a rehearsal of the son's unresolved feelings and complexes? Dorval's Chantale is often subdued, passive and distracted, a mother who most often acts *in response* to her son's constant demands, defiance, and insults. And yet, in the booklet accompanying the DVD, Dolan insists: "For those who haven't understood, the hero of the affair is my mother." In this narrative propelled by Hubert's tirade of rage and ambivalence directed at his mother, it is Chantale who, in a sense, gets the last word. After Hubert runs away from boarding school, Chantale responds fiercely to the school principal's suggestion that her son would benefit from a male presence at home:

> Who the fuck do you think you are? Do you teach "Mothering 101"? . . .
> I married a coward who left because fathering wasn't his cup of tea. Fifteen years I've been waking up at 5:30 to get to work and drive through goddam traffic so my son can eat and go to school! Goddam stupid-ass machos! You're always quick to judge us as you strut around in your goddam Bugs Bunny ties! You throw your red underwear in with the whites! . . . So don't tell me that my son ran away because I'm a single mother. You all have 150 IQs and you, you . . . auto-congratulate yourselves with your endless diplomas, and when a 17-year-old escapes from your establishment you dare tell me that I'm a bad mother?

In a dramatic shift from a resigned mother struggling to deal with a difficult son, Chantale speaks truth to power in this scene (Figure 2.2). Seated at her desk where she holds a generic administrative position, wearing a fuzzy pink sweater covered with large protruding black vinyl bows and braids, Chantale delivers this resounding monologue from a lowly socio-economic position as a single mother and clerical worker. While to this point Chantale's taste and limited cultural capital have been the butt of Hubert's judgment and a source of humor for the audience, in this sequence they become a badge of honor. Jack Babuscio describes how irony operates in camp to highlight "incongruous contrast . . . between an individual/thing and its context/association."[59] In this scene of Dolan's first feature, and in *Mommy*, it is the contrast between the marginal social status of the single mother, and her nobility and strength that generates a critique of "the world as it is."[60]

Figure 2.2 Chantale Lemming speaks truth to power.

Figure 2.3 "You! . . . Do I look fucking dead to you?"

Two stylized sequences bypass the poignant impasses of spoken communication in *J'ai tué ma mère*, and encapsulate the intense and strange mother-son relationship. First, after discovering that her son had informed the teacher she was dead, Chantale interrupts Hubert's class: "You! I'll talk to you after class. Do I look fucking dead to you?!" Wearing a leopard skin coat and a white fuzzy hat covered in knitted spikes, the furious Chantale makes for quite a spectacle (Figure 2.3). The class laughs and Hubert rolls his eyes, mortified. After the bell, Hubert runs down the hallway to escape his mother. The chase sequence converts to slow motion with slow violin music in the style of Wong Kar-wai's

Figure 2.4 Queer relations? Hubert in hot pursuit of his mother dressed as a bride.

In the Mood for Love (2000). This stylistic device accentuates the burlesque scene, at once funny and disturbing, where Chantale lumbers awkwardly after Hubert in her bulky coat and clogs. She briefly catches hold of him but he pushes her roughly to the ground. No longer laughing, Hubert's favorite teacher and classmates are shocked witnesses to this violent scuffle.

Near the end of the film, a fantasy sequence mirrors the first pursuit transposed to a pastoral setting known as Hubert's "kingdom" in reference to the Québec discourse of the self-centered and demanding "enfant roi" (infant-king). Again in slow motion, to a dissonant instrumental soundtrack, Hubert, dressed vaguely as a medieval prince or a king, ardently pursues Chantale who is dressed in a white wedding dress (Figure 2.4). Running through autumn woods and open fields, he reaches out to catch her white-gloved hand, and she eludes him; he catches her again and, in a reversal of the first chase, she pushes him roughly to the ground. Taken together, these pursuits and flights enact the complex, ambivalent, and shifting dynamics of attachment, of desire and flight. In a respite from the film's continuous rapid-fire dialogue, these wordless performances of the body in movement intensified by slow motion accentuate intensity and affect, feelings and sensations that escape conscious articulation. The teenager's passionate pursuit of his mother in the guise of a "bride" perversely skews fairy tale and generational orderings of desire, parenting, and power. Here, the Dolandrama performs strange affective intensities and qualities of relationality reminiscent of Weiner and Young's account of "queer bonds" as

> social bonds coequally constituted by the corrosive and adhesive pressures of eroticism. Queer bonds . . . are what come into view through

the isometric tension between queer world-making and world-shattering, naming a togetherness in failures to properly intersect, the social hailing named by recognition as well as its radical occlusion."[61]

MOMMY AND THE DOLANDRAMA

Dolan has often remarked that he made *J'ai tué ma mère* to punish his mother and *Mommy* to avenge her.[62] In line with the venerated and long-suffering French Canadian mother, Dolan describes Die, Dorval's character in *Mommy*, as a kind of "mother courage" who "fights like a devil in holy water to keep her honor. I wanted to show a heroic mother figure."[63] Like Chantale in *J'ai tué ma mère*, Die is a larger-than-life mother figure that sacrifices almost everything for her son. Yet in contrast with the timidity of her earlier role, Dorval's Die is a vibrant, sexy, straight-talking, hard-working, and fun-loving mature woman. Returning to Dolan's account of the endless possibilities of the cinematic mother—and I would add the mother-son dynamic—the visceral ambivalence between Hubert and Chantale in *J'ai tué ma mère* becomes in *Mommy* a sensual mutual infatuation. Dolan no longer privileges the teenaged boy's point of view, opting for a more fluid focalization that alternates between Die and Steve (Antoine Olivier Pilon)—and, at times, Kyla (Suzanne Clément). In an extension of her role as sympathetic teacher in *J'ai tué ma mère*, Kyla functions as a second mother figure in *Mommy*, a confidante, teacher, and above all, a witness and buffer to Die and Steve's intense relationship. Kyla's stutter—seemingly a symptom of post-traumatic stress related to the loss of a child—foregrounds the powerful register of what cannot be said.

The Dolandrama, as a cinema of affect and performance, crystallizes in many ways with *Mommy*. Dolan's signature dialogue and dialect recur with a far more accomplished expressive deployment of music, dramatic mise-en-scène and performance. The stunning scene where Steve rides the shopping cart to the tune of "Wonderwall" exemplifies Elena Del Río's account of how the "gestures and movements of the performing body, incorporeal forces or affects become concrete expression-events that attest to the body's powers of action and transformation."[64] In order to explore Dolan's mobilization of performance, gestures, and music to dramatize the mother-son dynamic, I turn to the scene where Steve dances seductively to Céline Dion's "On ne change pas" (Figure 2.5). This sequence coincides with Kyla's first proper visit, and begins with the two women chatting in the kitchen as Die chops vegetables for dinner. If in Dolan's films the clothes go a long way toward making the character, Die's black lace blouse worn over a black bra contrasts starkly with Kyla's pastel sweater set. As Steve inserts a homemade CD into the stereo, Die comments wryly to Kyla: "Not a dull moment with Steve." The diegetic opening bars of

Figure 2.5 A queer bond? Steve and Die dance to "On ne change pas."

the Dion song fade in, gradually drowning out the women's conversation. Cut to a series of close-ups of Steve, his hair slicked back, made up with pale pink lipstick, black eyeliner, black nail polish, and a black tank top; he does a sultry dance to the music, singing along. Steve sidles up to Die and nuzzles her neck from behind, reaching his hands around her torso and touching her breast; she brushes his hand away firmly but without breaking the mood: "Hey, don't touch that asshole!" As Die begins to dance in rhythm with Steve, he gently but firmly withdraws a large knife from her hand. This gesture evokes the very real possibility of violence that erupts periodically in *Mommy*, but the boy puts the knife down.

These shots of Steve are intercut with close-ups of Kyla as witness to the strange mother-son dynamic: surprised and visibly uncomfortable with his unexpected behavior, she is nevertheless drawn in by the duo's magnetic intensity. Steve invites Kyla to sing along, reminding him that Dion is "a national treasure," and she joins in, gradually losing her stutter. Steve approaches her, kneeling at her feet, and gently takes her hands to encourage her to dance. As he lets go of her hands, the camera pulls back to frame all three characters dancing and singing to the music, which shifts from diegetic to resonant non-diegetic sound. Steve's performance exudes a generalized eroticism, and he sets out to seduce or charm the two older women. His unexpected and exuberant dance generates an infectious and sublime moment of pleasure and complicity, cementing a compelling threesome.

Despite *Mommy*'s pervasive affective qualities of claustrophobia and desperation carried through the mise-en-scène and the constrained 1:1 aspect ratio, this scene crystallizes how music, as a melodramatic element, contributes to "a system of punctuation, giving expressive color and chromatic contrast to the story-line, by orchestrating the emotional ups and downs of the intrigue."[65] Similarly, other scenes from *Mommy* featuring songs by Oasis and Counting Crows project an affective, utopic sense of possibility at odds with the numerous obstacles faced by the characters. Shadowing Die and Steve's precarious situation and Steve's raw energy (Dolan describes the character as a "free electron"), the roller coaster rhythm of *Mommy* alternates between desperation and sublime scenes of pleasure. Rare and precious in their fleeting quality, these moments of expression and liberty recall what Del Río calls the "affective event," where "the body's expressions are not exhausted by the pressures to perform according to cultural, linguistic, or ideological requirements. Rather, alongside the inevitability of conforming to these pressures, there always lies the possibility that affective intensity may provide lines of escape."[66]

The maternal melodrama has historically explored themes of class ascendancy and racial passing, as well as ambivalent and disturbing mother-child relationships; examples include both versions of *Imitation of Life* (Stahl, 1934, and Sirk, 1959), to *Stella Dallas* (King Vidor, 1937), to *Mildred Pierce* (Michael Curtiz, 1945), and Todd Haynes's 2011 mini-series reprise. These films commonly foreground the hopes and dreams of working-class experience set against the impossibilities of escape. *Mommy* translates this melodramatic mode to contemporary suburban Montréal, where Die and Steve experience a slide from the middle class toward socio-economic precarity. After the sudden death of her husband, Die is saddled with his debts; she subsequently loses her job and is unable to find resources to help her "difficult" son. Earlier in this chapter, I identified Claude Jutra as a precursor to Dolan as a Québec queer auteur and genius. Furthermore, Michel Tremblay who is renowned for his affinity to women and penchant for all-out affective expression voiced in *joual*, offers another touchstone for thinking about the dynamics of gay authorship and strong working-class female characters in Québec culture.

In his early work in particular, Tremblay created a rich theatrical world peopled by extraordinary working-class heroines. Anchored within the milieus and experience of working-class women, Germaine Lauzon, Sainte Carmen of the Main, alongside the waitresses Françoise Durocher and Lise Paquette, are key cultural references in Québec. Returning to the dilemma of female enunciation, Lucie Robert recognizes the strength and rebellion expressed by Tremblay's superb female characters. She argues, however, that these characters are unable to express their demands for change in a language that is their own; moreover, the playwright "systematically orchestrates the destruction of each character by destruction, by silence or by death."[67] Erin Hurley grapples with this problem by arguing against dominant realist and allegorical nationalist readings of Tremblay's oeuvre. For Hurley, the narrative realism of "Les Belles-soeurs," for instance, is interrupted by a series of "rhapsodic monologues" by female characters foregrounding "the desire for something different . . . they point to a life more fundamentally fulfilling on the level of feeling."[68]

As with my brief reference to Jutra, the parallel between Dolan and Tremblay is not an easy or obvious one, and falls outside the scope of this chapter. Nonetheless, it is important to note that Hurley frames the problem of working-class women's enunciation in Tremblay's plays as a melodramatic structure of feeling that sets in tension what is and what could be. Tremblay's characters often express superficial desires associated with consumer culture: Germaine Lauzon is convinced that modcons will transform her life, Hosanna dreams of becoming Elizabeth Taylor's Cleopatra for a day, while Lise Paquette ardently desires the pale yellow dress displayed in a storefront. Amidst *Mommy*'s horrific climax during which Steve is violently controlled and institutionalized, Die imagines a "normal" heterosexual and successful middle-class life path for her son, where he moves euphorically from success to success, from graduation to a scholarship to Julliard, to a perfect wedding. Returning to Dolan's "queer art of success" overturning the "arrested development" of queer masculinity in a Québec context, Steve's fate in *Mommy* offers a dystopic reversal of Dolan's real-life fairy-tale trajectory from delinquent to celebrity auteur— another potential future.

And yet, there is a queer ambivalence to Steve's fate. Die's daydream reflects what J. Halberstam calls a heteronormative "schedule of normativity" enforced by "punishing norms that discipline behavior and manage human development with the goal of delivering us from unruly childhoods to orderly and predictable adulthoods."[69] Die's flash-forward to Steve's "successful" life poignantly inscribes the ways that social norms seem to project a "life more fundamentally fulfilling on the level of feeling." And yet, perhaps Steve's eventual leap through the window and into the void, far more than an "orderly" life path, resonates with the bravado of the outlaws of *Butch Cassidy and the Sundance Kid* (George Roy Hill, 1969) or *Thelma and Louise* (Ridley Scott, 1991). Shot in slow motion, Steve's final escape from the guard and his leap through the window recall the affective event as a line of escape that is irreducible to "happy endings."

Mommy develops not one but two "extraordinary" women's roles. According to Dolan, these characters are not based on individuals, but "their music, their tones and intonations, are inspired by women that I know. They are fictional characters full of hope, humor, wisdom, salaciousness and energy. I love them and I admire them. They exist for themselves . . . without the gaze of men. Without men." Even so, in the same article Dolan describes *Mommy*'s mirrored mother figures in this way: "It's the teenager who holds out the mirror. As soon as he disappears from this threesome, their friendship is over. These women stop seeing each other when they can no longer help one another.

It's an ephemeral friendship."[70] If Steve's presence is the lynchpin of Die and Kyla's friendship, does *Mommy* ultimately fail the Bechdel test as a measure of women's representation in fiction? Very simply, the Bechdel test asks whether a work features at least two women who talk to each other about something other than a man. In some sense, Dorval and Clément's roles have been created *because of* and *for* the autobiographical characters of Hubert and Steve. Returning to the kitchen scene where the three characters dance to the Dion tune, it is Steve's unstable and dynamic energy that propels the scene, and ultimately, it is Steve's fate that hangs in the balance. On this reading, rather than being "all about the mother," are *Mommy* and *J'ai tué ma mère* "all about the boy"?

CONCLUSION

This chapter has explored two interrelated themes: first, a critical account of Dolan's self-fashioning as a queer celebrity auteur; and second, an interrogation of the young director's "bonds" with his leading ladies. Pivotal to this two-pronged analysis are Claire Moran's notions of "self-fictionalizing" and "self-posturing" as overlapping practices that lead to ongoing, contradictory and contingent, "performances" of authorship. As a young filmmaker whose public persona and films project passionate, problematic, and complex relationships between mothers and sons, Dolan lends himself to this reading of filmic text, commercial intertext, and performance. Of particular interest here are the articulations of gender, sexuality, and class as negotiated through Dolan's author persona alongside the autofictional diptych of *J'ai tué ma mère* and *Mommy*, the two films that have decisively put him on the map of transnational auteur cinema as a young director to watch. I explore these two films as vehicles for an intermedial staging of Dolan as an emerging artist. Given his youth, his prolific production record, and his penchant for the limelight, Dolan's auteur persona may well continue to unfold in a baroque layering of biography and fiction.

This chapter also coins the term "Dolandrama," reading Dolan's works with reference to melodrama, exploring Dolan's self-fashioning as a young queer male auteur in relation to his fabulous leading ladies. Drawing on accounts of the queer melodrama, I interrogate Dolan's dramatization of women's experience in critical tension with the recurring superficial and celebratory argument that he writes pithy roles for women of different ages. I mobilize extensive textual and intertextual evidence in order to trace and evaluate the relationships of power, desire, and projection and identification between Dolan and his leading ladies whom he celebrates as "neither objects nor victims." In posing the question as to whether Dolan's leading ladies can speak, I develop a multiform reflection on language and enunciation, foregrounding mise-en-scène, music, and the performative power of speech to delve into complex and unspeakable emotions. Also, given that much of the first wave of scholarship on Dolan tends toward more or less celebratory queer readings, and to a lesser degree, his place in a transnational Québec national cinema, I hope to contribute to a more robust discussion of gender and sexuality in the Dolandrama by setting in dialogue feminist and queer thought.

NOTES

1. Caroline Besse, "Anne Dorval et Suzanne Clément—actrices-muses de Xavier Dolan. Elles l'inspirent, il les met en valeur," *Télérama*, May 23, 2014. Available at <http://www.telerama.fr/festival-de-cannes/2014/anne-dorval-et-suzanne-clement-actrices-muses-de-xavier-dolan,112857.php> (accessed March 23, 2018). Unless otherwise indicated, all translations from French-language sources are by the author.
2. Paul Julian Smith, *Desire Unlimited: The Cinema of Pedro Almodóvar*, 2nd edn (London: Verso, 1994), pp. 1–7. See also Paul Julian Smith, "Almodóvar's self-fashioning: the economics and aesthetics of deconstructive autobiography," in Marvin D'Lugo and Kathleen M. Vernon (eds), *A Companion to Pedro Almodóvar* (Cambridge: Blackwell Publishing, 2013), pp. 21–38.
3. Christine Gledhill, Introduction to *Gender Meets Genres in Postwar Cinemas*, ed. Christine Gledhill (Chicago: University of Chicago Press, 2002), p. 10.
4. Jack Babuscio, "The cinema of camp (AKA camp and the gay sensibility)," in Fabio Cleto (ed.), *Camp: Queer Aesthetics and the Performing Subject* (Edinburgh: Edinburgh University Press, 1999), p. 134.
5. Ibid. p. 134.
6. Stephen Maddison, *Fags, Hags and Queer Sisters: Gender Dissent and Heterosocial Bonds in Gay Culture* (New York: St. Martin's Press, 2000), p. 12.
7. Bill Marshall, "Spaces and times of Québec in two films by Xavier Dolan," *Nottingham French Studies* 55/2, 2016, pp. 198–208.
8. Gérard Grugeau, "Xavier Dolan: l'accélérateur d'intensité," *24 images*, 165, December 2013, p. 40. My translation.
9. Claire Moran, *Staging the Artist: Performance and the Self-Portrait from Realism to Expressionism* (New York: Routledge, 2017), p. 17.
10. Ibid. p. 17.
11. Janet Staiger, "Authorship studies and Gus Van Sant," *Film Criticism*, 29/1, Fall 2004, pp. 1–22.
12. Timothy Corrigan, "The commerce of auteurism," in Virginia Wright Wexman (ed.), *Film and Authorship* (New Brunswick, NJ: Rutgers University Press, 2003), p. 98.
13. Diane Taylor, *Performance* (Durham, NC: Duke University Press, 2016), p. 6.
14. Richard Dyer, *Heavenly Bodies: Film Stars and Society* (Basingstoke: Macmillan, 1986), pp. 17–18.
15. Stephen Maddison, *Fags, Hags and Queer Sisters*, p. 140.
16. Andy Medhurst, "That special thrill: *Brief Encounter*, homosexuality and authorship," *Screen*, 32/2, July 1991, p. 198.
17. Romain Blondeau, "Xavier Dolan: 'Je fais des films pour me venger,'" *Les Inrockuptibles*, October 1, 2014. Available at <https://www.lesinrocks.com/2014/10/01/cinema/xavier-dolan-fais-films-venger-11520012/> (accessed March 17, 2018).

18. Geneviève Sellier, *Masculine Singular: French New Wave Cinema*, trans. Kristin Ross (Durham, NC: Duke University Press, 2008), pp. 221–2.
19. Gabriel Roy quoted in André Ducharme, "L'étrange histoire de Xavier Dolan," *L'Actualité*, July 3, 2010. Available at <https://lactualite.com/culture/2010/07/03/letrange-histoire-de-xavier-dolan/> (accessed March 30, 2018).
20. Blondeau, "Xavier Dolan: 'Je fais des films pour me venger.'"
21. Xavier Dolan quoted in Vanessa Schneider, "L'exception Dolan," *M Le Magazine du Monde*, May 28, 2016.
22. Alexandre Fontaine Rousseau, "Culte de la personnalité: le cinéma de Xavier Dolan," *24 images*, 173, September 2015, p. 11.
23. Translated roughly as "hewers of wood and drawers of water" or "a destiny of little importance," in this context I propose the more literal translation of this idiomatic expression as "born for a small loaf."
24. Grugeau, "Xavier Dolan: l'accélérateur d'intensité," p. 40.
25. Xavier Dolan quoted in Vanessa Schneider, "L'exception Dolan."
26. Xavier Dolan and Anne Dorval quoted in Vanessa Schneider, "L'exception Dolan."
27. Ducharme, "L'étrange histoire de Xavier Dolan"; Michael Bodey, "Xavier Dolan: Mommy's boy," *Australian*, April 11, 2015. Available at <https://www.theaustralian.com.au/arts/review/xavier-dolan-mommys-boy/news-story/19802488896925f55ca966bd83ebe2ac> (accessed April 3, 2018); Luc Boulanger, "Xavier Dolan: tout sur la mère," *La Presse* (Montréal), September 15, 2014. Available at <https://www.lapresse.ca/cinema/cinema-quebecois/201409/15/01-4800386-xavier-dolan-tout-sur-la-mere.php> (accessed April 3, 2018); Ben Walters, "All about my mother," *Sight & Sound*, 25/4, April 2015, pp. 32–5.
28. Peter Bradshaw, "Interview. Xavier Dolan: 'If I didn't make movies, I would be a very angry man,'" *The Guardian*, February 22, 2017. Available at <https://www.theguardian.com/film/2017/feb/22/xavier-dolan-if-i-didnt-make-movies-i-would-be-a-very-angry-man> (accessed March 5, 2018).
29. Julianne Pidduck, "The 'Affaire Jutra' and the figure of the child," *Jump Cut*, 58, Spring 2018.
30. Robert Schwartzwald, "'Symbolic' homosexuality, 'false feminine,' and the problematics of identity in Québec," in Michael Warner (ed.), *Fear of a Queer Planet* (Minneapolis: University of Minnesota Press, 1993), pp. 267–9.
31. The first part of Dolan's speech from May 2014 was rebroadcast on the French television talk show *On n'est pas couché* in October the same year, where Dorval made this response as a guest on the show. *On n'est pas couché*, host Laurent Ruquier, produced by Catherine Barma, October 4, 2014 (France: France 2).
32. Fulvia Massimi, "'A boy's best friend is his mother': Quebec's matriarchy and queer nationalism in the cinema of Xavier Dolan," Special Issue, *Synoptique*, 4/2, Winter 2016, p. 27.
33. See, for instance, the memo presented to the provincial Minister of Culture and Communications by Réalisatrices équitables in 2016. Isabelle Hayeur, Marie-Hélène Panisset, and Nicole Giguère, "Enfin l'équité pour les femmes en culture?," *Réalisatrices équitables*, April 5, 2016. Available at <http://realisatrices-equitables.com/wp-content/uploads/2017/02/memoire-enfin-equite-pour-les-femmes-en-culture-2016.pdf>.
34. Stephen Maddison, "All about women: Pedro Almodóvar and the heterosocial dynamic," *Textual Practice*, 14/2, 2000, p. 269.
35. Ibid. p. 272.
36. Sellier, *Masculine Singular*, pp. 150–1.
37. Louis Guichard, "L'urgence, son moteur," *Télérama*, 3353, April 19, 2014.

38. Nathalie Baye quoted in Brigitte Baronnet, "Nathalie Baye et son look dans *Juste la fin du monde*: 'C'est Xavier Dolan le patron!,'" *Allociné*, September 25, 2016. Available at <http://www.allocine.fr/article/fichearticle_gen_carticle=18656162.html> (accessed March 15, 2018).
39. Xavier Dolan quoted in Philippe Rouyer and Yann Tobin, "Entretien avec Xavier Dolan: 'Je me pose des questions sur chaque plan,'" *Positif*, October 2014, p. 18.
40. Suzanne Clément quoted in Steve Bergeron, "Suzanne Clément: construire Kyla ensemble," *La Tribune* (Sherbrooke, QC), September 12, 2014. Available at <https://www.latribune.ca/arts/suzanne-clement--construire-kyla-ensemble-63991e2289310f0f985b5d2f75de70ac> (accessed March 17, 2018).
41. Anne Marie Withenshaw, "Les femmes de Dolan," *HuffPost*, Edition QC, February 7, 2012. Available at <https://quebec.huffingtonpost.ca/anne-marie-withenshaw/xavier-dolan-lawrence-anyways_b_1237021.html> (accessed March 15, 2018).
42. Nicolas Gendron, "'J'avais envie de montrer une figure maternelle héroïque,'" *Ciné-Bulles*, 32/3, Summer 2014, pp. 4–9.
43. Xavier Dolan quoted in Allard Clémence, "Xavier Dolan: le talent de mettre en lumière les femmes," *Tribune citoyenne*, May 18, 2016. Available at <https://latribunecitoyenne.wordpress.com/2016/05/18/xavier-dolan-le-talent-de-mettre-en-lumiere-les-femmes/> (accessed March 12, 2018).
44. Maddison, *Fags, Hags and Queer Sisters*, pp. 10, 12.
45. Ibid. pp. 71–2
46. Heinz Weinmann, *Du Canada au Québec: Généalogie d'une histoire* (Montréal: Éditions de l'Hexagone, 1987); Christian Tremblay-Daviault, *Un cinéma orphelin: structures mentales et sociales du cinéma québécois (1942–1953)* (Montréal: Éditions Québec/Amérique, 1981).
47. Schwartzwald, "'Symbolic' homosexuality, 'false feminine,'" pp. 267–9.
48. Lori Saint-Martin, *Le nom de la mère: Mères, filles et écriture dans la littérature québécoise au féminine* (Montréal: Éditions Nota bene, 1999), p. 25.
49. Patricia Smart, *Écrire dans la masion du père: l'émergence du féminine dans la tradition littéraire du Québec* (Montréal: XYZ éditeur, 2003), p. 29.
50. Ibid. p. 31.
51. Thomas Elsaesser, "Tales of sound and fury: observations on the family melodrama," in Christine Gledhill (ed.), *Home is Where the Heart Is: Studies in Melodrama and the Woman's Film* (London: British Film Institute, 1987), p. 51.
52. Judith Butler, *Excitable Speech: A Politics of the Performative* (New York: Routledge, 1997).
53. Xavier Dolan quoted in Schneider, "L'exception Dolan."
54. Elsaesser, "Tales of sound and fury," p. 51.
55. Butler, *Excitable Speech*, p. 11.
56. Ibid. p. 2.
57. Ibid. p. 2.
58. Pierre Bourdieu, *Outline of a Theory of Practice*, trans. Richard Nice (Cambridge: Cambridge University Press, 2012), pp. 122–4.
59. Jack Babuscio, "The cinema of camp (AKA camp and the gay sensibility)," in Fabio Cleto (ed.), *Camp: Queer Aesthetics and the Performing Subject* (Edinburgh: Edinburgh University Press, 1999), p. 119.
60. Ibid. p. 120.
61. Joshua J. Weiner and Damon Young, "Queer bonds," *GLQ*, 17/2–3, 2011, pp. 223–4.
62. See, for example, Gilles Médioni, "Xavier Dolan, le (ciné)fils prodige," *L'Express*, 3229, September 30, 2014. Available at <https://www.lexpress.fr/culture/cinema/xavier-dolan-le-cine-fils-prodige_1578803.html> (accessed March 17, 2018).

63. Xavier Dolan quoted in Gendron, "'J'avais envie de montrer un figure maternelle héroïque,'" p. 7.
64. Elena Del Río, *Deleuze and the Cinemas of Performance: Powers of Affection* (Edinburgh: Edinburgh University Press, 2008), pp. 3–4.
65. Elsaesser, "Tales of sound and fury," p. 50.
66. Del Río, *Deleuze and the Cinemas of Performance*, p. 6.
67. Lucie Robert, "L'impossible parole de femmes," in Gilbert David and Pierre Lavoie (eds), *Le monde de Michel Tremblay Tome II: Romans et récits*, 2nd edn (Carnières: Éditions Lansman, 2005), pp. 185–91.
68. Erin Hurley, *National Performance: Representing Québec from Expo 67 to Céline Dion* (Toronto: University of Toronto Press, 2011), Kindle.
69. Judith Halberstam, *The Queer Art of Failure* (Durham, NC: Duke University Press, 2011), p. 3.
70. Dolan quoted in Médioni, "Xavier Dolan, le (ciné)fils prodige."

CHAPTER 3

Xavier Dolan's Backward Cinema: Straight Spaces, Queer Temporality, and Genealogical Interruptions in *Tom at the Farm* and *It's Only the End of the World*

Florian Grandena and Pascal Gagné

> Over the last century, queers have embraced backwardness in many forms: in celebration of perversion, in defiant refusals to grow up, in explorations of haunting and memory, and in stubborn attachments to lost objects.[1]

> Queer time for me is the dark nightclub, the perverse turn away from the narrative coherence of adolescence—early adulthood–marriage–reproduction–child rearing–retirement–death, the embrace of late childhood in place of early adulthood or immaturity in place of responsibility.[2]

> Not only do the living come to talk to the dead (to their dead), but they also meet other people, individuals that history forbids them to befriend.[3]

In a contemptuous tirade against the Queer Palm won for his film *Lawrence Anyways* (2012), Xavier Dolan expressed his "disgust" for such supposedly divisive awards, favoring instead a more ecumenical spin (that is, a less exclusive or limited approach). Although Dolan may have a point regarding the queer nature of his movies[4]—they may not fall neatly into the "gay cinema" category—there is certainly homosexuality *in* them.[5] Take the protagonists of his first two feature films, *J'ai tué ma mère* (2009) and *Les Amours imaginaires* (2010): both are self-accepting gay men who certainly do not shy away from their desires for other men and neither project nor embody a conflicted homosexuality.[6]

At first glance, the Dolanian representation of homosexuality seems, on the one hand, to deterritorialize same-sex desires from the (self-)pathologizing discourse frequently found in many international *auteur* films,[7] and to depo-liticize male homosexuality on the other. Such an attempt to normalize and "de-problematize" male homosexuality does not mean, however, that Dolan's film representation of gay male characters is coy or trite. Beyond the playful ostentatiousness, if not garishness of their often visually pleasing mise-en-scène and their characters' heightened emotions (two of many formal characteris-tics of the Dolanian cinematic world), viewers can *feel* and acknowledge the "weight" of queerness[8] in some of the young director's melodramas.

The melodramatic genre is indeed an important and appealing one that is close to many queer spectators searching, in the cinematic play of heightened emotions, a figment of truth, a fragment of authenticity, and consequently giv-ing extra validity and meaning to specific lived experiences. Themes of failed romance, love made difficult or even impossible, and strained familial rela-tionships are the backbone of a great many melodramas. Such focus on tense and emotional situations can eventually allow many LGBTQ+ spectators who previously felt silenced and disenfranchised, if not threatened by a prevailing patriarchal or heteronormative order, to situate themselves, to reiterate their place in a queer historic continuum.[9]

Gay history, enacted through many casual stories and, to a certain extent, a rather considerable number of fictional works (whether movies, novels, or other) is predicated upon feelings of loss and melancholy, stigma and sorrow, and the secrecy and fear of being found out. It is also a fact that numerous queer cultural productions are often embedded in painful and complex emo-tions partly inherited from disparaging and discriminatory discourses (ranging from medical, legal, or popular sources), social attitudes, and policies defined and perpetuated by the sexual gender-conformist majority. It should then come as no surprise that "for groups constituted by historical injury, the chal-lenge is to engage with the past without being destroyed by it."[10] Therefore, given that "the history of Western representation is littered with the corpses of gender and sexual deviants,"[11] queer stories and fictional representations can often convey a real and powerful sense of pathos (e.g. dramatic signs of exem-plar suffering as in Ang Lee's celebrated *Brokeback Mountain*).

Of course, many gay writers—whether novelist or screenwriter—have attempted, and still do attempt, to oppose this intense, sometimes morbid, legacy by developing ostensibly empowering characters, nuanced situations and life-affirming storylines, thus positioning themselves along a fundamen-tal tension between "the need to resist damage and affirm queer existence."[12] From such a perspective, queer individuals' relation to their past, present, and future certainly is a complicated one: it understandably means evoking memo-ries laden with fear, pathos, and damage, yet without reviving or resuscitating them—by letting tangled memories flow back into the present—it undoubt-edly makes it a delicate and uncertain enterprise.

In many queer-themed feature films such as Xavier Dolan's, queer characters do often embody and perform a damaged subjectivity that is in line with a
queer history stamped with loss and melancholy as well as survival and hope.
Often predicated upon imminent or effective danger, many queer narratives
focus on suffering as much as they dwell on untold stories and suppressed emotions, that is, a specific queer experience of life often accompanied with danger,
illness (one almost inevitably thinks of AIDS) or tragic death. Although she
analyzes queer texts of the late nineteenth to early twentieth centuries, Heather
Love describes such a take on queer life and history as "feeling backwards,"
that is, the formation of "significant points in a tradition of queer experience
and representation that I call 'feeling backward' . . . they describe what it is
like to bear a 'disqualified' identity, which at times can simply mean living with
injury—not fixing it."[13] Such texts, Love continues, "choose isolation, turn
toward the past, or choose to live in a present disconnected from any larger
historical continuum."[14]

Such a definition of backwardness seems particularly relevant to discuss
the representation of male homosexuality in some of Dolan's feature films. In
the following pages, we explore and discuss the ways that Dolan's movies contribute to a "backward cinema" by putting great emphasis on feelings of loss,
temporary isolation from chosen communities and metronormative culture, as
well as the inability to express one's emotions in an often inimical familial context. In the two films of interest here, *Tom à la ferme* (2013) and *Juste la fin du
monde* (2016)[15] (henceforth *Tom* and *Juste la fin*), there is a discernible, uneasy
relation to temporality that the protagonists—and to a certain extent their
entourage—entertain. These two narratives of regress are replete with many
"negative" feelings such as deception, peer pressure, and endangerment. To
make sense of those queer attachments to objects of misguided affection, Ann
Cvetkovich suggests that examining an archive of feelings consists in looking
at the productive cultural and political value of trauma, which contributes to
the constitution of queer communities as public cultures.[16] The present analysis of Dolan's films follows Cvetkovich's insights. In the context of the two
films' metronormative narratives, intense emotions are both symptomatic and
constitutive of an uneasy bond, an unsettling connection to time and place:
through a reductive depiction of rural spaces, *Tom* and *Juste la fin* emphasize
genealogical discontinuity, ultimately contributing to and enriching an already
dense cinematic archive of melancholic feelings.

QUEER FOLKS IN RURAL LANDSCAPES

Although different in cinematic style,[17] both *Tom* and *Juste la fin* are
firmly rooted in a specific familial context. The films' protagonists are two

successful gay men having to (re)connect with close-knit, yet dysfunctional, families. Montréal-based Tom (Xavier Dolan) meets the family of
his recently deceased partner, Guillaume, for the first time, in order to give
a eulogy at the latter's funeral, whereas Louis (Gaspar Ulliel), an interna-
tionally renowned playwright, pays an unexpected visit to his mother and
siblings after a twelve-year absence: dying from an unnamed illness, Louis
wants to tell his relatives that his days are numbered. Thus, the thwarting of
possibilities and futurity itself frames the arrival or the return of the two gay
men to the family and countryside: for these two queer protagonists, their
relation to time is anything but linear as their trajectories are punctually
interrupted by melancholic affects and distant memories.

Both films are rooted in rural spaces, that is, geographic locations historically and ideologically disconnected from urban ones that are either indifferent
to queerness (*Juste la fin*) or unconditionally hostile toward gay men (*Tom*).
Particularly in *Tom*, the rural space is synonymous with personal alienation
and self-censorship, if not danger and fear. Coming (back) from the city to
the countryside is certainly not an innocent move for either Louis or Tom
as it entails leaving a chosen community behind (an urbanite life presumably
more open to the gay community, where taken-for-granted anonymity allows
for the possibility of a more peaceful queer existence) for a smaller and less
welcoming environment. In *Tom* and *Juste la fin*, rural spaces are represented
as the loci where interpersonal relations are obstacles to the queer protagonists'
happiness, and emotional and physical well-being. Uprooted and repeatedly
silenced, Tom and Louis are forced to withdraw to a regressive and agencyless
temporality; they inhabit, albeit for a short time—one painful day for Louis, a
few harrowing weeks for Tom—a seemingly infantilizing past deprived of possibilities and openings toward the future.

Shortly after his arrival on the farm, Tom is constrained to live in an
undesired temporality mainly determined by and dependent upon natural cycles (daylight, animal rearing). The spatial move to the countryside
implies a fundamental compromise that is temporal, personal, and ideological all at once: Tom must momentarily turn his back on both, his personal history (his feelings of mourning, his career, his social scene), and an
urbanity-based present synonymous with liberation and professional success. Louis, the protagonist of *Juste la fin*, spends the day with his mother,
his two siblings, and his sister-in-law in the hope of telling his family of
his impending death. The few hours with his relatives, however, happen
to be more demanding than expected, and do not allow Louis to reveal his
condition (of which we know nothing). Coming out of the city and into the
countryside (visually reduced to a few shots of country roads and isolated
houses) leads to a constant silencing and infantilization for Louis, who is
consequently pushed back to an adolescent-like state. In other words, both

Tom and Louis inhabit a kaleidoscopic temporal territory torn between the chosen "positive" space (the city, a haven dearly missed) and the imposed "negative" space (the countryside, offering little to Louis and synonymous with harassment and personal alienation for Tom).

TOM AT THE FARM

After the accidental death of his boyfriend, Guillaume, Tom arrives at the farm belonging to his recently deceased partner's family. The farm is inhabited by Guillaume's single mother, Agathe (Lise Roy), a hardworking woman in her fifties, and her other son, Francis (Pierre-Yves Cardinal), a brooding and manipulative man with more than one chip on his shoulder. Convinced that the news of her dead's son queerness would kill her, Francis becomes overprotective of his mother, who seems to purposely ignore, or be unaware of, her younger son's homosexuality. Francis controls her by strategically entertaining delusory fantasies, going to great lengths to reinvent Guillaume's past life, and consequently reformulating his brother's sexual identity by confabulating a heterosexual romance between his late brother and Tom's former colleague Sarah (Évelyne Brochu), who makes a brief appearance at the farm to rescue Tom but is eventually compelled to have sex with Francis in order to return to Montréal. Troubling his brother's past by revisiting it and reformulating it at his will, Francis carries a picture in his wallet of Guillaume kissing a young woman. Spending several days at the farm to overcome his grief, Tom is tormented by Francis on a daily basis, suffering severe psychological—as well as some physical—abuse. Francis repeatedly violates Tom's privacy (during sleep, in the shower, as well as in public restrooms) and relentlessly threatens and roughs him up.

Tom is a disquieting thriller relying greatly on the psychological tensions inherent in the Stockholm syndrome, with the young, emotionally distressed protagonist developing ambiguous feelings toward his attractive persecutor. Whenever Tom is about to leave the farm, Francis insists that he stay in attempts to reconstitute his disrupted family line, albeit in a rather disconcerting manner. Strangely, Tom is quick to buy into Francis's manipulative tale, seemingly convincing himself that a real life (or a real man) is bound to be rural. This is suggested by many visual and narrative cues throughout the film: the country bar's giant yellow neon sign, "*Les Vraies affaires*" (The Real Thing), implies that the dive bar is the most propitious place to expose family secrets, and the laminated poster hanging above the two brothers' single beds, where Francis and Tom sleep every night, reads "Feel Real," as if the rural lifestyle felt more concrete, more authentic than the alienating life of the city. Although Tom becomes complicit in the seductively perverse game of push and pull (a necessary coping mechanism), he eventually escapes after having heard a rather disturbing account of Francis's physical violence. Indeed, nine years prior, Francis disfigured a young man during a particularly violent fight. Shaken and scared, Tom unceremoniously leaves the farmhouse with nothing but a shovel to defend himself, should he run into his de facto captor. An enraged Francis then relentlessly pursues Tom with his pick-up truck until he sees him walking along the road. Tom finds refuge in a nearby wood whereas Francis, increasingly disoriented, pathetically ends up, both feet in a stream, shouting at Tom and threatening him, eventually admitting, "I need you!" Tom at last succeeds in escaping Francis's clutches by stealing his pick-up truck left on the side of the road.

Francis's very first appearance on screen occurs in the outdated family kitchen where, wearing only low-waisted sweatpants, he nonchalantly stands, torso bare, right behind Tom's chair; from the onset, the younger man is coerced into self-effacement and lies by Francis's psychological brutality and domineering demeanor. During this introductory scene, Francis's face is obscured,[18] and the subsequent objectification of his "manly" body suggests that it may be less Francis *per se* who poses a direct threat than rural men's reiterated enactment of an utterly toxic and menacing masculinity. With his pushy, unrefined manners, the man certainly embodies a stereotypical masculinity, all at once seductive, dangerous, and hostile. Here, the body of the Québécois redneck epitomizes the apprehensions and fears of homophobic violence as experienced by many a queer folk in a rural setting.

Tom inhabits a kaleidoscopic temporal territory torn between the chosen "positive" space (the yearned-for city, a haven that is dearly missed and which represents both the present and a utopian future) and the imposed "negative" space (the dystopian countryside in tune with a past that is both ideologically regressive and historically queer). In *Tom*, queerness is a cognitive dissonance: the countryside cannot be a safe and appropriate space where queer folks can express themselves and their desires on their own terms. Far from urban cultures and the city—the historical metronormative locus of queer self-affirmation and happiness—Tom is deprived of his own language and pushed back into a regressive state stamped with fear and self-repression. Such an intense accumulation of tense and damaging or damaged feelings and experiences (related to his partner's sudden death, the obligation to silence his sexual orientation, Francis's constant bullying) constitutes a personal archive of harsh feelings, bridging past and present, the latter being constantly informed and enriched by the former. The traumatic qualities of such feelings still do characterize some aspects of contemporary queer life, and this consequently places Tom, as well as his dead boyfriend, in an eminently queer historic continuum, trauma being "the subject of a discourse that has a history."[19] Trauma—in this instance, death/bullying bullying-related trauma—can [challenge] common understandings of what constitutes an archive. Because trauma can be unspeakable and unrepresentable and because it is marked by forgetting and dissociation, it often seems to leave behind no records at all. Trauma puts pressure on conventional forms of documentation, representation, and commemoration, giving rise to new genres of expression, such as testimony, and new forms of monuments, rituals, and performances that can call into being collective witnesses and publics.[20]

Here, it is Tom's very body that effectively documents—temporarily or permanently—trauma: his skinny figure, his increasingly disheveled appearance, and his greatly restricted freedom of speech and movement are induced by his excruciating rural experience. For Tom, hope and survival mean leaving the repressive/regressive, seemingly stuck-in-time countryside. Torn between backward rurality and negatively reconfigured families where traditional hierarchies are challenged by absent fathers, damaging brothers, and emotional mothers struggling to hold their remaining household together, gay subjectivities are inevitably damaged. In order to survive and eventually thrive, queer folks such as Tom (but also Louis) must move back to a safer space that, in both films, seems to hold the key to self-realization: the city. In that sense, both *Tom* and *Juste la fin* are metronormative tales *par excellence*, underlining the "conspicuous urbanity of queer life,"[21] and confirming the twofold literal and figurative movement that brings about the liberation of the gay subject: *out of the closet* and *into the city*. As J. J. Halberstam puts it, metronormativity

> reveals the conflation of "urban" and "visible" in many normalizing narratives of gay/lesbian subjectivities. Such narratives tell of closeted subjects who "come out" into an urban setting, which in turn, supposedly allows for the full expression of the sexual self in relation to a community of other gays/lesbians/queers. The metronormative narrative maps a story of migration onto the coming-out narrative. While the story of coming out tends to function as a temporal trajectory within which a period of disclosure follows a long period of repression, the metronormative's story of migration from "country" to "town" is a spatial narrative within which the subject moves to a place of tolerance after enduring life in a place of suspicion, persecution, and secrecy.[22]

The two films take place far away from urban centers and cities that, from a metronormative perspective, have long been understood as breeding grounds of gay rights and activism, as well as the main loci of gay histories and History. The city, the almost mythical location where, supposedly, all things queer are born and thrive, is only alluded to in dialogues. Physically absent from the two films (Montréal only appears at the end of *Tom* during a nocturnal tracking shot, and the city is an even more ambiguous, unspecified locale in *Juste la fin*), the Dolanian cinematic city is mostly constructed through verbal allusions and references that indirectly structure the narrative.

What is repeatedly suggested throughout the two films, however, is that rural space, inseparable from death, family drama and self-censorship/self-hatred, can only be detrimental to the two gay protagonists' freedoms of self-expression. This is a stereotypical take on the dialectic relation between queerness and rural space: as Colin R. Johnson et al. warn us, one cannot reify or have a homogenized look at space, as "'urban' and 'rural' are dynamic terms rather than static ones."[23] This is not to deny or minimize the violence that some queer folks can experience in a conservative rural area (let us remember the tragic fate of Matthew Shepard and Brandon Teena in the North American context). Nevertheless, it is important to bear in mind that perceptions of rurality are constructed through metronormative lenses:

> Naturalizations come in the form of typological renderings of the metronormative, which are their most easily identifiable because they are the most visible. Typologies of metronormativity produced by specific historic moments seen as sociopolitical positives—Stonewall, ACT UP New York—normalize an urbane sexual/gender expression. The naturalization of rural heteronormativity finds its footing in the equally negative experiences of violence, intolerance, and right-wing discourse. The rural queers lack visibility not only because of local hostility, but also because the absence of visibility is as a structural component of metronomativity.[24]

Despite the two films' metronormativity, homosexuality still remains somewhat subversive as it opens up a time and place for family drama and repressed fantasies, simultaneously erotic and traumatic. Indeed, in Dolan's cinema, gay male protagonists destabilize straight characters, as queerness resists family tradition and genealogical affiliation. In many ways, homosexuality remains unclassifiable, if not undesirable, in conventional temporalities and, by going against the procreative nature of heteronormative sexuality, it has customarily been conceived as a perversion in conflict with the community's expectations of a quiet and reassuring present/historicity. In Dolan's two films, such a reluctant rooting in rural heteronormativity prevents queer subcultures from thriving or appearing *at all*. An alternative history of queer subcultures, J. J. Halberstam tells us, cannot be about the family, the act of reproduction, heterosexual norms, locations, or identification processes; rather, an alternative history of queer subcultures concerns a critical examination of archives of feeling: "queer subcultures produce alternative temporalities by allowing participants to believe their futures can be imagined according to logic that lie outside of those paradigmatic markers of life experience—namely, birth, marriage, reproduction, and death."[25] Homosexuality, although acknowledged and seemingly accepted, remains wrapped in the mystery left by words unspoken. Truth and authenticity, thereby, can be found in stutters and silences, in implicatures and innuendos, but not in the characters' repetitious statements.[26] The geographical dislocation characterizing *Tom* and *Juste la fin* echoes the two respective families' genealogical interruption and disruption. Indeed, the representation of the two fragmented or disintegrating families (characterized by absent fathers and domineering brothers) takes place in environments that, from the outset, appear cut off from the rest of society—that is, isolated from other rural pockets as well as from urban centers and suburban networks. Cinematic space is here unclear if not confused: there is no precise indication about the location of the family house in *Juste la fin* whereas the farm in *Tom* seems lost in vast cornfields.

The locations of both films point to the fact that, as previously discussed, homosexuality is placed outside of the usual networks of signification, detached from urban stories and histories of homosexuality as well as disconnected from the struggles and tensions along the path to LBGTQ+ rights. It also suggests that, in such a context, homosexuality relies on different types of temporalities: in *Tom*, life is dependent on the farm's various activities, mostly animal rearing, which allows Dolan to provide his viewers with accessible if not obvious life and death symbols. For instance, in *Tom*, homosexuality is associated with death, and Francis cruelly reminds Tom that his sperm has no use, that he can contribute to neither the family's survival nor the perpetuation of his own genealogy and temporal line. Yet, Tom refuses to leave the farm; just like Francis, he is trapped in this seemingly frozen-in-time landscape. Francis himself confesses, during a troubling scene, while the two dance tango to very loud music, that he wants to leave, admitting his secret desire to give his mother a quick death and to be free of people's judgment. Unaware that his mother has entered the room, Francis attempts to change the subject and talks about a newly born calf named "Cul-de-bitch" (son-of-a-bitch). Agathe replies angrily: "Did you hear what I said? . . . I said: 'It's no name for a calf.'" The name of the newborn calf is a point of contention: Francis tries to emphasize its bastard origins, but Agathe rejects the misnaming of the animal. As a bastard son is better than no son at all, she will welcome anyone somehow related to Guillaume into her house. The calf's birth as well as its prompt passing represents the futility and impermanence of Tom's affective attachments, their lack of futurity.

If Tom repeatedly refuses to leave, it is also because he finds in Francis an amorous and erotic substitute, who smells and sounds like his late lover. Whereas Francis is too self-conscious to leave home, Tom is too fascinated to return to his life in the city.[27] Time and queer history are not linear, as any relationship to the past is iterated through multidirectional movements.[28] The backwardness that Francis shows toward the farm, and the ambivalence toward Tom, is characteristic of a traumatic relationship to the past, entertained by fantasies of a different life.

In Dolan's cinema, past and present are engaged in a touching dialogue through objects and sensuous cues that bridge these two temporalities, thus contributing to a hauntological calling. From their first encounter, Agathe is aware that Tom's cologne is the same as her late son's. Guillaume's death, then, does not appear to be a permanent or even insurmountable obstacle as his presence can be felt through Tom's scent. The connection between the past, to which Guillaume is supposed to be relegated, and the present that supposedly belongs to the living, is effectively established, making him not quite absent, nor present. As a result, the conventional temporal dichotomy of past and present is destabilized and challenged; spectrality becomes a coping mechanism for Agathe as well as for Tom himself.

Spectral sensuousness also finds its way into Tom and Francis's intense and utterly problematic relationship. Both men mourn Guillaume but for different reasons: Francis has lost his brother (and, perhaps, lover) whereas Tom grieves his lover. Their problematic closeness being portrayed as a textbook manifestation of the Stockholm syndrome, Tom and Francis entertain an ambiguous and dangerous rapport where sexual and psychological tensions go hand in hand. If Francis enjoys showing off his body or harassing Tom in the most private situations (in the shower or in public restrooms), he devotes some of his time to paraphilic activities: after an evening of heavy drinking, Tom permits Francis to engage into a game of erotic asphyxiation that, although not taken to an irremediable point, appears to sexually arouse both Francis (the strangler) and Tom (the strangled). This erotic exchange between the two men allows Tom to revive and continue his sexual relationship with Guillaume by using Francis as a familial substitute: sex with a dead boyfriend by proxy. Francis entertains similarly spooky fantasies with Tom: by dancing with him, like he used to with his brother Francis revisits and reenacts the trauma of violence, disfigurement, and betrayal suffered nine years before at the village bar, Les Vraies affaires.

IT'S ONLY THE END OF THE WORLD

In a similar vein, the second screen adaptation of Jean-Luc Lagarce's play, *Juste la fin du monde*,[29] relates Louis's unexpected visit after a twelve-year unexplained absence from his family. During that time, the protagonist has become a famous and celebrated playwright, whose various artistic achievements have been duly followed by Suzanne (Léa Seydoux), his immature younger sister, and Martine (Nathalie Baye), his brash and unconditionally loving mother. Although the two women first seem to easily reconnect with Louis, his brother Antoine (Vincent Cassel), an angry, disparaging man who continuously and gratuitously dismisses those around him, quickly becomes a challenge for Louis and the rest of the family.[30] At the film's outset, the expository intertitle, "somewhere, a while ago already," explicitly points to an indeterminate place and time, thereby purposely confusing traditional unity of time and space, and resulting in a spatial and temporal uprooting that relegates the whole narrative to an archetypical, almost fable-like context. The film's first images continue to build on this ambiguity by contrasting Québec visual tropes (typical small-town Québec architecture, a speeding Sea-Doo), and an all-French cast. In other words, though the film may vaguely "feel Québécois," deploying some of Dolan's signature visual tricks, it sounds "authentically French."

In *Juste la fin*, Antoine continuously projects his angst and frustration on those he is supposed to care for the most: he constantly silences and humiliates his relatives, and abruptly leaves rooms only to return to cause further pain and embarrassment. In sum, through the absence of fathers,[31] and the reiterated performances of both Francis and Antoine's inadequate masculinity, the traditional family unit is challenged head-on without being positively redefined or reconfigured. It is reformulated by default (the brothers replace their dead fathers) and becomes the locus of queer alienation *par excellence*; the parochial, homophobic place where queerness is constantly ignored or even smothered. The symbolic space of the family and the geographic locus that is the countryside thus collapse into each other, resulting in a representation of queer subjectivities as relentlessly silenced, censored (by the families or by the queer characters themselves), and inevitably rooted in stigma, pain, and a backward relation to familial temporality.

Louis's coming-back narrative becomes one of failed coming out, not as a gay man *per se* but as a gay man dying from an unnamed illness. Viewers are informed about the looming event by a voice-over, yet are not given any specific details. Since many parallels exist between Jean-Luc Lagarce and his protagonists this illness could very well be AIDS. That it remains unmentioned and unidentified allows Dolan to both depoliticize and deterritorialize it, arguably giving it a universal sheen. The only character aware of Louis's fate is a mysterious interlocutor with whom Louis speaks on his cellphone (we do not know, however, whether the person is a friend, a lover, an agent, or all at once). Although Louis's family is at first genuinely happy to see him again, his mother, sister, brother, and newly acquainted sister-in-law, Catherine (Marion Cotillard), all wonder what has prompted his sudden return. If no one understands why Louis kept to himself for so long, he alludes to his family's responsibility for the situation, of their never having made the effort to come and see him.[32]

One of *Juste la fin*'s early scenes focuses on Louis's sister-in-law, Catherine, who is meeting him for the first time. Eager to both welcome Louis and prevent awkward silences, she is happy to chitchat about her children, and brings up her daughter's physical resemblance to her husband. However, she promptly dismisses the fact that, on the actual photograph, the little girl looks like her father at all: such an odd, seemingly hesitant, if not contradictory, monologue sets the tone for the rest of the film, and also introduces a fundamental tension between kinship—membership in specific familial networks—and the impossibility of belonging. Indeed, Catherine suggests that in her family, and maybe by extension in all families, a fragmented and uncertain linearity is bound to manifest itself and destabilize familial continuities, affiliation and chronology. Her own family tradition requires that a newborn boy be named after his father, but as Catherine explains in a bitter and vexed tone, Antoine refused. Although Louis has stayed away from his family for twelve years, he is given a privileged place in heteronomative time and space as Catherine eventually gave his name to her youngest child. Louis's nephew, whom he has never seen, so becomes his "child," and allows him to re-imagine himself and his place within his family's broken genealogy. What was supposed to be a father-to-son transmission becomes instead an uncle-to-nephew "transfiliation" that partly transcends linear genealogy, which allows queers (like Louis) to consider and enact different types of transmission and kinship. By transfiliation, Denis M. Provencher refers to processes involving

> the creation of filial ties through subversive and transgressive artistic and cultural productions, and the transmissions of those models across genres and generations of producers and consumers, and across transnational networks of communication . . . [Transfiliation] also involves reaching across generations and is transgressive because of its potential to reverse the direction of the transfer of knowledge, tradition, and symbolic heritage between parent and child. It ushers in new forms of heritage and transmission.[33]

Transfiliation is another way to transcend temporality. It brings the past to the present in a subversive form. The spectrality of the interaction and the coexistence of present and past in blood kinship are made possible precisely because homosexuality disrupts the traditional model of genealogical affiliation. In the absence of a clear progeny to homosexual protagonists, family members seek to offer an alternative, and replace queer socio-affective relationships with other forms of identification, reproducing heteronormative order. For instance, Catherine destabilizes and complicates Louis's connection to familial chronology and kinship further by awkwardly discussing Louis's relation to parenthood, legitimacy, and transmission. She cannot imagine a future in which Louis is disconnected, cut off from the family tree. She brings up Louis's perceived infertility, but then immediately acknowledges that male homosexuality and paternity do not have to be antonyms: "Since you people don't have kids, we thought we weren't depriving you of anything . . . But . . . I mean, we say that but, of course, you can . . . have children. Everything's possible nowadays. You'll have some, I'm sure. You're still young. Would you have named him Louis?"[34] Catherine associates the act of naming a child with depriving someone of immortality, because the newborn baby named after his father lives to remember and pursue his genealogy. Louis's sperm is deemed useless, and only his name retains a semblance of value: it evokes memories of an alternative time and place (when the family was together).

Juste la fin also gives some screen time to the revival of past affections and attachments through nostalgic references to specific objects, experiences and locations: given his discontinuous relationship to his family (communication reduced to eloquent postcards), Louis has a conflicting relationship to his own past and physical environment. Through his prolonged absence, Louis has left both his youth and his life lie fallow. The house he grew up in no longer belongs to the family, and, according to Martine, has been literally abandoned by the new owners. As a result, the belongings of his younger self sit, boxed up, in a tiny dusty room in the basement of the family's current home. Still, the boxes act as a reconciling hyphen between two conventionally opposed tempo-ralities: Louis can look at the physical remains of his teenage years as well as remember his first love (who, Antoine tells him, only recently died of cancer). Such a "restorative nostalgia"[35] thus becomes a way to positively bridge differ-ent temporalities.

Nostalgia drives the family's rituals, as its members are fully immobilized in their obligations toward one another, floating in an ethereal space and time. Much to Antoine's displeasure, Martine enjoys reminiscing about the Sundays she, her late husband, and their children would spend together. He gets furious every time someone attempts to situate events and reconnect the past with the present. In one instance, he blows up at his mother, shouting that nostalgia is boring and unproductive, a charge she vehemently opposes.

> "Why tell stories we already know?"
> "We do that in life, stop being so stiff! We recall and relive the things we love. That can't hurt! I know she [Catherine] knows about the Sundays, but I enjoy telling her again. There, that's why we remember! For me. Ha! Happy?"[36]

The relationship to time and memory seems as fragmented as language. Dia-logues are filled with tirades and stutters, with everyone speaking out loud without listening. In a telling scene, at a moment when Louis is about to disclose his illness to his mother, he falls silent upon realizing that she does not know her own son's age, and is unable to quite place him on the family temporal line. At a loss, Martine fills the silence with a lecture about his responsibility as the substitute head of the family, adding prophetically: "I know you won't come back."

Louis has little time left with his family as the day and his life draw to a close. Such a problematic relationship to time is emphasized by recurring shots of the tacky, old-fashioned cuckoo clock, its kitsch unmistakably imbued with a strong sense of nostalgia. Not unlike camp, kitsch can be said to mediate a specific relation to both past and present: "Camp, for instance, with its tender concern for outmoded elements of popular culture and its refusal to get over childhood pleasures and traumas, is a backward art."[37] Against the background of old-fashioned, brownish flowery wallpaper, the clock appears several times throughout the film, working metonymically to represent the house's supposed lack of refinement and overall kitsch style. The cuckoo clock is also an obvious nod to the indubitable passing of time: by stressing the clock's relevance through reiterated forward tracking shots and close-ups, Dolan graphically reminds viewers that Louis's visit and life are bound to end soon. However, the final countdown metaphor toward the end of the film is given when a sparrow suddenly escapes out of the clock and starts to fly around the house in panic. The bird rapidly runs out of energy though and in the film's concluding shot, lies on the floor, breathing rapidly from either exhaustion or impending death. Family life is not only noxious and dangerous, the bird's broken body seems to imply, but also incapable of recognizing its queer son's own fragility and finitude.

As the clock shots emphasize the impending end of the family reunion and of his life, Louis announces that he will be back more often, invites Suzanne to come and visit him and tacitly reconciles with Antoine, offering to continue their conversation. This is, of course, wishful thinking, Louis's final, bittersweet, attempt to speak and to transcend his own death by projecting himself, along with his family, into an impossible but temporarily pleasing future. After a few silent shots of each family member (filmed in slow motion in a typical Dolanian contrast of speed between scenes), Louis reveals that he has to leave: "The truth is that I have to go."

BACKWARDNESS AND POSTPONED DEPARTURES

As previously mentioned, the premises of both *Tom* and *Juste la fin* are predicated upon loss and reluctant, if not forced, concealment, and such a *queer aesthetic of absence* is enhanced by the fact that fathers are nowhere to be seen: Agathe experienced her youngest son's and her husband's passing over a short period of time, whereas Louis's father died many years before. As a result, the traditional family genealogy and linearity are permanently disrupted as no family member has been able to successfully or positively compensate for the fathers' permanent absence, which remains unresolved despite (or perhaps due to) the overwhelming presence of the elder brothers.

The dystopian countryside in *Tom* and the heteronormative, unwittingly repressive family in *Juste la fin* subject the queer characters to physical and psychological violence. Immobilized and isolated in remote landscapes, gay characters wrestle with a traumatic past and its violent reminders, and ambivalently oppose and espouse a backward mindset: they ignore the harshness of name-calling, and recollect bittersweet memories of former innocence through futile attempts at evasion either in drugs or fugitive orgasms. As a result, Louis and Tom need to overcome the traditional family model of inter-individual/ trans-generational exchange and transmission: they have to establish transfilial relations to other beings—animals, nephews yet-to-be-met, ghosts—so that they can survive and exist within a space that leaves little room for hope, self-affirmation, and happiness.

Tom and *Juste la fin* both document the vicissitudes of retreat, each film stressing the necessary but alienating movement back into shame and self-censorship, one into which many "liberated" urban queer folks are forced upon a return to the country and to family obligations, when illness and imminent death strike them or their loved ones. The countryside is thus an agrestic closet larger than queer life where hegemonic voices unrelentingly muzzle queer ones, and where the violent norms and actions of heterosexual, toxic masculinity await Louis and Tom. On the one hand, Dolan's queer characters are deprived of their own voices and agency, and are consequently infantilized, regressing into a desexualized and disempowering temporality. On the other hand, their families expect them to conform, to assume the role of provider, and carry on family duties including household chores, facilitating communication, attending to family ritual, reproducing the social and symbolic order, and possibly even productively using their own sperm to procreate and continue the family line. Thus, social and family control is deeply imbued with the expression of unnatural desires and unwelcome identities alongside the maintenance and reproduction of the "adolescence-early adulthood-marriage-reproduction-child-rearing-retirement-death"[38] heteronormative time sequence.

Homosexuality in both films is repressed since it is perceived as an unproductive act yielding no future. However, its very muzzling is symptomatic of homosexuality's destabilizing power and heterosexuality's fragility, as queerness supposedly threatens to shatter the illusions sustaining futile familial obligations that coerce individuals into a dystopian territory and *trans-temporal* existence (the hegemonic family temporality interspersed with a forced return to an adolescence-like state and a queer history stamped with trauma, loss, hope and survival all at once). If they choose to blend in, queer individuals thus have to find a substitute for their impossible progeny—by raising cattle on a farm or inquiring about their nephews. But this bond or attachment is soon cruelly gone, as symbolized by the dead calf and the final shot of the dying sparrow. Dolan's films seem to imply that there is no future for gays: as a result, withdrawing and leaving are often easier than speaking the truth about oneself.

Nevertheless, the subversive quality of homosexuality is not completely lost in *Tom* and *Juste la fin*. Despite its reiterated smothering, queerness eventually succeeds in disrupting the cyclical time of agriculture, traditional rites, and genealogical reproduction, indicating that queerness can belong to an indefatigable history.[39] Because gays have sex for the sake of pleasure rather than for family continuity and reproduction, their arrivals and departures can nonetheless open up spaces for new beginnings. A feeling of hospitality can be nurtured by queer individuals when the straight spaces they inhabit are fraught with shame, and haunted by spectral figures that seep through the cracks of the broken temporality of trauma.

There is indeed a tension between hospitality and hostility that makes home a place of grief and miscommunication. Making a home in a hostile place sometimes entails a forced return to the closet, which, deeply imbued with the repressive spirit of a backward hinterland and the tragic feelings of mourning, becomes a prison cell (for Tom) and a coffin (for Louis). Although such a backward move may be motivated and justified by the resistance to family feuds, it remains unbearable and morbid. When Louis says to his brother: "It's not the end of the world to come here," he speaks to deceive. Homecoming, when coupled with secrecy and self-censorship, *feels* like the end of the world.

Because the queer protagonists leave no trace behind but unauthorized memories of their own otherness, there are no official versions, no testimonies of their stories, only a trail of bruises that both acknowledges and represses their queer existence. Such violence is never named but it has a face: their loved ones'.

NOTES

1. Heather Love, *Feeling Backward: Loss and the Politics of Queer History* (Cambridge, MA: Harvard University Press, 2007), p. 7.

2. Judith Halberstam, "Theorizing queer temporalities: a roundtable discussion," *GLQ*, 13/2–3, 2007, p. 182.

3. Mireille Rosello, *France and the Maghreb: Performative Encounters* (Gainesville: University of Florida Press, 2005), p. 129.

4. In Dolan's words: "I'm just trying to blur this very clear line we've drawn and are drawing over and over again between communities. Saying those are queer films and those are films. I would love for that line to disappear. For that frontier to be abolished once and for all. I would love to stop putting names on things and claiming things. There is a lot of work to be done, let's be honest. I am queer, but the films are for everyone to see. I don't

think I can help a kid in Texas or in Utah or Colorado or Idaho or Ohio who is struggling with his identity, as a queer filmmaker. Or because my films have been, what, labeled as queer? He'll go and Google 'queer films?' I doubt he will ever do that and if he does he'll probably end up hearing about me. But what I'm trying to do because I feel pretty helpless with that, with those cases and those kids out there, what I'm trying to do on the other hand is to widen the minds of people who think in a more narrow way of homosexuality by trying to depict and illustrate relationships between men as not the central narrative, theme or line of the film. And making it secondary. Making it not unimportant, but not stressing. And with these tags and labels are achieving is exactly the opposite of what I'm trying to do. I'm trying to incorporate it in people's minds and societies imagination that it is normal and doesn't need to be named. Not out of shame or because I'm cool, but this is not where we are at anymore. At least not in these cinematic circles where people can see these films. Does that make sense?"; Eric Eidelstein, "*Mommy* director Xavier Dolan doesn't want you to label his films," *IndieWire*, January 19, 2015. Available at <https://www.indiewire.com/2015/01/mommy-director-xavier-dolan-doesnt-want-you-to-label-his-films-2-66142/> (accessed August 20, 2018).

5. See, for instance, Clément Giuliano, "Xavier Dolan ou l'évidence de l'homosexualité," *Medium*, September 18, 2016. Available at <https://medium.com/@clemgiu/xavier-dolan-ou-lévidence-de-l-homo sexualité-a49248cf385a> (accessed September 10, 2018).

6. If the protagonist of *J'ai tué ma mère* is first unable to come out to his mother, it is mostly because his relationship to the woman is considerably strained and smudged with many trust and communication issues. Homosexuality per se is not portrayed as being problematic.

7. *Beach Rats* (Eliza Hittman, 2017) and *Heartstone* (Guðmund Arnar Guðmundsson, 2016) both focus on their protagonists' intense (self-)repression and self-hatred. The two characters (a young unemployed man and a teenager) find themselves unable to overtly express their desires for other men in an environment little open to sexual nonconformists (the Brooklyn suburbs and an isolated fishing village in contemporary Iceland respectively).

8. Here, we use queer as a synonym with homosexuality.

9. Eve Kosofsky Sedgwick, *Epistemology of the Closet* (Berkeley: University of California Press, 1990).

10. Love, *Feeling Backward*, p. 1.

11. Ibid. p. 1.

12. Ibid. p. 3

13. Ibid. p. 4

14. Ibid. p. 8

15. (Dolan's two screen adaptations of contemporary theatrical plays.)

16. Ann Cvetkovich, *An Archive of Feelings: Trauma, Sexuality, and Lesbian Public Cultures* (Durham, NC: Duke University Press, 2003).

17. *Tom* is a Hitchcock-like drama in which mise-en-scène focuses on a subdued color palette and restrained acting performances. In contrast, *Only the End* is an affected family melodrama and it does not spare spectators with its garish colors and ostentatious characters in line with Dolan's usual flamboyant cinematic world.

18. One of the first close-ups of Francis's face occurs when, rather perversely, he surprises Tom in the shower, his odd and predatory demeanor enhanced by his destabilizing odd-eyed gaze.

19. Cvetkovich, *An Archive of Feelings*, p. 17.

20. Ibid. p. 7.

21. Colin R. Johnson, Brian J. Gilley, and Mary L. Gray, "Introduction," in Mary L. Gray, Colin R. Johnson, and Brian J. Gilley (eds), *Queering the Countryside: New Frontiers in Queer Studies* (New York: New York University Press, 2016), p. 9.
22. Judith Halberstam, *In a Queer Time and Place: Transgender Bodies, Subcultural Lives* (New York: New York University Press, 2005), pp. 36–7.
23. Johnson et al., "Introduction," in *Queering the Countryside*, p. 19.
24. Ibid. p. 13.
25. Ibid. p. 2.
26. In contrast with Ducastel and Martineau's earlier version of Lagarce's play, Dolan's screen adaptation does not aim to stick to the original text word for word. On the contrary, Dolan manipulated and partially rewrote some of the dialogue, simplifying it by minimizing one of the linguistic characteristics of Lagarce's admirable prose (the characters often intersperse the fluidity of the conversation with many stylistic stutters and hesitations).
27. In *Tom*, the return to the closet is a form of *servitude volontaire*. See Romain Ferreira, "*Tom à la ferme,*" *La Kinopithèque* (blog), May 24, 2014. Available at <http://www.kinopitheque.net/tom-a-la-ferme/> (accessed September 10, 2018).
28. Michael Rothberg, *Multidirectional Memory: Remembering the Holocaust in the Age of Decolonization* (Stanford, CA: Stanford University Press, 2009).
29. Olivier Ducastel and Jacques Martineau directed their own screen adaptation of Lagarce's play in 2010.
30. Lagarce initially wrote the play in 1990 in Berlin as he was living with AIDS. Annelise Roux, "'Juste la fin du monde': l'impossible annonce faite à Martine," *La République du cinéma*, September 20, 2016. Available at <http://larepubliqueducinema.com/juste-la-fin-du-monde-limpossible-annonce-faite-martine/> (accessed September 25, 2018).
31. Absent fathers are a recurrent theme in many an international queer production such as *Beach Rats*, *Drôle de Félix/The Adventures of Felix* (Olivier Ducastel and Jacques Martineau, 2000), *Quand on a 17 ans/Being 17* (André Téchiné, 2016), and *Beautiful Thing* (Hettie Macdonald, 1996), to name a few.
32. Louis says, "Vous vous imaginez que j'habite loin" (You imagine that I live far away).
33. Denis M. Provencher, *Queer Maghrebi French: Language, Temporalities, Transfiliations* (Liverpool: Liverpool University Press, 2017), pp. 46–7.
34. "Et puisque vous n'aurez pas d'enfants, on s'est dit qu'on ne vous volait rien. Mais enfin, on dit ça, mais en même temps, vous pouvez. Évidemment, tout est possible. Avoir des enfants. Et vous en aurez même. Vous êtes encore jeune. Vous les auriez appelés Louis."
35. Svetlana Boym, *The Future of Nostalgia* (New York: Basic Books, 2008).
36. "C'est quoi ce truc de toujours raconter des histoires qu'on connaît déjà?"
ANTOINE: "Mais on fait ça dans la vie, t'es bête ou quoi? On se rappelle des choses qu'on aime. Ça fait pas de mal! Je sais qu'elle connaît les dimanches, mais moi je suis contente de lui redire. Voilà, voilà pourquoi on raconte les dimanches. Pour moi. Ha! T'es content?"
37. Love, *Feeling Backward*, p. 7.
38. Halberstam, "Theorizing queer temporalities: a roundtable discussion," p. 182.
39. Lawrence R. Schehr, *Parts of an Andrology: On Representations of Men's Bodies* (Stanford, CA: Stanford University Press, 1997), p. 182.

PART 2

Local Auteur

CHAPTER 4

Spaces and Times of Québec in Films by Xavier Dolan

Bill Marshall

The success of Xavier Dolan since his breakthrough film, *J'ai tué ma mère* (2009), made when he was only nineteen, has been one of the most striking developments in Québec cinema over the past decade. Culminating in the shared Prix du Jury at Cannes in 2014 for *Mommy*, following *Les Amours imaginaires* (2010), *Laurence Anyways* (2012), and *Tom à la ferme* (2013), this triumphant tale has been, needless to say, accompanied by much journalistic chatter and cliché, and some, but so far relatively limited,[1] published academic attention. The former has often dwelt on the youth angle (the term wunderkind is repeated *ad nauseam*), and, relatedly, a certain skepticism regarding his talents as a filmmaker, the expressive maximalism of much of his directorial style read as often undisciplined and even immature.[2] The first stirrings of academic attention have focused on the queer angle, as we shall see, including this director's take on the family and mother/son relationship,[3] on his ability to reach a diversity of audiences beyond the frontiers of Québec,[4] and on his relation to music.[5]

Certainly, the Dolan phenomenon joins certain (mainly) globalizing trends in Québec cinema since 2000: an on average significantly increased share of the domestic box office by local films; prizes and nominations not only at Cannes but at the Oscars;[6] the Hollywood careers of Jean-Marc Vallée, Denis Villeneuve, and now, Dolan;[7] the transnational success of *La Grande Séduction/ Seducing Doctor Lewis* (Jean-François Pouliot, 2003) and the English-Canadian, French, and Italian remakes it has spawned.[8] However, it would be inappropriate to speak of a "post-national" cinema. Rather, we might examine re-shapings in that risky category, a Québec national narrative, or more specifically, in shifts in perceptions of self and the world among (largely white) French-speaking Québécois audiences. Critical discussion[9] has speculated about what changes have taken place that have enabled this opening up of new audiences. In 1982, Ginette Major had posited that, rather than the resigned and fatalistic, slow and intimist dramas of current auteur production, Québec cinema would "rediscover its lost audience when it stops being the complacent mirror of an enfeebled society."[10] Christian Poirier later identified a tension in Québec film narratives between "a hegemonic narrative of emptiness and lack, of being prevented from existing, and a narrative of plurality, of a positively embraced ambivalence, of delight in existing."[11] Jocelyn Létourneau has in turn identified a number of factors that are contributing to what he refers to as a contemporary *révolution silencieuse* (silent revolution) in Québec society.[12] The evidence of polls and voting patterns suggests that the sovereigntist project is the preference of the baby boomer generation but no longer that of those aged eighteen to thirty-four. A Léger poll conducted for the Institut du Nouveau Monde in February 2015 indicated that since 1995 support had fallen in the lower age group from 63 percent to 41 percent, and actually risen in the higher from 25 percent to 37 percent.[13] The 2012 provincial election put the Parti Québécois (PQ) just 0.75 percent and four seats ahead of the Liberals, battered by scandals and weeks of student protests, and eighteen months later the PQ government was replaced by the PLQ (Parti Libéral du Québec/Liberal Party of Québec) with a convincing majority. Moreover, it is becoming clear that, freed from the colonial reference, English is ceasing to be perceived as the language of the Other by younger Québécois, but is rather seen as a pragmatic vehicle to access the world—of opportunity and of culture.[14] What we now witness is a pluralization of references—what Létourneau refers to as "interferences" or even "inter(re)ferences"—which mark at once a shift in the self-perception(s) of the white francophone majority, and a continuity in relation to that community's sempiternal navigation between sedentarism and nomadism, Frenchness and Americanness, tradition and opening to otherness.[15] In *Quebec National Cinema*, I sought to trace these "national-allegorical tensions" as expressed in film, that is tensions between forces that would gather identity into something fixed, finished, and unified, what we might call centripetal or territorializing tendencies, and forces that would undo, unravel, disperse, the national, what we might call deterritorializing or centrifugal tendencies.[16]

In the rest of this essay, I wish to investigate how two films by Xavier Dolan, *Laurence Anyways* and *Tom à la ferme*, with some glances at *Mommy*, might be examined in relation to these concepts and contexts. I shall argue that a productive way forward is to read the films at the convergence of two approaches, the sexual and spatial.

Dolan himself famously refuses the categorization of "gay" or "queer" filmmaker, while being at ease with his queer identity/identification as such.[17] In this he is not untypical of various cinematic auteurs, particularly in the French-speaking world. Here we are obliged neither to sanctify these authorial protests, nor to lose sight of their relation to a social and generational context in which identities—sexual and national—are pluralized and recognized as performative, provisional, and relational. Given the symbolic weight of both gender roles and the family in the elaboration of wider identities, and the way in which sexualities are crucial sites within the unceasing and unfolding textual patterns noted above, it is legitimate therefore to pause and reflect on the place of Dolan's films in a history of queer filmmaking in Québec. However, what understanding of "queer" is to be wielded?

At one level, "queer" can simply be a shorthand term that is understood to assemble the categories collected under "LGBT," with the added piquancy of a general challenge to heteronormativity and its assimilations (a challenge unlikely to warm to, for example, the institution of gay marriage): this concerns "the possibility of distinguishing between, on the one hand, a queer politics that can easily be reduced to lesbian and gay identity interests and on the other, a 'properly' queer politics that seeks to disrupt the police order that is regimes of normalized sexuality."[18]

Dolan himself seems to understand the term to refer to identity, but a question posed of the two films is whether his "queerness" also encompasses that disruption of heteronormativity. "Queer" might also be used more productively here for the way in which it problematizes identity itself and even summarizes some of those millennial shifts noted earlier. The term has always embodied the tension that a return to the contemporary origins of these debates highlights: as Eve Sedgwick noted in *Epistemology of the Closet*:

the contradiction between seeing homo/heterosexual definition on the one hand as an issue of active importance primarily for a small, distinct, relatively fixed homosexual minority (what I refer to as a minoritizing view), and seeing it on the other hand as an issue of continuing determinative importance in the lives of people across the spectrum of sexualities (what I refer to as a universalizing view).[19]

That "trans" preposition in "across the spectrum" perhaps announces the development in Sedgwick's thought, via "queer," into ideas of movement: "Queer is a continuing movement, moment, motive—recurrent, eddying, *troublant* [*unnerving*]. The word 'queer' itself means *across*—it comes from the Indo-European root – *twerkw*, which also yields the German *quer* (transverse), Latin *torquere* (twist), English *athwart*."[20]

The broad lines of a history of queerness in Québec cinema would go something like this. An originary discourse in 1960s (pre-feminist, pre-Stonewall) nationalism posited the father/son relationship as perpetuating a masculinist vision of national emancipation, with queer subjects as the threatening or comic Other (fathers and sons in *Le Temps d'une chasse/The Time of the*

Hunt, Francis Mankiewicz, 1972, and *De père en flic / Father and Guns*, Émile Gaudreault, 2009; with added homophobia in *Un Zoo la nuit / Night Zoo*, Jean-Claude Lauzon, 1987; 1970s sex comedies such as *La Pomme, la queue et les pépins / The Apple, the Stem and the Seeds*, Claude Fournier, 1974). Later, homosexuality, in films such as *Le Déclin de l'empire américain / The Decline of the American Empire* (Denys Arcand, 1986) and *Le Confessionnal / The Confessional* (Robert Lepage, 1995) became the emblem of a successful Québec modernity and modernization, or at the very least a marker of the distinction between a clerical past and a secularized present, and of the road travelled. The apogee of this process is *C.R.A.Z.Y.* (Jean-Marc Vallée, 2005), when the narrative journey of the gay son—born at the birth of the Quiet Revolution—is folded back, indeed assimilated, into a national family romance, and, needless to say, a father-son reconciliation. But there is also a history of alternative, sporadic queer filmmaking in terms of form as well as content (of which *Le Confessionnal* partakes, to be fair), beginning with Claude Jutra's astonishing *À tout prendre / Take It All* (1963), and continuing with André Brassard's *Il était une fois dans l'est / Once Upon a Time in the East* (1974), which adapted several Michel Tremblay plays to depict a pre-Stonewall world of working-class queer outcasts who could stand for national alienation as well as, by foregrounding gender as performance in the person of the drag queen, hinting intriguingly at the performativity of both national and sexual identities.

The lack of resolution in queerness (between identity and its undoing) means that it can, as well as a refusal of normative, Oedipalized identity trajectories (Dolan famously focuses on the gay or trans-/mother dyad), become a touchstone for these wider uncertainties of the national, rather than the antithesis of its unified and heteronormative assertion or the embodiment of its modernizing trajectory. This is immediately apparent in *Laurence Anyways*. Ambitiously spanning a ten-year period in the 1980s and 1990s, the narrative recounts the decision by a thirtysomething male writer and literature teacher, Laurence (Melvil Poupaud), to change sex and live as a woman. The film charts the turbulent effects of this decision on Laurence's career and moreover on his passionate relationship with a woman, Fred (Suzanne Clément), who eventually accepts the situation and for a time remains with him and supports him in his transformation.

As Thomas J. D. Armbrecht has pointed out, the emphasis here is on "trans" rather than "sexual," in that the prefix's relation to its root word is a pre(-)text, or even a metaphor, for any process of transformation or becoming.[21] We would seem here to be in very Deleuzian territory, in which becoming is a process that does not end with a new identity one has become, and in which *le devenir femme* or "becoming woman" is considered to be the key to those minoritarian movements which would undo "major" identities and positions based on mastery or domination. To that extent, those close to Laurence—Fred, and his mother

Julienne (Nathalie Baye)—are also swept along in a movement of change which disrupts the fixities by which they have lived and injects them with a renewed belief in the world in contrast with previous assumptions about gender binary polarizations and/or domestic stasis. (However, Fred is ultimately peripheralized by the narrative, and this opens up a whole other set of debates about socially and historically situated women faced with this ontology and even metaphysics of becoming which are best joined in other contexts.)

At some levels, *Laurence Anyways* is an obvious text in which to consider the "national-allegorical tension" noted above: centripetal forces of identity recognition (for a Québec film audience faced with its own cultural references, mirrored by the main protagonist's quest), references to Québec film history (Denise Filiatrault in the role of a waitress providing a direct link to *Il était une fois dans l'est*), and an emphasis on orality, on Québec speech as marker of belonging and even authenticity, co-exist with centrifugal tendencies (the never-ending becoming, the diversity of Montréal, the alternative families, the co-production with France, two French stars [Poupaud and Baye] and appeal to international audiences, the eschewal of depth models in favor of a proliferation of surfaces that can be said even to generate a queer style, as in the bravura party scene and 1980s pop video aesthetic to Visage's "Fade to Grey"). However, given the marked dominance of the centrifugal along with a decidedly non-erasure of Québec specificity, the question begins to arise as to whether this transnationalism in Dolan is actually generating a paradigm shift. For Valérie Mandia, the emphasis is on language in Dolan's films. The mix of registers, the irruption of English, the code-switching, all contribute for her to an adaptable, mobile, and protean attitude to Québec language(s) which prioritizes intercommunication (and "inter(re)ferences," in Létourneau's terms) over "authenticity" and identity, quotations by Dolan *à l'appui*: "The protection of Québec identity implies an opening out to other identities, that's how identities are enriched and truly elevated."[22] Mandia even extends the analysis to include questions of space:

> The hybridity which characterizes his works becomes more acute, and allows him to situate himself in a much vaster space than Québec. In so doing, he gives his characters a ubiquity, as if they could be located in more than one place at once.[23]

Space is a preoccupation in Dolan's films in terms of cinematic form, geographies of Québec, and queerness. The bravura moments, briefly marking euphoria, in *Mommy* when the 1:1 aspect ratio—associated with portraiture, mobile phone photography, and confinement—is opened out to widescreen are just two examples of the way in which Dolan manipulates the frame to establish structure and pattern, and to explore themes associated with movement and stasis. Figures 4.1–4.3 from *Laurence Anyways* illustrate this first of all in relation to domestic space. Coming at the opening of the film when Laurence, as we later learn, has moved back to Montréal, the shots of apartment interiors are typically ambivalent: interiority and even enclosure mitigated by an underlining of the relation between interior and exterior spaces; the view of the door as something that is passed through rather than shuts in. Moreover, the *emboîtement* (nestling) of frames within frames[24] hints at relays of interconnectedness with what is out-of-field, which, following Deleuze's analysis in *L'Image-mouvement*, "refers to what is neither seen nor understood, but is nevertheless perfectly present":[25]

Figure 4.1 Frames and spaces. *Laurence Anyways.*

Figure 4.2 Interiors. *Laurence Anyways.*

Figure 4.3 Doorways. *Laurence Anyways.*

The divisibility of content means that the parts belong to various sets, which constantly subdivide into sub-sets or are themselves the sub-set of a larger set, on to infinity. This is why content is defined both by the tendency to constitute closed systems and by the fact that this tendency never reaches completion. Every closed system also communicates.[26]

I wish to link this evocation of cinematic frames and spaces to organizations—and imaginations—of space in Québec, but via Foucault, who reminds us of the imbrications of space and power, and how contemporary distributions have their origins at the end of the eighteenth century, with "the disposition of space for economico-political ends":[27]

There emerged a new form of social spatiality, a certain way of socially and politically distributing space, and to show that one could write the whole history of a country, of a culture or of a society, based on the way space is valuated and distributed.[28]

The distributions and (re)organizations of space in Québec are of course traced across the differing strategies of New France, the British Empire, Canadian Confederation, industrialization and the rural exodus, the Quiet Revolution, technocracy, and so on, and result in familiar mappings, including the class and linguistic divisions in urban space. Foucault's notion of differentiated space includes, also, of course, the demarcations between "normal" and "marginal," how these are defined, and how they are organized spatially. The three examples of "Québec space" I shall take at this point are to be found in *Laurence Anyways* and *Mommy.*

Figure 4.4 *Balconville* encounters. *Laurence Anyways.*

Near the end of the former film, Laurence has returned from living in Vermont and moves into the Montréal apartment, backing on to the Parc du Mont-Royal, which was glimpsed at the outset. Laurence is out on the rear balcony, and is glimpsed by a neighbor, a young teenage boy who blows her a kiss from the heart in a playful, amorous gesture (Figure 4.4). The scene sums up many of the film's ambiguities, and in a very Montréal context. Laurence has achieved that recognition as a woman in the *regard de l'autre* (eye of the other) that he had sought throughout the film, and which the editing had heavily thematized, with numerous shots of Laurence being *gazed at* by people at his/her school and in the street. However, the fact that this seemingly identitarian moment takes place on the balcony is significant. In *Outside Belongings*, Elspeth Probyn uses the Montréal summer phenomenon of *balconville*—when households often decamp to the ubiquitous balconies that originally imitated the galleries of rural and village life—as a point of departure, in its blurring of private and public space, for the exploration of the ambiguities of identity, or, preferably, "belonging": for her, the Montréal balcony exemplifies "a certain movement as different and distinct elements are brought together. Lines of class, gender, sex, generation, ethnicity, and race intermingle as people hang out. The balcony is . . . a site where one sees an ongoing inbetweenness."[29] Adopting perspectives drawn from queer theory, Probyn argues that "belonging therefore points, rather than to a finished and fixed position or 'identity', to an always incomplete 'yearning', a 'movement of desiring belonging'"[30] whose "threads . . . lead us into unforeseen places and connections."[31] The balcony scene in *Laurence Anyways* thus prolongs the numerous scenes of thresholds that pepper the film, including those outside the door to Fred's house in Trois-Rivières as Laurence renews contact with her (Figure 4.5).

Figure 4.5 Suburban thresholds. *Laurence Anyways.*

Secondly, Dolan's films are significant for their representation of suburbia. This is more visible in *Mommy* than in *Laurence Anyways*, but even in the latter the traversals of the metropolitan area of Montréal (Centre-Sud and Plateau-Mont-Royal, Longueuil and Laval) are marked by motor vehicle spaces, including garages and carwashes (two contrasting scenes place the car as site of romantic and erotic complicity followed by that of confession, in both cases marked by a literal fluidity which characterizes the film's approach to belonging), and suburbs stand in for other sites such as Trois-Rivières. In *Mommy*, the action largely takes place in a residential area on the south shore of Montréal, with filming in Longueuil, Chambly, and Oka.

The urtext of representations of suburbia in Québec fictional feature films is an inaugural sex comedy, *Deux femmes en or / Two Women in Gold*, directed in 1970 by Claude Fournier, in which two bored housewives living in Brossard on the south shore avenge a husband's infidelity by sleeping with the various handymen and delivery boys that come their way. Nationalist in its perspective in its targeting of the English language, Ontario, and federal Canada as butts of humor, the film depicts a society that is emerging from Catholicism and is extensively modernizing (and suburbanizing) itself, and is negotiating change through a play of autonomy and dependency for women, a debunking of traditional machismo, and an ironic take on the *banlieue* (suburb). In an early fictional feature by Denys Arcand, *Réjeanne Padovani* (1973), the suburban family home is associated with municipal corruption and organized crime. However, in the decades since, Québec cinema has witnessed a "normalization" of the suburbs, represented in diverse ways, as a site of social aspiration, of boredom certainly, of childhood memories (*C.R.A.Z.Y.* but also, for example, *1981*, Ricardo Trogi, 2009). By the 2000s, the suburbs have tended to become, as Andrée Fortin argues, the "default" setting for the representation of family life, including single parenthood. In addition, a metropolitan space that includes both the city and its suburbs has become the point of reference in relation to elsewhere, be it the countryside or the wider world, rather than simply "Montréal" (or, within it, the Plateau and/or "the east end").[32] The *banlieue* in cinematic representations seems to have simply become the place where dwell the white Franco-Québécois majority, the national "we" so artfully addressed and constructed in *C.R.A.Z.Y.*, with the gay son, born on Christmas Day 1960 at the dawn of the Quiet Revolution, by the end re-integrated into the contemporary national family romance. Robert Schwartzwald argues that Stéphane Lafleur's 2007 film, *Continental, un film sans fusil/Continental, a Film Without Guns*, in its depiction of the suburban loneliness of four white Franco-Québécois central characters, portrays the inhabitants of the *banlieue* as representing a "homogenous 'nous' [we/us] *à la dérive* [adrift],"[33] in which the multicultural, global, "de-nationalized" city is the absent Other.

This symbolic investment in the suburbs is a significant shift, which it may be possible, however, to link to the 'post-national' or 'inter-referential' tendencies noted above. As Daniel Laforest points out, the overwhelming critical consensus within literary culture toward the *banlieue* has been to deride its supposed ahistoricity and to limit an understanding of its culture to that of "North American"—that is simply *états-unien* ("American")—meanings.[34] A solution he proposes is a new emphasis on "ordinary life," which will be able to grasp the sets of affects that could invest new forms of literary realism. Dolan's *Mommy* in particular suggests some ways forward in its depiction of its *banlieue* characters. Its story of a dysfunctional mother-son relationship and the temporary alliance with a female neighbor suffering from some unspecified post-traumatic stress is bathed in affect, in ways that sidestep the conventional depiction of American suburbia which, *Desperate Housewives* in mind, delves into the secrets and neuroses behind the calm and ordered picket-fence exterior. As Joachim Lepastier argues in his review in *Cahiers du Cinéma*, thanks to Dolan's characteristic film style, the reverse is true: his "fetishism of surfaces and gorgeous images," along with the excesses of the protagonists' emotion and self-expression, grants the film a distinctiveness which also extends to its articulation of Québécois "belonging."[35] We recall Probyn's emphasis on surface, on "modes of belonging as surface shifts" rather than grounded in "deep" authenticity: "particularity and sensuality, surfaces and the outside, images that hit and move one to return to the minuteness of the social surface."[36] Let us then connect this to the "de-nationalized" view of Québec identity that Dolan articulates above. His use of language in *Mommy*, as we have seen, and his eclectic, translinguistic choice of musical elements on the soundtrack, suggest that the national "we" now so at home (in diverse, contradictory, and even conflictual ways) in the suburbs is located in a space which, thanks to audio-visual media, internet networks, and a *décrispation* (thawing) of relations with the English language, is in a position to relay the multiple surfaces of belonging which constitute the new horizons of "Québecness." *Mommy* ends with an example of Foucauldian confinement, in which the mentally troubled son is sent to a psychiatric institution, where he commits suicide. The film's exploration of the boundaries of "normality" refuses, however, any attempt at (national) allegorization, rendering it radically distinct from *C.R.A.Z.Y.*

The third spatial element that *Laurence Anyways* articulates connects with another Foucauldian concept, that of heterotopia. When Fred runs off with Laurence after they meet again in Trois-Rivières, they head in the depths of winter for the "Île au Noir," variously interpreted as l'Île aux Noix on the Richelieu River, but, given that these sequences were shot in Charlevoix, resembling more the Îsle-aux-Coudres, famous for the documentaries of rural life, folklore, and fabulation filmed there in the 1960s by Pierre Perrault. Rather than an actually existing "place," Dolan here sets up a space which is not utopian (Fred is mortified by its *faux* bohemian nature and returns to her husband and son) but which constitutes a narrative pause where Laurence's quest for recognition and for a non-differentiation in difference, in other words a difference of transgender which makes no difference in the world, is momentarily satisfied in the friendship with the transgender couple. In the highly influential 1967 essay, "Of other spaces," Foucault wrote of those spaces which do not quite fit into the contemporary regime of classifying and establishing relations between sites. These other spaces are

> something like counter-sites, a kind of effectively enacted utopia in which the real sites, all the other real sites can be found within the culture, are simultaneously represented, contested and inverted. Places of this kind are outside of all places, even though it may be possible to indicate their location in reality.[37]

In our desanctified world, these "heterotopias" hark back to sacred spaces, real but "elsewhere"—the mirror, the honeymoon, later commentators even suggest theme parks—which can have a double function. The first, which mainly concerns us here, is as "a space of illusion that exposes every real space, all the sites inside of which human life is partitioned, as still more illusory":[38] the Île au Noir imperfectly fulfills this role in *Laurence Anyways*. It is tempting, however, to invoke also the other "pole" of Foucault's reflections in this section of his essay: the heterotopia of compensation which he associates with the colony. Here the Puritans in New England, the Jesuits in Paraguay, and why not also Jeanne Mance founding Montréal, conjoin to add greater suggestiveness, given Dolan's predilection for polyvalent images, to the Île au Noir (both the Île aux Noix with its fortress and the Îsle-aux-Coudres described by Jacques Cartier)

Figure 4.6 To and from an island. *Laurence Anyways*.

and to the enigmatic photographic image of it, which introduces the first references to it in the film, framed behind a sugar jar. What is more, Foucault concludes his essay by invoking the ship as heterotopia, "a floating piece of space, a place without a place, that exists by itself, that is closed in on itself and at the same time given over to the infinity of the sea."[39] Dolan makes much of Laurence's maritime journey to and from the island, witness the characteristic framing shot in Figure 4.6.

The pre-credit sequence of *Tom à la ferme* sees Tom (Xavier Dolan), in his car, frantically scratching on a tissue, in extreme close-up, a eulogy for his dead boyfriend Guillaume, which is to take place at the latter's family home on a poor farm in rural Québec. There this city boy, who works in advertising, is drawn into the world of Guillaume's widowed mother, Agathe (Lise Roy), who has no idea of her son's sexual orientation, and his violent brother Francis (Pierre-Yves Cardinal), who intends to keep it that way. Tom never gives his eulogy at a tense church service, and is pressured to stay at the farm by Francis, momentarily succumbing to a form of "Stockholm syndrome" in his relationship with him, to the point of inviting a friend from Montréal (Évelyne Brochu) to impersonate Guillaume's supposed girlfriend, Sarah. Finally, however, Tom makes his escape back to Montréal in Francis's pick-up truck after learning of an extremely violent past incident, which explains why the local community has shunned the family.

The immediate post-credit sequence features an aerial tracking shot of Tom's car that swoops over a body of water, and follows him driving down a rectilinear road through fields and farms (Figure 4.7). No doubt this is the Richelieu, as much of the film was shot in the area of Saint-Blaise. Here are embedded the spaces of Québec: the division into *rangs* beginning at the

Figure 4.7 Embedded spaces of Québec. *Tom à la ferme.*

waterside that characterized New France's cadastral system, the twentieth-century network of paved roads for motor traffic. In Deleuze and Guattari's sense, these are striated rather than smooth spaces, the product of administration and regulation. There is more in play, however: the shot is very reminiscent of opening scenes of Stanley Kubrick's *The Shining* (1980) as the car journeys to the Overlook Hotel where the film's horrors will take place. Indeed, *Tom à la ferme* is replete with references to American cinema, notably Hitchcock (the shower scene from *Psycho*, the chase through a cornfield in *North by Northwest*, the Bernard Herrmann-like score by the well-established international film composer Gabriel Yared). In addition, Tom's journey is accompanied by an *a cappella* rendition (in the Eddy Marnay French version) by the Québécoise Kathleen Fortin of the 1960s Michel Legrand/Marilyn and Alan Bergman song "Windmills of Your Mind"/"Moulins de mon cœur." Not only does this soundtrack add to the plurality of cultural references, its vocabulary of turns and spirals—*manège* (carousel), *anneau de Saturne* (ring of Saturn), *chemin de ronde* (circular guard walk), *écheveau de laine* (skein of wool)—not only evokes a mental landscape of love lost (if not, as with Tom, through bereavement), but also announces a relationship to movement and space that differs from the linear trajectory of the opening shot, a shift confirmed as the filming of the car journey shifts to bends on unpaved roads.

The narrative in *Tom à la ferme* can of course be inserted into a history, not only of representations in Québec fiction of the countryside (such as the *roman du terroir*—rural novel—in which an older clerical nationalism invested its hegemonic values and imaginings), but also of the (re)transplantation of the urban subject/protagonist into a rural setting. This is a vast topic, but the main argument to be made about cinematic representations of this theme is how their ambiguity and complexity can be traced to contradictions in Quiet Revolution discourse between a heartland—and therefore "past"—left behind in the face of modernity, and a persistent, even necessary, reference to that past for constructions of a national narrative based on authenticity and origins. Recent, very popular audio-visual texts representing Québec's rural past (*Séraphin: un homme et son péché/Séraphin: Heart of Stone*, Charles Binamé, 2002, remains the biggest box office success ever for a Québec film in the domestic market) hover textually between the past as authenticating origin, as identity and identification therefore, and the past as difference, even unlivable because of the lack of, or restricted access to, "the modern," in terms of, for example, free heterosexual couple formation. *Tom à la ferme* joins a rich array of Québec films that problematize the journey to the countryside: Perrault's *Pour la suite du monde/For Those Who Will Follow* (1963) avoids the more facile versions of "authenticity" by building into the film's architecture the problematic relationship of the urban documentary filmmakers to their rural subjects; Mankiewicz's *Le Temps d'une chasse* has its urban working-class men embark on a disastrously fatal hunting trip; Gilles Carle's *La Vraie Nature de Bernadette/ The Real Nature of Bernadette* (1972) satirizes naturalistic theories of *le retour à la terre* (return to the land). Even *La Grande Séduction*, while investing heavily in the "authentic," communitarian associations of village life, is careful not to oversimplify its reliance on binaries of truth and lies, and connects the local and global in surprising ways.

It is queerness, of course, which intensifies the drama of *Tom à la ferme*, a dimension well explored in the source play and in other works by Michel Marc Bouchard (notably *Les Feluettes*, 1996, made in English as *Lilies* by John Greyson, one of the major representatives of that decade's New Queer Cinema). Here, questions of space again both illustrate and qualify the thematics of Dolan's film. In recent years, relations between sexuality and space, and conceptions of "queer geographies," have brought new debates to the fore. "The critical role of place and space in the production of sexual identities, practices, communities, subjectivities, and embodiments"[40] forces the consideration of how Tom's narrative is constituted spatially in the film, and this goes well beyond a simple urban/rural dichotomy. Most notably, the film is dominated by the space that the household and Francis demand, namely the closet, that is a massive re-calculation of where it is safe to be "out" or not. In *Closet Space: Geographies of Metaphor from the Body to the Globe*, Michael P. Browne argues for the need to take seriously the spatial implications of the metaphorical use of "closet" that dominates its use both in everyday language and in scholarly discourse ever since Eve Kosofsky Sedgwick's pioneering work. Rather than as a rhetorical flourish, Browne, in very Foucauldian terms, sees the closet as "a manifestation of heteronormative and homophobic powers in time-space, and moreover . . . this materiality mediates a power/knowledge of oppression":

the closet is a *spatial* metaphor: a way of talking about power that makes sense because of a geographic epistemology that is largely taken for granted. It is a sign that—often surreptitiously—alludes to certain kinds of location, space, distance, accessibility and interaction . . .

This demands an "appreciation of the ways that power/knowledge signified by 'the closet' work because they/themselves are always some*where* (and at some scale), and that whereness enables and constrains social relations." He proceeds in his study to take examples from urban space, censuses and travel to demonstrate that "certain spaces and spatial relations do conceal, erase, and deny."[41]

If it is not a question of rural versus urban—the rural space outside the farm is seen to be distinct from what is going on in the Longchamp household—then how to understand Tom's relationship to space-time? He is in mourning, his journey to his boyfriend's past becomes also a journey to his own, in terms of a return to the closet (it might be presumed), and in fact to a version of Guillaume: Tom is attracted to Francis—he did not know he existed—who resembles his brother and who wears the same scent. (In fact, the countryside for Tom is valorized, not as "authentic"—the play-acting Sarah effectively bursts that balloon—but as a sensorium of new and familiar stimuli.) The sadomasochistic relationship which develops between them is also characterized, of course, by an always potential reversibility. It becomes clear that Francis has his own vulnerabilities, left to run the farm alone with an increasingly mentally fragile mother, and his emotionally desperate pleas to Tom as he flees through woods are credible. Psychological ambiguities are translated spatially in the film not through lines, binaries, and boundaries but through loops, spirals, departures, and returns, as in the opening song. Tom at first drives away from the returning funeral party, but then goes back, ostensibly to pick up his luggage. The framing of Tom in the car, in right profile, is repeated after the closing credits in the film, when in Montréal Tom again stops his car. This shot is followed by a close-up of his hands gripping the steering wheel, and a point of view shot of the open road (Figure 4.7). Whether his intention is to return to Francis or not, we witness here, far from a linear *aller-retour* (round trip), the initiation of another loop.

The most eloquent expression in the film of the imbrication of mindscapes, soundscapes, and spiral movement in space is the scene in which Tom and Francis dance the tango. Whatever the debates about the history of men dancing with men at the dance's origins (as here, Francis insists it is to practice for when he dances with women), tango's spatial metaphor for sexual attraction, danger, and ambivalence, and a play of intimacy and distance, perfectly matches the scene. In contrast to the dance sequences in *Laurence Anyways* and *Mommy*, which respectively feature a version of a heterotopic space (the party where Fred meets her future husband) and an innovative movement through a domestic space previously dominated by confrontation, both Tom and Francis here dance around the closet, they spatialize the closet through dance. Francis here speaks his own previously unspoken agenda—his unhappiness with his mother: Agathe's appearance at the entrance re-asserts the closet's presence.

The tango scene takes place in a separate section of the barn: emptier, and, in a familiar Dolan flourish, which is illuminated by a series of rectangular openings in the side of the barn which continue his use of frames within frames, and which here render the space almost abstract. As in *Laurence Anyways*, Dolan in *Tom à la ferme* emphasizes the space of the threshold (the protracted early scene where Tom arrives at an empty house), and in a striking shot he films a conversation between Agathe and Tom where she is framed in the kitchen window as he sits on the rocking bench outside. We have seen how these ambivalent images in Dolan paradoxically combine connotations of separateness and connectedness. I wish to end this essay by speculating about an even more daring example, in my view, of Dolan's practice of *emboîtement*. Whereas the opening of *Tom à la ferme*, pluralistically as we saw, spoke to a history of Québec, Dolan chooses to end his film with, on the soundtrack as the camera follows Tom into and within Montréal, Rufus Wainwright's 2007 "Going to a Town" ("I'm going to a town that has already been burnt down/I'm so tired of you, America/Making my own way home, ain't gonna be alone/I've got a life to lead, America"), a song very explicitly about Dolan's fellow gay but anglophone Montrealer's disillusionment with the United States and the Bush years. This *états-unien* aspect of the closing sections of the film (Francis in fact wears a "USA" denim jacket during the final pursuit sequence) seems surprising only if we forget the tendency in Dolan not to allegorize but to construct multiple horizons of belonging, or, in geographers' terms, the way that "places result from a spatial 'framing' of a particular scale, from the nation-state, to regions, communities, and neighborhoods, and even to the microsettings within a house,"[42] to which we must add "the world," "the continent," "the anglosphere," and so forth. It is not, then, that Dolan is setting up, in the manner of Denys Arcand in *Le Déclin de l'empire américain* (1986) or *Les Invasions barbares/The Barbarian Invasions* (2003) a critique or analysis of Québec's relations with American society, via a depiction of rural violence. Rather, we are in frameworks of space which speak to interconnecting and overlapping surfaces, parts of wholes that touch or do not touch according to position: outside belongings indeed. It remains to be seen whether Dolan's global trajectory and penchant for this *emboîtement* of frames and surfaces will permit a defamiliarization of white Francophone identities which goes further than the ethnic pluralism of the gaze upon Laurence on the streets of Montréal.

NOTES

1. See the special issue of the online journal *Synoptique* devoted to Dolan. Kester Dyer, Andrée Lafontaine, and Fulvia Massimi (eds), "Locating the intimate within the global: Xavier Dolan, queer nations and Québec cinema," *Synoptique*, 4/2, Winter 2016. Available at <http://synoptique.hybrid.concordia.ca/index.php/main/issue/view/9>.
2. Liam Lacey, "Xavier Dolan: enfant. Terrible?," *Globe and Mail* (Toronto), May 24, 2012; Peter Knegt, "Xavier Dolan gets respect," *Film Quarterly*, 68/2, Winter 2014, pp. 31–6.
3. Hannah Vaughan, "Filming fracture in Xavier Dolan's *J'ai tué ma mère*," Special issue, *Québec Studies*, Winter 2013, pp. 107–15.
4. Valérie Mandia, "Le septième art hors des frontières nationales: le pouvoir de la langue et de l'imaginaire culturel dans les films du cinéaste québécois Xavier Dolan," *Francophonies d'Amérique*, 37, Spring 2014, pp. 105–32.
5. Gabriel Laverdière, "L'esthétique rock queer, de C.R.A.Z.Y. à Xavier Dolan," *Nouvelles Vues*, 16, Spring-Summer 2015. Available at <http://www.nouvellesvues.ulaval.ca/no-16-printemps-ete-2015-musique-rock-et-cinema-dirige-par-j-p-sirois-trahan-et-e-fillion/articles/lesthetique-rock-queer-de-crazy-a-xavier-dolan-par-gabriel-laverdiere/>.
6. *Les Invasions barbares* (Denys Arcand) for best foreign language film in 2004 (with nods at Cannes for best screenplay and best actress), and three consecutive nominations in 2011, 2012, and 2013 for *Incendies* (Denis Villeneuve, 2010), *Monsieur Lazhar* (Philippe Falardeau, 2011), and *Rebelle* (Kim Nguyen, 2012).
7. *Dallas Buyer's Club* (2013) and *Wild* (2014), Villeneuve's *Prisoners* (2013), and *Sicario* (2015).
8. *The Grand Seduction* (Don McKellar, 2013); *Un Village presque parfait* (Stéphane Meunier, 2015); *Un paese quasi perfetto* (Massimo Gaudioso, 2015).
9. For example, Gabrielle Trépanier-Jobin, "Le Cinéma québécois: un succès réel ou imaginé?," *Nouvelles Vues*, 9, Autumn 2008. Available at <http://www.nouvellesvues.ulaval.ca/fileadmin/nouvelles_vues/fichiers/Numero9/TrepanierNVCQ9.pdf>.
10. Ginette Major, *Le Cinéma québécois à la recherche d'un public. Bilan d'une décennie: 1970–1980* (Montréal: Presses de l'Université de Montréal, 1982), p. 153.
11. Christian Poirier, "Le cinéma québécois et la question identitaire. La confrontation entre les récits de l'empêchement et de l'enchantement," *Recherches sociologiques*, 45/1, 2004, p. 11.
12. Jocelyn Létourneau, "Le Québec, la révolution silencieuse," *Québec Studies*, 56, Winter 2013, pp. 97–111.
13. Léger poll, Institut du Nouveau Monde. Available at <http://inm.qc.ca/wp-content/uploads/2015/03/sondage-l%C3%A9ger_1304.pdf> (accessed February 27, 2016).
14. This includes of course music, as the conservative nationalist Société Saint-Jean-Baptiste fretted in 2011, about 75 percent of young Québécois preferring to listen to music in English. *Sondage: les jeunes Québécois préfèrent écouter de la musique en anglais.* Available at <http://ssjb.com/sondage-les-jeunes-quebecois-preferent-ecouter-de-la-musique-en-anglais/> (accessed February 27, 2016).
15. Jocelyn Létourneau, *Que veulent vraiment les Québécois?* (Montréal: Boréal, 2006), p. 24.
16. Bill Marshall, *Quebec National Cinema* (Montreal: McGill-Queen's University Press, 2001).
17. Xavier Dolan, "Director Xavier Dolan on *Laurence Anyways* and the ghetto of queer cinema," interview by Tyler Coates, *Flavorwire* (blog), June 27, 2013. Available at <http://flavorwire.com/400845/flavorwire-interview-director-xavier-dolan-on-laurence-anyways-and-the-ghetto-of-queer-cinema> (accessed February 27, 2016).

18. Samuel A. Chambers and Michael O'Rourke, "Introduction: Jacques Rancière on the shores of queer theory," in Samuel A. Chambers and Michael O'Rourke (eds), "Jacques Rancière on the shores of queer theory," *Borderlands*, 8/2, 2009, p. 4.

19. Eve Kosofsky Sedgwick, *Epistemology of the Closet* (Berkeley: University of California Press, 1990), p. 1.

20. Eve Kosofsky Sedgwick, *Tendencies* (London: Routledge, 1994), p. xii.

21. Thomas J. D. Armbrecht, "'On ne se baigne jamais deux fois dans le même fleuve': l'ontologie trans- de *Laurence Anyways*," *L'Esprit Créateur*, 53/1, Spring 2013, pp. 31–44.

22. Xavier Dolan, interview by Marie-France Bazzo, *Bazzo.tv*, Télé-Québec, September 27, 2012, quoted in Valérie Mandia, "Le septième art," p. 115. Available at <http://dx.doi.org/10.7202/1033977ar>.

23. Valérie Mandia, "Le septième art," p. 124.

24. Gilles Deleuze, *Cinema 1: The Movement-Image*, trans. Hugh Tomlinson and Barbara Habberjam (Minneapolis: University of Minnesota Press, 1986), p. 14.

25. Ibid. p. 16.

26. Ibid. p. 16.

27. Michel Foucault, "The eye of power," trans. Colin Gordon, in *Power/Knowledge: Selected Interviews and Other Writings 1972–1977*, ed. Colin Gordon, trans. Colin Gordon, Leo Marshall, John Mepham, and Kate Soper (New York: Pantheon Books, 1980), p. 148.

28. Michel Foucault, "The stage of philosophy: a conversation between Michel Foucault and Moriaki Watanabe," April 22, 1978, trans. Rosa Eidelpes and Kevin Kennedy, Scenes of Knowledge, *New York Magazine of Art and Theory*, 1.5.

29. Elspeth Probyn, *Outside Belongings* (London: Routledge, 1996), pp. 5–6.

30. Ibid. p. 20.

31. Ibid. p. 21.

32. Andrée Fortin, *Imaginaire de l'espace dans le cinéma québécois* (Sainte-Foy, Québec: Presses de l'Université Laval, 2015), pp. 121–2.

33. Robert Schwartzwald, "Explorations of suburban non-space in Stéphane Lafleur's *Continental*," *Québec Studies*, 48, Fall 2009/Winter 2010, p. 30.

34. Daniel Laforest, "La banlieue dans l'imaginaire québécois. Problèmes originels et avenir critique," *Temps zéro*, 6, April 2013. Available at <http://tempszero.contemporain.info/document945> (accessed February 27, 2016).

35. Joachim Lepastier, "*Mommy* de Xavier Dolan: en fusion," *Cahiers du Cinéma*, 704, October 2014, pp. 6–9. My translation.

36. Probyn, *Outside Belongings*, pp. 19–20.

37. Michel Foucault, "Of other spaces," trans. Jay Miskowiec, *Diacritics*, 16/1, Spring 1986 (March 1967), p. 24.

38. Ibid. p. 27.

39. Ibid. p. 27.

40. Susan Mayhew, *A Dictionary of Geography*, 4th edn (Oxford: Oxford University Press, 2009), p. 409. See also Lynda Johnston and Robyn Longhurst, *Space, Place and Sex: Geographies of Sexualities* (Lanham, MD: Rowman and Littlefield, 2009); Kath Brown, Jason Lim, and Gavin Browne (eds), *Geographies of Sexualities: Theory, Practices and Politics* (Aldershot: Ashgate, 2007).

41. Michael P. Browne, *Closet Space: Geographies of Metaphor from the Body to the Globe* (London: Routledge, 2000), pp. 1–3.

42. Wolfgang Natter and John Paul Jones, "Signposts toward a poststructuralist geography," in John Paul Jones, Wolfgang Natter, and Theodore R. Schatzki (eds), *Postmodern Contentions: Epochs, Politics, Space* (New York: Guilford Press, 1993), p. 170.

CHAPTER 5

Xavier Dolan's *J'ai tué ma mère* and Québec's New Cinema of mise-en-scène

Liz Czach

In 2011, a number of Québec publications, including the film magazines *24 images* and *Séquences*, the online academic journal *Nouvelles Vues*, and the daily newspaper *Le Devoir*, undertook a joint examination of an undeniable resurgence in Québec cinema. Using 2005 as a starting point of this renaissance, their combined effort aimed to chart the first inklings of what appeared to be an identifiable aesthetic movement.[1] Differentiated from filmmakers such as Denis Villeneuve, Manon Briand, and André Turpin, who formed part of Québec's New Wave of the 1990s, this new generation of filmmakers, including Denis Côté, Stéphane Lafleur, Maxime Giroux, Sophie Deraspe, and Rafaël Ouellet, amongst others, were forging a seemingly different path. Unquestionably a diverse group of directors, this group of *cinéastes* was seen to be rejecting Québec's commercial cinema, the stylized cinema of the previous generation (Villeneuve, Turpin, et al.), as well as the socially conscious strand of Québec filmmaking exemplified by the work of Bernard Émond, Louis Bélanger, and Denis Chouinard. Upon reflection, the critics participating in the discussion observed that this new assemblage of auteurs were undeniably cinephiles who evinced less of an interest in a cinema of the image and more in a cinema of mise-en-scène. Evoking the work of André Bazin, Jean-Pierre Sirois-Trahan has suggested there is "a cinema that aestheticizes its subject and another in which 'the form of film doesn't serve the story, but is the story.'"[2] The aesthetic ground for this *renouvellement* (renewal), and for this cohort of filmmakers, is an evident attention to mise-en-scène—where formal matters not only aid the narrative but also become it. To put it simply, the form becomes the content.

In his recent book *Mise-en-Scène and Film Style* (2014), Adrian Martin somewhat irreverently titles his opening chapter "A term that means everything, and nothing very specific," capturing the difficulty in employing such a malleable term.[3] Any introductory film studies textbook reiterates the well-trodden path of defining mise-en-scène as the contents of the frame and how they are organized.[4] Keeping with this basic definition, elements such as props, costumes, staging, figure placement, and lighting are included. Of course, all films create a profilmic world that is recorded, thus *all films* engage with mise-en-scène. Mise-en-scène, as Martin reminds us, is a term that was eagerly employed by filmmakers and critics in the 1950s and 1960s to "combat the idea that a film is essentially its *screenplay*."[5] A focus on mise-en-scène in film criticism and analysis draws attention to the fact that *style matters*. Martin quotes Sam Rohdie's characterization of how attentiveness to mise-en-scène in the 1950s gave rise to stylistic criticism. Rohdie writes:

> In general, *mise-en-scène* denotes a new attitude to the cinema opposed to the literary cinema of the 1930s that turned scripts into images . . . *Mise-en-scène*, as used by the Nouvelle Vague critics, referred to a specifically "cinematic" and natural, realistic rendering of emotion and expression *conveyed less by dialogue and the script, than by décor, performance, expression linked to the actor, to his movements and gestures, also to the settings and the use of the camera and lighting.*[6]

The cinema of mise-en-scène in the films of Côté, Lafleur, Giroux, Ouellet, and Deraspe (amongst others) does not easily translate to an identifiable group style, but rather loosely characterizes the approaches these filmmakers take. Overwhelmingly, if not exclusively, these filmmakers share an unflinching and uncompromising cinema that is, as Helen Faradji characterizes it, "first and foremost a cinephilic cinema."[7] The approach to mise-en-scène of these films aligns with contemporary art cinema practices as reflected in their being selected for numerous European film festivals as well as garnering prestigious prizes. To mention but a few, Stéphane Lafleur's *En terrains connus/ Familiar Grounds* won the Ecumenical Prize at the Berlin Film Festival in 2011, Rafaël Ouellet picked up the Best Director and Ecumenical Prize for *Camion* (2012) at the Karlovy Vary Film Festival, and Sophie Deraspe was awarded the FIPRESCI Prize for *Les loups* at the 2015 Torino Film Festival. Amongst the most successful on the European film festival circuit is Denis Côté who garnered the Best Director Prize at Locarno for *Curling* (2010) and the Alfred Bauer Prize for *Vic + Flo ont vu un ours/ Vic + Flo Saw a Bear* (2013) at the Berlin International Film Festival. Côté's uncompromisingly cinephilic oeuvre is undoubtedly the most prominent example of Québec's current cinema of mise-en-scène. His films partake of an elliptical narrative style employing sparse dialogue that generates uncertainty. Images and situations, more so than words, convey the films' meanings, or perhaps more accurately, create scenarios that resist easy interpretation. For example, Côté's pared down scripts and cinematic naturalism render much of their narrative thrust ambiguous. Dialogue is kept to a minimum and what the characters express is rarely sufficient as explanation or motivation for the plot.[8]

Equally successful on the festival circuit, yet radically different in style, has been Xavier Dolan, who burst onto the film festival scene in 2009 with the Cannes premiere of his first feature film, *J'ai tué ma mère*. His relationship with Cannes was solidified when he won the Jury Prize for his 2014 film *Mommy* (shared with Jean-Luc Godard's *Goodbye to Language*), and cemented further with the prestigious Grand Prix for *Juste la fin du monde* (2016). Dolan's international success at Cannes has placed him somewhat paradoxically at the center of this cinematic resurgence since his films do not at first consideration sit comfortably under the umbrella of a cinema of mise-en-scène. Jean-Pierre Sirois-Trahan differentiates the uncompromising cinema of Côté et al. as being "un noyau dur" (hardcore) whereas Dolan is characterized as an outsider in his production of a "cinéma plus *artiste*" (a more *artistic* cinema).[9] In contradistinction to the minimal scripts, slow pacing, and long-duration shots of Côté's films, Dolan's films are much "talkier" with frequent use of voluminous and frenetic dialogue. In *J'ai tué ma mère*, for example, effusive outbursts between the main protagonist Hubert, played by Dolan, and his mother Chantale (Anne Dorval) are common.[10] Unsurprisingly, scholars and popular critics alike have debated and studied this verbosity, and how Dolan's use of Anglicisms, code-switching, colloquialisms, and cursing function in his films.[11] The prominence of dialogue and emphasis on what characters *say* seems to position Dolan's films outside of the current cinematic renewal in that his films appear to communicate meaning primarily through dialogue with a lesser emphasis on mise-en-scène. In what follows, I examine Dolan's first film, *J'ai tué ma mère*, as demonstrating a keen understanding of how mise-en-scène works not only to reinforce dialogue, but also to communicate in more subtle, independent ways.

Made when Dolan was just nineteen years old, *J'ai tué ma mère* (2009) was lauded for its audacious semi-autobiographical portrayal of the complex relationship between a combative gay teenager and his frustrated mother. The film's story of a homosexual teen apparently seeking acceptance from his mother touched a chord with audiences and critics alike for the manner in which it caught "something . . . universal about the rope-a-dope dance between sullen adolescent and parent."[12] Over the course of the film, mother and son dramatically fluctuate between moments of tender understanding and hostility before settling upon a tentative reconciliation at the film's conclusion. Much of this "rope-a-dope dance" between mother and son is effectuated through dialogue, but less commented upon has been Dolan's deliberate and repetitive use of framing and composition to illustrate the push–pull that characterizes their tempestuous relationship. When careful attention is paid to

Dolan's mise-en-scène, it becomes evident that Hubert's teenage outbursts and aggression are not due to his mother's disapproval of his homosexuality, but rather the result of Hubert's disapproval of and shame at his mother's lower middle-class status, and the attendant assumption that she is homophobic. If Hubert feels stigmatized and humiliated it is not because he is gay, but because his mother is an embarrassment. While Dolan's attentiveness to the class status of his characters is unmistakably communicated through mise-en-scène elements such as decor and costume, these more overt elements are bolstered by a repetitive framing of his characters against backdrops of paintings, which, as I argue, position them within a class hierarchy. Furthermore, the paintings illuminate not only what class status the characters enjoy, but what role they play in Hubert's emotional journey as he seeks to transcend his mother's lower middle-class position.

Dolan's careful use of mise-en-scène in *J'ai tué ma mère* is unsurprising as the film displays a wide range of stylistic flourishes that demonstrate Dolan's skill in using a full slate of cinematic techniques including shifts to a black and white video diary confessional (echoing films like *Tarnation*, Jonathan Caouette, 2003), grainy home movie footage, slow motion tracking shots of characters (reminiscent of Wong Kar-wai), and Nouvelle Vague-inspired jump cuts. Other techniques include unconventional shot compositions: for example, Dolan dispenses with the classic over the shoulder shot-reverse-shot composition for conversation scenes, preferring instead to frame characters in a two-shot facing the camera with each pushed to the opposing outer edge of the frame—a technique that suggests Hubert's acute feelings of disconnection. The film also includes what appear to be non-diegetic inserts of random images of butterflies, cherubs, cupids, etc., but that are revealed to be elements of Chantale's home decor. Dolan employs quick close-up insert shots of such various elements of decor to suggest a space *before* an establishing shot thereby evoking space through fragmented details rather than the whole. Additionally, the film uses a number of surrealistic fantasy sequences that hint at Almodóvarian melodramatic excess (smashing dishes in slow motion, imagining his mother in Carmen Miranda-esque costume or dead in a coffin). In effect, Dolan displays a surfeit of stylistic flourishes leading some critics to suggest this overindulgence as symptomatic of directorial immaturity. *Variety* critic Jay Weissberg asserts that "Dolan's hunger to prove his talents results in a superfluity of styles,"[13] whereas Rick Groen of *The Globe and Mail* contends that "the techniques all seem a little self-conscious."[14] The film is undisputedly, even perhaps excessively, stylish, yet there is a simple and consistent use of framing amongst these devices that effectively communicates Hubert's frustrations with his mother's lower middle-class status.

In one of the first published scholarly articles to address the film, Hannah Vaughan analyzes the film's form, focusing primarily on the film's editing, to claim that *J'ai tué ma mère* embraces a radical avant-garde style that connects the film's "relatively radical content to similarly radical form."[15] "Stylistically," she argues, "the film's techniques frequently disrupt the classical continuity editing system, creating visual and narrative discontinuity that mirrors Hubert's constant fluctuation of emotion, and reflects the discontinuous, fractured nature of the mother-son (and father-son) relationship."[16] *J'ai tué ma mère*, she continues, exhibits a non-normative, anti-conformist filmmaking in which the film's radical gay content is matched by its radical style. In effect, the film "essentially functions as the anti-paradigmatic Hollywood film."[17] In arguing for the film's anti-Hollywood aesthetic Vaughan bypasses European art cinema as a source of influence and argues, instead, that *J'ai tué ma mère* exhibits characteristics of the radical avant-garde. The film does indeed dispense with some continuity editing techniques (delayed establishing shots, seemingly non-diegetic inserts, and jump cuts, for example), but the film's use of these techniques places it firmly within contemporary art cinema practices. Indeed, when mise-en-scène, rather than editing, is closely analyzed, *J'ai tué ma mère*'s potential "radicality" is considerably muted by the fact that Hubert's class shame strains his relationship with his mother.

In an interview with *The Hollywood Reporter*, Dolan states: "For me, *I Killed My Mother* was the impossible love story of a teen and his mother."[18] But what makes this love impossible? First impressions may suggest that Hubert's homosexuality is the source of conflict. Hubert is gay but has not come out to his mother, which is somewhat surprising given how "out" and untroubled he is with his sexuality. He is at ease with his orientation; he has a boyfriend, Antonin (François Arnaud), and scenes of them together at school, as well as at Antonin's home, where his mother, Hélène (Patricia Tulasne), warmly embraces their relationship, suggests that he is far from closeted. Refreshingly, the film lacks any teenage coming out angst and nary a word is spoken about feelings of guilt, doubt, or anxiety about being gay. Given this openness, why Hubert has not come out to his mother is somewhat perplexing since she does not exhibit any behavior nor does she say anything that would suggest homophobia. Furthermore, there is no indication that she would not accept her son's sexual orientation. Yet, as Vaughan suggests, we are invited to interpret Chantale as "socially conservative."[19] This assertion is not necessarily based on anything she says or does, but rather on how she looks and lives. Chantale's social conservatism is thus assumed not because of her actions, but because of the way she dresses, her home decor and her "bad taste." Vaughan's reading falls in line with André Loiselle's observation that post-1980s representations of working-class people in Québec cinema tend to be based on spectacle and how they *look*, whereas before 1980, how characters figured in the narrative, that is, how they *acted*, was central to their representation.[20] Furthermore, Loiselle contends: "On the one hand, workers are seen as being more genuine and honest than members of the upper classes. But simultaneously, they are shown as *lacking social awareness*, as *displaying bad taste*, and as being often politically ineffectual and at times *profoundly conservative*."[21] To view Chantale as socially conservative is to reflexively align the working class, or in this case the lower middle class, with conservatism even though there is nothing in Chantale's actions that indicates she is either homophobic or conservative. Yet, this mischaracterization of Chantale and her assumed homophobia is to some degree understandable given that it is predicated upon Dolan's extremely subjective portrayal of her character through Hubert's eyes. For the first third of the film, audience knowledge about Chantale is restricted almost exclusively to her interactions with Hubert. From these interactions, we learn that the two have a profoundly antagonistic relationship, one that she continually exacerbates. When we learn that Hubert has a boyfriend but has not come out to his mother, we might assume that he fears her reaction—that she is homophobic. Yet, when Chantale inadvertently does learn that Hubert is gay, she does not display any signs of moral consternation; rather she sees it as a personal failing for not having realized this earlier. This then becomes a pivotal (and for Chantale, deeply hurtful and humiliating) moment in the film, as it untethers the long-standing association of being lower class with moral conservatism, and dispels any presumptions that Hubert's reticence (if there is any) about coming out to Chantale has anything to do with her social morality. That Hubert, unaware of his mother's knowledge about his orientation, continues to rail against her, then becomes about his hostility toward her way of life, and her class affiliation.

Throughout *J'ai tué ma mère*, Hubert exhibits profound class anxiety. The antagonism and arguments that pervade the film's narrative are often spurred by the shame Hubert feels toward his lower middle-class mother. While Chantale is obviously at ease and happy in her modest home, Hubert is ashamed of what he perceives as her lack of taste and class. In what follows I will first address the more overt mechanisms of mise-en-scène such as the decor of Chantale's modest home, her costuming, and behavior, all of which position her, in Hubert's view, as a risible lower middle-class figure. I then move on to an analysis of the use of repetitive framing and shot composition, and how this creates parallels and distinctions between characters, so that I may illuminate how the film's characters function narratively vis-à-vis their relationship with Hubert, what place they occupy in class hierarchy, and how this reveals Hubert's own class aspirations.

The film begins with one of the black and white confessional sequences that intermittently punctuate the film. Evoking the form of a video-diary, Hubert faces the camera in close-up and speaks directly to the camera/audience. "I don't know what happened," he explains, "when I was little we loved each other. I still love her. I can look at her, be next to her. But I can't be her son. I could be anyone's son. But not hers." This establishes the film's central existential questions: why can't Hubert love his mother as a son, and what makes life with her so intolerable? Almost as if in direct response, this sequence is followed by a series of short shots of cherubs, cupids, figurines, and butterflies, which we later identify as Chantale's tacky *tchotchkes* that decorate her home. At this point in the film, these shots seem to operate as part of a non-diegetic transition from Hubert's video-diary confessional to Hubert and Chantale eating breakfast together. Slow motion close-up shots alternate between Chantale's mouth and his eyes as he watches her eat, with disgust. A close-up of her mouth shows her biting into an orange wedge and then licking the juices off of her lower lip; another shot depicts her eating a bagel with cream cheese, the cheese smearing on her lips and catching in the corner of her mouth. A two-shot of Hubert and Chantale follows with them sitting beside each other at the table and Hubert telling her about the cream cheese on her mouth. She attempts to clean it, but somehow keeps missing the right spot. He grows irritated. His repeated instructions, her repeated attempts to remove the cream cheese, and his increasing frustration veer toward the absurd, taking on a somewhat comical edge. Part farcical comedy, part overwrought melodrama, this first scene of the film effectively establishes the rapport between mother and son. Hubert perceives Chantale as undignified; as the film unfolds, the way she acts, dresses, eats, and talks, as well as what she watches, listens to, and does for fun, are a source of derision and scorn for him. Her class, and how it is reflected in her tastes, and more specifically, how she dresses and decorates her home, openly provoke his contempt.

If *J'ai tué ma mère* has been interpreted as a film about a son's difficulty in coming out to his mother, it is filtered through Hubert's profound class shame. This is established most tellingly in an early scene in which Hubert "kills" his mother. The matricide evoked by the film's provocative title is, of course, metaphorical and Hubert only figuratively kills his mother. The impetus for Chantale's death is a two-part class assignment in which Hubert must first provide his parents' annual salary, work conditions and benefits, and second, interview them. After the details of the assignment are announced, Hubert tentatively approaches his teacher to inquire if he can use his aunt's profession instead. His teacher insists that it must be his parents. By way of explanation, Hubert tells his instructor that he does not see his father very often and then, after a long pause and some hesitation, says "and . . . my mother is dead." The teacher is flustered by this revelation but also deeply sympathetic to his predicament, and accommodates his request. That Hubert would rather kill off his mother, even symbolically, rather than divulge her salary and work conditions suggests a profound discomfort with her job and wage earnings, that is, her class status. When she learns that her son has killed her off, Chantale responds by appearing unannounced at Hubert's school. The ensuing scene is one of the most dramatic instances of her portrayal as an embarrassing figure. In an embarrassing (for Hubert) display of crass taste and lack of decorum, Chantale arrives at his classroom unannounced, bangs on the door, and bursts in without waiting to be invited. She wears a puffy white fur hat and leopard print coat. She yells at Hubert about needing to talk to him after class and finishes by screaming, "Do I look fucking dead, for Christ's sake?" before storming off. The classroom, unsurprisingly, erupts in laughter, and Hubert is mortified. When he emerges from the classroom he immediately takes flight to escape her. She pursues him and the slow motion chase ends when Hubert pushes her down to the ground and runs off. Humiliated in front of a group of students and a teacher, she pulls herself up off the floor, brushes herself off, straightens her hat, and exits the frame. Hubert's heartless and cruel rejection of his mother is, in many respects, devastating, but his classmates, teacher, and the audience are drawn into a kind of sympathy with Hubert by positing Chantale as a figure whose dress and behavior, as shorthand for her class position, are deserving of disapproval.

Yet, Chantale's class position is never clearly explicated. The exact nature of her job isn't specified albeit she wears "tacky" attire to work rather than sporting a typical business casual wardrobe. Her nondescript, cubicle-like office features a drab standard issue desk, filing cabinets, and phone to suggest some sort of low-ranking administrative support position. She is not, however, identifiably "working class." Unlike the predominately male proletarian protagonists of 1960s and 70s Québec cinema, Chantale does not toil in a factory, work on a farm, or drive a cab, but rather, works in an office. Chantale is representative of a shift in the nature of work in twenty-first-century Québec (as well as across North America). With the disappearance of manufacturing jobs and the abandonment of rural agricultural communities for urban life, the working classes are no longer only blue-collar workers or farmers, but increasingly, the underpaid white-collar precarious workers of the contemporary information and service economies. Chantale's life, however, appears somewhat financially stable as she seems to own her duplex (in a nondescript semi-suburban neighborhood), she can afford the occasional indulgence in new clothes (while always mindful of getting a good bargain), and seems to be living a modest lower middle-class lifestyle. While her work environment may not adhere to a dated stereotype of what constitutes a working-class occupation, Chantale does conform to a stereotypical perception of how working-class characters behave.

The most overt manner in which Chantale is cast as a lower-class figure is through her wardrobe and home decor. She is tacky, or as the Québécois put it, her home, behavior, and clothing could be described as *quétaine*—an adjective describing something that is kitschy or lacking refinement. Chantale's home is chock-full of kitsch: decorative figurines, wall hangings, flower and feather arrangements, blankets and throw cushions abound, and a bookcase stuffed with a doll collection features prominently. In short, her home is a shrine to bad taste. She shows affection for animal prints both in her wardrobe and her home, in one scene arriving home with a shopping bag and showing Hubert her most recent purchase: a lampshade with a zebra-like print on it. "I'm sure you'll hate it," she says anticipating Hubert's disapproval. Hubert, attempting to be somewhat conciliatory replies, "I don't hate it." Trying to find something kind to say, he struggles and notes, "it's kind of . . . it's kind of safari." Continuing to admire the lampshade Chantale admits that she likes animal prints and bought it to coordinate with a painting of tigers that hangs prominently above the couch. This scene, like several others in the film, highlights how at odds Chantale's aesthetic taste is from Hubert's. His mother's lack of sophistication is an embarrassment. She watches tacky television shows (featuring laugh tracks) while eating cheese puffs and playing computer solitaire. Chantale, together with her best friend Dédé (Monique Spaziani), who is equally loud and bombastic, go on shopping excursions or to the tanning salon. Hubert clearly can't abide his mother's poor taste and his inability to love her as a son is imbedded in his dislike of her lifestyle. The conflict between them relies principally on this disjuncture in taste. When Chantale returns home with a new jacket she purchased at Suzy Coquette (a fictional store, whose very name evokes *quétaine* fashions), she is delighted with her purchase, noting she got a jacket worth $40 for $8, and that it fits her perfectly. "It's cute," she declares, using the English word—one of the many Anglicisms peppering Chantale's French. Hubert, sulking in the dark, declares: "It's ugly." He has learned that he is being sent off to boarding school. "I'm pissed off," he continues, "but I still have taste." This exchange is subdued compared to the invectives he unleashes later on when she drops him off at the bus that will take him to boarding school. Distraught over his impending departure, he tells Chantale that he will have nothing to do with her once he turns eighteen. He makes it clear that she disgusts him. "And those crumbs on your face when you eat like a pig . . . your revolting clothes that make me want to barf, your ignorant suburbanite expressions [*tes expressions b.s.*], your manipulation, you can shove it up your ass!" These exchanges make painfully clear the class rage Hubert feels at her lack of refinement, sophistication, or taste. She is not a mother he can seemingly love.

If Chantale is the "bad mother" that Hubert is ashamed of, Antonin's mother, Hélène, is the "good mother" who displays the taste, refinement, and liberal values Hubert seeks. The distinction between the two mothers is rather crudely mapped out by their names: Chantale's last name, Lemming, suggests sheep-like qualities and a lack of critical awareness whereas Hélène's family name, Rimbaud, evokes the libertine values and artistic-poetic nature of Arthur Rimbaud. This simplistic juxtaposition is further entrenched in the less than subtle manner in which Hélène embodies (in the eyes of a rebellious sixteen-year-old, in any case) all the attributes of the ideal, upper-class mother. Hélène is worldly and sophisticated in ways Chantale is not; she orders sushi for dinner, is encouraging of Hubert and Antonin's relationship, lets them smoke pot in her house, and is supportive of their artistic endeavors. The class and taste differences between the two mothers are made patently clear when they meet, the only time in the film, by chance at a tanning salon. Hélène, recognizing Chantale from PTA meetings enthusiastically greets her, but quickly asserts that she is not at the salon to get a tan but merely waiting for her mother. "She likes getting a tan, it's not my thing," she explains. Hélène, it is clear, is a bit of a class snob. Chantale, not immune to these moments of judgment, looks awkwardly away. An embarrassing pause ensues and to clear the air Hélène enthuses: "Our boys . . . Two months in a week!" Chantale, unaware of her son's relationship with Antonin, is confused. Hélène clarifies and Chantale is at a stupefied loss—she has only now learned Hubert is gay, and from his boyfriend's mother. The contrast between the two could not be more definitely drawn: one is open, liberal, worldly, while the other is tacky, unrefined, and (it is assumed) homophobic. Yet, in the following scene showing Chantale and Dédé discussing Hubert's homosexuality, Chantale does not condemn her son's orientation but rather quickly accepts it, moreover recalling in retrospect the "signs," like Hubert's earlier obsession with Leonardo DiCaprio in *Titanic*. Chantale is crushed by her son's emotional withdrawal; they have grown apart not because of his sexual orientation, but because he is ashamed of her. Dolan's mise-en-scène in these instances operates to reinforce what is happening at the level of dialogue and plot. That is, Hubert's hostility to Chantale is seemingly justified by how she is depicted through decor and costume, and explicitly realized at the level of dialogue in Hubert's many tantrums during which he criticizes Chantale, in every possible way, for her lack of refinement and poor taste. In what follows, I shift my attention to Dolan's more understated use of mise-en-scène—specifically his attention to framing—to propose how this more subtly evokes the class antagonism at the film's core.

In his now classic study of the role that taste plays in class formation, *Distinction: A Social Critique of the Judgment of Taste*, Pierre Bourdieu writes: "Taste classifies, and it classifies the classifier. Social subjects classified by their classifications, distinguish themselves by the distinctions they make, between the beautiful and the ugly, the distinguished and the vulgar, in which their position in the objective classifications is expressed or betrayed."[22] Dolan, mindful of the role taste plays in class distinctions, uses paintings as signposts to distinguish his characters' class status. This is achieved through a careful and repetitive mise-en-scène in which characters often occupy the center of the frame, facing the camera, with a painting (or paintings) behind them, which not only positions them within their social milieu, but also defines their relationship to Hubert. As we have seen, Hubert seems acutely aware of the role that taste plays in class distinctions as evidenced by his perpetual mortification over his mother's tastes. Indeed, the centrality of visual art in the film's mise-en-scène is moreover reflected in Hubert and Antonin's artistic pursuits: they exuberantly paint, in the mode of Jackson Pollock, to decorate Hélène's office, thereby actively producing their own cultural capital. Taste formation and cultural capital shape Hubert's relationship to his mother and the film's other characters: his boyfriend, his teacher, his father, and his boarding school principal. Each character, as I elaborate below, is positioned within a class hierarchy via framing, setting, and the use of decor—most pertinently, the aforementioned use of visual art.

As I have argued, Hubert's relationship with his mother is strained by the profound class rage he feels toward her. He expresses his disgust with her verbally on the occasion of his being sent off to boarding school, but this is preceded by visual evidence of his revulsion (the depiction of his mother's eating habits, her television viewing choices, taste in decor, clothes, etc.). And while Chantale's lack of culture is most evident in her fondness for animal print clothing, junk food, and tanning salons, early in the film, the mise-en-scène of Chantale's home is the first instance of framing that will be repeated to establish class and status. In an early scene, Hubert looks through a family photo album while waiting for his mother to return home. He sits on a couch, facing the camera, in the center of the frame, with an image of tigers (it is not entirely clear whether this is a painting, print, or rug/tapestry) behind his head. The scene's framing reiterates the animal print motif, established through Chantale's wardrobe, and solidifies her home as a place that embarrasses Hubert. This framing then comes to dominate the mise-en-scène in a number of key scenes in the film to efficiently communicate class and status as well as Hubert's relationship to the established milieu.

Hubert's profound discomfort in his mother's home expresses itself not only in the verbal attacks he launches, but in his active desire to escape it; he makes plans to move out on his own, frequently hangs out at his boyfriend's house, and takes refuge at his teacher's house. In these other environments, Hubert finds some escape; as if offering an antidote to the stifling interior of his mother's house, Antonin's mother, for example, is framed in front of a reproduction of Gustav Klimt's *Mother and Child*, a painting forcefully establishing her as not only in possession of cultural capital and class, but also associating Hélène with a vision of idealized motherhood. Likewise, Julie (Suzanne Clément), his sympathetic social studies teacher, is a figure that similarly offers Hubert a refuge. At the film's mid-point, Hubert has grown increasingly estranged from his mother and shows up at Julie's apartment. They sit together in front of a fireplace where a large painting hangs over the mantle (Figure 5.1). As the teacher explains, the house belonged to her grandmother and is still decorated with her items. It's a little "old fogey" she states by way of an apology. The

Figure 5.1 Hubert at Julie's "old fogey" house.

Figure 5.2 Chantale and the pitiful Pierrot.

old-fashioned upper middle-class decor is tasteful, if not a little stodgy, but it provides the sanctuary Hubert seeks from his mother's lower class tasteless residence.

Although sympathetic to Hubert's distress, Julie commonsensically notes that he can't just run away and insists he call his mother, which Hubert reluctantly does. Chantale is shown speaking to Hubert on the phone in her bedroom, propped up on the bed in the center of the frame with a painting above her, again repeating the framing motif (Figure 5.2). Chantale's mood moreover appears to be reflected in the image of the sad Pierrot clown who waits pitifully, like she does, for unrequited love to be returned.

The Pierrot figure's pathetic countenance mirrors Chantale's abjectness—an ungenerous parallel that is in keeping with Hubert's characterization, and Dolan's framing, of her as lonely and undeserving of love. The next morning, after spending the night at Julie's house, Hubert awakens on his teacher's couch to be framed, yet again, by a number of paintings. Here, however, the paintings are oils with a decidedly nineteenth-century aesthetic in keeping with the grandmotherly decor of Julie's house. The paintings of bucolic pastoral scenes and turn-of-the-century urban landscapes suggest the safety and comfort of the teacher's home and the potential of a retreat from the malaise Hubert feels at home.

Having tangibly established this pattern of framing, Dolan's recursive use of it gathers greater prominence and momentum through the rest of the film with each instance recalling previous compositions while revealing the class and socio-economic particularities of the new mises-en-scène. Its iterative operation of revealing class status is employed when Hubert goes to visit his father Richard (Pierre Chagnon)—a figure who has been absent until this point. Upon arrival, father and son greet awkwardly, clearly ill at ease with each other. Hubert's attempt to embrace his father leads to a fumbled hug. Their limited contact partially accounts for this estrangement and lack of affection, but their discomfort is also a product of their differing class status. In a study of the use of different language registers in the films of Dolan, Valérie Mandia points out Richard's use of a "refined French." She notes that Richard's "surname, his accent, and his largely Continental French vocabulary allows us to confirm his nationality."[23] Indeed, Richard speaks a polished, elevated French lacking a noticeable Québécois accent and devoid of the Anglicisms, colloquialisms, or Québécois *joual* that pepper Hubert and Chantale's speech. Language establishes Richard as a French snob. But language is not the only way in which Richard's class distinction is established; visual art and character placement in the mise-en-scène again signal the class and power dynamic at play. On arrival Hubert expresses excitement about having been invited over for dinner, but this is quickly quashed by the realization that not only is his mother present, but that his parents have agreed to send Hubert off to boarding school. Upon announcement of this decision, Hubert is framed sitting below an idyllic painting of country life similar to the paintings in Julie's home (Figure 5.3).

The comfort that similar paintings implied at Julie's home now suggest, not a respite, but rather a casting out. "They're fucking rednecks!," screams Hubert when told the school he'll be attending. "Can we talk like civilized adults?," asks Hubert's father, his tone even-tempered and reserved, albeit faltering, as he tries to master the tense situation with an appeal to decorum. His taste and propriety are further accentuated in a shot of Chantale sharing

Figure 5.3 Hubert at his father's house.

the frame with a cubist-style painting, signaling Richard's possession of cultural capital and class. This scene concludes with a final image of Hubert in the same position below the bucolic painting, but now with his back turned to the camera suggesting a despondent resignation and that the symbolic pastoral retreat has transformed into a rural backwater.

The film's denouement features two more prominent examples of Dolan's systematic placement of a character against the backdrop of a painting. As with previous instances, class and status are reflected in the paintings and help situate the character's relationship to Hubert. In one of the film's most pivotal scenes, Chantale receives a phone call from the principal of the boarding school to inform her that Hubert has run away. The ensuing shot of the telephone conversation alternates between Chantale in her office at work and the principal similarly positioned at his desk in his office. He is seated in front of a large abstract painting that consists predominately of muted blues and greys (Figure 5.4). The painting is tasteful, but unremarkable, its somber color palette matching the office walls as well as the principal's suit, and suggesting a cold utilitarianism. The painting appears purely functional, seemingly chosen because it complements the office and thus corresponds with his personality and position. This painting stands in stark opposition to a brightly colored painting of flowers found in Hubert's childhood home, the film's final location and the place to which Hubert and Antonin, having come to his rescue after escaping the boarding school, have fled (Figure 5.5). The rustic home on the shore of the St Lawrence River is a source of bucolic tranquility and comfort for Hubert—a return to the site of familial plenitude. The flower painting is neither overly abstract nor too stuffy (or "old fogey" as Julie would say) and

Figure 5.4 Principal's office.

Figure 5.5 Floral middlebrow middle ground.

hits the right note of warmth and charm. The flowers and the country home
are a fitting site for Hubert and Chantale's tentative reconciliation. It is against
the backdrop of flowers, sky, rocks, sun, and river that nature can provide the
haven and comfort Hubert has been seeking. In the class battle waged between
Hubert and Chantale, a tentative detente is reached in this space. The home,
landscape, and painting offer a safe middlebrow middle ground between Chantale's kitschy duplex and the austere, cold, high-class tastes of his father and
his boarding school principal. It is with their tentative reconciliation that we

get the first glimpse of Hubert understanding what we have known since the salon scene, that despite her seemingly tasteless appearance and crass actions, that is, her lower middle classness, Chantale accepted his homosexuality from the moment she learned about it.

At first blush Dolan's place as a key figure of Québec's new cinema of mise-en-scène is not immediately apparent. The use of dialogue to propel his films' narratives, as well as the unambiguous use of mise-en-scène to highlight his characters' social status, belie the more understated use of figure place-ment (particularly in relationship to visual art) evident in *J'ai tué ma mère*, and Dolan's more subtle expression of his characters' class—and, in Hubert's case, class anxiety. It is clear that Dolan is still much of an "outsider" to Québec's *renouvellement* as his films mostly do not adhere to the austere and elliptical use of mise-en-scène characterizing much of the other directors' work of this group. Yet, as Bill Marshall has shown, paying attention to the spatial dynam-ics of Dolan's films can be a productive approach to reading his films.[24] Thus, while *J'ai tué ma mère* has been interpreted by some scholars (such as Vaughan) as a film about estrangement between a gay son and his socially conservative mother, Dolan's use of mise-en-scène points to a tale of how Hubert eventually uncouples the presumed association of lower-class social conservatism and homophobia, to overcome his profound class anxiety and shame.

NOTES

1. Jean-Pierre Sirois-Trahan noted the emergence of the "renouveau de cinéma québécois" (renewal of Québécois cinema) in a 2010 article in *Cahiers du Cinéma*. See "La mouvée et son dehors: renouveau du cinéma québécois," *Cahiers du Cinéma*, 660, October 2010, pp. 76–8. My translation.
2. Jean-Pierre Sirois-Trahan, "Table ronde sur le renouveau du cinéma québécois," *Nouvelles Vues*, 12, Spring-Summer 2011. Available at <http://www.nouvellesvues.ulaval.ca/le-renouveau-dirige-par-jean-pierre-sirois-trahan/table-ronde-sur-le-renouveau-du-cinema-dauteur-quebecois-avec-martin-bilodeau-philippe-gajan-marcel-jean-germain-lacasse-sylvain-lavallee-marie-claude-loiselle-et-jean-pierre-sirois-trahan-organisee-par-bruno-dequen/>. My translation.
3. Adrian Martin, *Mise-en-Scène and Film Style: From Classical Hollywood to New Media Art* (Basingstoke: Palgrave Macmillan, 2014).
4. The popular textbook *Film Art: An Introduction* defines mise-en-scène as "All the elements placed in front of the camera to be photographed: the settings and props, lighting, costumes and make-up, and figure behavior." See David Bordwell and Kristin Thompson, *Film Art: An Introduction*, 9th edn (New York: McGraw-Hill, 2010), p. 492.
5. Ibid. p. 4.
6. Sam Rohdie quoted in ibid. p. 5. Italics added.
7. Helen Faradji, "Les cinéastes cinéphiles," *24 images*, 152, June–July 2011, p. 24. My translation.
8. For an analysis of one of Côté's films that in part addresses this elliptical storytelling approach, see Dominique Fisher, "*Vic + Flo ont vu un ours* de Denis Côté: histoire de femmes cruelles ou esthétique de la cruauté?," *Québec Studies*, 60, 2015, pp. 67–82.

9. Jean-Pierre Sirois-Trahan, "Le renouveau du cinéma d'auteur Québécois," *24 Images*, 152, June–July 2011, pp. 15–16. The other outsider of this group is Sophie Deraspe, who is deserving of her own consideration. My translation.
10. *Juste la fin du monde* is equally "talky" if not more so than *J'ai tué ma mère*, but is based on a play by Jean-Luc Lagarce although Dolan wrote the screenplay.
11. See Valérie Mandia, "Le septième art hors des frontières nationales: le pouvoir de la langue et de l'imaginaire culturel dans les films du cinéaste québécois Xavier Dolan," *Francophonies d'Amérique*, 37, Spring 2014, pp. 105–32. See also Andrée Lafontaine's contribution to this volume.
12. Rachel Saltz, "A mother-son dance with many awkward steps," review of *Mommy*, directed by Xavier Dolan, *New York Times*, March 12, 2013. Available at <http://www.nytimes.com/2013/03/13/movies/i-killed-my-mother-a-xavier-dolan-film.html?partner=rss &emc=rss>.
13. Jay Weissberg, "I Killed my Mother," *Variety*, May 18, 2009. Available at <http://variety.com/2009/film/markets-festivals/i-killed-my-mother-1200474797/>.
14. Rick Goen, "I Killed my Mother," review of *J'ai tué ma mère*, directed by Xavier Dolan, *Globe and Mail* (Toronto), February 5, 2010. Available at <https://www.theglobeandmail.com/arts/i-killed-my-mother-jai-tue-ma-mere/article4304732/>.
15. Hannah Vaughan, "Filming fracture in Xavier Dolan's *J'ai tué ma mère*," *Québec Studies*, Winter 2013, p. 109.
16. Ibid. p. 109.
17. Ibid. p. 109.
18. Xavier Dolan, "Cannes 2012: Canadian director Xavier Dolan on 'Laurence Anyways' (Q&A)," interview by Etan Vlessing, *Variety*, May 18, 2012. Available at <https://www.hollywoodreporter.com/news/cannes-festival-xavier-dolan-qa-326081>.
19. Vaughan, "Filming fracture," p. 108.
20. André Loiselle, "*Look* like a worker and *act* like a worker: stereotypical representations of the working class in Quebec fiction feature films," in Malek Khouri and Darrell Varga (eds), *Working On Screen: Representations of the Working Class in Canadian Cinema* (Toronto: University of Toronto Press, 2006), pp. 208, 209
21. Ibid. p. 210. Emphasis added.
22. Pierre Bourdieu, *Distinction: A Social Critique of the Judgment of Taste*, trans. Richard Nice (Cambridge, MA: Harvard University Press, 1984), p. 6.
23. Valérie Mandia, "Le septième art hors des frontières nationales: le pouvoir de la langue et de l'imaginaire culturel dans les films du cinéaste québécois Xavier Dolan," *Francophonies d'Amérique*, 37, Spring 2014, p. 120. Available at <http://dx.doi.org/10.7202/1033977ar> (accessed September 20, 2018). My translation.
24. Bill Marshall, "Spaces and times of Québec in two films By Xavier Dolan," *Nottingham French Studies*, 55/2, 2016, pp. 189–208.

CHAPTER 6

Transcreating *Tom à la ferme* and *Juste la fin du monde*

Marie Pascal

The comparison between plays *Tom à la ferme* (Michel Marc Bouchard, 2011) and *Juste la fin du monde* (Jean-Luc Lagarce, 1999) is justified, among other reasons, by the fact that both have attracted Xavier Dolan's attention. Although they belong to different traditions (one being a drama, the other a tragedy), both plays similarly neglect the traditional *mimetic* aspect of theatre, a crucial point as the action will then be based on language. Yet, evolving around the problem of expression (censured acts of speech, discordance between different characters' voices, long soliloquies and monologues), the two plays develop a similar *leitmotiv*, which finds its counterpart in the approximation of stage directions, be they chronological, as in Lagarce ("one Sunday, obviously, or else something like a whole year"), or spatial ("a dairy farm somewhere in the countryside"), as in Bouchard. These features raise another concern when it comes to their on-screen adaptation. According to André Gaudreault and Philippe Marion, texts can be more or less "adaptable" depending on how much they resist their transposition into another medium. Given Lagarce's and Bouchard's esoteric styles, Dolan's choice of plays adds yet another difficulty to the adaptation process. *Tom à la ferme* (2012) and *Juste la fin du monde* (2016) can therefore be considered highly "mediagenic" as each of them "is literally shaped by the medium in which it found its first expressive form."[1]

The plays' targeted audience may be reluctant to watch these filmic versions, fearing that the spirit of the originals has been disregarded or alienated—a displeasing experience as the film then "fails to realize or substantiate what we most appreciated in the source novel."[2] But most will be surprised to find that the tone in Dolan's films resembles that of the plays they adapt, that the stories seem immutable and, just as importantly, that the dialogues are respected to an unusual extent as far as adaptations go. Yet, as the plays are elliptical, both stylistically and diegetically, as I will show, the director resorts to some transformations and continuations which will be studied in detail.

Instead of solely concentrating on the extent to which the director is "faithful" to the texts,[3] I propose to base my analysis on the way Dolan adapts the "style" of the plays, to then turn to other components that had to be "discarded, supplemented, transcoded, or replaced," to use Robert Stam's formula.[4] In this chapter, I will therefore consider the numerous though minute changes between the original texts and Dolan's films, in order to highlight the different adaptation processes at stake and see if the public's perception of the stories and protagonists is transformed from one medium to another, hence inviting the reader to reconsider the relevance of the term "transcreation" as opposed to the dominantly used one, "adaptation."

TWO MEDIAGENIC PLAYS

Although it is broadly agreed that theatre and cinema are inherently compatible (mimesis, actors, and audience are at the forefront), some critics focus on the differences that make filmic adaptation of plays a complicated process. As Linda Costanzo Cahir argues:

> Ironically, it is the inherent compatibilities of the two forms that, also ironically, present the greatest difficulties for the transition of a play to the screen, as the filmmaker must find the means of making the movie something more than simply a filmed stage play. The movie must negotiate specific ways of eliminating the stagy feeling that would seem disruptive and discrepant in a film.[5]

Others distinguish the two forms by saying that cinema is an art of image and action, whereas drama is an art of language and speech.[6] In this respect, the two plays present a particular set of difficulties as they both evolve around the protagonists' inability to express a secret that may disappear with them, and put forth the question of language and its inherent flaws. In *Tom à la ferme*, Tom needs to clarify the nature of his relationship with Agathe's recently deceased son, Guillaume; in *Juste la fin du monde*, Louis comes back after a decade to tell his family that he is about to die. Although the storylines can be summarized in a few words, the playwrights have taken it upon themselves to make the plays verbose, poetic, and complex, thanks to an always-shifting pattern of lingering on, and overabundance of, details, which, paradoxically, restricts the flow of information, and reduces the characters to silence in the final words of each play. In what follows, I describe the textual patterns, which appear most mediagenic in order to build an argument regarding Dolan's methods for transcoding such elements.

SPECTATOR-CENTERED INFORMATION

André Bazin initiated the typological comparison between theatre and cinema, explaining the "psychological difference" that opposes them: while drama "is based on the reciprocal awareness of the presence of the audience and actor,"[7] when spectators go to the movies, "alone hidden in a dark room, [they] watch through half-open blinds a spectacle that is unaware of [their] existence and which is part of the universe."[8] The stage direction in *Tom à la ferme* indicates that the spectator will indeed receive more information than any of the characters: "The lines that Tom addresses to himself or to his deceased lover, should not be played like traditional direct asides to the audience. Tom should instead deliver these lines in ongoing interaction with the other characters."[9] This notable process of making Tom's inner life transparent to the public is present throughout the text. For example, Tom examines the house of the departed, starting from the description of the kitchen and eventually inventing Guillaume's past life: "Butter. Butter on the table . . . I think of something else. I say I'm thinking of something else, and the other things rush back to haunt me. Obsess me. Torment me. A fly that won't go away. (*Beat*) I imagine you when you were little. You're trying to climb onto the kitchen counter."[10] The character's train of thought takes shape on stage through these verbalized items whose only receptor is the public. This first example of the play's *mediagenia*—this singular relationship between a character and the spectator—seems unlikely to be transferred to a cinematic context where nods to the audience sitting in a dark room are much more rare.

It is through very long soliloquies that Lagarce's play *Juste la fin du monde* acknowledges the importance of spectators, as no other character is privy to Louis's thoughts. Inside such introspective scenes, the main character details his past, sheds new light on his present behavior, and sometimes projects himself into the future, despite the prospect of his imminent death. The first soliloquy happens as a "Prologue,"[11] and the audience is made aware of Louis's "imminent and irremediable death," his excuse for returning home. No character ever understands why Louis comes back, and their lack of comprehension resonates throughout the play. Later on, after a long discussion with his mother, the protagonist offers a hypothesis to explain his death: "I am dying of vexation, I am dying of nastiness and pettiness. I sacrifice myself. You will suffer longer and harder than I."[12] In this occurrence, the spectator, as the only entity able to receive his justification, is called upon to judge Louis. Finally, in the epilogue, Louis pictures himself in a tunnel in the most eccentric of these asides: "I should burst out with a big, beautiful shout, a long and joyful shout that would resonate along the valley, this is the happiness that I should offer myself, but I don't. I haven't . . . This is the kind of omission I will regret."[13] In this last passage, Louis projects himself in death and still cannot imagine his own freedom. As a dramatic feature, the soliloquies deny the dying charac-ter an audience inside the story—be it his mother or siblings—and, therefore, deny him peace of mind. Moreover, these soliloquies dispense with the impres-sion of reality by addressing an extradiegetic instance, which will have to find a complicated counterpart in the movie.

Spectators of the plays are hence given access to intimate (nearly subcon-scious) thoughts that Tom and Louis share only with them. Yet, while the play's main characters reveal themselves through a flood of internal informa-tion, which a spectator may use to understand them, their dialogues are fraught with language inefficiency, a contradiction to which I now turn.

INEFFICIENCY

Entangled discussions and struggles to find the right words leave the characters of the two plays unsatisfied but the impasse of language leaves its biggest mark on the plays' conclusions: both Louis and Tom realize that any attempt to mas-ter their acts of speech is futile, and lies and silence ultimately win the day. In *Juste la fin du monde*, Louis's siblings are silently begging him to acknowledge why he abandoned them; they remain unsatisfied and hurt, as only the audi-ence ever hears Louis's justifications in the soliloquies. The family's frustra-tion takes shape in Antoine's final reaction, when his older brother is about to leave forever. Antoine then bursts into words:

> You're here, in front of me, I knew you would be so, accusing me without a word, standing there in front of me in order to accuse me without a word, and I feel sorry for you. I have pity for you. This is an old word, but I have pity for you, and I have fear too, and worry, and despite all this anger, I hope nothing bad is happening to you, and I am already reproaching myself (you haven't left yet) the wrong that today I am doing you.[14]

In this passage of dramatic irony, Antoine is torn between the need to express his frustration and his intuition of the truth (something bad is happening to Louis). As soon as he breaks his silence, he engages in a monologue so tangled with linguistic reformulations that he will eventually be unable to express his fury. Although the monologue's placement at the end of the play points to its importance, Louis's behavior reveals its uselessness. Instead of reacting to or refuting Antoine's accusations, Louis dives further into his lie and, on the edge of his permanent departure, pretends he will be back: "I promise there won't be much time before I am back, I am lying, I promise I will be here, very soon, and other such words."[15] In this last speech to the family, Lagarce's play mingles the content of direct speech (what Louis tells his family—that he will be back soon) with his thoughts (what he shares with the audience—that all this is a lie). Only Louis and the audience know that he is dying, and this knowledge gives meaning to the metaphor of the tunnel which otherwise would have remained unintelligible.

Although Tom and Louis both lie, Tom's situation is different as it is forced upon him by another character. His lie is born in a remote village, a milieu where homosexuality is considered morally wrong. Thus, Guillaume *cannot* be homosexual (and consequently, Tom *cannot* be his boyfriend). The tale that Francis, Guillaume's brother, makes up for his mother (that her son had a girlfriend named Sarah[16]) is meant to protect family cohesion as well as their alignment with the village's moral views. The lie pre-exists Tom's arrival at the farm, which explains why he is immediately required to embody the role of the deceased's *best friend*. Because of it, Tom is deprived of his right to mourn Guillaume, as well as of the possibility of creating a true relationship with his in-laws. Despite the fact that the truth is partially uncovered at the end of the play, when Agathe reads Guillaume's diary, the play ends with the genesis of another lie: according to the stage directions, Tom, about to kill Francis, is considering telling Agathe that her son left with Sarah. This last line indicates that lying has the last word, something only the spectator is entrusted with. *Tom à la ferme* ends elliptically: neither Francis's murder nor Tom's liberation is shown on stage, presenting another complication in need of reformatting before being adapted.

If monologues and dialogues may at first glance seem reliable, omissions and lies act as a counterpart to the overabundance of language. Stated at the outset of each play (in the prologue for *Juste la fin du monde* and in the first scene for *Tom à la ferme*), the protagonists' purposes are never discovered by the group each is meeting: the plays are built on tacit and unexpressed content to which only the audience has access. In order to address the dialogue between plays and films, I will correlate the adaptive processes put forward by Robert Stam and the typology on "filmic translations" drawn by Linda Costanzo Cahir. I aim to depict the choice of cinematic techniques in order to see whether Dolan's adaptive style is closer to "literal translation" (a mere *transcoding*), "traditional translation" (operating *discarding* or *replacing*) or "radical translation" (where a *supplementation* occurs), a method explored in the last section of this chapter.

TO TRANSCODE, DISCARD, AND REPLACE

Despite Dolan's success and recognition for his original screenplays, his first adaptation, *Tom à la ferme* (2013), was most likely a challenging task, not only because of the text's aforementioned difficulties, but also due to the particular skills required for adaptation. The adapter must first produce an analysis of the text, and then determine what will be kept, changed, or eluded. With all the linguistic difficulties of the plays in mind, including their intrinsic "artificial" qualities, I first examine how Dolan transcodes most of the plays, but also recreates entire passages and replaces others, without tone or style disruptions, all the while being true to the new medium of cinema.

LITERAL TRANSLATION

According to Cahir, "literal translation," the most unrefined type of adaptation, "reproduces the plot and all its attending details as closely as possible to the letter of the book."[17] Although it may sound challenging to figure out how words could literally be transcoded on screen, the question is perhaps less relevant for drama, where stage actors can simply be replaced by screen actors. But Dolan did not offer a "filmed drama," the mere recording of the play, although he did reproduce several scenes in their entirety. This pattern is more frequent in *Tom à la ferme* (2013), perhaps as a result of Michel Marc Bouchard's involvement with the script. The similarities between the dialogues in the text and their filmic counterparts are striking, as the tango scene exhibits. As they get physically closer, Francis (Pierre-Yves Cardinal) and Tom (Xavier Dolan) discuss the sad reality of Francis's life, secluded on the farm and unlikely to find a partner thanks to his mother's presence. At the end of this discussion,

> *Tom and Francis notice Agathe, who has heard everything.*
>
> AGATHE: I was looking for the two of you.
> FRANCIS: Where were you?
> AGATHE: I was looking for you . . .
> FRANCIS: She had a beautiful calf. We baptized it: Baby-butt.
> AGATHE: That's no name for a calf.
> FRANCIS: You heard what I was saying just now?
> AGATHE: Come eat now. The pies are hot.
> FRANCIS: Did you hear what I was saying?
> AGATHE: (*coldly*) Yes! I heard everything and I said Baby-butt is no name for a calf! The pies are hot.[18]
>
> AGATHE: I made some pies.
> FRANCIS: What?
> AGATHE: I made . . . (*irritated pause*) pies.
> FRANCIS: She had a big calf, we named it Bitch-Ass. (*the two boys laugh*)
> AGATHE: (*cold*) That is not a name for a calf.

FRANCIS: You heard everything I said before? Agathe . . . (*he runs after his mother*) Agathe . . . did you hear everything I was saying?

AGATHE: Yes, I heard it all and I said: That is not a name for a calf. (*pauses*) You'll come get your pies, they're getting cold. (53:22 to 54:20)[19]

While Francis opens up to Tom for the first time, Agathe (Lise Roy) is shown standing at the back of the barn, listening. In the play, the stage directions explain that she was there the whole time and heard everything; in the film, Agathe appears in the background after a cut, the editing thus conveying the effect of the original scene. Moreover, apart from minor reformulations and contractions (in the film), the important component of the scene (namely, Agathe's pretense that she didn't overhear Francis's desire to be rid of her) is retained. This occurrence is one of many passages, which Dolan transcodes with little change, transposing the setting, the character's position, and most of the dialogue. Having thus been "literally translated," this passage proves to be a pivotal moment in the story.

As regards Lagarce's play, Dolan tightened the massive acts of speech, a transcoding that can still be considered a "literal translation" although it is not as close to the word of the text as in *Tom à la ferme*'s case. However, this reduction of the monologues does not affect the reception of the message nor the vivid impression left on the spectator, and it remains clear that the characters are struggling to express themselves. Some languid exchanges result, such as Catherine's (Marion Cotillard) struggle to explain her children's absence to Louis (Gaspard Ulliel), in the play and in the film:

CATHERINE: They are at their other grand-mother's house, we couldn't have known you were coming, and taking them back at the very last second, she wouldn't have allowed it. They would have been very happy to see you, we don't doubt that.—No?—and me too, Antoine as well, we would have been very happy, obviously, that they'd finally meet you. They can't imagine you. The eldest is 8. People say, but I don't realize, I am not in my right place to speak, everybody says that, they say, but these things don't seem too logical to me—just a bit, how to say? To be funny, no?—I don't know, people say and I won't contradict them, that she looks like Antoine, they say that she is exactly like him, as a girl, the same person. One always says such things, about every child, I don't know, why not?[20]

CATHERINE: —They are at their other grandmother's house, my mother . . . obviously. But we weren't aware, it was so, and you couldn't get them back or else, she would have made a scene. So there. But they

would have been happy to see you. And I would have been happy too
. . . well, Antoine and I would have been happy for them to meet you.
So, the eldest is eight and everybody says she looks like Antoine. That
she is exactly like him. People say such things about all children, true
or not true, people say that, don't they? (8:22 to 9:02)[21]

Although Dolan kept the playwright's style and words, the tendency is to
shorten long sentences and paragraphs, a procedure which necessitated some
re-writing. In the filmic scene, Catherine's uneasiness is accompanied by her
husband's ferocious interventions, which are far less frequent in the text.
Moreover, Dolan's decision to have Catherine and Louis filmed together in
close-ups, Cotillard's hesitant, blubbering way of talking, as well as her nervous
swallowing and sighs, all channel the awkwardness of the situation, and give
shape to what we will later examine as a silent understanding between Catherine and Louis. All the aforementioned filming techniques also emphasize the
director's efforts to alter some of the play's information to adapt the source
material to the new medium. As Cahir announces, cinema has several possibilities that are denied to drama:

> [It can] change the audience's perspective by moving and reposition-
> ing the camera; manipulate emotional responses through such devices
> as extreme close-ups, high angles, and editing; create more subtlety of
> performance through the small gestures and facial movements that the
> camera can record, but which would be lost on the stage.[22]

From this thorough description of the cinematic possibilities over drama, one
can deduce that the term "literal translation" is not conceptually broad enough.
A singular focus on dialogues and monologues, which is essentially all the
information that can be extracted from a written play, will not take into account
other types of transformations. Even if Dolan remains true to both Bouchard's
and Lagarce's original texts while channeling their styles, the choice of camera
position, editing, as well as the actors' performance, have additional impacts on
the film's audience. It is therefore difficult to narrow this analysis to a simple
"transcoding," as some information is discarded, and some is replaced.

TRADITIONAL TRANSLATION

Cahir defines the "traditional translation" as an adaptation "which maintains the overall traits of the book (plot, setting and stylistic conventions), but
revamps particular details in those particular ways that the filmmaker sees as
necessary and fitting."[23] Although this definition does not explore the actual

methods in place, Cahir's quote complements André Gardies's conception of adaptation, that

> one should not conceive of the source text as a semiotic object, full and unique, needing to pass from one medium to another thanks to a trans-semiotic operation, but, in a much more pragmatic way, as a reservoir full of instructions, a kind of database from which the director-adaptor can freely draw.[24]

According to Gardies, the adaptor is given complete freedom with regards to what is to be used or discarded, to which I would add the displacement of some elements into other strata of the film. I will therefore focus on the elements which seem absent from the films, as if discarded during the adaptation process, to then consider the cinematic means used to express the texts' ideas. I then examine some of the liberties taken in thoroughly transforming scenes and patterns so as to render them nearly unrecognizable: from such creative reinterpretation derives one of the main pleasures of studying adaptations, according to Linda Hutcheon.[25]

In Bouchard's version of *Tom à la ferme*, Agathe is a devout Catholic, a reference to the lasting influence of Catholicism in Québec's rural areas. Agathe's monologue concludes the play with a biblical reference explicitly likening Tom to a martyr: "Go get Tom! 'He entered the house. No one recognized him. He sat down at our table. No one recognized him. He spoke to us of love. No one recognized him and those who were mourning him went to his grave, but it was empty.'"[26] Agathe had earlier quoted from memory a similar passage from the Bible. The thematic pattern of martyrdom is a recurrent though implicit reference in the play, as in each of the scenes where Francis hangs Tom by the feet above a stinking cow pit, a punishment formerly reserved for his younger brother. While this sadistic action aims at objectifying Francis's antagonist as well as proving his cowardice, Agathe's actual reference to the martyr implies that Tom's secret (his love for her departed son) has been understood. This relevance of religion—and, more importantly, Tom's martyrdom—seems absent in the movie. The omission is glaring as such a deletion would have greatly changed the reception of the story, but it becomes evident that the religious trope has in fact been displaced or rather, disseminated, as it reverberates in several scenes. It first appears during the funeral scene, which spans over three minutes (19:10 to 22:49) while it is an ellipsis in the play. Moreover, Tom's identification with a martyr is displaced to the numerous scenes where he is subjected to Francis's punches, spits, and insults. Close-ups or extreme close-ups give an impression of claustrophobia or being trapped in the frame, together with the victim and his torturer. For instance, as he gets into bed on his first night at the farm, Tom is intimidated by a figure that chokes him and admonishes him for coming to the farm (14:50). Francis here makes it clear that Tom must speak at the funeral. Immediately after the service (23:50), Francis beats Tom in the toilet for not speaking. The latter tries to escape through a cornfield (39:38) and is beaten again. Every one of these scenes—Dolan's additions—can hence be seen as a dissemination of the violence evolving around the metaphor of the textual cow pit. Although it first seems to be eluded, Dolan chooses to disseminate the representation of martyrdom throughout the film instead of keeping one explicit reference as in the play.

This inclination to replace or displace elements can be similarly observed in *Juste la fin du monde*, a prime example of which occurs in the long monologue delivered by Antoine, who scarcely speaks in the rest of the play. As already mentioned, he then decries Louis's inconsiderate attitude toward the family, and especially toward himself. Although Antoine (Vincent Cassel) rebels against his family's implication that he is a violent and mean person, his anger and violence are disseminated throughout the film as provocations, excesses of rage, insults, and otherwise passive aggressive behavior. Listing these numerous occurrences is maybe not of primary interest, but suffice it to recall Antoine's more egregious reactions—all Dolan's (or Cassel's) additions—first, to Catherine's rhetorical question ("Do you remember how your daughter looked so much like you?"), to which he responds "no, I don't, I love forgetting the things that are most important to me" (10:01);[27] and, second, the supremely inappropriate, "and what am I supposed to do, jerk off?" (17:01), when his mother asks everyone but him to help with dinner preparations.[28] Antoine's exceptional anger is not only visible in minor exchanges: a sequence showcases his excess of rage through elaborate cinematic techniques, demonstrating Dolan's great imagination when it comes to replacing the violence of Antoine's final soliloquy. When the two brothers eventually get to speak to each other midway into the movie, Antoine asks his brother if he would go get cigarettes with him (1:03:00). True to Lagarce (though the scene is totally Dolan's), the characters express themselves with difficulty and to Antoine's elliptical "in the car, we could . . ." Louis languidly completes with " talk?" Cinematic choices converge to illustrate Antoine's importance as a strong-willed character. First, the actors' positions clearly indicate who is the focus: Cassel is in the foreground, occupying his entire half of the frame, while Uriell is squeezed into the right half, in the background. The camera is steady but the focus alternates, following the speaker. Up to this point, the disparity remains minor. But when Antoine punctuates his brother's acceptance to come along with "So then, it's decided," the non-diegetic music abruptly vanishes with the end of the sentence.

Antoine's peremptory conclusion seems to initiate a struggle between the diegetic (manifested in his voice) and the extradiegetic machinations (the interruption of the non-diegetic music). This clash between diegetic and non-diegetic devices, which appears to give Antoine a sort of "metafilmic" control over the film, replaces Antoine's monologue in the play, not in terms of content but in terms of emphasis. Thanks to this, the spectator is able to grasp the character's importance.

Despite the plays' mediagenia, Dolan therefore succeeds in reintegrating most of the apparently discarded elements through cinematic techniques, be they elaborations of a theme by way of cinematography (as in the ana-lyzed scenes in *Tom à la ferme*) or inventive editing (as in *Juste la fin du monde*'s sequence described above). Moreover, such creative and memorable sequences also coincide with the qualities Cahir highlights for a successful "translation":

> The film must communicate definite ideas concerning the *internal* meaning and value of the literary text as the filmmaker interprets it . . . exhibit a collaboration of filmmaking skills . . . demonstrate an audacity to create a work that stands as a world apart, that exploits literature in such a way that a self-reliant, but related, aesthetic offspring is born.[29]

All these qualities are enhanced by Dolan, who remains close to the spirit of the plays all the while audaciously replacing the original world with his own. Because they engage in such interplay with the original texts, Dolan's two films "involve both (re-)interpretation and then (re-)creation" and can therefore be labeled "appropriation and salvaging, depending on your perspective."[30]

TRANSCREATION: THE SHIFT IN "SPIRIT"

Investigating this interplay between media shows the importance of analyzing adaptation as an inherently intertextual practice and to consider the position of "radical translation." Cahir defines this type of adaptation as one "which reshapes the book in extreme and revolutionary ways, both as a means of interpreting the literature and of making the film a more fully independent work."[31] Dolan's take on the plays tends to complement his films, by trans-creating rather than trans-coding the stories, initiating the idea that neither the book nor the movie supersedes the other. Unexpectedly, one soon under-stands that the cause of such differences does not lie in what Dolan alters in the playwrights' messages, but rather in tenuous changes and subtle addi-tions, what Genette calls "continuations," and Stam "supplementations." In this last section, I focus on the most important filmic continuations, coupled with several minor changes, which distinguish the two transcreations from the texts.

TOM: FROM VICTIMHOOD TO EMPOWERMENT

As mentioned earlier, Tom's status as a martyr in the play is linked to Agathe's final interpretation of his behavior (that he is the Christ who came to talk about love and tolerance). Moreover, related to her faith, Agathe's disclosure of the deceased's diary allows her to finally understand that her departed son was gay and, consequently, that Tom came to visit her as a "widow," as he calls himself. Finally, the very reason for Guillaume's desertion from his hometown is implied in this scene: his older brother Francis, a redneck who strived to keep homosexuality out of his family, assaulted Guillaume's first boyfriend, Paul. This too is revealed in Agathe's reading:

> AGATHE: (*still quoting from the diary*) "He tore Paul's beautiful face apart. I saw the whole thing. I didn't lift a finger. I could see he was suffering, I could hear him screaming, I didn't defend him. I didn't do a thing. I think we should never tell the truth. Never." (*The silhouette of Tom holding the shovel disappears.*)
> FRANCIS: If I hadn't shut Paul up, someday, someone would've shut your little boy up for good! Let them do that stuff in the city, but not here. Let's keep the little we've got left here clean.[32]

This scene not only gives Agathe and Tom the possibility for redemption, it also grants Francis the space to explain why he felt he had to brutalize Paul. Yet, Tom is not fully aware of the details of Francis's assault, as he is absent in this scene. The last lines of the play describe Tom about to kill Francis with a shovel in the cornfield (the location of his first defiance in the film) but it does not explain why Tom would now kill his torturer.

As this scene is eluded from the film, the first consequence is that Agathe is never given the satisfaction of knowingly having met Guillaume's widow. The second consequence is that Francis does not get to explain his crime, and it is unclear why Guillaume left his family. The film then ends with an entirely different resolution, in an original sequence. After deciding that nobody will read the diary, Francis drives Sarah (Évelyne Brochu) to the bus station. While she and Francis have sex in the car, Tom is sent to the nearby pub, from which, as he discovers, Francis is banned. Tom questions the bar owner (Manuel Tadros) who witnessed Paul's mutilation and clearly remembers it. The changes operated are of great importance: not only does Tom "want to know" the scabrous details of Francis's crime, but the latter is not given any space in which to express his motives or express remorse for what he did.

Once a martyr, Tom here becomes gifted with knowledge, which prompts his escape, in a scene so seamlessly fitting into the story that one would struggle to notice its absence from the text. Where the victim is empowered and willful, the torturer is sentenced to silence.

In light of this addition, it is worth looking closer at the shift in Tom and Francis's relationship between text and film. Whereas Tom is a passive victim of the sadistic compulsions of a homophobe in the play, in the film, he tries to escape multiple times.[33] Although he is gradually subdued by Francis's power and resemblance to the departed, Tom confronts him several times, gathers clues regarding his violent behavior, and eventually asks for an explanation in the pub. But more importantly, the accumulation of these subtle additions has a logical impact on the ending. In the film, after his discussion with the bar owner, Tom decides to go back to Montréal. As Francis chases him, Tom takes shelter in the woods, armed with a shovel. He doesn't kill him, however; instead, he steals his truck and leaves the shovel behind. The scene preceding Tom's escape (1:34:35 to 1:37:02) is singled out with a horizontal curtain slowly narrowing the screen and creating an impression of imprisonment. The curtain eventually lifts as Tom escapes Francis's reach. This second to last sequence ends with a fixed camera showing a desperate Francis running toward the shovel, an ironic reminder that he is a farmer, while the play's omnipresent coyotes begin to howl (1:38:00). In the last sequence, Tom is at a gas station where he chances upon Paul (Olivier Morin) and sees his disfigured face. The young man is depicted as having taken shelter in this deserted area, between the farm and the city, and the spectator only gets a short glimpse of his scar. This sequence is *Tom à la ferme*'s most important "paraliptic continuation," a concept presented by Genette as a "desire to fill eventual paralipsis or gaps of some importance."[34] In other words, the sequence introducing Paul can be understood as fulfilling a desire to supplement an ellipsis: this paraliptic continuation reinforces Francis's monstrosity, makes Tom's newfound power to leave more credible, and possibly represents the director's reflection on homophobic behavior. Such a reading is reinforced by Rufus Wainwright's end credit "Going to a Town." The song's lyrics, especially the line "Do you really think you'd go to Hell for having loved?," seem to consolidate the film's themes of martyrdom and homosexuality into a call for open-mindedness.

If the final change in Tom's behavior in the play seems incongruous, it is imposed by the medium: the theatre audience is indeed aware that "dramatic illusion is never the illusion of reality: it is always imaginative illusion, the illusion of a period of make-believe."[35] It then makes sense that Tom's redemption, now that Agathe understands who he is, is consummated by his killing of the wrongdoer. In a similar fashion, the title "Tom *à la ferme*" implies the timelessness of his stay, refusing the character any life outside the farm. The film's take is quite different, as Tom is shown both on his way to the farm (opening sequence) and on his exit from it (last sequence). Since he will not kill Francis nor pretend to stay with him, his stay at the farm is but a cathartic period where

Tom learns firsthand about homophobia and captivity. The reason why Tom has to escape in the film is implied by Bazin's claims that "there can be no cinema without the setting up of an open space in place of the universe rather than as part of it."[36] Thus, Tom's final journey from the farm to the forest, then to the gas station, and eventually to Montréal, substitutes the single-setting action of the play with a wider setting. In this light, Dolan's discarding of the play's final scene, and his replacement with a myriad of additional scenes, are essential for the narrative coherence of his transcreation.

LOUIS: FROM PAST INJUSTICE TO REDEMPTION

Though Dolan is faithful—stylistically—to Lagarce's *Juste la fin du monde*, a reading from stage to screen leads to opposing analyses of Louis, thanks to two concomitant adaptive elements: first, the removal of a scene, and second, the use of paraliptic continuations.

In Lagarce's play, the tragic tone is implemented through the following repetitive pattern: every scene where Louis argues with a family member is followed by a monologue about his past, always macabre. The repetition of this pattern (deteriorating dialogue leading to hateful explanations in soliloquy) throughout the play enhances the tragic tone as well as the feeling that Louis is doomed from the start. Given this pattern, *Juste la fin du monde*'s ending is pessimistic even if this is expected of a tragedy. In Dolan's film, Louis addresses the audience solely in the scene preceding the opening credits where, as he is flying back home, his voice-over states the imminence of his death and the reason for his visit to "them"—his mother and siblings. Saying that the other soliloquies are completely eluded from the movie is not completely accurate, however, for Louis's past is recounted by two added flashbacks. Although these are not explicitly singled out from the main narration (as they would be with titles or slow motion), Dolan distinguishes them visually from the main story by introducing events that trigger Louis's recollection of the past, depicted in flashbacks. In order to smooth out the transition between present and past, the audio track bridges the scenes. For instance, in the scene where his mother, Martine (Nathalie Baye), recalls the family's weekend trips, O-Zone's "Dragosta Din Tei" (2004) can be heard from the radio, and mother and daughter Suzanne (Léa Seydoux) start dancing after turning up the volume (32:10). The camera then turns to Louis's face and the radio music becomes distorted (32:12), implicating the protagonist's subjectivity, before finally transforming into non-diegetic music (32:14) in a flashback of an adolescent Antoine and a young Louis playing together during one of these weekend trips. As in the play, the flashbacks are therefore linked to events prior to the main narrative in the same way that a soliloquy follows an argument in the play.

Yet, there is a difference between text and film in the tone of these recollections: in the play, the soliloquies are essentially tragic and convey Louis's desolate feelings; in the film, the flashbacks refer to a happy past, an optimism further enhanced by the choice of filters and soundtrack. Similarly, the second flashback shows Louis with his late boyfriend, Pierre (59:32), right before Antoine tells him the latter has passed away from a rare form of cancer. Surrounded by his old belongings, Louis dreams of his nights with Pierre in the aforementioned style of vivid colors, romantic music (a remix of Françoise Hardy's "Une miss s'immisce," 1988), and an arc shot conveying a feeling of unity. In the filmic "pastness," Louis is thus pictured as capable of love and laughter, and the palpable uneasiness one feels toward the written character is partially eluded. From text to film, these flashbacks transpose Louis's negative vision of his past to a positive though melancholic version of it.

This element initiates a shift in the audience's reaction toward the story, sustained by two additional important transformations occurring during the "transcreative" process. First, Antoine is older than Louis: in the play, Antoine's anger is justified by Lagarce because he is the middle child, subjugated by his elder brother's unhappiness. In Dolan's film, there is little to justify Antoine's resentment and feelings of abandonment, especially given that the flashback emphasizes their close relationship. However, the most important supplementation, one that will completely invert the reception of the ending, concerns the relationship between Louis and Catherine, his sister-in-law. Although Catherine is nearly elided from the text, she is of prime importance in the movie, and placed at the center of two notable scenes—two "paraliptic continuations," as it were—distinguished by their unique arrangement of cinematic techniques.

The first instance occurs in the third scene (starting 8:22), as the characters are waiting for appetizers. Catherine is discussing her children with Louis when she is interrupted by a violent off-screen verbal intervention from her husband that triggers a change in the audio (11:30 to 12:00): progressively, the diegetic noises and voices fade out, giving way to what Michel Chion calls "*empathetic* sound," one that "directly participates in the characters' emotions, prolongs and amplifies them."[37] Dolan's innovative sound editing has been touched upon in the analysis of the cigarette scene, but it now goes beyond the dialogue between diegetic and non-diegetic devices. Giving way to a metaphysical space, the muting of all other diegetic voices allows Catherine's whispered "Louis" (11:42) to be audible. The calling of the name, uttered in an echoing whisper, is intended to remove this scene from the "realistic" world, a thread which is uncoiled in the next scene of interest (1:01:00). It takes place when Louis wakes up from the second flashback/dream: Catherine's worried face appears behind Pierre's evanescent one and, after letting him know dessert will soon be ready, she mutters a mysterious question: "How much longer?" (1:01:40). Dreamily, Louis seeks clarification and asks in turn, "how much longer what?" (1:02:00), to which Catherine never gives an answer. One can interpret this elliptic dialogue and Catherine's muteness as the impossibility for the truth (Louis's agony) to be unveiled. Nothing is ever clarified until the last sequence, where Louis, deserted by his angry family, simply gestures to Catherine to remain silent (1:26:40), possibly expressing his desire for secrecy. Bathed in a sunset light, Louis then turns his back and leaves the house forever, accompanied by Moby's optimistic "Natural Blues" (1999).[38]

There is thus a threefold process in the transcreation of *Juste la fin du monde*: first, the added flashbacks, which can be seen as simple filmic transpositions of a literary device (the soliloquies); second, the swap between the brothers' ages (an elaboration on sibling relationships); third and most important, the scenes depicting Catherine and Louis's special relationship (a continuation granting Louis's suffering a diegetic audience). All these supplementations direct our interpretation in the same direction: Dolan's transfiguration of the pessimistic tone of Lagarce's tragedy. Although Louis is filmed as a very ill character— he throws up in the bathroom (32:57), is bathed in sweat until the end—his departure appears as undramatic, nearly casual. While Lagarce's drama builds an unhappy character, muted and imprisoned in his lies and upcoming death, Dolan's film allows Louis to remember a happy past and to be less alone with his secret, thanks to Catherine, who is but a secondary character in the play.

This twofold analysis centered on Dolan's transcreative power allows us to consider cinema's richness as a medium. As Stam notes:

> As a rich, sensorially composite language, the cinema as a medium is open to all kinds of literary and pictorial energies and symbolism, to all collective representations, to all ideological currents, to all aesthetic trends, and to the infinite play of influences within the cinema, within the other arts, and within culture generally.[39]

Dolan addresses most of Stam's points, whether by including his moral views as in *Tom à la ferme*, or reflecting on the impact of music in *Juste la fin du monde*'s last scene. Furthermore, in 1952, Bazin had explained that "the more important and decisive the literary qualities of the work, the more adaptation disturbs its equilibrium, the more it needs a creative talent to reconstruct it on a new equilibrium, not identical with, but the equivalent of, the old one."[40] Xavier Dolan seems to have found this equivalent equilibrium in his transcreations of these plays.

CONCLUSION

"For a phenomena to be transformed, something belonging to it needs to remain, needs to be extended," claim Gaudreault and Marion.[41] Thus, transformations can only be witnessed if enough of the text persists, explaining Dolan's retention of much of the body of the original works. Yet, one also has to take into account Dolan's distance from the originals, which makes the films intrinsically contrasting (if not conflicting, as the last part of my argument seeks to show) to the plays. Though the director remains faithful to the word of the original works, he departs from their spirit. However, these transformations are so subtle that they can only be identified through a close examination of various scenes' cinematographic choices, sound design, as well as the transformation of purely dramatic forms (such as soliloquies and stage directions) and the attenuation of pathos. To us, this is the main relevance of Dolan's work, a director who won the 2016 Grand Prix at Cannes for *Juste la fin du monde*; a prize awarded to the most *original* film in competition.

From this "appropriation/salvaging" process to which Hutcheon refers, one can argue that both stories, and their reception, are so transformed that the texts and the films are made "divergent" rather than "convergent," despite first impressions of the films as "literal" or "traditional translations" due to the survival of style and whole fragments of text. Dolan's two films prove that the attempts of typology in cinematic adaptation so far developed miss the point of such works. In this respect, despite the intellectual value of critiques such as those offered by Cahir and Stam in sparking the debate on adaptation, the field could benefit from perspectives of more cinematographic depth. By this I mean that consideration should be given not only to the "faithfulness" to the word or the story but to the different layers of creative construction, which lead to the final product. This brings us back to the more fitting title of "transcreator," as opposed to "adaptor," for directors such as Dolan. It also brings our focus to a particularly stimulating theory by Gaudreault,[42] which, in conjunction, with Cahir and Stam's previous work, can add a new level of precision and profundity to the study of transcreation.

NOTES

1. André Gaudreault and Philippe Marion, "Un art de l'emprunt: les sources intermédiales de l'adaptation," in Carla Fratta (ed.), *Littérature et cinéma au Québec (1995–2005)* (Bologna: Pendragon, 2008), p. 18. (La condition d'un texte qui serait littéralement coulé dans le média par lequel il a trouvé sa première forme expressive.) My translation.
2. Robert Stam, "Introduction: the theory and practice of film adaptation," in Robert Stam and Alessandra Raengo (eds), *Literature and Film: A Guide to the Theory and Practice of Film Adaptation* (Malden, MA: Blackwell, 2005), p. 14.
3. As too many critics have already written since the dawn of adaptation, associating this artistic practice to a rigid and moral relationship owed by the film (the parasite), to the text (the untouchable original). From André Bazin's 1950 article "Pour un cinéma impur" to Robert Stam (*Literature and Film*, 2005, and *Literature Through Film*, 2004), it is

generally accepted that a debate on faithfulness will not be fruitful in film studies: as Stam argues, "the mediocrity of some adaptations should not lead us to endorse fidelity as a methodological principle." Robert Stam, *Literature Through Film: Realism, Magic, and the Art of Adaptation* (Malden, MA: Blackwell, 2004), p. 3.

4. Ibid. p. 6.

5. Linda Costanzo Cahir, *Literature into Film: Theory and Practical Approaches* (Jefferson, NC: McFarland, 2006), p. 145.

6. I refer here to the central thought which Michel Marc Bouchard puts forward in his contribution to the debate in *Littérature et cinéma au Québec* (2008). At the time, he had not yet worked with Dolan on his play *Tom à la ferme*, but his earlier drama, *Les Feluettes ou la répétition d'un drame romantique* (1996), had not only been adapted but also translated into English by Paul Greyson (*Lilies*, 1998). In his article, Bouchard explains, amongst other things, this crucial distinction between cinema ("art d'images et d'actions") and drama ("art de parole"). The playwright goes further and stipulates that while cinema shows, drama evokes. Michel Marc Bouchard, "Le théâtre au cinéma ou le dramaturge déviant scénariste!," in Carla Fratta (ed.), *Littérature et cinéma au Québec (1995–2005)* (Bologna: Pendragon, 2008), p. 43. My translation.

7. André Bazin, "Theater and cinema," in *What Is Cinema?*, vol. 1, trans. and ed. Hugh Gray (Berkeley: University of California Press, 2005), p. 102.

8. Ibid. p. 102.

9. Michel Marc Bouchard, "Performance note," in *Tom at the Farm*, trans. Linda Gaboriau (Vancouver: Talonbooks, 2013), n.p.

10. Ibid. p. 1.

11. The play explores a form that drama usually does not use as such, the prologue normally being uttered by an external form of narration (a chorus for instance). This excess of information has been adapted by Dolan in the form of pre-credits in both adaptations, and could be explored in further research.

12. Jean-Luc Lagarce, *Juste la fin du monde* (Québec: Hamacs, 2007), p. 66, "Je meurs par dépit, je meurs par méchanceté et mesquinerie, je me sacrifie. Vous souffrirez plus longtemps et plus durement que moi." My translation.

13. Ibid. p. 114, "Je devrais pousser un grand et beau cri, un long et joyeux cri qui résonnerait dans toute la vallée, c'est ce bonheur-là que je devrais m'offrir, mais je ne le fais pas, je ne l'ai pas fait . . . Ce sont des oublis comme celui-là que je regretterai."

14. Ibid. p. 111, "Tu es là, devant moi, je savais que tu serais ainsi, à m'accuser sans mot, à te mettre debout devant moi pour m'accuser sans mot, et je te plains, et j'ai de la pitié pour toi, c'est un vieux mot, mais j'ai de la pitié pour toi, et de la peur aussi, de l'inquiétude, et malgré toute cette colère, j'espère qu'il ne t'arrive rien de mal, et je me reproche déjà (tu n'es pas encore parti) le mal aujourd'hui que je te fais."

15. Ibid. p. 91, "Je promets qu'il n'y aura pas tout ce temps avant que je revienne, je dis des mensonges, je promets d'être là, à nouveau, très bientôt, des phrases comme ça."

16. The girl's name changes in the play: where the metatext (foreword and stage directions) calls her "Sarah," Francis presents her as "Ellen" (Nathalie in the English translation) even though he says her real name is Sarah (p. 25). Dolan simply uses "Sarah," which I will also use henceforth.

17. Cahir, *Literature into Film*, p. 16.

18. Bouchard, *Tom at the Farm*, p. 39.

19. Xavier Dolan, *Tom à la ferme* (Canada and France: Sons of Manual; MK2 Films, 2013), 53:22–54:20, "AGATHE: J'ai fait des tartes. FRANCIS: Quoi? AGATHE: J'ai faite . . . *(ton irrité)* des tartes. FRANCIS: Elle a eu un beau veau, on va l'appeler cul de bitch! *(les garçons rient)* AGATHE: C'est pas un nom pour un veau. FRANCIS: T'as-tu entendu

ce que j'ai dit tantôt? Agathe . . . *(il court après sa mère)* Agathe . . . t'as-tu toute entendu ce que j'ai dit? AGATHE: Oui, j'ai toute entendu, pis j'ai dit: 'C'est pas un nom pour un veau.' *(pause)* Vous viendrez manger, les tartes vont refroidir." DVD subtitles.

20. Lagarce, *Juste la fin*, p. 18, "CATHERINE: Ils sont chez leur autre grand-mère, nous ne pouvions pas savoir que vous viendriez, et les lui retirer à la dernière seconde, elle n'aurait pas admis. Ils auraient été très heureux de vous voir, cela, on n'en doute pas une seconde. – non ? –, et moi aussi, Antoine également, nous aurions été heureux, évidemment, qu'ils vous connaissent enfin. Ils ne vous imaginent pas. La plus grande a huit ans. On dit, mais je ne me rends pas compte, je ne suis pas la mieux placée, tout le monde dit ça, on dit, et ces choses-là ne me paraissent jamais très logiques – juste un peu, comment dire? pour amuser, non? – je ne sais pas, on dit et je ne vais pas les contredire, qu'elle ressemble à Antoine, on dit qu'elle est exactement son portrait, en fille, la même personne. On dit toujours des choses comme ça, de tous les enfants on le dit, je ne sais pas, pourquoi non?" My translation.

21. Xavier Dolan, *Juste la fin du monde* (Canada and France: Sons of Manual; MK2 Films, 2016), 8:22–9:02, "CATHERINE: Ils sont chez leur autre grand-mère, ma mère . . . évidemment. Mais on ne pouvait pas savoir, c'était tellement, et tu pouvais pas les lui retirer parce que sinon elle m'aurait fait une scène. Alors là. Mais ils auraient été heureux de vous voir. Et j'aurais été heureuse moi aussi . . . enfin, Antoine et moi, on aurait été heureux qu'ils vous rencontrent. Alors, la plus grande elle a huit ans et tout le monde dit qu'elle ressemble à Antoine. Mais qu'elle est exactement son portrait. On dit ça de tous les enfants, vrai ou pas vrai on le dit, non?" DVD subtitles.

22. Cahir, *Literature into Film*, p. 151.

23. Ibid. p. 16.

24. André Gardies, "Le narrateur sonne toujours deux fois," in André Gaudreault and Thierry Groensteen (eds), *La transécriture: pour une théorie de l'adaptation* (Québec: Nota bene, 1999), p. 68. (Il ne s'agit pas de concevoir le texte source comme un objet sémiotique plein et unique ayant à passer d'un médium à un autre grâce à une opération transsémiotique, mais, de façon beaucoup plus pragmatique, comme un réservoir d'instructions, une sorte de banque de données, dans lequel puise librement le réalisateur-adaptateur). My translation.

25. In the first chapter of her book on adaptation, Hutcheon states: "part of this pleasure, I want to argue, comes simply from repetition with variation, from the comfort of ritual combined with the piquancy of surprise." Linda Hutcheon, *A Theory of Adaptation* (London: Routledge, 2006), p. 4.

26. Bouchard, *Tom at the Farm*, p. 78.

27. Dolan, *Juste la fin du monde*, 10:01, "Tu te souviens Antoine?" / "Non, j'adore oublier les choses qui sont les plus importantes pour moi." DVD subtitles.

28. Ibid. 17:01, "Et moi, qu'est-ce que je fais? J'me branle?" DVD subtitles.

29. Cahir, *Literature into Film*, p. 99.

30. Hutcheon, *A Theory of Adaptation*, p. 8.

31. Cahir, *Literature into Film*, p. 17.

32. Bouchard, *Tom at the Farm*, p. 78.

33. When they return from the funeral after Francis has bullied him in the bathroom, Tom is left alone in his car and, after a long inner conflict as he is driving off, finally obeys the tacit order to be back at the farm. After the tango scene, Tom tries to escape again through a cornfield (the same one where he eventually kills Francis in the play's last scene, a transfer of this eloquent setting).

34. Gérard Genette, *Palimpsestes: Littérature au second degré* (Paris: Seuil, 1982), p. 242 (combler d'éventuelles paralipses ou ellipses latérales). My translation.

35. Allardyce Nicoll, "Film reality: the cinema and the theatre," in Bert Cardullo (ed.), *Stage and Screen: Adaptation Theory From 1916 to 2000* (New York: Continuum), p. 74.

36. Bazin, "Theater and cinema," p. 110.

37. Michel Chion, *Le son au cinéma* (Paris: Éditions de l'Étoile, 1985), p. 123 (la musique qui participe directement aux émotions des personnages, les prolonge, les amplifie). On the other hand, "anempathetic" music is referred to as "counterpoint music," as is the case with the use of Moby's "Natural Blues" in the exit scene. My translation.

38. One could argue that the lyrics sustain the narration, the reference to God reads as Louis's deliverance when exiting: "Oh Lordy, Trouble so hard / Don't nobody know my trouble but God / Went down the hill, the other day, soul got happy and stayed all day."

39. Robert Stam, *Literature Through Film*, p. 7.

40. André Bazin, "In defense of mixed cinema," in *What Is Cinema?*, vol. 1, trans. and ed. Hugh Gray (Berkeley: University of California Press, 2005), p. 68.

41. Gaudreault and Marion, "Un art de l'emprunt," p. 14 (Pour qu'un phénomène puisse se transformer, il faut que quelque chose qui lui est propre se perpétue, se prolonge). My translation.

42. I refer here to the typology offered by Gaudreault on filmic narrators, which would need reformulation in order to be practically used by researchers. See André Gaudreault, *Du littéraire au filmique: Système du récit* (Paris: Méridiens Klincksieck, 1988).

CHAPTER 7

Xavier Dolan in India: The Alchemy of Film Viewing

Navaneetha Mokkil

Xavier Dolan's *Laurence Anyways* (2012) has been one of the most debated texts in my syllabus on "Gender and Visual Culture," a post-graduate course I have taught during the last three years at the Center for Women's Studies, Jawaharlal Nehru University, New Delhi, India.[1] The film garnered a range of responses—from bewilderment to fascination, headiness to indignation. When a still image from the film, of the Mona Lisa painting with *liberté* (freedom) scrawled on it, later appeared as a poster for the classroom wall it was clear that the film had made a deep impact on the students. An engagement with the sensual texture of the film—its pulsating music, shaky and intimate camera movements, caress of fabric and burst of colors, the surge and pull of bodies and desires in ceaseless motion—led to discussions on the potential of the cinematic medium and its unsettling explorations of gender, sexuality and subjectivity. This chapter will analyze the dynamic world of Xavier Dolan's cinema, primarily focusing on the formal aspects of *Laurence Anyways* and *Mommy* (2014), in order to explore how Dolan's films engage viewers located in India.

Since 2012 Dolan's films have garnered attention in film festivals in India such as the International Film Festival of India (IFFI), Mumbai Film Festival (MAMI), International Film Festival of Kerala (IFFK), and Bangalore Queer Film Festival (BQFF). *The Navhind Times* places *Mommy* on the list of "Ten Best Films from MAMI 2014" and says that it shows how "actor-director Xavier Dolan has 'prodigy' written all over his work."[2] The 2016 IFFI showcased Dolan's *It's Only the End of the World* (2016) in the "Masterstrokes" category.[3] Publicity materials underlined that *It's Only the End of the World* was directed by the "most exciting contemporary voice in Canadian film"[4] and won the Grand Prix at Cannes. The IFFI blog states "Director

Xavier Dolan was just 25 when he stunned the world with *Mommy* (2014) for which he won the Jury Prize at Cannes."[5] Thus in the film festival publicity materials and media reportage in India, Dolan is celebrated as an auteur, noted for his bold breakthroughs with the cinematic form. These reports underline that he has won accolades in European centers of accreditation such as Cannes and Venice. This shows how European film festivals and awards continue to play a dominant role in shaping the circuits of world cinema. Along with Canadian cultural and economic collaborations with India in terms of film production and distribution,[6] French cultural institutions such as the Alliance Française also play a role in the circulation of Dolan's films in India.[7] The media often celebrates Dolan as a "prodigy" and a "wunderkind." Therefore the tendency to focus on authorship and biography and the presumption of the "director as both generator and locus of meaning"[8] has dominated the reception of his films.

This chapter firmly moves away from those trends by focusing on how the aesthetics of his films is mediated in international scenes of reception. The studies on the global effect of Québec national cinema often circles on European and North American configurations of cinema. I shift the focus to map the hitherto understudied area of the trajectories of Dolan's cinema in the global south.

The reception of Dolan's films in India is linked to the circuits of world cinema,[9] the global expansion of the film festival phenomena,[10] the increasing popularity of film festivals in different contexts in India since the 1990s, digital technologies of film circulation and exhibition,[11] and the emergence of queer film festivals.[12] Multiple film enthusiasts in India traverse the terrains of world cinema along with an everyday embeddedness in film cultures in different languages.[13] The spaces of screening are also quite varied—ranging from single-screen theaters, multiplexes, film festivals, academic institutions, cultural institutions, film clubs, and more private modes of viewing. It is within this vibrant culture of proliferation and consumption of different forms of cinema that Dolan's films meet viewers in India.

While Québec's cultural specificity plays a crucial role in the making of Dolan's films, critical reception also points to its "universality" and "resonance" across cultural borders. Universality is often an opaque category—an epithet deployed as an explanatory framework to explain the success of select films and directors in the international market. My attempt in this chapter is to flesh out the aesthetic dimensions of the "universal" appeal of Dolan's cinema. I will analyze how the repeated thematic and formal concerns of his film, such as the melodramatic rendering of romance and the raw edges of intimacy that disrupt the bounds of "normalcy," reach out to a film-viewing audience in India. I specifically focus on *Mommy*, along with *Laurence Anyways*, because these films offer an entry-point to analyze how the movement of cinema plays a crucial role in creating a corporeal and intimate relation between the spectators and the screen. I draw on recent scholarship that focuses on the sensual and embodied experience of film viewing for my analysis. Jennifer Barker argues that the kinaesthetic, reciprocal, and visceral interaction between the viewer and the "cinematic lived-body," that she describes as the "film's body," can connect the human and the machine in an intimate exchange.[14] Scholars observe how the viewer moves, inhabits and gravitates toward the skin and musculature of the film itself that is cast as a non-human yet animate body.[15] The impassioned responses to *Mommy* (2014) on the part of the audience in the International Film Festival of India (IFFI) 2014 point to the affective dimension of the cinematic experience.

Through an analysis of formal aspects such as editing, cinematography, and mise-en-scène of *Laurence Anyways* and *Mommy* I speculate on how "stutter" and "sweep" become two devices through which we can unpack how an Indian audience might be immersed in the body of Dolan's cinema. The sensual overtones and formal experiments of *Laurence Anyways* and *Mommy* are central to my analysis. I am interested in the varied circuits and scenes of viewing of Dolan's films, such as a classroom or a film festival in India. I attempt to link these experiences of film reception to a range of broader questions about the technology of cinema and its capacity to move viewers in different global contexts. The attempt in this chapter is to engage with conceptions of the viewing body as a located one, embedded in mediated cultures of cinema in different global contexts, and place this in conversation with theoretical approaches that investigate the visceral and reciprocal relation between the viewer's body and the cinematic medium. I try to underline how the body as a cultural formation, laden with specific histories of being immersed in cinematic forms, has to be taken into account even as we draw on scholarship that explores sensory and embodied modes of spectatorship.

THE RECEPTION OF DOLAN'S FILMS

The experience of viewing a film is shaped by the cultural, economic, and political locations of the subjects who encounter a film and also the material space of the screening itself. The power of *Mommy* to make a visceral impact on the audience was palpable as I watched the film during the IFFI 2014 in a packed auditorium in Goa. I could sense the collective tension and exhilaration in the audience and see the shaken faces and bleary eyes as we walked out of the hall, not yet ready to look at each other. All of us were still caught in the vortex of an emotional storm that was difficult to translate into words. Later, the casual conversations on the film in the venue of the festival focused on the formal aspects—especially the impact of the shifts in aspect ratio.

When I taught the "Gender and Visual Culture" course in 2015 and 2017, to a group of ten to twelve students, some of them were familiar with Xavier Dolan's films and had watched *Mommy* since it had come to film festivals and was also available via digital networks. Most of them saw *Laurence Anyways* for the first time during the screening in the classroom. In the syllabus this film was placed along with *Paris is Burning* (1990) and *Qissa: The Tale of a Lonely Ghost* (2013)—two other films that disrupt the binary oppositions of masculinity and femininity and explore the fragmented terrains of desire, embodiment, and subjectivity. The dramatic tenor of *Laurence Anyways*, its over-saturated use of colors, opulent and highly stylized sequences, the use of stimulating music, its quick cuts and "music video" aesthetics, piqued the curiosity of the students and also led to debates on the location of the filmmaker. The sensory overplay[16] was perceived by some students to be an impediment that stopped short of telling a searing story of transgender lives and struggles. This film was also placed in contrast to *Paris is Burning* with its documentary investment in recording the experiences of transgender communities in 1980s New York that centrally engages with questions of race and class. Some of them perceived the spectacular form of the film as a whimsical indulgence available to an upper class, white Canadian filmmaker.[17] In a Women's Studies classroom where there is often an overwhelming tendency to place cultural texts as offering a direct commentary on the social, this film posed a challenge because of its unabashed investment in spectacle and aesthetic experimentation.[18]

In spite of these reservations, many students said that the film drew them in and touched them in ways they did not anticipate. The fantasy sequence of a multicolored butterfly popping out of Laurence's mouth in the scene of parting between Fred Belair (Suzanne Clément) and Laurence Alia (Melvil Poupaud) was an arresting moment that they returned to in conversations after the screening—almost like a visual puzzle that was difficult to contain and give fixed meanings to. When I designed the syllabus through my inclusion of *Laurence Anyways* I aimed to engage with the question of gender, embodiment, and subjectivity—yet, the responses often revolved on the impossibility of romance and how cinema can weave a fabric that wraps us into the pain and pleasure of acts of loving. Questions of location that accentuate the distance between the viewers and the cinematic world of *Laurence Anyways* became less significant when students spoke about the emotionally fraught experience of viewing the film. Rather than framing filmmakers through categories such as nationality and geopolitical location, how can we enter into the body of cinema to speculate on how and why it might affect a wider audience? What are the ways in which the technical devices in Dolan's films cut across cultural and geographical boundaries?[19] I will now explore the aesthetic codes in two of his films to analyze the interlinkages between form, spectatorship, and the cross-cultural networks of cinema. Dolan's films travel and reach out to spectators in different contexts of the world who are embedded in their own ecology of film viewing, aesthetic categories, histories of the body, sexuality, subjectivity, and desire. Mapping the presence of Dolan in India will allow me to point to how the universal is not produced by an erasure of the specificities of local contexts but through the alchemy between different film cultures.

THE CHIAROSCURO OF MELODRAMA

By repeating actors, storylines, and settings Dolan's films create a world that is citational and relational. Recurring tropes in his films pay homage to the genre of melodrama. The powerful emotional impact of Dolan's films is closely connected to how their formalist aesthetics are intertwined with a melodramatic *topos*. From *I Killed my Mother* (2009) to *It's Only the End of the World*, his films draw on and recast the structures of melodrama in thematic and formal terms. Scholars have argued that the "use of emotional excess and the formal and affective elements of a critically denigrated lowbrow genre such as melodrama, conventionally seen as being antithetical to the aesthetic of art cinema"[20] has to be brought in to pry open the "impure" transnational trajectories of the category of art cinema. The tenuous binds of love and responsibility between mothers and sons, the obsessive staging of domestic dramas, the tempestuous sequences of emotional outburst, the recurring scenes of confrontations and reunions, the haunting presence of death, the circular dramas of doomed love—Dolan's films share these tropes that are central to the genre of melodrama in different film cultures. His films also reinvent the generic features of melodrama such as sentimental identification with characters, the sensory opulence of the mise-en-scène, and the stirring use of music and song for "visceral cinematic effect."[21]

In one of the initial sequences in *Mommy*, Steve (Antoine Olivier Pilon) asks for his father's photographs soon after he reaches his mother's new apartment. Soft yellow light suffuses his mother's bedroom as Steve settles into the silk bedspread surrounded by framed photographs of his father, who is no more, and Steve's face is reflected on the photograph of the familial unit from earlier times. The tenderness of this scene is triggered via tropes of familial warmth such as the nostalgic appeal of "family" photographs, and the intimate recall of the caress of the mother's body recreated through the enveloping effect of the bedspread. Steve's gift to his mother, of a shiny necklace with the cursive word "Mommy" fashioned into a pendant, is the hyperbolic, almost kitschy, crystallization of the mother-son bond. But this cocoon of sentiment is splintered as the gift giving ceremony goes awry and ends in a panic stricken confrontation between Steve and Diane (Anne Dorval). Shaky camera movements show a scuffle between the mother and son and as Steve tries to choke Diane in a fit of rage, she grabs a photograph (belonging to the same genre of family memo-ries) from the wall and hits him on the head with it, and the glass splinters. As objects in the house literally come tumbling down we see the intense close-ups of both their agitated faces. In this scene Diane refers to herself as "mommy" and says, "mommy was scared," "mommy isn't mad," "mommy doesn't know what to do anymore." The sequence stages the breakdown of the sentimental universe of domesticity and points to the essential instability of familial roles and bonds.

In *Laurence Anyways*, the relationship between Laurence and her mother Julienne (Nathalie Baye) evolves over the course of the film and traverses the fractured terrains between intimacy and distance. In the scene after Lau-rence breaks the news to her mother about the decision to undergo transition, Julienne walks into the cooped-up space of a rectangular kitchen. We see a back-shot of Julienne's tense body in a black coat as she lights and smokes a cigarette. Laurence enters the kitchen and there are mid-shots of both of them as they exchange heated words—her mother says that while she doesn't care because she suspected all along, Laurence's father will never accept it. She will therefore not open her door to Laurence if she shows up dressed as a woman. But as the conversation continues the mother voices her feelings of hurt and betrayal in a marriage that gives priority only to the husband's needs. The camera moves behind Laurence and there are multiple shots of the two of them in the same frame. The focus seems to be on the space between the two bod-ies tenuously facing each other. As the question of love is posed by Laurence and answered by the mother affirmatively, and in a characteristically ironic fashion, the camera still holds in the same position but the gap is lessened as the mother comes close to Laurence and lights her cigarette. The gap between them lessens and we see a frame in which they smoke together. Later in the film Julienne says that she never saw Laurence as her son: "But I do see you as my daughter." Yet, in the same conversation she does not hesitate to point out that Laurence takes for granted the understanding and care of her girlfriend Charlotte (Magalie Lépine-Blondeau). The interactions between Julienne and Laurence do not reify the roles of mother or son; in fact at one point in the film Laurence remarks that she never saw Julienne as her mother only as a woman who lived in the house.

The melodramatic in Dolan's cinema may engender a range of responses as it encounters different publics. For most viewers in India who are familiar with the form of maternal melodramas in different Indian language films as well as in Hollywood cinema, a film in which the maternal is reassembled might have a powerful appeal. Both these films use emotional registers and corresponding visual and aural tropes that are intimately familiar, but break away from any romantic visions of the mother-son bond and make us come face to face with their raw edges.[22] In fact there are multiple instances in *Mommy* that stage this discordance between the soft-focus visions of motherhood and its heart-numbing realities. The film begins with a statement referring to a new bill (S-14) in a fictionalized Canada in the near future, which allows parents to commit children with behavioral problems to a public hospital without due process of law. Thus *Mommy* locates itself directly in the governmental structures of biopower. The opening shot of the film shows a bucolic scene on a sunny day, clothes drying on the line, an apple orchard and a blurred shot of a woman's hand reaching out to pluck a ripe apple. The camera pans slowly over her body and then shows us Diane's face as she closes her eyes and smells the air. The title of the film, *Mommy*, comes soon after this sequence. This opening scene of plenitude is in sharp contrast to the penultimate sequence of the film where Diane breaks down and weeps in an inconsolable and uncontrolled fashion after committing Steve to the mental health institution. The camera is unflinching as it shows us the messy contortions of her face and her flailing hand gestures as we bear witness to her unraveling. This sequence is so hard-hitting because of the contrast built within the film that recalls "invincible"[23] and beatific visions of motherhood as in the opening sequence. Thus both *Laurence Anyways* and *Mommy* draw on the tropes of motherhood that are central to the genre of melodrama, but the maternal is stretched, dismantled, and recast as we inhabit the gaps and excesses of dominant figurations of femininity.

THE STUTTER IN *MOMMY*

Dolan creates a cinematic form of movements that break the linear flow of time in order to recast the idioms of desire and intimacy. The techniques in Dolan's films, that stagger or accelerate time, inject a sense of instability into the viewing experience. Cinematography and editing, such as abrupt zooms, a still frame, or a sudden shift in aspect ratio, can physically jolt the viewer and produce a multisensory impact. One of the main characters in *Mommy*, Kyla (Suzanne Clément), the perceptive neighbor who steps into Steve and Diane's troubled lives, stutters when she speaks. In this section, I draw attention to how Kyla's stutter and the effect it has on viewers and listeners, both inside and outside the film text, is emblematic of the dynamics of Dolan's cinematic style and its capacity to reach out to a wide audience. The formal staging of stutter in *Mommy* positions the viewer as vulnerable and open to a multisensory encounter with cinema—this cinematic mode could be central to the potential of *Mommy* to reach out to a varied audience. I link the narrative function of Kyla's stutter to the movements in the film's body that immerse the spectator in the embodied experience of film viewing.

Kyla's stutter becomes a bridge between the teenager Steve, who is diagnosed with ADHD and other emotional problems, and has been sent back to live with his mother after he is evicted from the juvenile rehabilitation center, and Kyla, who is on leave from her teaching job and caught in a web of sadness and alienation. In the constant flow of clashing music and loud expressions of love and rage between Steve and his mother, Kyla's "partial aphasia"[24] forces a sense of calm and quietude as both mother and son have to pause to let her enunciate. In a climactic sequence, toward the end of the film, when Steve cuts his wrist, and lies, bleeding, on the supermarket floor, the jerky camera movements show Kyla rushing toward him. This is cut to an extreme close-up and we see the torsion in her facial and throat muscles caused by the physical pressure of calling out for help. In this scene speech is interlinked with other sensations such as tactility. Steve, keeled over on the floor, says through his pain: "you can do it, just say the fucking words." Thus even in this scene that marks the denouement of Steve's shattering recognition that he cannot function within the available social network, Kyla's struggle to vocalize forces him to enter into the circuit of speech and language.

We pause when we speak, but a stutter is an unsettling pause where the speaker labors to produce the next word and that labor is made evident. A stutter makes us acutely aware of the mechanics of speech; it dislocates vocalization from any presumption of "naturalness" or "ease."[25] It disrupts the durational rhythm of speech and slows it down, creates pregnant silences, half-words, garbled sounds, and repetitions. This struggle to enunciate can produce an intensely interdependent relationship between the speaker and the listener. Can the camera stutter? Can editing styles compel us to lean into the body of the film to watch it with such care that we feel our anticipation and participation is essential to making the film unfold? Formal devices of what I would like to term as "cinematic stuttering" may play a crucial role in global practices of reception of Xavier Dolan's *Mommy*.

I use a term linked primarily to practices of vocalizing but expand its critical potential to think about the "stutters" in cinema and how they produce embodied modes of spectatorship. Cinematic stuttering disturbs the seamless stitching together of sequences that is characteristic of classical narrative cinema.[26] For example, the abrupt and sharp zooming in and out of the camera in the direct interview sequences in *Heartbeats* (2010) make us register the presence of the camera and interject a disruption in a single take. In *Mommy* there are two instances that stage the dramatic shift of the aspect ratio from the unconventional square box (1:1 ratio), the format that Dolan uses for most of the film, to the standard widescreen ratio. In an iconic moment in this film, written about by multiple critics and reviewers, skating on a wave of happiness and a feeling of belonging we see Steve literally push the edges of the box screen to make it widescreen.[27] This formal transition jolts the viewer, who is carried away by the tactile capacity of the film to open up before our eyes. The moment also arrests our gaze and makes us aware of our relation to the

Figure 7.1 Fantasy sequence in *Mommy*.

cinematic screen and how our affective responses are determined through the materiality of cinema.

In a long fantasy sequence toward the end of the film we see Diane imagining a golden future for her son—graduation, college admission, a girlfriend, and a marriage ceremony all shot in soft and iridescent colors (Figure 7.1). The uplifting piano score sutures these scenes together as we traipse through them.

The shift in aspect ratio in this sequence contributes to a heady feeling of hope, but also signals how these scenes fit into the scale of a domestic drama of aspiration, heterosexuality, and success within which both Diane and Steve cannot be housed. Thus the technical modes are tied to the power of this film to make the spectators intimately encounter relationships and subjectivities that do not fit into the standard format. Toward the end of the sequence the camera pans over the orange silhouette of Diane's face and the aspect ratio shifts again. The screen shifts back to the square box (1:1 aspect ratio). The fantasy ends and we wake up to find Diane at a traffic light. Steve tells her that the light has changed to green. The camera moves to the front of the car and we see the worried exchange of looks between Kyla and Diane. This cuts again to a shot of Diane's hand as she drives on. Suddenly there is an abrupt cut to a blank screen—a microsecond of blackness followed by another shot of the car now being driven to the mental health facility where Steve is admitted against his will.

The black screen functions as a sharp tear in the fabric of the film after which the brutal reality of governmental structures of law and health care take over. "I sent him there because I have hope," Diane later tells Kyla. But the editing of this sequence pushes us to inhabit the dark zone between hope and hopelessness. It is through these staccato movements that Dolan's films compel viewers to immerse themselves in an excruciating and intense world of relationships. In viewing Dolan's films we are placed in the scene of bodies, desires, and affects that cannot be contained within pre-existing edifices. As Rancière observes:

> The film mobilizes forms to work bodies up into a frenzy, to use pathologies and language to create something like a choreography . . . It is an emotional cinema that plays on the surplus of emotions, with this "hyperactive" teenager who explodes the normal functions of bodily gestures in cinema. There is a direct—or at least unsaid—play of physical emotions, which the viewer needs to reinvent.[28]

Rancière suggests that the frenzied choreography of this film triggers an overflow of emotions and places viewers in a realm that exceeds the bounds of normalcy. The corporeality of uncontained bodies is captured through the formal gestures of the cinema itself.

In *Mommy* there are particular sequences when movement is arrested,[29] such as when Diane, Steve, and Kyla pose for a group selfie during an effervescent lunch party. We see a slow motion sequence as they playfully try out different poses and then the camera holds still as they hold the pose while Steve takes the photo. There is a repetition of the same composition later as the two women drag a bleeding Steve out of the supermarket after his suicide attempt. From the quick movements of the camera in the earlier sequence, now the pace is intensely slow. The mournful piano score accentuates the stasis of the sequence. The camera tracks backward extremely slowly while holding these three bodies in the frame, stretching the dimensions of time to produce an intense sense of claustrophobia and desperation as if there is no escape, no possibility of redemption for subjects that are marked as disorderly and delinquent. On the other hand, sometimes the film picks up a giddy pace—as in the sequence when Steve is on the longboard and Diane and Kyla are cycling, and as we watch we see him accelerate to widen the aspect ratio of the film. We respond to these sequences by being immersed in the sheer movement of the body of the film that pulls us along or makes us stay still. The frenetic energy of Steve and his mother contrasts with Kyla's silences and unspoken sadness—but together they create a universe that compels the viewers to reinvent their own emotional registers. The choreography of the film creates a force field through which the spectators participate in the labor of fleshing out worlds that dismantles the frames of normalcy.

THE BREATHLESS SWEEP OF *LAURENCE ANYWAYS*

Questions of memory, the reworking of tropes of romance, and the play with cinematic movements could be central to the ways in which *Laurence Anyways* captures the imagination of film viewers in India. Falling leaves, tumbling clothes, cascading waterfalls, the shower of snow, the swish of coats, the dance of tassels, the rain of kisses, bodies and emotions colliding and becoming new—every time I watch *Laurence Anyways* I catch my breath as I try to keep up with its pace. Reflecting on how certain films can inspire and draw us in Jennifer Barker writes:

> A "breathtaking" film not only makes us gasp in astonishment at what we're watching; it also takes our breath in and gives it back to us in cinematic form. We take in its color, light, movement, drama, music, violence, eroticism, grandeur, intimacy or immensity, for example. At the same time and in the same, bi-directional movement, we express these qualities back to the film in our own human form, and the film draws these things from us.[30]

Thus, Barker argues that this intersubjectivity between the viewer and the viewed can open up something larger than either film or viewer.[31] This bidirectional and constitutive relation between the film form and the viewer is central to my analysis of *Laurence Anyways*.

The film begins with a conversation without a corresponding visual image—a question and an answer:

> "What are you looking for, Laurence Alia?"
> "I'm looking for a person who understands my language and speaks it. A
>   person who, without being a pariah, will question not only the rights
>   and the values of the marginalized, but also those of the people who
>   claim to be normal."

We move into the opening sequence of the film where we see a window with white translucent curtains fluttering in the wind—the camera slowly moves backward to capture the light that seeps in through the curtains. An opening shot that reminds us of the magic of cinema itself, its power to capture the moving play of light and shadows and make it come alive on a screen. This meditative frame is followed by the slow wandering of the camera that shows us different parts of the interior of a house that we see through closing doors and door-hangings. This is a sequence that makes us aware of our position as spectators and voyeurs peeping into private spaces.[32] This is cut to close-up shots of a series of people staring at the camera. But soon we realize that these could be stares of curiosity, shock, bewilderment, or disgust directed at Laurence. The close-up shots are intercut with shots of Laurence—but she is shot from the back, covered in a mist of smoke or from a distance. Even as the camera moves closer and zooms in on the back of her head, it is cut to another long shot before we can see her face. At that instance the spectator is also made aware of our desire to see, categorize, and unveil the bodies we encounter in the street and on the screen. The relational practices of looking and remembering are central to the opening sequence of *Laurence Anyways* and it is integral to the structure of the film.

In the director's statement on *Laurence Anyways*, Dolan notes: "my film is an homage to the ultimate love story: ambitious, impossible, the love we want to be sensational, boundless, the love that we don't dare hope for, the love that only cinema, books and art provide."[33] Thus love for cinema and the utopic terrains of romantic love are tied together in this film. If the stutter becomes the critical device I use to explore the dynamics of *Mommy*, the epic scale of *Laurence Anyways* forges a cinematic style that is marked by a breathless sweep. It is a film that works through the dynamics of interconnections, memory, and relationality. Tracking a decade of transformation in the life of the poet and teacher Laurence Alia as he/she transitions from man to woman, and her attempts to keep alive her romantic relationship with Fred Belair, this film is circular in its form. It is organized as chapters in Laurence's life, with the year appearing in block letters like the title of a book chapter and time-periods are codified via the bridge of memory and story-telling as the narrative is framed through an interview. Thus it draws the spectator in through habits of viewing cinema as well as practices of reading and listening.

In discussions and interviews Dolan states that he is more influenced by still images in magazines than by films and has had limited exposure to "serious films."[34] Yet, the experience of watching this film reverberates with memories of other films. For a film enthusiast in India who is exposed to different bodies of global cinema there might be multiple axes of entry into the world of this film. One of the primary modes of mediation is through the works of other filmmakers who have a dominant space in the circuits of world cinema in India such as Rainer Werner Fassbinder, Pedro Almodóvar, and Wong Kar-wai. For example, the specific techniques in *Laurence Anyways*, such as the "affective charge and meanings"[35] conveyed through the use of color, throb with visual echoes of Wong Kar-wai's signature style. This is a style that has made an impact on Indian filmmakers, with films such as Anurag Kashyap's *Dev D* (2009), which deploys over-saturated color schemas that correspond to each character's story.[36] Thus, *Laurence Anyways* draws in viewers through connections with other filmmakers who conjure up the fragile world of ceaseless and impossible desires. The drama of doomed romance is an intimately known terrain to film viewers in India through their recurring habitation of the shimmering space of love as an embodied experience, as well as a sphere of fantasy staged in multiple Indian films.[37] The performance of desire in *Laurence Anyways* draws on the conventions of romance in different film cultures and reinvents it.

The aesthetic of the film hinges on the trapeze acts of relationality; the framing and editing works in such a manner as to produce a tense dynamic between reaching toward and distancing. This dualism of connection and gap, absence and presence is key to the composition of multiple frames in the film. In the tense meeting in a café where Fred tells Laurence that she has met another man and has decided to move to another city and break her ties with Laurence, the shots are framed in such a way that the impression of one person impinges upon the another. In a scene of seeming dissolution of their relationship, their entanglement with each other is retained via the visual frames that literally hold them together even as the words and acts tear them apart. Thus the composition of the frames places the spectator in the space of the relational, which is at the same time one of possibility and that of intense yearning. Instead of a linear flow of events where bodies pull apart never to meet again, in the world of this film, the repetition of gestures, objects, and scenes smudge this supposition of linearity.

Each frame triggers multiple associations with other visual media experiences that range from cinema to advertisements, such as the closing shot of the scene of confrontation between Laurence and Fred after he/she tells her about the decision to transition. In the final shot Laurence kneels down near Fred, hands clasped together in a gesture of desperation as Fred sits down on the floor looking defeated.

The camera focuses on this spellbinding tableau of flesh and clothing, the stylized image looking like it is right out of a glossy fashion magazine. Laurence's upper body is naked and Fred is drenched in a plethora of colors: red hair, a tri-colored top with blocks of pink, orange, yellow, green and a peacock blue jacket. Even as we witness the emotional outburst, the throbbing play of colors and textile adds another layer to this dynamic. We are not merely participating in the drama of the relationship but we are also dazzled by the sensory quality of this romance. What we see and feel on screen itself triggers desire. After a long period of separation Fred reads the book of poetry penned by Laurence while sitting in her well-ordered beige and cream living room. The words of poetry acquire a multisensory quality as the camera slowly zooms in and we hear the sound of gushing water. A cascading waterfall washes over Fred capturing the overpowering force of her desire for Laurence. This is repeated in other sequences in the film that mark their coming together and tearing apart—the slow motion sequence in the dreamscape on the Isle of Black in 1996 where multicolored clothes float in the air and fall on the jubilant faces of Fred and Laurence, dressed in rich purple and blue with hints of red; golden autumnal lighting, bursts of wind, and a cascade of falling leaves as Laurence and Fred meet and part toward the beginning of a new millennium. In all these sequences, the vibrant colors, and sensuous setting propel the viewers into the scene of desire. Thus cinema's sensory capacity to immerse the viewers in a passionate relationship with what unfolds before them and to rekindle memories of other scenes of on-screen romances meld together in their experience of watching *Laurence Anyways*.

Therefore the reception of *Laurence Anyways* by an Indian audience works through multiple processes. Viewers might place Dolan's film alongside other noted filmmakers of "serious" cinema, but also within popular depiction of doomed romances in films such as *Titanic* (James Cameron, 1997). The visual and tactile presence of certain larger-than-life objects fills the screen and bears the weight of shifting scenarios in *Laurence Anyways*. The repeated use of the chandelier in the party sequence where Fred breaks out of her lonely and depressed state and makes a grand entry into the Cinébal is a case in point. In this high-decibel party, Fred's sheer sequined dress is synchronized with the gigantic chandelier in the party hall. The dissolves between the scene of the party and the battered Laurence sitting alone in a bus is done using shots of the chandelier as a transition device. Fred and Albert's (David Savard) embrace melts into the body of the chandelier, the vision of this shimmering ornament of light and glass parting and melding the worlds of Fred and Laurence. This use of opulent objects, made of glass or mirrors, synchronized with shimmering costumes is an oft-used technique in popular Indian cinema especially in dance sequences that are performances and celebrations of romantic desire. So memories of archetypal scenes of romance from other film cultures also bleed into the experience of watching *Laurence Anyways*. The citational quality of the film and its capacity to trigger memories of cinematic spaces that are saturated with the pulsating energies of romance itself cuts across different worlds of cinema.

CINEMA THAT MOVES US

The transnational circuits of Dolan's films show that cinema draws its power, not because it addresses and moves different audiences in the same way, but because it can use formal devices to tap into the embodied histories of different film viewers. I explore how the reception of *Laurence Anyways* in India hinges on the breathless sweep in the film, its capacity to place us in relational spaces, and its ability to invoke and reanimate the sensory repositories of film viewing. In my analysis of the viewing experience of *Mommy* I draw on theories of embodied practices of spectatorship and the sensory and reciprocal relationship between the viewer and the mechanisms and technical instrumentation of cinema. I point to how the choreography of this film is pivoted on stuttered movements that immerse the viewer and position him or her in a vulnerable relation with the "film's body." I also examine how both these films are centrally concerned with the relational structures of memory and recast the genre of melodrama by taking us to the stark and serrated terrains of motherhood.

While teaching *Laurence Anyways*, when the question of difference is foregrounded, broad categories such as "nation" and "queer" are brought in to quickly categorize the film and its maker. These categories often do not give us the space to account for practices of viewing in different global contexts that are embodied and intimate. For some of the students in the class that I taught in 2015, the image of the Mona Lisa with *Liberté* (Freedom!) scrawled on it beckoned to them in ways that made it travel back as a memento—a poster in the classroom. Tracking the material circuits of Dolan's films allows us to record embodied histories of affective processes of cinematic engagement. My aim in this chapter has been to speculate on what produces this chemistry between the screen and the viewers as Dolan's films find a space within different communities of viewers in India, whether in a classroom, digital media networks of cinephiles, or film festival audiences. From cinematic stuttering to breathtaking sweeps, from the reinvention of melodrama to the recasting of mother figures, from memories of romance to memories of cinema, there are tantalizing ways in which Dolan's films animate the spectators in India.

NOTES

1. Coming into being in 1969, this is one of the most significant universities in India that has students from all parts of the country.
2. Sachin Chatte, "10 best films from MAMI," *Navhind Times* (Goa), October 24, 2014. Available at <http://www.navhindtimes.in/10-best-films-mami/> (accessed October 12, 2017).
3. This category of films is described in the IFFI catalogue as the "latest essays from world cinema's most celebrated auteurs." Available at <https://iffigoa.org/2016-international-cinema-catalogue/> (accessed October 1, 2017).
4. This was the description given on the IFFI blog in 2016 of the films in the Masterstrokes category (accessed October 1, 2017).
5. IFFI, "12 Cannes 2016 film to be screened at IFFI Goa 2016" (blog). Available at <http://iffigoa.org/12-cannes-winning-films-screened-iffi-goa-2016/> (accessed October 2, 2017).
6. "Canadian producers in Canada-India Business Council," *On Screen Manitoba*, November 10, 2014. Available at <http://onscreenmanitoba.com/canadian-producers-in-the-canada-india-business-council/?doing_wp_cron=1539521920 .1354639530181884765625> (accessed October 1, 2017).
7. Local cultural events website announces *Laurence Anyways* screening in March 2016 at the Alliance Française, in Hyderabad, "The Mint Planner, 4 March 2016," last updated March 17, 2016, 1:41 IST. Available at <http://www.livemint.com/Leisure/

d2K366wVC62QPNtrvPT94N/The-Mint-Planner-4-March-2016.html> (accessed October 6, 2017).

8. Mark Betz, *Beyond the Subtitle: Remapping European Art Cinema* (Minneapolis: University of Minnesota Press, 2009), p. 8.

9. The concept of world cinema "contributes to the work of redrawing the maps of cinema, of cinema as an experiential space, of cinema as an object of affect and perception, and of cinema as a cultural object." Vinzenz Hediger, "What do we know when we know where something is? World cinema and the question of spatial ordering," *Screening the Past*, 21, 2013, p. 5. Available at <http://www.screeningthepast.com/2013/10/what-do-we-know-when-we-know-where-something-is-world-cinema-and-the-question-of-spatial-ordering/> (accessed March 2, 2017). For an expanded discussion of the category of "world cinema" see: Dudley Andrew, "An atlas of world cinema," *Framework*, 45/2, Fall 2004, pp. 9–23; Thomas Elsaesser, *European Cinema: Face to Face with Hollywood* (Amsterdam: Amsterdam University Press, 2005); Stephanie Dennison and Song Hwee Lim (eds), *Remapping World Cinema: Identity, Culture and Politics in Film* (London: Wallflower Press, 2006).

10. Marijke de Valck, *Film Festivals: From European Geopolitics to Global Cinephilia* (Amsterdam: University of Amsterdam Press, 2007).

11. Biswas discusses the new cinephilia that has emerged in the last two decades of people gathered around the LCD projector and DVD player and holding screenings in small groups that has produced a younger generation of viewers "who are conversant with contemporary films from across the world" as members of DVD sharing groups and Bit Torrent harvesters. Moinak Biswas, "Teaching Film Studies in India: curricula and crises," *Journal of the Moving Image*, 2012, p. 17.

12. From the 1990s queer film festivals have been organized in different parts of India and they have become more established since 2010.

13. Analyzing the regional configurations of cinephilia in India, Ratheesh Radhakrishan observes: "the cinephile and the film festivalgoer are co-constituted with a notion of 'world cinema,' as formed in and through the contingencies of their cultural/geographic/political location." Ratheesh Radhakrishnan, "Kim Ki Duk's promise, Zanussi's betrayal: film festival, world cinema and the subject of the region," *Inter-Asia-Cultural Studies*, 17/2, 2016, p. 210. Thus there is no homogeneous film viewing culture or archetypal cinephile that cuts across different locations in India. In this chapter my observations are based on the circulation of Dolan's films primarily through film festivals, DVDs, piracy networks, and screenings at cultural and educational institutions. Therefore, I refer to a privileged group of film viewers who have access to such spaces and technologies. Rather than solidifying the "Indian film viewer," my attempt is to explore how Dolan's films find a place in the heterogeneous film culture in India.

14. Jennifer M. Barker, *The Tactile Eye: Touch and the Cinematic Experience* (Berkeley: University of California Press, 2009), p. 9.

15. Vivian Sobchack, *The Address of the Eye: A Phenomenology of Film Experience* (Princeton, NJ: Princeton University Press, 1992); Laura U. Marks, *Touch: Sensuous Theory and Multisensory Media* (Minneapolis: University of Minnesota Press, 2002); Barker, *The Tactile Eye*.

16. Multiple reviewers also categorize *Laurence Anyways* as an "enormous (excessive?) audio-visual outpouring." Leigh Singer, "Ten great modern films shot in Academy ratio," *British Film Institute*, updated August 10, 2017. Available at <http://www.bfi.org.uk/news-opinion/news-bfi/lists/10-great-modern-films-shot-43-academy-ratio> (accessed October 2, 2017).

17. The specific contours of Dolan as a filmmaker do not enter into the present discussion where he is primarily positioned as a "Canadian filmmaker." The questions about his Québec identity and how that informs his cinematic universe are brushed aside in his categorization as a "Canadian auteur" in publicity materials in India. The slippages in the process of how "Québec and other cinemas navigate between (would-be) 'major' and 'minor' configurations of nationhood" acquire new dimensions when we look at sites of reception in India where Dolan's films are still subsumed within the overarching framework of Canadian cinema. Bill Marshall, "Interview with Bill Marshall," interview by Kester Dyer, Andrée Lafontaine, and Fulvia Massimi, *Synoptique*, 4/2, Winter 2016, p. 117. Available at <http://synoptique.hybrid.concordia.ca/index.php/main/article/view/127/139> (accessed May 10, 2017).

18. This film was shot in the squarer aspect ratio of 1:33 often termed "Academy ratio." Leigh Singer describes this as a bold gesture by a director who sets out to make a film "so operatic in its emotional register . . . that it sometimes feels that anamorphic widescreen would scarcely be enough to contain it, let alone the cropped aspect ratio." Singer, "Ten great modern films."

19. Ashish Rajadhyaksha, "Why film narratives exist," *Inter-Asia Cultural Studies*, 14/1, 2013, pp. 62–75. Rajadhyaksha observes that in Paul Willemen's conception of the project of comparative film studies, the transposition of narrative-technical devices across different cultural locations is of crucial significance.

20. Manishita Dass, "The cloud-capped star: Ritwik Ghatak on the horizon of global art cinema," in Rosalind Galt and Karl Schoonover (eds), *Global Art Cinema: New Theories and Histories* (Oxford: Oxford University Press, 2010), p. 249.

21. Christine Gledhill, Introduction to *Gender Meets Genre in Postwar Cinemas*, ed. Christine Gledhill (Chicago: University of Chicago Press, 2012), p. 9.

22. Another direction of analysis that is beyond the scope of this chapter is about how Dolan's films are embedded in queer film cultures in India. His films circulate within queer film festivals and informal screenings by queer collectives. One can find similarities between Dolan's cinematic explorations and autobiographical documentaries from India such as *Summer in my Veins* (Nish Sharan, 1999) and *Snapshots from a Family Album* (Avijit Mukul Kishore, 2004) that explore the terrains of queerness and the formations of the family. For an analysis of the circuits of world cinema and queer film cultures in India, see Navaneetha Mokkil, "Queer encounters: film festivals and the sensual circuits of European cinema in India," *Studies in European Cinema*, 15/1, 2018, pp. 85–100.

23. In the beginning of the film the director of the detention center asks Diane whether she has considered the provisions available under the S-14 law to commit her son to a public hospital and Diane replies, "I'll never do that to my son." The director answers, "Don't consider yourself invincible—loving people does not mean you can save them. Love does not have a say unfortunately." This is a statement that comes back to haunt us at the end of the film.

24. Jason D'Aoust, "The queer voices of Xavier Dolan's *Mommy*," *European Journal of American Studies*, 11/3, 2017, p. 17.

25. Jason D'Aoust argues "it is precisely the notion that voices are 'natural' with static and stable identities that produces the cultural biases that endure and continue to foster discrimination against people who do not identify with normative vocalities." Ibid. p. 10. The breakdown of "normative vocalities" is a significant way in which the film stages the affinity between Kyla and Steve.

26. Discussing the category of art cinema and how it is experienced by its audience Mark Betz underlines how this cinema renegotiates "the formal mimicry of the subjective experience of time—as flying, as dragging—the cinematic representation of which invites, compels

the viewer to reflect on the time of the film itself, and, by association, cinema itself." Mark Betz, *Beyond the Subtitle*, p. 6. Thus my analysis of Dolan's films needs to be placed within studies on forms of cinema that "work[s] the extremes of the temporal-spatial-narrative continuum" (ibid. p. 5), aesthetic construction and spectatorial engagement.

27. Digital media sites on cinema in India also note the impact of this scene, one blogger calling it "the show stealer." Moifightclub, "VTOD: Dharam Paaji's *Sitamgar* > Xavier Dolan's *Mommy*," F.I.G.H.T C.L.U.B. (blog), October 24, 2014. Available at <https://moifightclub.com/2014/10/24/votd-dharam-paajis-sitamgar-xavier-dolans-mommy/> (accessed August 8, 2017); an article on the open platform *Youth Ki Awaaz* describes the use of the unconventional aspect ratio as a "radical technique" that produces empathy with the characters. Rachit, "A gripping tale about how far a mother would go for her son," *YKA: Youth Ki Awaaz* (blog), 2016. Available at <https://www.youthkiawaaz.com/2016/05/comedy-drama-mommy-xavier-dolan/> (accessed September 27, 2017).

28. Jacques Rancière, "It's up to you to invent the rest," interview by Stéphane Delorme and Dork Zabunyan, *Cahiers du Cinéma*, 709, March 2015, in Emiliano Battista (ed. and trans.), *Dissenting Words: Interviews with Jacques Rancière* (London: Bloomsbury, 2017), p. 298.

29. This is a repeated technique used in Dolan's earlier films such as *I Killed my Mother* and *Heartbeats* when the camera freezes on objects: ceramic cherubs, butterflies, modernist paintings, vintage wallpaper, clothes on a line—still-life portraits in a moving cinematic form.

30. Barker, *The Tactile Eye*, p. 147.

31. Ibid. p. 148.

32. Bill Marshall, "Spaces and times of Québec in two films by Xavier Dolan," *Nottingham French Studies*, 55/2, July 2016, pp. 189–208. Marshall offers a detailed discussion of spatiality in Québec cinema.

33. Xavier Dolan, "Director's statement," official film site. Available at <http://laurenceanywaysthemovie.com/directors-statement/> (accessed July 26, 2017).

34. Xavier Dolan quoted in "Interview: Xavier Dolan," interview by Emma Myers, *Film Comment*, June 24, 2013. Available at <https://www.filmcomment.com/blog/interview-xavier-dolan/> (accessed July 26, 2017).

35. Shohini Chaudhuri, "Color design in the cinema of Wong Kar-wai," in Martha P. Nochimson (ed.), *A Companion to Wong Kar-wai* (Chichester: Wiley-Blackwell, 2016), p. 178.

36. Yellow, pink, and red dominate respectively in different segments of the film. These formal codes in *Dev D*, which is a contemporary reworking of one of the most celebrated tragic love stories in Indian literature and cinema, can be seen as an homage to Wong Kar-wai's aesthetic practices.

37. Moinak Biswas, in his study of the highly popular Bengali film *Harano Sur* (1957), observes that the journey from the familial to the conjugal remains largely unfulfilled in popular Bengali cinema in this period. In fact, he suggests that the lasting popularity of the film is because it finds a way to recognize and articulate the absent space of the couple. Moinak Biswas, "The couple and their spaces: *Hurano Sur* as melodrama now," in Ravi Vasudevan (ed.), *Making Meaning in Indian Cinema* (New Delhi: Oxford University Press, 2000), pp. 122–42.

PART 3

Millennial Auteur

CHAPTER 8

Joy, Melancholy, and the Promise of Happiness in Xavier Dolan's *Mommy*

Mercédès Baillargeon

Melancholia is the joy of feeling sad.—Victor Hugo

Mommy (2014) is the story of Diane (Anne Dorval), nicknamed Die, and her teenage son Steve (Antoine Olivier Pilon). After Steve gets kicked out of the juvenile detention center, where he was institutionalized, Die struggles to provide for and take care of her son. Steve is violent and cruel when he is in one of his fits, even choking his mother in one scene. But when he has calmed down he is sweet and enthusiastic, and possesses a killer charm, not unlike his mother who also has a bit of an explosive temper. Die befriends Kyla (Suzanne Clément), the overly shy neighbor from across the street, a teacher who suffered a nervous breakdown two years prior—the chief symptom of which is stammering—to help homeschool Steve. From then on, it seems as though the three of them set out to do only one thing as they struggle—make it through, keep going, and find a little solace in each other.

It is with his fourth feature film, *Mommy*, that Québec filmmaker Xavier Dolan finally attains a larger critical acclaim. Although he shared the Prix du Jury with Jean-Luc Godard, many, including Dolan himself, have expressed outrage at *Mommy* not winning the Palme d'Or at the Cannes Film Festival that year.[1] This arrogance, or entitlement, is one of the many characteristics that make Dolan a representative of the millennial generation, as decried on the May 2013 cover page of *Time Magazine*, entitled "The Me Me Me Generation." With research to back him up, Joel Stein claims that millennials are "entitled, selfish and shallow."[2] As Malcolm Harris points out, however, "often stereotyped as lazy, narcissistic, entitled, and immature, Millennials are in fact the hardest working and most educated generation in American history."[3] Indeed, although the millennial generation has invested time and money in hopes of living the American dream, neoliberalism has, in fact, failed them in terms of job security, student debt, and upward social mobility. *Mommy*, in this perspective, appears as a tale of neoliberalism's failed promise as its main characters—Die, Steve, and Kyla—try to nurse each other back to a sense of "normalcy," aspiring to the dream of the "good life," while never entirely achieving it. I propose to examine the humanistic dimension of Dolan's film through the lens of affect theory, and more specifically of melancholy as a structural affect in today's neoliberal rat race, of promises made and unfulfilled.

A tension between the dream of the good life, as it appeared during the 1950s and 1960s for baby boomers, and the looming feeling of those days being left behind ties the future to the past; because desire—a drive forward—remains, what we see emerging then is a complicated emotional relationship with time that manifests as melancholy. Looking at Dolan's camp aesthetics of failure, this chapter will examine the tension between joy and melancholy that traverses *Mommy* through both narrative and aesthetic strategies, and steers the film's plot to a seemingly inevitable ending. Using Emily Brady and Arto Haapala's "Melancholy as an aesthetic emotion" as a starting point,[4] I will look at how *Mommy* creates a skewed relationship with time closely resembling that of melancholy—a present-time longing for something in the past, yet also complicating it. I will then present a close reading of a specific scene to demonstrate how Dolan's camp aesthetic plays with our perception of time, all the while conjuring contradictory emotions of joy, loss, familiarity, discomfort, hope, and despair. Lastly, I will show how, though the viewer cannot help but sympathize with the main characters, the "promise of happiness," to use Sara Ahmed's expression,[5] operates as a driving force throughout the film, albeit inevitably leading to disappointment. The complicated relationship of affect and time, through melancholy, established in *Mommy* leads to the confirmation of a mother's worst fears, fears alluded to in the opening scene, which create a sense of fatality that lingers throughout the film. In this way, we will see how Dolan's film is laced with questions of politics, power, legitimacy, and marginalization, which are problematized through aesthetics and formal experimentation.

MELANCHOLY AND TIME

From the outset *Mommy* creates a skewed relationship with time on multiple levels, and sets up a melancholic relationship to the story being told through a distortion of time. In "Melancholy as an aesthetic emotion," Brady and Haapala propose to consider melancholy not from a clinical perspective associated with depression—"a feeling of pensive sadness, typically with no obvious cause"[6]—but as a complex feeling akin to Kant's "sublime." Indeed, melancholy differentiates itself from depression and sadness for two main reasons: first, it comprises both positive and negative aspects, which "involve the pleasure of reflection and contemplation of things we love and long for, so that the hope of having them adds a touch of sweetness that makes melancholy bearable,"[7] and second, it is innately reflective in the sense that "rather than being an immediate response to some object that is present to perception, melancholy most often involves reflection on or contemplation of a memory of a person, place, event, or state of affairs."[8] The fascination that melancholy inspires, in addition to its dual and reflective nature, makes it such that it can be considered an aesthetic emotion.[9] Thus, if melancholy is awakened by thinking in the present about events in the past, *Mommy* constructs a similar, alternative, disjointed temporality through a series of aesthetic and narrative strategies, including speculative fiction, music, and design.

As the opening scene of the film states, *Mommy* takes place in a not-so-distant future in which parents are allowed to institutionalize their children in cases where they have become unable to care for them. In *Mommy*, reality is "speculative" in the sense that, though it *could*, it hasn't yet and might *never*, happen. Some critics argue that this device was unnecessary, that it makes the film overly complicated without bringing much to the story, and that the film would otherwise have made sense without it.[10] Others criticize this as a gauche strategy, the sign of a still weak or immature filmmaker. Some, however, make the case that the kitsch (or even camp) nature of this addition functions to bolster the fictional and speculative dimensions of the film (as opposed to auto-fictional or autobiographical). Indeed, all of Dolan's aesthetic choices feed into a camp aesthetic based on exaggeration, over-stylization, and self-conscious artificiality.

Susan Sontag points out in her 1964 article "Notes on 'camp'" that a term such as camp is hard to define. She proposes to see it as an aesthetic sensibility rather than a concept, and conceives camp largely as "artifice,"[11] a sensibility well portrayed in Dolan's films. With *Mommy*, the director appears to have mastered the art of excess—not only in his use of warm colors (yellow and orange hues), of costume design, acting, and music, but also in terms of language (both Die and Steve have a colorful vocabulary filled with swear words, colloquialisms, and English-language expressions). As Fabio Cleto puts it in the introduction to *Camp: Queer Aesthetics and the Performing Subject*, camp uses "representational excess, heterogeneity, and gratuitousness of references, [which] . . . constitute a major *raison d'être* of camp's fun and exclusiveness," and makes it, in his terms, "an *aesthetic of (critical) failure*."[12] From the outside, camp can often be perceived as artificial, vulgar, or banal to a viewer who is not a part of the code of reference it is borrowing from, or winking at. To be decoded properly, both sender and receiver must share the camp frame of reference, creating a fun interplay within the members of a same group.

Dolan, moreover, is often embraced as a hipster filmmaker,[13] and his penchant for elaborate aesthetics has often been criticized as superficial or kitsch, some critics denouncing his preference of formal exploration over content, social commentary, and narrative development.[14] Sontag claims that "it goes without saying that the Camp sensibility is disengaged, depoliticized – or at least apolitical,"[15] because it emphasizes style over content. I argue that Dolan's camp aesthetic, winking to *passé* trends in popular culture, actually plays an important role in creating a distortion in time, which contributes greatly to the film's melancholic affect. In this regard, one of the most striking aspects of Dolan's film, which generated quite a buzz on the festival circuit, is the film's 1:1 aspect ratio. This uncommon format, likened to that of a selfie,[16] creates a much tighter frame around the characters than used in conventional cinema. The effect is a sense of nervousness akin to claustrophobia, which accentuates the viewer's impression that these characters are caged in—a metaphor signifying how they are prisoners of their problems, be it their struggling social class, or Steve's behavioral and mental health issues. This impression is made all the clearer when Steve physically widens the screen to a conventional aspect ratio, thus signaling his sense of hope and freedom, a sense of relief and anticipation meant to be transmitted to the viewer, but that somehow does not feel quite right.

Though it is explicitly mentioned that the film's actions are placed in the future, there is something fundamentally misleading in the aesthetic choices Dolan makes in this film. CDs, a flip-phone, Die's wardrobe, and the musical soundtrack—including 90s "tubes" from Québec such as "Provocante" by Marjo (1990) and "On ne change pas" by Céline Dion (1999), and international English-language hits like "Colorblind" by the Counting Crows (1999) and "Wonderwall" by Oasis (1995)—are all elements that lead us to believe that the movie is set in suburban Québec in the late 1990s or early 2000s. As Patrick McDermott puts it, "the soundtrack to *Mommy* is a music snob's worst nightmare,"[17] yet it also creates the emotional landscape of the movie as a reflection of these characters' personal crises, which I will discuss further in my scene analysis. For now, let us note that the film's editing alternates between scenes in which discourse plays a crucial part and long scenes in which songs are almost played in their entirety. Some of these scenes, especially the ones where dialogue is prevalent, can be endearing. For example, Die yells from the kitchen, over the radio playing "Provocante" by Marjo, to Steve to turn down the volume of the music in his room. Another amusing exchange between them is when she barges into his room to pick up his dirty laundry and walks in on him masturbating. In others, the screaming is brutal, like when Die confronts Steve over stealing some groceries and a kitschy golden necklace with "Mommy" written in cursive lettering. The exchange turns violent, and she hurts him in self-defense by knocking over a bookshelf before locking herself in a room in the basement. In contrast, the scenes where music is prevalent provide the viewer some respite from the film's emotional intensity.

It has often been mentioned that Dolan is considered to be quite obsessive when it comes to creating complex costume and set designs,[18] and this is no less the case in *Mommy*. Along with these aesthetic choices, the film privileges Québec's vernacular, *joual*, and colloquialisms rather than a more "neutral" or "bourgeois" language; a choice that necessitated French-language subtitles for the larger French-speaking markets. In two separate articles, Jason R. D'Aoust[19] and Pierre-Alexandre Fradet[20] focus on the contentious question of language in Dolan's *Mommy*, identifying it as the root of *Mommy*'s controversial reception, especially in the Québec media. As they both point out, Dolan's use of *joual* walks right into an age-old dichotomy in Québec between high (i.e. with Continental French) and low (popular, vaudeville-type theater) culture and blurs the lines between the two, in line with camp aesthetic.

In addition, Dolan's kitsch aesthetic choices are also meant to be frank representations of an underprivileged social class. In doing this, as he mentions in a *Vulture* interview, one of his biggest difficulties was to avoid making stylistic decisions at the cost of the film's characters and their humanity.[21] Similarly, he explains his costume design by saying that, "given the background and social strata that the characters come from, you can't really imagine that they've gone shopping lately, so we went for that very normcore, fashionless era in history, the early 2000s, which was completely transitional."[22] Thus, Anne Dorval's character "looks cheap," as one would say in Québec, which is a derogatory expression meaning that she is showing too much flesh, and that she looks overdone. Her streaked, dyed hair and fake nails, skin-tight embroidered jeans, and tacky jewelry make her look more like a teenager than a mother in her forties. Added to this is the ambiguous nature of her relationship to Steve, who at times acts more like a father or husband. As he pats dry Die's tears after she loses her job, he tells her, "It ain't our first ride, Diane, is it? Look at me. We gonna be a team. The two of us! I'm gonna control myself and I'll take care of you . . . I'mma protect you,"[23] and kisses her on the mouth on top of his hand, creating one of the film's most iconic images, which appeared both on the movie's poster and DVD cover.

Beyond being a reminder of social class and evoking a kind of nostalgia (especially for the Québécois viewer) for the places, music, and fashion of an earlier (perhaps childhood) era, such aesthetic references to the past create temporal confusions. Rather than placing the viewer in a "real-time" relationship to the action of the film (or the illusion thereof) and letting her share the experience *simultaneously* with the characters as it unfolds, the film adopts what I see as a retrospective perspective, akin to a third-person narration in the past tense. These aesthetic choices thus create a paradox in which the viewer is projected into a fictitious future all the while being given the impression of taking place in the past. From the very retro-kitsch opening notice announcing that Die's destiny is intrinsically tied to the S-14 law—"This is the story of Diane 'Die' Després, a woman whose fate appears to be intimately tied to this affair"[24]—the film creates a *regard de biais*, a sideways glance, suggesting that this is a story that has already been played out. The destiny of its characters has already been sealed, thereby tying the film firmly to melancholy as a retrospective emotion. As such, there exists a *décalage*—a discrepancy—between the story being told (of Die, Steve, Kyla, and the unexpected bond they develop) and the story as it is being recounted. This narrative strategy plays with the distinction made by Tzvetan Todorov between "*histoire*" and "*discours*." Todorov explains:

> At the most general level, the literary work has two aspects: it is at the same time a story [*histoire*] and a discourse [*discours*]. It is story, in the sense that it evokes a certain reality . . . But the work is at the same time discourse . . . At this level, it is not the events reported which count but the manner in which the narrator makes them known to us.[25]

In *Mommy*, the discrepancy between the two not only creates a distance between what is being shown and the viewer's experience, but also gives an impression of fatalism, the viewer witnessing the characters' vain attempts to find equilibrium and a sense of normalcy in their lives.

MELANCHOLY AND EMOTION

Another way *Mommy* wells up melancholy is by combining powerful, yet contradictory emotions. As Brady and Haapala point out, melancholy

> does not involve a single emotion, rather it is an emotion with various shades: a shade of longing; a shade of sadness; and a shade of feeling uplifted, or even a subtle sense of excitement . . . it has both displeasurable and pleasurable shades of feeling.[26]

This can be said of *Mommy* too. There are scenes of hope, pleasure, and joy, as well as scenes of extreme tension, anger, frustration, and complete misunderstanding between the characters. For this reason, the film can be difficult for more sensitive viewers. Die and Steve are constantly screaming at each other, conjuring a sense of total alienation, and yet, despite their yelling matches and Steve's unpredictable temper, they share a lot of love—the kind of love only a mother and son can feel for each other. As Die tells him at the end of the movie, right before driving him to the psychiatric hospital without his knowing,

"A mother doesn't wake up one morning not loving her son. Do you get that?"[27] The use of *joual* and a camp aesthetic of exaggeration also serves to transmit an excess of emotion permeating the film. Emotions run high between Die and Steve, and the film is punctuated with outbursts of love, desire, and anger. "You're always in my head,"[28] says Steve to his mother with excitement, bopping up and down, his arms around her, and words coming out of his mouth at machine-gun speed as they leave the juvenile detention center from which Steve has been expelled. As the social worker who signs off on Steve's release cautions Die, "Don't consider him or yourself invincible. That's the worst thing you could do. Loving people doesn't save them. Love has no say. Unfortunately."[29] And although Die challenges her, telling her that skeptics will be proven wrong, we cannot help but feel that, no matter how hard she tries, this story will not end well. As such, *Mommy*'s affective dimension creates an effect on viewers through contradictory emotions. This is particularly obvious when Kyla stays for dinner after having come over to help in the afternoon after one of Steve's fits of violence, and she gets to know this dynamite mother-son duo. While Kyla and Die are talking in the kitchen, Steve disappears only to come back with his hair slicked back, eyeliner under his eyes, and a mixed CD his father had burnt for them before his death, aptly entitled "Steve + Die 4ever." He puts on Céline Dion's "On ne change pas"—a decidedly camp reference, as Carl Wilson states in his *Let's Talk About Love: A Journey to the End of Taste*[30]—off the album *S'il suffisait d'aimer* (an ironic allusion to the social worker's warning at the beginning of the movie), and starts a dramatic lip synch. As Die, Steve, and Kyla sing along, the song appears to articulate an eerie prophecy:

> We do not change / We simply put the costumes of others on ourselves / We do not change / A jacket simply hides a little of what we see / We do not grow up / We simply get a little taller, just barely / The time of a dream, of a little dream / And touch them with our finger / . . . We do not change / We put on airs and combat poses / We do not change / We do not let it show, we believe / That we make choices.[31]

The lyrics, by iconic French songwriter Jean-Jacques Goldman, foreshadow the film's outcome: as Céline Dion sings, we might think that we can change, that we are self-governed and free-willed individuals, but that is little more than a mere illusion, especially in the case of Die and Steve, who constantly seem to be fighting an uphill battle—against psychology, against the limits of what love can fulfill, and especially, against the contradictory emotions that hold families together while simultaneously threatening their survival.

Dion's song brings the viewer to start wondering if Die's love for her son will be enough to save him. Steve comes over to the kitchen, trying to get his mother and Kyla to dance with him. He dances sensuously with Die, who is wearing a skin-tight black lace top and micro-skirt, touching her breasts from behind. Die laughs it off and tells him that he is not supposed to touch those, and the group carries on dancing and singing. At this point, the camera goes between the characters, which serves as a connection between them—from Steve, to Kyla, to Die, and Steve literally going from one woman to the other. Kyla, despite her speech impediment, seems to finally be finding her voice, singing along to the song, slowly freeing herself from her trauma. Then, in a slow traveling shot, the camera pulls back from the kitchen and shows the trio as they appear united for the first time in the film. The impression this creates is unsettling, combining a feeling of joy (are they not free, and having fun, at last?) and a sense of doom (yes, they are, but for how long?). An uncanny feeling emerges, especially for the millennial Québécois viewer for whom this song is almost inevitably associated with childhood memories. Indeed, for Freud, the experience of the uncanny, which arises when the familiar is experienced as strange or unknown, confronts the subject with unconscious, repressed impulses, and arises in two specific contexts: when the distinction between imagination and reality is erased, and/or through the evocation of infantile complexes (such as the Oedipus complex) and surmounted infantile beliefs[32]—all of which are suggested by Steve's sexualized rapport with his mother as well as his omnipotent, charming, and manipulative ways. The camera pulling away, giving us a *vue d'ensemble*—an overview—of the three characters dancing, creates an uneasy feeling. While we get a sense of togetherness, we simultaneously get the impression that something about this picture is off, that something doesn't feel quite right. What is more, the viewer is left to deal with these contradictory feelings without the filmmaker's intervention. This scene thus showcases what I would call Dolan's "cinéma humaniste," in which the camera, at medium distance, is meant to show an objective, humanizing perspective on its characters by forcing neither viewer identification nor a particular point of view on what is being shown.[33] In this case, Dolan shows without judgment Kyla, Steve, and Die's moments of joy while we are all the while reminded of the fate that will befall them. This strategy allows for the viewer to truly experience the scene, putting the focus on his/her own affective response to the scene—an affective response that summons contradictory feelings of joy and sadness, not unlike melancholy.

MELANCHOLY AND THE "PROMISE OF HAPPINESS"

It is only with the arrival of shy neighbor Kyla that hope of getting their lives back on track appears for Die and Steve. She first intervenes to stitch up Steve's thigh after the first physical altercation between mother and son, subsequently taking on the job of homeschooling Steve while Die is out working. It could seem unusual, almost impossible, that a woman from the suburbs of Québec City, who has recently moved to the Montréal area, would jump in so quickly to help out this odd duo, if it wasn't that Kyla herself is working through her own trauma, her loss, by integrating this ad hoc proxy "family." Indeed, Kyla, who is on leave from work, is an almost mute, ghostlike figure when she is with her own family, distant and detached from her husband and daughter. With Die and Steve though, she starts living again; she laughs, participates, cares about them, and regains her voice, her stutter gradually fading away. After a fight with Steve, the camera shows a picture of a little boy whom we have never seen on her dresser, suggesting that she lost her own son, and that her recovery involves "saving" another boy since she could not save her own. However, rather than taking the psychoanalytical route, which would very well be possible given that psychoanalytical references abound in Dolan's oeuvre, I will take a detour through queer theory and Sara Ahmed's proposition in *The Promise of Happiness.*

Combining philosophy and feminist cultural studies, Sara Ahmed looks at how the individual's desire, or social imperative, to be happy, is actually conditional to the fulfillment of affective, moral, and ideological conditions, chief of which is the belief that we will be made happy by taking part in that which is deemed good, and that by being happy ourselves, we will make others happy. For Ahmed, happiness is a promise that directs us toward certain life choices and away from others, and is promised to those willing to live their lives in the "right" way. Thus, family is often ideologically constructed as a fundamental site of happiness—it is an assured place of belonging, if only one can adhere to the model of (still mostly heteronormative) nuclear family. If Ahmed looks at feminist killjoys, unhappy queers, and melancholic migrants as three categories who are alienated from the family's "promise of happiness," we may add *Mommy*'s ad hoc family as also being excluded from the said promise that the traditional family normally encapsulates. It makes the tragedy of the film's ending—after Steve tries to commit suicide in a big-box retail store, Die decides to have him committed—all the more bittersweet.

One of the most powerful scenes in this film, which is also deeply driven by music, is near the end, as Kyla and Die are driving Steve, unbeknownst to him, to a psychiatric hospital. As Dolan explains, the song, "Experience," by Ludovico Einaudi inspired him to write this scene, which consequently led to writing the whole screenplay.[34] Die daydreams about the future she hopes for her son—we see Steve getting his high school diploma, being accepted at Juilliard, leaving for New York City, and we witness him growing up all the way to his wedding day. The music swirls and accelerates in an almost anxious tone, accentuating the vertigo from the milestones being shown, jumping from one to the next in rapid succession. Out of focus like a dreamscape, the shots show

Die, Steve, and Kyla in close-ups, with a very short depth of image, creating an unsettling feeling of uncertainty since we cannot actually see what is going on around the characters, creating only an impression, a dream, a hope—an affect. Superimposed on this vision, we hear again some dialogue between the three characters—words of love, but also screams of anger. This serves as an eerie reminder that the past is never very far behind, while at the same time it makes us wonder if it is possible to free oneself from the past entirely. As Dolan points out, this scene "is almost oneiric, because it's so positive, it's so optimistic, it's so bright and tacky and perfect."[35] It is so far from their reality, yet, as a viewer, you want to believe this is possible, you want to believe that it is the actual future, and not just a mere fantasy. This not only creates a sense of hope, but also a malaise because we realize that this "perfect" outcome is more likely than not out of reach for the trio. The scene ends with a subjective shot from Die's perspective in which the camera goes around in circles, and what she sees is a vertigo-inducing blur. Then, the camera stops on a close-up of Die's face at Steve's wedding, her expression decomposing, a sense of disillusionment, disappointment, and heartbreak, as if she is realizing that this dream life she constructed for Steve was actually escaping her. Die is called back into reality when a stoplight turns green and Steve asks her where she has been, without knowing that she is, in fact, driving him to a State facility to have him interned, further adding to the heartbreak since the viewer is in the know while Steve is not.

In line with his tendency toward "cinéma humaniste"—a film genre which, according to Michel Estève, focuses on humanistic values of dignity, tolerance, and respect for others, and the Other[36]—one of Dolan's feats is to show Die's dilemma between turning her son's care over to the public authorities, or to keep struggling to keep him safe and to try to care for him *from her perspective*, without any judgment or blame. I believe that Die's lose–lose situation embodies the paradox of "melancholic universalism," which, according to Sara Ahmed, is "the requirement to identify with the universal that repudiates you."[37] Indeed, as Ahmed elaborates in *The Promise of Happiness*, the paradox is that this "promise" actually conceals its own failure; for Ahmed, "the promise of the universal is what conceals the very failure of the universal to be universal."[38] Furthermore, this supposedly "universal" promise of a "good life," to allude to Lauren Berlant's proposition in *Cruel Optimism*,[39] also excludes people that it claims to be including, making it a "cruel optimism" because it can never be more than an unattainable object of desire, a mirage one keeps striving for without ever succeeding, for it is systemically out of reach.

In this case, Die cannot help but wish for a certain kind of "happiness," often seen as "universal," for her son, based on success, self-realization, love, and marriage. A couple of weeks after Steve has been committed to psychiatric care, Kyla comes over to tell Die that she is moving to Toronto the following weekend. She stutters that she cannot abandon her family, implying that it is what her friend did, or that the time they spent together was akin to her "abandoning her family." Die grins, and explains the reasons behind her decision:

> You know, Kyla . . . There's just so many ways to deal. You deal with your life, I deal with mine. That's it. I sent him there because I have hope. I'm full of hope, okay? This world ain't got tons of hope. But I like to think that it's full of hopeful people, hoping all day long. Better off that way 'cause us hopeful people can change things. Hopeful world with hopeless people, that won't get us far. I did what I did, so that way, there is hope. So I win. All the way. It's a win-win. For everybody.[40]

Indeed, it is the prospect of hope—of a happy life, of a future—that leads Die to her decision to have Steve institutionalized. It is as though, once she realizes that she is powerless to help her son, and especially that she is helpless in trying to protect him from himself after his suicide attempt, what Die ends up holding on to is the mere possibility of a better future for Steve, no matter the way, to help herself cope with her own powerlessness. She cannot relinquish the possibility of a happy future for Steve even though the odds at this point are undoubtedly stacked against him. The fact that she insists on the expression "winning"—she wins, everybody wins—also shows close ties with neoliberal values that emphasize success. However, she is very well aware that her situation is far from being that of "a winner," which is shown in her exaggerated reactions, the incisiveness of her monologue, and her need to hide the way she authentically feels (revealed by her meltdown after Kyla leaves). Although she refuses to relinquish her aspirations, it becomes clear that, for people like Die and Steve, the kind of happiness they pursue—which, in this case, is also overlaid with a traditional "redemption narrative," of someone overcoming their personal issues and context to "succeed" against all odds—is not attainable for everyone even though its "universal" dimension seems to imply it is. Kyla gets to escape, returning to her nuclear middle class family after she has worked through her traumatic experience enough to rejoin them, while the film ends on a grim scene in which, after leaving an apology on his mother's voicemail, Steve frees himself from a straightjacket and jumps through a large window at the end of a hospital corridor. All the while, the song "Born to Die" by Lana Del Rey breaks with Dolan's late 1990s and early 2000s aesthetics, and all but prophesies Steve's fate (the title of the song is, after all, "Born to Die"), the film's message seemingly being that there is actually no promise of happiness for people like Die and Steve, who occupy a marginal space (from the perspective of mental health, traditional family, and class) within society, or at least, not in the way that the universalist promise of happiness seems to offer. In the end, it is the coexistence of contradictory emotions, and the contradictions inherent in Die's message of hope and its concurrent undermining by its actual function as bravado, a coping mechanism for guilt and loss, as well as the pain hinted at in Die's face and her exaggerated, forced joy on learning of Kyla's impending move, that make Steve's suicide at the film's end all the more predictable—and bittersweet.

To conclude, I would like to return to Brady and Haapala's definition of melancholy. They write: "when mourning transforms itself into melancholy, when the desperation of a loss has calmed down and is mixed with pleasurable memories, then we have an instance of melancholy, which in itself seems to create an aesthetic context of its own." It appears then that in this tragic story of Die and Steve's struggles to aspire to a certain "promise of happiness" (to reiterate Sara Ahmed) and create a life for themselves, *Mommy* borrows heavily from an aesthetics of melancholy. By enabling a "sideways glance" (*regard de biais*) that distorts past, present, and future, Dolan creates the distance necessary for melancholy to emerge. The film's camp aesthetics, its soundtrack filled with turn-of-the-millennium hits, its timeless, "normcore" costumes, and the use of *joual* all serve to clearly mark these characters' social belonging, as well as their belonging to a time foregone. Language and music moreover serve to exacerbate the raw emotionality of the film, transferred to the viewer through affect, but also with a certain distance precisely because of its complicated temporality. Placed in the future, the film transpires a kind of fatalism, but also carries a sense of hope; a sense of cruelty as well for people who are relegated to a melancholy rapport to universalism because they are not actually included in its narrative. The film's complicated emotions—those of the characters, but also those the viewer is moved to experience—also accentuate a sense of melancholy, the joy of being sad for this beautiful story of a mother's love for her son. In the end, the viewer is allowed to experience the film fully, thanks to Dolan's "cinéma humaniste" which does not offer a judgment over these characters' tragic tale; only a sympathetic gaze to honor their struggle.

NOTES

1. Peter Knegt, "Xavier Dolan gets respect," *Film Quarterly*, 68/2, 2014, pp. 31–6.
2. Joel Stein, "The me me me generation," *Time*, May 21, 2013. Available at <http://time.com/247/millennials-the-me-me-me-generation/> (accessed June 24, 2018).
3. Malcolm Harris, *Kids These Days: Human Capital and the Making of Millennials* (New York, Boston, London: Little, Brown, 2017), back cover.
4. Emily Brady and Arto Haapala, "Melancholy as an aesthetic emotion," *Contemporary Aesthetics*, 1, 2003). Available at <https://contempaesthetics.org/newvolume/pages/article.php?articleID=214> (accessed March 24, 2018).
5. Sara Ahmed, *The Promise of Happiness* (Durham, NC: Duke University Press, 2010).
6. *English Oxford Living Dictionary*, s.v. "melancholy" (n.). Available at <https://en.oxforddictionaries.com/definition/melancholy> (accessed March 24, 2018).

7. Brady and Haapala, "Melancholy as an aesthetic emotion," par. 9.
8. Ibid. par. 12.
9. Ibid. par. 12.
10. Adam Nayman, "Imaginary love: Xavier Dolan's *Mommy*," *Cinema Scope*, 60, Fall 2014, p. 48; Zoé Protat, "L'Amour fou: *Mommy* de Xavier Dolan," *Ciné-Bulles*, 32/3, Summer 2014, p. 10.
11. Susan Sontag, "Notes on 'Camp,'" in *Against Interpretation and Other Essays* (New York: Octagon Books, 1978), pp. 272–89.
12. Fabio Cleto (ed.), *Camp: Queer Aesthetics and the Performing Subject. A Reader* (Ann Arbor: University of Michigan Press, 1999), p. 3.
13. Laure Magnier and Matthieu Amaré, "Xavier Dolan et le cinéma français: amour imaginaire?," *Café Babel*, December 6, 2011. Available at <http://www.cafebabel.fr/culture/article/xavier-dolan-et-le-cinema-francais-amour-imaginaire.html> (accessed March 24, 2018); Alison Willmore, "The 25-year-old filmmaker who's the king of Cannes," *Buzzfeed*, May 22, 2014. Available at <https://www.buzzfeed.com/alisonwillmore/the-25-year-old-filmmaker-whos-the-king-of-cannes> (accessed March 24, 2018).
14. Logan Hill, "*Enfant terrible* Xavier Dolan is a director who really wants to act," *Vulture*, February 25, 2011. Available at <http://www.vulture.com/2011/02/enfant_terrible_xavier_dolan_i.html> (accessed March 24, 2018).
15. Sontag, "Notes on 'Camp,'" p. 287.
16. Peter Bradshaw, "*Mommy* review – outrageous and brilliant, a daytime soap from hell," review of *Mommy*, directed by Xavier Dolan, *The Guardian*, March 19, 2015, 16:00 GMT. Available at <https://www.theguardian.com/film/2015/mar/19/mommy-xavier-dolan-film-review> (accessed September 26, 2018).
17. Patrick D. McDermott, "The soundtrack to 'Mommy' is a music snob's worst nightmare," *Fader*, January 30, 2015. Available at <http://www.thefader.com/2015/01/30/xavier-dolan-mommy> (accessed March 24, 2018).
18. *The Canadian Encyclopedia*, s.v. "Xavier Dolan," last edited March 14, 2017. Available at <http://www.thecanadianencyclopedia.ca/en/article/xavier-dolan/> (accessed March 24, 2018).
19. Jason R. D'Aoust, "The queer voices of Xavier Dolan's *Mommy*," *European Journal of American Studies*, 11/3, 2017. Available at <https://doi.org/10.4000/ejas.11755>.
20. Pierre-Alexandre Fradet, "Le parler québécois, du Roi Soleil à Xavier Dolan," *Positif: revue mensuelle de cinéma*, 674, April 2017, pp. 69–72.
21. Kyle Buchanan, "Xavier Dolan on *Mommy*, art, and his *Harry Potter* tattoo," *Vulture*, January 21, 2015. Available at <http://www.vulture.com/2015/01/xavier-dolan-mommy-interview.html> (accessed March 24, 2018).
22. Xavier Dolan quoted in ibid.
23. *Mommy*, directed by Xavier Dolan (2014, Montréal, Québec; Les Films Séville, 2015), DVD. "Toi pis moé, Diane, c'est pas notre premier tour de char, hein? . . . Moi, je vais apprendre à me contrôler, je vais prendre soin de toi, je vais te protéger, okay?" DVD subtitles.
24. Ibid. "Voici l'histoire de Diane 'Die' Després, une femme dont le destin semble directement lié à cette affaire." DVD subtitles.
25. Tzvetan Todorov, "The categories of literary narrative," trans. Joseph Kestner, *Papers on Language and Literature*, 16, 1980, p. 5.
26. Brady and Haapala, "Melancholy as an aesthetic emotion," par. 24.
27. "Ça arrive pas dans la vie d'une mère qu'elle aime moins son fils, comprends-tu, ça?"
28. "T'es toujours dans ma tête."

29. *Mommy* (Les Films Séville, 2015), "La pire chose qu'on puisse faire à un enfant malade, c'est se croire ou le croire invincible. C'est pas parce qu'on aime quelqu'un qu'on peut le sauver. L'amour n'a rien à voir là-dedans, malheureusement." DVD subtitles.
30. Carl Wilson, *Céline Dion's Let's Talk About Love: A Journey to the End of Taste* (33 1/3) (London: Continuum, 2007).
31. Céline Dion, *S'il suffisait d'aimer*, produced by Erick Benzi and Jean-Jacques Goldman, written by Jean-Jacques Goldman (Columbia Records, 1998).
     On ne change pas / On met juste les costumes d'autres sur soi / On ne change pas / Une veste ne cache qu'un peu de ce qu'on voit / On ne grandit pas / On pousse un peu, tout juste / Le temps d'un rêve, d'un songe / Et les toucher du doigt / . . . / On ne change pas / On attrape des airs et des poses de combat / On ne change pas / On se donne le change, on croit / Que l'on fait des choix . . . (My translation).
32. Sigmund Freud, *The Uncanny* (New York: Penguin Books, 2003), pp. 10–17.
33. Michel Estève, *Un Cinéma humaniste* (Paris: Septième Art, 2007).
34. Knegt, "Xavier Dolan gets respect," p. 34.
35. Xavier Dolan quoted in Michelle Lanz and Cameron Kell, "Xavier Dolan talks about his Oedipal drama, 'Mommy,'" *The Frame*, January 22, 2015. Available at <http://www.scpr.org/programs/the-frame/2015/01/22/41203/xavier-dolan-talks-about-his-oedipal-drama-mommy/> (accessed March 24, 2018).
36. Estève, *Un Cinéma humaniste*, p. 11.
37. Sara Ahmed, "Melancholic universalism," *Feminist Killjoys*, December 15, 2015. Available at <https://feministkilljoys.com/2015/12/15/melancholic-universalism/> (accessed March 24, 2018).
38. Ibid.
39. Lauren Berlant, *Cruel Optimism* (Durham, NC: Duke University Press, 2011).
40. "Die's speech to Kyla," *Mommy*.
     Tsé, Kyla, on a toutes nos façons de dealer. Toi, tu deales avec ta vie. Moi, je deale avec la mienne, c'est de même. Si je l'ai placé là, c'est parce que j'ai de l'espoir, comprends-tu? Que je suis pleine d'espoir, ok? Le monde, c'est une place où qui a pas beaucoup d'espoir. Ben moi j'aime ça penser, qu'il est rempli de monde rempli d'espoir qui espère, qui espère. C'est aussi ben de même parce que à nous autres on peut changer quelque chose. . . . Moi, j'ai fait ce que j'ai fait parce que de même, il y a de l'espoir, ok? Faque je gagne, sur toute la ligne, tsé. Tout le monde est gagnant. . . DVD subtitles.

CHAPTER 9

"I am looking for someone who understands my language and speaks it": Dolan's Excessive Dialogues

Andrée Lafontaine

> I spoke *joual*, and spoke poorly, I swore like a sailor, sometimes talked in English, and often out of turn, I suppose . . .[1]

Dolan's deft use of language is one of the most commonly praised elements of his films. Critics have noted the writer/director's sensitive ear for street talk, his ability to develop powerful verbal sparring, and his gift for rendering "oh-so-real dialogues." In Québec, however, discussions of Dolan's use of language have centered on *jurons*, *Franglais*, and *joual*—that is, his use of profanity, English words, and Québec's popular sociolect. Far from attracting universal praise, Dolan's dialogues have sparked lively exchanges and reignited old debates over the quality of the French language spoken and used in Québec's cultural output. Criticism of Dolan's dialogues, in fact, reverberated in Canada's federal capital, where a Senatorial Committee meeting was called to examine the disbursement of public monies for films displaying poor or "bad" French.[2] Asked to explain his concerns, Senator Ghislain Maltais echoed the opinion of many film critics, stating that Dolan's films are great, but they could be so much better if only he would get rid of this bad habit of excessively peppering French dialogues with English and profanity. "Is there really no way," asked the senator, "to make a film without involving the whole sacristy?" One must ask, however, whether language is just another stylistic excess from a famously excessive director. In this chapter I explore Dolan's creative use of language to argue against this position, showing how code-switching and *joual* are strategically used to establish and break down interpersonal and emotional boundaries. In the first section, I offer an overview of the debate over *joual* in artistic productions, situating Dolan within the context of Québec's linguistic history. In the following three sections, I examine distinct facets of Dolan's dialogues, focusing respectively on the emotional and nostalgic powers of *joual*, its connection to class and motherhood, and Dolan's strategic use of code and register switching.

JOUAL, FROM TREMBLAY TO DOLAN

> Between my mother's language and standard French, I will always choose my mother's language.[3]

Québec has long struggled to define the distinctiveness of its national character. While its French heritage and Catholic roots gave substance to national claims in the pre-modern context, starting in the mid-twentieth century, these stopped being effective means of solidifying the social and political body. As the province gained political, social, and economic autonomy, it focused increasingly on linguistic specificity: the fact that Québec is predominantly francophone (French-speaking). Since the 1960s, the French language has served as a marker of both personal and national identity, and has established a direct link between individuals and community. Consequently, the nascent nationalist project, advocating greater self-determination as well as political, legal, and economic independence from the rest of Canada, defined itself largely as a defense of the French language and of the right of francophones to enjoy full citizenship. Indeed, proudly affirming oneself as a French speaker, and affirming one's right to participate fully in the political, social, and economic spheres *in French*, was an integral part of early nationalist claims.

Despite social consensus over the desirability of establishing French as a common public language, divisions abounded to determine *which* French should serve as Québec's national language—proper, standard French spoken in France and by the elites, or the French spoken on the street and by the working class? Indeed, in addition to not being English, Québec French is also not Continental ("European") French and, by definition, deviates from "standard" French. In the last forty years, several attempts to standardize Québec French have been made (through dictionaries and other reference manuals, for instance), all attracting some level of criticism and acceptability. The point of contention typically concerns how much of Québec's unique *joual* is to be admitted into standard French. "*Joual*" designates various characteristics of Québec French that, while forming a unique sociolect, can be perceived as stigmatizing.[4] *Joual* includes various elements of everyday vernacular Québec French, including slang, archaic words, curses, slurred diction, and Anglicisms. For Jacques Godbout and Henri Wittmann, *joual* essentially designates a type of "Franglais"—a mixture of French and English—spoken mostly in Montréal.[5]

In *La langue et le nombril* (1998) and *Méchante langue* (2011), sociolinguist Chantal Bouchard traces the evolution of Québec French and people's attitudes toward it, which she views through William Labov's concept of *linguistic insecurity*: "the feeling some people have that they can't speak 'well.'"[6] Bouchard's insightful analysis makes two important points: first, Québec French truly became *joual*, complete with Anglicisms, following the British Conquest and the ensuing English language dominance of the legal and economic spheres of society. English words then further penetrated Québec French as workers were forced to use English in the workplace. Through this process there developed two strands of French along class lines: "proper" French, spoken by the elite and the educated, and *joual*, spoken by the working and less educated classes. Bouchard's second point is that the negative opinions toward *joual*, which developed in the 1950s and 1960s, echoed negative opinions toward French Canadians: "French Canadians saw themselves as a dominated people, poor, ignorant and condemned to mediocrity."[7] Their language, by extension, was seen as equally poor; a constant reminder of a lack (of education, refinement, self-mastery), *joual* became a source of shame, something to be hidden and not displayed. Consequently, "the discourse about language could be described as a discourse on identity. Whenever the Québécois talked about their language, they described themselves."[8]

Québec's first recorded linguistic quarrel dates as far back as 1841, when various clerics, teachers, and journalists argued over proper pronunciation and local usage of certain words.[9] Far from receding, these linguistic quarrels intensified throughout the 1960s as the Quiet Revolution was unfolding. In his October 21, 1959 editorial, André Laurendeau, then chief editor of the French-language Montréal daily, *Le Devoir*, ignited the linguistic fire when he complained about the "awful accent" kids were acquiring in school.[10] Within days, Jean-Paul Desbiens, writing under the pen name "Frère Untel," mounted the first systematic critique of Québec students' poor language skills and the overall quality of Québec's education system. Already at its inception, the term was embedded with negative sentiments toward the working class and its children's "contaminating" those from good families through intermingling in the public school system. Under *joual* opponents' penships, dehumanizing words—"barking" (Laurendeau)—and words indicative of disease and death—"gangrene" (Brault), "contamination" (*Grand dictionnaire*), "disability" (Dor) and "decomposition" (Desbiens)—were commonly used to describe the destructive effect of *joual* on Québec culture and society. The situation was so bad, Laurendeau claimed, that some parents were sending their kids to English school; they would rather see French die than hear it being tortured. Given *joual*'s close ties with the working classes and the implicit class dimension of the debate over *joual*, Gilles Lefebvre (1965) and Jean-Claude Corbeil (1976) questioned whether, under the guise of critiquing the use of *joual*, the elites and intellectuals were not in fact criticizing the predominant *users* of *joual*, Québec's working classes.

Joual grew to split Québec intellectuals along lines that defied the simple nationalist/federalist divide. Indeed, *joual* generally divided along class, rather than political lines. *Le Devoir*, the elite paper at the forefront of the Quiet Revolution, was staunchly opposed, and *Parti pris*, the Marxist journal, saw in *joual* a truly national language. While the first saw in *joual* the expression of a colonized people, the latter saw it as a force of de-colonization.[11] Despite its poor press, a handful of artists and intellectuals spoke out in defense of *joual* as a legitimate form of expression. The year 1968 marked the entry of *joual* into the mainstream with the premiere of comedy show *L'Osstidcho*—spoken entirely in vernacular Québec French—and Michel Tremblay's landmark *joual* play about working-class women, *Les Belles-sœurs/The Sisters-in-law*. It certainly was no coincidence that Tremblay chose women to voice his play: in an interview, the playwright explained that *joual* originated with working-class women who were determined to preserve French despite their husbands' increasing use of English.[12]

Contemporary Québec French is, for the most part, "*joualisant*," that is, a grammatically correct French, which integrates some *joual* and vernacular with only minimal efforts to camouflage Québec's distinct accent. Nevertheless, Québec French deviates in significant ways from the French spoken in France, so much so that the "Québécois accent" can make communications challenging between Quebecers and Continental French-speakers. A number of non-standard usages produced by co-mingling with neighboring English have entered common parlance and become part of the Québec lexicon. One is more likely, for instance, to see "hot dog steamé" and "hot dog toasté" than "chien chaud vapeur" and "chien chaud grillé" on menus. Criticism of non-standard French has gradually shifted in recent years from *joual* to Franglais, the mixing of French and English that is most typical of how young Montrealers speak today. Tremblay's *joual*, some have claimed, has been replaced by Dolan's Franglais, and the defenders of "correct" French have redirected their efforts accordingly:[13] like the *joual* of the 1960s, *modern* Franglais is perceived by its detractors as a handicapped expression of a colonized people, with similarly deleterious effects on society.

Today's proponents of standard French lament lazy pronunciation, poor syntax, the declining quality of written French, liberal use of expletives and, finally, the use of Anglicisms and English words. In this sense, the quarrels over Franglais echo Frère Untel's old complaints. In addition to Dolan, other young artists have been criticized for "mauling" the French language with Acadian singer Lisa Leblanc, and hip hop artists Radio Radio and the Dead Obies among the biggest targets of opprobrium in recent years. While *joual* used to be associated with a specific social class—the working class—today's

Franglais is linked above all else with a generation—the millennials. One could argue that, in an ironic turn, Franglais is in fact a by-product of Québec's efforts to promote French as a national language. Indeed, the Franglais generation is also the "Bill 101 generation." Adopted in 1977, Bill 101 made schooling in French mandatory not only for francophones but also for school-aged immigrants and/or their children, ensuring their integration in wider society and the sustainability of the French language in Québec. In an open letter addressed to his detractors, Yes Mccan (then Dead Obies member) explains that the Franglais used in their music is a reflection of the multilingual environment in which the band's members grew up and of their understanding of Québec identity: "Some of the Dead Obies were raised by a francophone mother and an anglo[phone] father, or vice versa." Echoing Mccan's account, linguist Mela Sarkar further notes the inclusive character of multilingual Montréal rap: "Montreal rap proposes a new model of social belonging which takes into account the complex linguistic, ethnic and racial reality considered taboo in dominant discourse."[14]

In this context, the deluge of criticism of Franglais, which inundated the Québec press after 2010, took on additional generational and national connotations, not to mention moralistic overtones. Franglais is lamented by its detractors as a neo-liberal phenomenon unique to the younger, urbanite set, a generation who blindly celebrates diversity and a naïve openness to the world. Commenting on her failure to pass on to her son her own deep commitment to the French language and to her roots, Josée Blanchette recently expressed surprise that her fifteen-year-old son, "who lives in a squeaky-clean White South Shore suburb," would be so fluent in "back alley" creole and Arabic-influenced French slang.[15] The intermingling, once again, is disturbing. When it comes to Dolan, what shocks many is precisely the fact that those characters in his films who use *joual* are *not* working class: it was okay for Tremblay to have his working-class characters speak *joual*, but Dolan's are from middle-class suburbs, and therefore have no business trading in *joual*.[16] "Colonized people" are very different today, notes sociologist and columnist Mathieu Bock-Côté: "they see themselves as the cream of the globalized crop, and they speak both English and French to let us know. Using Franglais, they send a signal: we are Cosmopolitans."[17]

While Dolan and he are only eight years apart, it is as if, as Bock-Côté puts it, several generations stand between them.[18] This younger generation, "brainwashed by talks of globalization and postmodernity, mindlessly abandons its national anchors and errs pointlessly in a soft, spineless society."[19] Using Franglais, according to Bock-Côté, is at once snobbish and foolish: "to dissolve the conqueror's language into one's own, like sugar cubes in coffee, is to elevate oneself above the plebs, to be supremely cool and in control of one's own alienation."[20] Indeed, the use of Franglais, whereby "English eats

French," "represents an implicit consent to English dominance and a sign of imminent assimilation."²¹ When considered alongside other criticisms of the director—Bock-Côté deplores the absence of father figures in his films, for instance—it becomes evident that it is not just about language. Along this line, Jason D'Aoust observes that criticism of *Mommy*'s vulgarity and poor diction display undercurrents of homophobia.²²

Already with his second film, *Les Amours imaginaires* (2010), disapproving voices decried the linguistic habits of Dolan's characters. Loosely borrowing from psychoanalysis, Marc Chevrier claims that the film's characters are swimming in "linguistic schizophrenia,"²³ their hybridized "Franglais," a language at the junction of "pure" French of yesteryear and *Real* American English, makes them perceive elevated Québec French (standard French) as a foreign language. What irks numerous critics, scholars, and intellectuals in *Les Amours* is not so much the use of *joual* and swear words, but the constant "code-switching," the alternation between two languages—in this case, French and English. Why, they ask, should people use English words and expressions when they could just as well use their native French? Why use the language of the colonizer? Chevrier is here unequivocal: Quebecers do not use English out of a pure, disinterested love of English culture, but rather out of laziness, a hedonistic desire for the riches of success. He finds himself in agreement with other intellectuals, who see the use of English words and *joual* as a way to lazily hide one's inability to use French properly.²⁴ Not only is the use of Franglais, despite its subtle manipulation of two sets of linguistic baggage, not perceived as a skill, it is even presented as an impoverishment. Chevrier is quick to add that the Franglais currently spoken in Québec bears no resemblance to the "snobbish" borrowings found in elite French literature, such as Proust. Rather, it is closer to what Albert Memmi describes in *The Colonizer and the Colonized* (1957) and *L'homme dominé/Dominated Man* (1968) as "colonial bilingualism," whereby "there is an official, foreign language, that of the ruling class, and a mother tongue, that has little or no currency in the conduct of urban affairs.²⁵ This purely Québécois Franglais is all the more criticized in that, in films like *Les Amours*, its use is qualified as *décomplexé*, uninhibited, unapologetic—proud, even.

With *Mommy*, criticism of the director's use of language reached new heights, as the film displays the most extensive use of *joual*, Franglais, and profanity, prompting the aforementioned Senatorial Committee meeting. The French spoken in *Mommy*, "shapeless and in larval state, closer to a rumbling noise than a full-fledged language" is both embarrassing and pure fiction, according to several critics; pure fiction because it in no way represents how people really talk, and embarrassing because it shows the world a poor image of Quebecers.²⁶ At issue was Dolan's excessiveness: too much English, too much cursing, and too much *joual*.

Beyond the shameful image of Québec it projects, the use of *joual* in film is denounced for the barrier it erects with rest of the *francophonie*, the French-speaking world at large. French, "the most beautiful language in the world," is widely used online and is in constant progression in Africa.[27] *Joual* and Franglais bars its users from participating in the francophone world, an argument presented by Telefilm Canada in its decision not to fund *J'ai tué ma mère*. The federal funding agency's readers' reports mention, among other problems, the film's poor dialogues, which "guarantee that the film has no chance to break on the international market and festivals."[28] A similarly devastating report for Émile Gaudreault's popular 2009 comedy, *De père en flic / Father and Guns*, criticizes the use of *joual* in the scenario: "Again, this stubborn idea that the only way to sound authentic is to use the Québec dialect. This choice makes it impossible for any non-native viewer to watch the film in its original version."[29] These reviewers' concerns, in retrospect, were largely unfounded. Not only were Dolan's films successful on the festival circuit and travelled well in Europe and Asia but the French press overwhelmingly praised *Mommy* precisely for its deft use of the local dialect.[30] They may not have understood most of it had it not been for subtitles, but they appreciated the authenticity and exoticism of their overseas cousins. Speaking of rhythm and emotions in film, French philosopher Jacques Rancière noted how Dolan's dialogues "[create] something like a choreography."[31]

EMOTIONAL WORDS

Words are, in my not-so-humble opinion, our most inexhaustible source of magic. Capable of both inflicting injury, and remedying it.[32]

Dolan's body, covered with words, is a testament to his deep attachment and passion for language. By tattooing the above Dumbledore quote—one of several words tattooed on his body—Dolan highlights the intersubjective power and dual nature of language. *J'ai tué ma mère*, a study of teenage rebellion against one's mother, can be read as an exposé of this twin power to both inflict and appease pain. From the very first scene, Hubert (Dolan) explains to the camera that though he once loved his mother, he now finds himself unable to love her as a son, and the subsequent scenes constitute so many tableaux of their impossible relationship. The close framing and claustrophobic mise-en-scène, each frame packed with carefully selected props, present Hubert and his mother Chantale as two animals trapped in a cage, constantly taunting one another. Although Hubert and Chantale (Anne Dorval) cannot stand each other, they are also linked by a deep affective bond, a complicated mix which manifests itself in a bipolar back-and-forth of "I hate you, I love you."

Early in the film, we witness their first argument over supper:

CHANTALE: "We could talk you know. We used to talk" (On peut se parler. On se parlait avant).

HUBERT: "*Used* to, yeah. When I was four and didn't have anyone else to talk to" (Avant. Ouains. Quand j'avais quatre ans pis que j'avais personne d'autre).

Quickly realizing he's gone too far, he immediately compliments her cooking skills. This is too little too late, though:

CHANTALE: "That's good. At least I didn't bust my ass for nothing. I fucking hate cooking" (Ben tant mieux. Au moins j'me force pas l'cul pour rien. Ça m'fait tellement chier d'cuisiner).

Here Chantale's switch to a much lower, vulgar, register both betrays the emotions stirred by Hubert's hurtful comment, but is also meant to return his retort's violence.

One can find countless examples in Dolan's films of words used to hurtful purpose; the director and screenwriter's talent is precisely in exploiting *joual*'s varying registers to pierce through conversations and attack others. In *Les Amours imaginaires*, Francis uses vulgar *joual* to break up Marie and Nicolas's intimacy. Interjecting abruptly with "gotta piss" (j'va aller pisser) Francis clearly intends to create discomfort. In *Juste la fin du monde*, this form of verbal sparring is taken to a level of intensity that proved too much for many, who described the experience as "excruciating."[33]

To be sure, however, Dolan's films also exploit language's healing, soothing powers. He in fact describes his films in a very similar therapeutic fashion, as objects people can "insert into their own lives in a moment of need, or in a moment of growth."[34] Therapeutic, his films use various strategies to comfort viewers, to nostalgically bring us back to a shared yet personal past.[35] The director explains how he deploys a number of aesthetic strategies to achieve this nostalgic feel, notably with his use of songs:

Movies are about . . . what I miss from when I was a kid. The textures, the colors, they're all things that I miss. All these movies are poured out of nostalgia, and so are these songs. They send us back to the precise moments where we first heard that song, where we made out to that song, where we had a breakup to that song. You soak it in and you never forget these things and suddenly you're in a dark theater room with all these people and you have nothing to do with this film, you didn't write this film. But here's our chance as the creators of the film to have you contribute to the story that we're telling because suddenly when you hear this song, it's your emotions, it's your sensibility, it's your memory of when your dad was rough, it's the pleasure you have when you think of the aunt who would always give you candies and that song would be playing in the background. It's all of these things and suddenly you become a writer of the film and we're writing it together.[36]

Like music, Dolan uses popular language to nostalgically bring the viewer back to intimate, personal childhood experiences. It is in fact significant that these memories evoked by Dolan are familial—"your memory of when your dad was rough . . . the aunt who would always give you candies"—as the characters that Dolan implicates most in his language politics are, precisely, parents. This statement about the role of music in his films is consistent with those made regarding other elements of mise-en-scène (notably costume design), which Dolan adamantly defends against accusations that we are meant to laugh at the horrendous fashions. Speaking of Diane's tacky and outmoded fashion in *Mommy*, Dolan states: "I love what she's wearing. I love her style. This is not a game for me. I'm not like, 'Oh, that's funny.'"[37]

I argue that Dolan proceeds in a similar way in his construction of dialogue: the director uses Québécois turns of phrase as memory vectors to bring us back in time to a parent's peculiar expressions. Quotidian language, it has been remarked, anchors us in concrete reality: "the closest you get to vernacular language, the more firmly anchored in a specific local context" you are.[38] In Dolan's case, we could add that *joual* summons memories of a nostalgic familial past, being used in the intimacy of the home, while standard French dominates public life.

THE POLITICS OF *JOUAL*

I might not speak the French they speak in France but yeah, I speak French.[39]

Mommy has often been described as a film about people's inability to communicate: while Kyla stutters, Die and Steve's *joual* functions as a symptom of their lack (of education, of English), a lack which condemns them to the lower rungs of society. Steve jokes openly about his complete inability to speak English ("I can't speak a fuckin' word of English" (j'parle pas un tabarnak de mot d'anglais), Kyla only painfully communicates with her family, and numerous scenes' dialogues are drowned in a sea of noise, screams, and music. These various lacks congeal in moments such as Die's attempts (and failures) to elevate her register, clumsily mixing formal and informal forms of address in the same sentence.[40]

And yet, despite their struggles to communicate, the three of them do form a strong community, albeit one cut off from, even in opposition to, the rest of society. Dolan sets this up early on in the film, when Die squares off with the condescending detention center director, who speaks with a Continental French accent:

> DIRECTOR: "Miss Després, do you understand French?" (Mme Després, est-que vous parlez français vous?).
>
> DIANE: "I might not speak the French they speak in France but yeah, I speak French" (Ben là j'parle peut-être pas l'français d'France mais oui j'parle français).

Shortly after, Diane proudly smiles as the director's walkie-talkie transmits Steve's colorful insults, as if impressed with his range: "I'm happy to see that you've improved his vocabulary."

In *J'ai tué ma mère*, language politics mirrors class politics. Hubert's adolescent lashing out is first and foremost a rebellion against his mother's lower middle-class status. Hubert hates how his mother eats, how she dresses, how she puts on her make-up while driving, and how she occupies her leisure time. On their morning commute, his mother's talk-radio show becomes the main bone of contention. As Hubert lambasts the inanity of the show, he uses the rarely used verb *pourlécher* (to lick) to qualify his mother's enjoyment in an effort to distance himself from the show's much lower language register. This won't be the only instance where Hubert signals his superiority by putting down other people's common tastes and poor linguistic abilities: when asked how his day at school went, Hubert calls his classmates "a bunch of morons who can only talk about hockey and sex and who get 35 percent on their French dictation."[41] His mother reacts by noting how Hubert uses the same kind of snobbish lingo his father uses, remarking "can't speak like normal people; always has to show off with his fancy words" (pas capable de s'exprimer comme tout l'monde; faut qu'ça épate la gallérie avec son vocabulaire). Hubert's father (Pierre Chagnon), like Antonin's mother Hélène (Patricia Tulasne), has a distinct *joual*-free accent. While the former's hints at his European background[42] and the latter's betrays bourgeois affect, they both clash with Chantale and her tacky sun-tanning friend Denise (Monique Spaziani), who refers to Hubert with the outmoded moniker *ti-coune* ("lil' rascal"). Despite Hubert's continuous efforts to set himself apart from his mother and his lower middle-class surroundings, the film makes clear that Hubert's attachment, albeit deeply troubled at this juncture, is with his tacky mother, not his bourgeois, distant father, or the free-spirited but mannered Hélène. Although Hubert enjoys his boyfriend's bohemian household, he also appears ill at ease around Hélène.

Joual, as we have defined it earlier, contains elements of code-switching and code-mixing—elements that have increasingly become the focus of *joual* skeptics and critics. Criticism of this tendency to mix languages within inter-actions, common in societies where two or more languages co-mingle, is far from unique to Québec society.[43] As observed by Alla Nedashkivska in her study of Ukrainian bilingualism, various definitions of "code-switching" have been offered.[44] While Valdes-Fallis,[45] Myers-Scotton and Ury,[46] and Baker[47] consider code-switching to be the alternation between two or more languages within a conversation (either intra clausal or at the sentential level), Hymes[48] adds that code-switching may also include the alternate use of different speech styles. Code-mixing, on the other hand, implies a *transfer* of linguistic aspects from one language, or code, to another (as when Steve coins the term "*obvi-ousment*," in *Mommy*.) Code-mixing therefore involves code-switching, but is distinct in that it results in the creation of an additional code.[49] As Meisel[50] points out, there has been a fair amount of confusion between code-switching and code-mixing, and some scholars use the two terms interchangeably.

Following Gumperz,[51] Auer,[52] and Myers-Scotton,[53] I see code-switching not as a passive occurrence or a sign of a lack in linguistic knowledge, but rather as an active and purposeful gesture at community building. Code-switching, notably, can be seen as a strategy to draw boundaries, to include and exclude interlocutors in communication communities. An example of this practice is when two native French speakers, who do not know each other, are interact-ing in English in a public space where English is the official, public language. Either interlocutor might switch to French at any point to establish or reflect a more intimate or friendlier tone, at which point the other interlocutor might engage in or refuse to switch, signaling an acceptance or a refusal of this dif-ferent level of interaction. In this sense, code-switching can be perceived as a conversational strategy. According to Gumperz,

> the tendency is for the ethnically specific, minority language to be regarded as the "we code" and become associated with in-group and informal activities, and for the majority language to serve as the "they code" associated with more formal, stiffer and less personal out-group relations.[54]

A wider definition of code-switching, following Eastman, not only implies the use of two or more languages, but also of various levels of language. This way of looking at language alternation sees it as a tool through which social identi-ties are negotiated and achieved. Indeed, individuals rarely establish their iden-tity, within social interactions, in direct linguistic terms ("I am an educated, white, married woman from a large, mixed, bilingual urban center"). Rather, non-referential ways of speaking are used to position and identify oneself, be it by indicating, using specific words and registers, a geographic region, ethnic background, socioeconomic status, subculture, etc.[55] What we see at work in Dolan's dialogues, and his code and register switching, is precisely the creation and breakdown of "we" and "in-groups" and, more specifically, an ambivalent back and forth toward origin. By its very nature, *joual* is at once political and aesthetic.

While many people criticize the use of English words in *Les Amours*, the film's young, millennial characters, living in a cool neighborhood of a metropolitan city, make little use of *joual*. The only *joualisant* character, tellingly, is Nicolas's mother Désirée (Anne Dorval). Désirée uses the whole gamut of language's possibilities, alternating between French and English, pronouncing French words with an English inflection for no apparent reason ("take care *mon beau*," "Francis" pronounced in English rather than French), using vulgarity and old expressions ("ça se prend pas pour un 7-up ça 'sti" ["that dick thinks he's King of the World"], "câlasse" [a modified version of the curse, *câlisse*]). Désirée being a stripper, code-switching might be explained by her frequent travels across North America, but her lower working-class status is certainly communicated by her *joual* pronunciation of certain words (heavily inflected "party," "père," and "rêve").

Much like in *Mommy* and *Les Amours*, the use of *joual* in *J'ai tué ma mère* is intimately linked with mothers, motherhood, and motherly love. In the latter, Hubert's mother is the character most associated with the use of *joual*, which Hubert also uses though only during his emotional spats with her. In contradistinction, his father sports an affected international French accent, which can be seen as indicating emotional distance between parent and child. Similarly, Fred's (Suzanne Clément/ *Laurence Anyways*) distant and ever so critical mother Andrée (Sophie Faucher) not only puts on a phony accent but also "pretends she's French."

In "Le Septième art hors des frontières nationales," Valérie Mandia reads Dolan's films along this line, arguing that his characters switch registers to indicate hybridity and universality. It is therefore not so much that they lazily use an impoverished, uneducated, version of French, but rather that they actively and skillfully engage with various codes and registers. "Code and accent-switching," she adds, "become metaphors for Québec's relationship to alterity."[56] For Mandia, this hybrid use of language goes a long way to explain Dolan's films' success in international markets.[57] While acknowledging Dolan's openness to a diverse world, the present chapter highlight his films' countermovement toward white, lower middle-class origins.

Love of mothers, and of origins, is deeply felt in Dolan's films. While the millennial filmmaker is firmly anchored in present-day society, and oriented toward the future, a deep—almost fetishistic—love of the past acts as a strong background and undercurrent in his work. Dolan's constant use of kitschy and nostalgic props could be perceived as a ridiculing of the past, but the tender sentiment organizing their use negates such a reading. This is done, notably, through his use of popular Québec songs that are as kitschy—what people in Québec would call *quétaine*—as the surrounding props. Use of music in his films, however, is skillfully done so as to convey a very different feeling; not a ridiculing of a kitschy past, but a tender remembering of the past and acknowledgment of a guilty pleasure.

Similarly, Dolan's use of *joual* acts, in many ways, as a nostalgic profession of love toward origins. The most unsophisticated manifestations of *joual*, the working-class French of those who didn't go to school and who associate literary French with the elites and the clergy, is the French many young Québécois who have had the chance to receive higher education and travel, associate with their parents. There is certainly a generational gap underpinning this linguistic gap, but Dolan's characters' constant fishing in both registers is certainly a gesture aimed at establishing bridges between past and future. Living in the present while acknowledging the past with a look toward the future, as Massimi puts it earlier in this volume.

BOUNDARIES AND CODE-SWITCHING

In this final section, I want to explore the affective dimension of Dolan's code-switching. Research on bilingualism shows that bilinguals report different perceived affective meaning in their first and second languages. According to neurolinguist Rafał Jończyk (2016), "bilinguals report to experience affective detachment when communicating in their second language while experiencing full-blown affective experiences when operating in their first language."[58] Jończyk's research shows the relationship between affect and language in bilinguals; the first language more readily associated with affect, "because it is deeply attached to affective experiences and memories."[59] Jończyk further shows how bilinguals may strategically use their second language precisely to distance themselves when dealing with traumatic or emotionally difficult situations.[60] The thesis put forward here is that alternating language levels is done for similar purposes as with language switching; to conjure affective experiences and memories or, alternatively, to distance oneself from them.

Monia Chokri's character in *Les Amours imaginaires*, Marie Camille, exemplifies this use of language to create emotional distance when situations become too intimate. Dolan's second film concerns two millennials' falling in and out of love with the same evanescent boy (Niels Schneider). This unspoken love triangle causes tension until they both profess their love for Nicolas, who turns them both away. The last scene of the film, showing that a similar scenario is about to begin once more—this time with Louis Garrel—implies that both get a kick out of the tension and euphoria caused by impossible romantic pursuits, and throws a new light on the preceding drama. Marie and Francis almost seem to have a code whereby they choose their next (non-)conquest, the object of their (impossible) desire. The fact that neither will ultimately win guarantees the longevity of their game, a game that can only be sustained if neither gets too close to Nicolas despite his constant physical breaches. Both Marie and Francis tense up whenever Nicolas gets physical or intimate, which both scares and titillates them. They like to circle around Nicolas, taking turns and alternating between closeness and exclusion.

Marie and Francis have no intentions of letting anyone in on their *folie à deux*, and must keep Nicolas safely at bay, while clearly visible. A control-freak, Marie creates a parallel alternate world, a bubble of her own making, which cuts her off from her environment. This world is anachronistic and theatrical, with disparate furniture, vintage clothes and jewelry, and 1950s hair and make-up. Much like Dolan, who excels in theatricality and mise-en-scène, Marie exerts control over every aspect of her environment, constructing elaborate scenarios in which every object is treated like a prop. In addition to her physical appearance, Marie uses language for similar purposes to cut herself off emotionally from her environment. In a short scene with a sexual partner who starts asking her personal questions, Marie, visibly annoyed by the breach, alternates between vulgarity and a high register. When he grows concerned with her excessive smoking, she snaps back:

> I love to smoke. Smoking a cigarette is like forgetting. When I hit rock bottom it's all I have. Light up, smoke, shut the fuck up. It hides the shit. The smoke hides the shit (J'aime ça fumer. Fumer une cigarette c'est comme . . . un oubli. Moé quand j't'au fond du câlisse de baril c'est ben juste ça qu'i'm reste; c'est m'allumer une cigarette, la fumer pis fermer ma gueule. Ça cache la marde. La smoke cache la marde).

Popular language, like *joual*, anchors us into quotidian reality.[61] She follows this outburst by listing the different flavors of cigarette—mint, vanilla, chocolate—which she pronounces with an increasingly affected high-register accent, as if coming back gradually to the safety of her staged mise-en-scène.

The film's narrative is interspersed with fictional interviews of people talking about past failed relationships. The first interviewee, played by Anne-Élizabeth Bossé, uses language in a similar way to Marie when shamefully recounting a painful love affair in which she, unbeknownst to her, turned into an obsessed stalker. When she first introduces the object of her obsession, she gets animated, angry with herself for always falling for men who treat her like shit. She wishes she would fall for the nice guy, but alas laments: "I fall for that fucking arrogant prick Jean-Marc Beaulieu who takes forever to answer my emails" (L'ostie d'chien sale à Jean-Marc Beaulieu à marde qui prend son temps à répondre à mes courriels ostie). The English subtitles here do not do justice to the raw vulgarity of the original French statement. Voicing this is emotionally painful, and so the interviewee follows this with "J'ai une inquiétude" (I get all worked up), pronounced in a marked high-register, Continental accent. Much like *J'ai tué*'s back and forth between love and hate, hurting and soothing, here the interviewee switches registers to release anger and then safely put the lid back on. Throughout *Les Amours imaginaires*, *joual* is used to express raw emotions, while a more international, or Continental, French is used to generate emotional distance.

CONCLUSION

In this chapter, I have explored the potency of Dolan's deft use of various linguistic strategies to both hurt and soothe, and to draw social and psychological boundaries. While many Québec commentators have criticized Dolan's use of *joual*, profanity, and Franglais—seeing them as lacks and faults rather than additions—few have focused on these as linguistic strategies for aesthetic and emotional effects. Language, in Dolan's films, works in tandem with other aspects of mise-en-scène (music, props, and wardrobe) to coherently convey characters' personality and interiority, and to establish powerful emotional bonds with the viewer. Associating *joual* with the lower, less educated class (*Les Amours*, *J'ai tué ma mère*, *Mommy*) and communication difficulties (*Mommy*), Dolan certainly emphasizes the limitations of an impoverished language, while at the same time claiming a definite sentimental attachment to the spoken language of yesteryear. The very expression "mother tongue" points to the intimate link between one's first language and one's mother. Through their use of language, Dolan's films powerfully convey a deep, passionate love of mothers, and of origins, where *joual* and Franglais can indeed be seen as nostalgic professions of this love. Though it might not be as used today, especially by the younger, urban, millennial generation, *joual* nevertheless has a way of reminding viewers of years past, of how their parents speak or used to speak. For these reasons, *joual* remains, for many, the true mother tongue.

NOTES

1. *Mommy* pressbook. All non-filmic translations are mine except when noted otherwise. The original reads: "J'ai parlé *joual* et j'ai parlé mal, j'ai sacré comme un charretier, parlé l'anglais parfois et parlé à travers mon chapeau plus souvent qu'à mon tour, je suppose . . . ."
2. "Films québécois: la question des jurons soulevée devant un comité sénatorial." Agence QMI, May 12, 2015.

3. *"Entre la langue de ma mère et le français standard, je choisirai toujours la langue de ma mère."* Claude Jasmin, "Pour en finir avec le bon parler français!," *Claude Jasmin, écrivain— Point comme* net (blog), August 28, 2001. Available at <http://www.claudejasmin.com/ wordpress/?p=260>.

4. *Petit Robert* (1993), s.v. *"joual."*

5. Jacques Godbout, "Entre l'Académie et l'Écurie," *Liberté*, 16/3, May–June 1974, p. 27 (16–33); Henri Wittmann, "Le *joual*, c'est-tu un créole?," *La linguistique*, 9/2, 1973.

6. Chantal Bouchard, *Obsessed With Language: A Sociolinguistic History of Quebec*, trans. Luise von Flotow (Toronto: Guernica, 2009), p. 7.

7. Chantal Bouchard, *Méchante Langue: La légitimité linguistique du français parlé au Québec* (Montréal: Les Presses de l'Université de Montréal, 2012), loc. 49 of 2674, Kindle.

8. Bouchard, *Obsessed with Language*, p. 260.

9. Chantal Bouchard, *La langue et le nombril: histoire d'une obsession québécoise*, Collection Nouvelles études québécoises (Montréal: Fides, 1998), pp. 66–9.

10. André Laurendeau (Candide), "La langue que nous parlons," editorial, *Le Devoir* (Montréal), October 21, 1959, p. 4.

11. See, for instance: Jean Marcel's *Le Joual de Troie*; Léandre Bergeron's numerous books on the subject; the journal *Parti pris*.

12. "Tout le monde en parlait," Season 1, episode 10, Radio-Canada, July 25, 2006.

13. Nathalie Petrowski, "Charlotte anyways . . .," *La Presse* (Montréal), January 30, 2012. Available at <https://www.lapresse.ca/ debats/chroniques/nathalie-petrowski/201201/30/01-4490635-charlotte-anyways.php>.

14. Mela Sarkar, "'Ousqu'on chill à soir?' Pratiques multilingues comme stratégies identitaires dans la communauté hip hop montréalais," supplement, *Diversité urbaine*, Fall 2008, pp. 27–44.

15. Josée Blanchette, "'Wipés' de la 'map,'" *Le Devoir* (Montréal), October 5, 2018.

16. See Christian Rioux, "L'enfant roi," *Le Devoir* (Montréal), October 10, 2014, A3; Christian Rioux, "Faire peuple," *Le Devoir* (Montréal), November 14, 2014; Petrowski, "Charlotte anyways . . ."; Christian Dufour, "La langue de *Mommy*," *Journal de Montréal*, October 1, 2014, p. 35.

17. Mathieu Bock-Côté, "Le franglais: le raffinement des colonisés," *Journal de Montréal*, July 12, 2014.

18. Mathieu Bock-Côté, "Voyage sur la planète Dolan," *Le Journal de Montréal*, May 25, 2016.

19. Mathieu Bock-Côté, "L'identité malheureuse au Québec aussi," *Le Figaro* (Paris), June 6, 2014; Christian Rioux, "Anyway!," *Le Devoir* (Montréal), July 20, 2012.

20. Bock-Côté, "L'identité malheureuse."

21. Bock-Côté, "Le franglais: le raffinement des colonisés"; Mathieu Bock-Côté, "Qui franglise s'anglicise," *Journal de Montréal*, July 27, 2014.

22. Jason D'Aoust, "The queer voices of Xavier Dolan's *Mommy*," *European Journal of American Studies*, 11/3, 2017, pp. 1–17.

23. Marc Chevrier, "Les français imaginaires (et le réel franglais)." Available at <http:// agora-2.org/francophonie.nsf/Documents/Anglicisme-Les_francais_imaginaires_et_le_ reel_franglais_par_Marc_Chevrier>.

24. See Gaston Bernier, "Pourquoi tant de mots anglais?," *Le Devoir* (Montréal), November 11, 2010.

25. Albert Memmi, "Are the French Canadians colonized?," in *Dominated Man: Notes towards a Portrait*, trans. Jane Brooks (Boston: Beacon, 1969), p. 75. [Published in French, Paris: Gallimard, 1968].

26. Jean Delisle, "La pseudo-langue de *Mommy*," *Le Devoir* (Montréal), October 16, 2014; Christian Rioux, "L'enfant roi"; Christian Dufour, "La langue de *Mommy*."

27. Christian Dufour, "La plus belle langue du monde," *Le Journal de Québec*, November 23, 2014; Christian Rioux, "Faire peuple."

28. Claude Jacqueline Herdhuin, "J'ai tué le cinéma," review of *J'ai tué ma mère*, directed by Xavier Dolan, *La Presse* (Montréal), July 1, 2010.

29. *J'ai tué ma mère*, the report reads, has "aucune chance de se démarquer tant sur les marchés internationaux que dans les festivals." Similarly, for *De père en flic*, "toujours cette idée tenace que seul le dialecte québécois est gage d'authenticité . . . Cet engagement élimine toute possibilité d'écoute, en VO, de tout spectateur autre que 'de souche.'" Anabelle Nicoud, "Le film qui n'avait 'aucune chance,'" *La Presse* (Montréal), June 22, 2010, Arts spectacles 1.

30. See Marc-Olivier Bherer, "Au Québec, Xavier Dolan ravive le débat linguistique," *Le Monde* (Paris), November 12, 2014, p. 14; Marie-Luce Maupetit, "*Mommy*, avec sous-titres," *Ouest-France* (Rennes), March 13, 2015; Pierre-Alexandre Fradet, "Le parler québécois, du Roi Soleil à Xavier Dolan," *Positif*, 674, April 2017, pp. 69–72.

31. Jacques Rancière, "It's up to you to invent the rest," interview by Stéphane Delorme and Dork Zabunyan, in Emiliano Battista (ed. and trans.), *Dissenting Words: Interviews with Jacques Rancière* (London: Bloomsbury, 2017), p. 298.

32. J. K. Rowling, *Harry Potter and the Deathly Hallows*. Quote tattooed on Dolan's body.

33. Peter Debruge, "Cannes film review: *It's Only the End of the World*," *Variety*, May 18, 2016.

34. Xavier Dolan quoted in "Xavier Dolan on Blink-182, bottoming, and being the world's biggest Kate Winslet fan," interview by Kyle Buchanan, *Vulture*, December 8, 2016. Available at <http://www.vulture.com/2016/12/xavier-dolan-on-his-new-film-critics-and-more.html> (accessed August 29, 2018).

35. "On est au fond du baril, on est désespéré, on a perdu son emploi, son amoureux, sa mère, son père. Puis, tout à coup, un billet de cinéma, on s'assoit dans le noir . . . 'Et par le pouvoir d'un mot, je recommence ma vie.' Paul Éluard écrivait ça dans le poème *Liberté*. Par l'art, oui, on peut décider de se changer, de changer sa vie." Noémi Mercier, "Xavier Dolan: 'Tout est possible,'" *L'Actualité*, September 15, 2017. Available at <http://lactualite.com/culture/2017/09/15/xavier-dolan-tout-est-possible> (accessed June 12, 2018).

36. Xavier Dolan quoted in Buchanan, *Vulture*, December 8, 2016.

37. Sophie Monks Kaufman, "Xavier Dolan: 'I've never experienced love as something calm and tender,'" *Little White Lies*. Available at <http://lwlies.com/interviews/xavier-dolan-mommy/> (accessed February 2, 2018).

38. Isabelle Collombat quoted in Stéphane Baillargeon, "Une chatte dans la gorge," *Le Devoir* (Montréal), January 28, 2017, B1.

39. Diane Després, *Mommy*. I am using a more literal translation than the DVD English subtitles.

40. For instance, when she greets Kyla ("Kyla, *vous* êtes pas venu avec *ton* chum?") and her husband.

41. Similarly, one of *Les Amours*' interviewees justifies not pursuing a relationship with a woman by reading a letter she wrote to him, emphasizing her poor command of the French language, spelling out how she wrote "Chans Élisés."

42. Richard Minel's high register accent could best be described as a Québec French equivalent to the 1940s mid-Atlantic accent: a consciously acquired accent intended as a blend of spoken American English and British Received Pronunciation, used primarily in media to denote class and sophistication.

43. Joseph Gararanga, "Code-switching as a conversational strategy," in Peter Auer and Li Wei (eds), *Handbook of Multilingualism and Multilingual Communication* (Berlin: Mouton de Gruyter, 2007), p. 279.

44. Alla Nedashkivska, "Symbolic bilingualism in contemporary Ukrainian media," *Canadian Slavonic Papers/Revue canadienne des slavistes*, 52/3–4, September–December 2010, pp. 351–71.

45. Guadalupe Valdes-Fallis, "Code-switching as a deliberate verbal strategy: a micro-analysis of direct and indirect requests among bilingual Chicano speakers," in R. P. Duran (ed.), *Latino Language and Communicative Behaviour* (Norwood: ABLEX, 1981).

46. Carol Myers-Scotton and William Ury, "Bilingual strategies: the social functions of code-switching," *Linguistics*, 193, June 1977, 5–20.

47. Colin Baker, *Foundations of Bilingual Education and Bilingualism* (Clevedon: Multilingual Matters, 1997).

48. Dell Hymes, *Foundations in Sociolinguistics: An Ethnographic Approach* (Philadelphia: University of Pennsylvania Press, 1974).

49. Edmund O. Bamiro, "The politics of code-switching: English vs. Nigerian languages," *World Englishes*, 25/1, February 2006, pp. 23–4 (23–5).

50. Jürgen M. Meisel, "Early differentiation of languages in bilingual children," in Kenneth Hyltenstam and Loraine K. Obler (eds), *Bilingualism Across the Lifespan: Aspects of Acquisition, Maturity, and Loss* (Cambridge: Cambridge University Press, 1989), pp. 13–40.

51. John Gumperz, *Discourse Strategies*, Studies in Interactional Sociolinguistics I (Cambridge: Cambridge University Press, 1982).

52. Peter Auer, *Bilingual Conversation* (Amsterdam: John Benjamins, 1984).

53. Carol Myers-Scotton, *Social Motivation for Code-Switching* (Oxford: Oxford University Press, 1993).

54. Gumperz, *Discourse Strategies*, p. 66.

55. Benjamin Bailey, "Multilingual forms of talk and identity work," in Peter Auer and Li Wei (eds), *Handbook of Multiligualism and Multilingual Communication* (Berlin: De Gruyter, 2009), p. 343.

56. Valérie Mandia, "Le septième art hors des frontières nationales: le pouvoir de la langue et de l'imaginaire culturel dans les films du cinéaste québécois Xavier Dolan," *Francophonie d'Amérique*, 37, Spring 2014, pp. 105–32.

57. Ibid.

58. Rafał Jończyk, *Affect-Language Interactions in Native and Non-Native English Speakers: A Neuropragmatic Perspective*, Bilingual Mind and Brain Book Series (Berlin: Springer, 2016), p. 75, eBook.

59. Ibid. p. 97.

60. Ibid. p. 97.

61. "Une langue populaire . . . nous enracine dans la quotidienneté même," in Fradet, "Le parler québécois," p. 70.

CHAPTER 10

Fade to Grey: Dolan's Pop Fashion and Surface Style

Nick Rees-Roberts

Pop art knows that the fundamental expression of the person is style.
—Roland Barthes

Clear from the quotation above by a canonical writer on the subject, this chapter examines Dolan through the superficial lens of style. His cinema to date has been celebrated for an elaborate conjunction of sound and vision, positioned by critics at the intersection of pop aesthetics and consumer culture. His films, moreover, have often either been praised or criticized for their heightened expressive stylization. In this chapter, I assess the relationship between the formal aesthetics of costume design and the social contexts of celebrity and consumerism. Drawing on Dolan's feature filmography, music videos, and commercial role as a model and ambassador for the luxury fashion brand Louis Vuitton, I explore the "fashionability" of the Dolan brand in the broader context of screen media culture. Can we think of Dolan as representing a specific form of popular auteurism that circulates in both the institutional spaces of world cinema and the globalized spaces of online social media? How does this type of pop cinema, at once local and transnational, intersect with the media discourses and cultural representations of celebrity and branding? Going beyond an inquiry into the formal centrality of costume in the production design of Dolan's films, I also seek to assess the director's public persona by examining his status within pop culture, a profile that far outstrips that of most world cinema directors. I also investigate the relationship between contemporary fashion and melodrama as a filmic mode, asking how contemporary fashion functions itself as a sort of melodrama, and how it cultivates a melodramatic sensibility. Contemporary consumer culture is often associated with notions of excess and exhaustion that are also shared historically by the filmic mode of melodrama. Taking the example of *Juste la fin du monde* (2016), which won the prestigious Grand Prix at the 2016 International Cannes Film Festival, I argue that the tropes of exaggeration, failure, and vulgarity—all elements of both the contemporary fashion system and the melodramatic imagination—structure Dolan's film world. If contemporary fashion interrogates the excesses of celebrity, the exhaustion of the designer system, and the hegemony of the global luxury brand—as, in essence, bound up in the cultivation of a melodramatic sensibility as the mode of fashion—Dolan's cinema of excess might also be symptomatic of this particular cultural configuration.

UGLY-PRETTY: DOLAN'S DESIGNS

Les Amours imaginaires (2010), is a tale of two arch and insecure friends living in Montréal's hip Mile End neighborhood, who both lust after the same guy. Midway through the film, there is a scene that visually translates the director's signature style—a contrived exuberance incorporating elaborate set pieces that fold style into the dramatic tension of the narrative. The rival characters, Francis (played by Dolan), and Marie (Monia Chokri), are at a party observing their prey, Nicolas (Niels Schneider), dance with his mother, Désirée (Anne Dorval), who is wearing an electric blue wig.

> "Who's that android?" [he asks her].
> "His mother" [she tartly replies]. "She's called Désirée. He just introduced us. She said I looked like a 1950s housewife. She can't talk; she looks like Captain Spock. At least I don't look like some lame New York try-hard."
> "Yeah, but your dress is slightly anachronistic though" [he observes snidely].
> "I beg your pardon," [she replies] "it is vintage, I'll have you know."
> "Yeah, but just because it's vintage, that doesn't means it's pretty, does it?" [Ignoring his comment, she exhales smoke back in his face.]

Prior to this curt confrontation the rivals are filmed picking out birthday presents for their beloved—Marie chooses a quirky straw boater; Francis goes for a costly cashmere sweater, the garish shade of which she calls out as a potentially risky choice. Their elaborate preparations for the party are meticulously shot in slow motion to amplify the growing antagonism between them. Francis hands a picture of James Dean to his coiffeuse for inspiration; he dresses up in a royal blue suit offset by Cuban heels to equal Marie's luminous pink gown and shiny gold pumps. Their obsessional rivalry is captured through a shared vanity as well as through the material and symbolic value of their gifts.

Dolan's strategy is to mock their pretensions while sympathizing with their predicament of unrequited love—an emotional balance that relies on the ironic distance of "camp" as a way of neutralizing the underlying bitchiness of much of their interaction. One might even say, to paraphrase Susan Sontag's famous "Notes on Camp," that the film's overall decorative sensibility is purposefully off, consciously designed to be so awful, it's good.[1] Therein lies, in my view, the aesthetic queerness of Dolan's cinema.

While they watch Nicolas dance with his mother, Marie and Francis fantasize about his body, producing mental images that Dolan captures in subjective counterpoint: the neon flashes from the dance floor alternate with a series of projections of Renaissance statues (for her) and Cocteau graphics (for him). The imaginary attachments of the film's original French title (the English, *Heartbeats*, loses in translation the element of cerebral fantasy in the original) involve the staging of erotic obsession, which contrasts the hyperbolic, aestheticized paraphernalia of vintage style with more ordinary elements of everyday clothing such as Nicolas's discarded shirt to which Francis furtively masturbates the next morning—a fetishism that Dolan realizes head-on by filming himself sniffing the worn garment, thereby revealing the more perverse drives at work beneath the polished veneer of control that both characters strive to project. Thus, the extended party sequence, from frantic anticipation to needy (albeit interrupted) release, crystallizes the film's overall vision of desire as a toxic blend of unrequited love and predatory lust; one that is contained behind the civilized mask of ironic self-fashioning.

The film ends with another party held one year later, a vengeful epilogue to the failed love triangle in which, out of social embarrassment, Nicolas attempts to make superficial peace with the duo, a gesture that is violently rejected by Francis who erratically spits his contempt back before resting his head on the shoulder of his confidante like a wounded animal. Nicolas is shown to be a manipulative and self-satisfied hipster and, like Tom, the urban ad exec out of his depth in *Tom à la ferme* (2013), he sports a sexy leather perfecto and ugly ironic knitwear. The predators meanwhile have upped their game with even sharper haircuts and more tailored outfits as they move onto their next subject, who is played in a cameo by the French actor Louis Garrel, whose teasing smile suggests that the pair have perhaps met their match. The film's parting shot heralds the return of slow motion (the predictable repetitiousness of which indicates the scripted performance of being in love), closing with an image of Marie and Francis as they head toward the new boy in a trance like moths drawn to a flame.

This example of Dolan's approach to narrative composition through camp styling and ironic wit shows how he places the "look" of popular fashion—part of the director's pronounced editorial sensibility—at the "heart" of his stories by making use of multiple surfaces to punctuate the dramatic tension and shape the worlds that he is imagining. Personal style and self-invention rub up against a more socio-historically inflected understanding of fashion as rooted in both milieu and modernity—the etymological root of the English word "fashion" is in the French for "shaping" (*façonner*), originally from the Latin verb "to make" (*facere*); whereas the French term for "fashion" (*mode*) defines it as emblematic of what it means to be modern. Critical suspicion of fashion in film has historically focused on the perceived over-investment in artifice and surface. Theorist of fashion and film Pamela Church Gibson has described the entrenched elitism in much academic film scholarship that leaves the study of costume design for fashion historians or journalists, thereby diminishing its disciplinary legitimacy.[2] Criticism is often directed at the sort of production design that submerges the narrative in a stagnant aesthetic coding that relies on the clichéd look of the still fashion image. In the case of Dolan, rather than adopting a glossy postmodern aesthetic to neutralize the impact of narrative by emptying it of its thematic content, his cinema of excess ambitiously deploys camp hyperbole and proliferating surfaces precisely as the formal means to embed individual stories of love, longing, and desire within broader cultural questions of conflict, constraint, and power, in relation to contemporary societal issues of identity, language, and location. By referring to camp I am following cultural critic Peter Wollen's definition of it as rooted in performance. With its "hyperbolic aestheticization" and its "playful connoisseurship of kitsch," camp, Wollen remarks, is geared toward "the theatricalization of everyday life."[3] But, as Sontag observes in her original sketch of camp as a specifically aesthetic sensibility rather than a queer subcultural strategy, the whole point of its investment in artifice is "to dethrone the serious," to accept "a victory of 'style' over 'content,' 'aesthetics' over 'morality,' of irony over tragedy."[4] However, I argue that by taking the perceived frivolousness of fashion seriously, by establishing it quite so consistently as a formal framework for his fictions, Dolan rejects the type of high modernist binary oppositions that support Sontag's more apolitical conception of camp, particularly the artificial distinction between style and content. Put simply, the affected surface style of *Les Amours*, for example, complements the film's ironic exposé of the illusions of love. Despite initially clocking Nicolas as a narcissist ("Who is that rather confident poser?" Marie asks Francis as they first spy on him at a dinner party as he plays with his luscious blond curls), they nevertheless fall headfirst for his superficial charms.

Dolan acts as the costume designer for all his films. He clearly not only loves fashion; it is also central to his aesthetic sensibility and worldview in both the lighter pop-inflected romantic dramas like *Les Amours*, the homoerotic thriller *Tom à la ferme*, or the more weighty domestic or relational melodramas, *Laurence Anyways* (2012), *Mommy* (2014), and *Juste la fin du monde*. Critics have remarked on how his breakthrough film *J'ai tué ma mère*, released in 2009—when Dolan was just out of adolescence—ambitiously set out his stand through a narrative that explored issues of intimacy, sexuality, and conflict within a stylized formal framework that showcased production design, and costume in particular. Dolan grew up wanting to be a fashion designer, and he has explained in interview that he sees costume, often overlooked by film directors, as central to the process of characterization:

> As a young boy I drew lots of fashion clothes. Terrible drawings, but I thought maybe I'd be a designer one day. I make film costumes myself because I love dressing up, love dressing up characters, love imagining what their taste is—where they shop, and how they see themselves. Fashion for characters is like who they want to be, how they want to be seen, or who they truly are. It tells you so much about a character and I think that's often belittled or neglected by directors. I just think it's so incredibly important and crucial in establishing who the character is.[5]

Transposing ideas and practices from fashion to cinema, Dolan's attention to decorative design through costume involves look books that are presented to actors to help flesh out characterization visually by imagining how characters might have acquired clothing or why they might adopt specific looks or might choose to wear specific garments. This approach to production design situates costume as more than a descriptive key to accompany dramatic storytelling, and more like a fundamental part of the designed spectacle of the film. Dolan's look books include fabrics as well as images gleaned from Instagram and old magazines to give performers the texture of the characters they are to interpret, to document his vision of specific social milieus or historical periods through the affective appeal of both fashion photography and pop music. Questioned by the French cultural magazine *Les Inrockuptibles* about how he researched and documented the style of *Laurence Anyways*, a film that covers the exhaustion of a relationship through the male-to-female transition of the protagonist, Laurence (Melvil Poupaud), from 1989 to the late 1990s, Dolan explains he used mostly fashion magazines to convey the mood of the decade rather than precise historical documentation from the era.[6] The film alternates between the more obvious kitsch clichés of the late 1980s and early 1990s—heavy on sequins and shoulder-pads—and less artificial, more realistic sequences in which the styles are less connoted or obvious to situate in time and place. The same approach is taken with regard to the choice of music: pop hits such as Céline Dion's anthem "Pour que tu m'aimes encore" ironically over-score the emotion of the couple's imploding relationship in conventional melodramatic mode while other set-pieces, such as the "Fade to Grey" ball scene, adopt music from earlier in the 1980s. In this remarkable spectacle set to the soundtrack of Visage's new wave hit, Laurence's partner, Fred (Suzanne Clément), momentarily escapes, or possibly fantasizes about escaping, to attend a formal ball, which is shot as a hip homage to the fashion show and the performance style of the early music video. In what follows, I assess Dolan's cinema through this particular lens of stylization to explore the relationship between the heightened artifice and surface glamour of fashion imagery and the melodramatic sensibility as a filmic mode in his work, fashioned as it is around excess and exhaustion.

POP STYLE: NARRATIVE AND IMAGE

In 2015, Dolan made his most widely viewed piece of work, the sepia-toned six-minute video for pop star Adele's hit single "Hello," and his most popular "film" in terms of visibility and recognition. "Hello" was the first single ever to sell a million downloads within a week and the video was seen over 27 million times in the first 24 hours on the entertainment platform Vevo. The singer's much anticipated return, partially shot in rural Québec using IMAX cameras, was the first music video to use such technology and, paradoxically, caused a stir on social media by including an anachronistic flip cell phone as part of its nostalgic decor for the romantic narrative of lost love.[7] The video also includes other vintage memorabilia such as a rotary dial phone and a red telephone box installed surreally in a forest, a strategic way of breaking the contemporary realist frame of reference (the "nowness" of representation being routinely indicated by the inclusion of up-to-the-minute technology) by emphasizing the re-evaluation of a forgotten object, seen as *démodé* and kitsch once relegated to the electronic trash heap. The design choice could also be part of a more calculated anti-commercial strategy to bypass the ubiquitous product placements embedded in contemporary screen fictions by tech corporations like Apple or Samsung.

This overarching tension between forms of mass commodification and authorial origination—between the serial and the individual—is not only germane to pop art and culture's reproductions of reality, it is also part of the broader aesthetic history of the decorative arts. Published in 1908, Georg Simmel's essay "The problem of style" first defined stylization as precisely the translation of an individual mode of expression, or personal point of view, to the "shared properties" of the applied arts, whose *raison d'être* is, after all, to reproduce functional objects of design; the "character of style" therefore replaces "the character of individuality," in Simmel's view.[8] Some fifty years later in her seminal dissection of late-modernist literary and visual culture, Sontag distinguished between style and stylization by defining the latter as "creative mistreatment" occurring "when style and subject are . . . played off against one another."[9] Stylization was subsequently the cause of hostility toward the glossy postmodern "cinema of the look" (*le cinéma du look*) in France in the 1980s with its aesthetic transposition of advertising, particularly associated with the impact of pop culture—and the postmodern sensibility of pastiche detected by cultural critic Fredric Jameson.[10] At its crudest, this parasitical visual sensibility still operates in the work of contemporary filmmakers who stylize their subject matter through surface design alone as, for example, designer-turned-director Tom Ford's superficial rendition of 1960s fashion and interior design in *A Single Man* (2010), in which cinematic narrative is embedded within a larger promotional branding strategy.

But if we accept the accessible formal style of Dolan's cinema (as well as the charge of narcissism—"you can kiss my narcissistic ass,"[11] he brazenly tweeted back to *The Hollywood Reporter* in 2013) to be in fact misleading, or "falsely superficial,"[12] then it's equally important to situate the filmmaker in the broader cultural-commercial context of advanced branding and digital self-promotion, in which, according to film critic Richard Brody, "the auteur's name seems more like a marketing strategy, the selling of a brand, than the reflection of an artistic practice."[13] Apart from fellow director Sofia Coppola, Dolan is perhaps the only high profile filmmaker to cultivate close ties to the fashion industry by acting as an "ambassador" for the luxury brand Louis Vuitton. And alongside consumer culture and fashion imagery, we might also ask how Dolan strategically reroutes the genres of mainstream narrative cinema back to their origins in the artifacts of pop art, music, and culture such as fashion design, advertising and magazine editorials, music video, and graphic design. What are the influences on his pop vision, or, in fashion-speak, what cultural representations is he "channeling"? The style of *Les Amours*—its *faux* glamour and arch-worldliness—is appealing precisely because the protagonists fail to get it quite right, and their excessive self-fashioning borders on brash. Dolan's inflection of pop lies in the interstice of these two tendencies: the heady style of his cinema is in essence a mix of the refined and the vulgar. The closed world of romantic citation in *Les Amours* is only revealed as such in ironic contrast to the documentary style of the fake testimonies that punctuate the story and provide some indication of a world outside the hermetic triangular relationship.

Beyond the allure of sophistication, seduction, and sexiness, pop is also about youth. By the time of his third film, *Laurence Anyways*, the *Cahiers du Cinéma* explained that in a short time Dolan had come to occupy a free space in international cinema: that of extreme youth.[14] This generational question is invariably raised in relation to Dolan, not just in the context of his output as a filmmaker, but also his role as a public personality, a star director, actor, and model, one whose media presence has included institutional award speeches, political comments on social media, and photographic appearances in numerous popular magazines and branded fashion advertisements. Despite his early successful positioning within the prestigious exhibition and distribution circuits of world cinema (all his films to date were first screened at the Cannes, Venice, or Toronto film festivals), his commercial (or, more precisely, self-pro-motional) status as a savvy impresario—not to mention his career as a child-actor—has yet to be examined. His public profile as an outspoken millennial voice—he is "out" despite rejecting the LGBT label of the Queer Palme award at Cannes in 2012—shows how his youth is constantly invoked in relation to his popularity. Born in 1989, Dolan's age is routinely cited as an underlying factor in his initial success and the mainstream press, especially, has focused on this issue much to his chagrin.[15] When he tied with the veteran Jean-Luc Godard for the Jury prize at Cannes for *Mommy* in 2014, the manifest age gap between the two directors was commented on. Godard made a backhanded compliment that the award united an old director who had made a young film with a young director who had made an old film—by old he meant old-fashioned, though also possibly accessible and commercial.[16] It is clearly not by chance that Dolan cites the global box office smash of the 1990s lavish romantic drama *Titanic* (James Cameron, 1997) as his main inter-text and narrative model. The tur-bulent adolescent, Hubert (Dolan), in *I Killed My Mother* also has a crush on Leonardo DiCaprio and desire for unreceptive or repressed straight men is a recurring motif in *Les Amours* and *Tom à la ferme*.[17]

The cultural span of Dolan's celebrity is such that his role as model and ambassador for Louis Vuitton menswear is unsurprising despite this being a rare occurrence for an international foreign language filmmaker. It also indi-cates how Dolan re-inflects the outmoded idea of the auteur as being more in tune with popular commercial discourses of consumerism and creativity in the contemporary digital context. His role as luxury ambassador shows how keen global fashion brands are to connect with a younger demographic (tomorrow's consumers of luxury goods) to move away from the problem-atic cultural connotations associated with brand devaluation across the globe through the spread of mass luxury, particularly in China. The point of celeb-rity branding is to consolidate the star's market value by creating "synergies" between the brand's heritage—its codes and values, in marketing terms—and the star's individual persona.[18] Dolan's local fame in Québec began as a child star in advertising and on television, where he dubbed roles and began acting from the age of four. He has claimed the lucrative contract with Louis Vuitton to be a childhood dream come true,[19] and his work modeling for the brand's menswear self-consciously taps into the commercial potential of his youth as a representative of his millennial generation without explicitly referencing the content of his cinema. The success of his films in East Asian markets also ensures a receptive audience and consumer base for the brand to reiterate its cross-cultural heritage of travel.

The ad campaign for the brand's *Ombré* collection of leather goods, shot by photographer Alasdair McLellan, emphasizes the subject's dynamic mobility as an urbane on-the-go international filmmaker producing films at a frantic pace, by promoting travel accessories such as leather bags, satchels, and backpacks and essentially foregrounding the product range vicariously through the appeal of the celebrity director. The campaign film—a montage of shots of Dolan modeling the designer Kim Jones's clothing and accessories—also highlights Dolan's persona through his informal English-language voice-over commentary, packaged as a mock interview, which talks of the need to surrender to the sensory experience of travel. This connoted image of normative (straight) masculinity, bold, energetic, and forward driving, contrasts with the more seductively subversive (queer) editorial shots of Dolan in style magazines as either a rebellious subject or a passive object, such as those taken by photographers Shayne Laverdière or Paolo Roversi to accompany features in *Man About Town* and *Égoïste* in 2018. These editorial images exploit the subject's edgier status as a disaffected cover boy through the homo-narcissism of fashion photography. Despite not being a conventional pin-up, Dolan is explicitly sexualized through the surface fetishism of Roversi's photos for *Égoïste*, which focus on his physique by combining a close-up of the filmmaker-as-tortured-artist with more sensual ones of his body, drawing haptic attention to his skin by showing off his tattoos and even revealing his naked ass.

SURFACE AFFECT

In addressing the visual matter of fashion, design, and style—the crucial question for a filmmaker, production, or costume designer being precisely how to convey their sensorial appeal to an audience—it is equally important to recognize their affective impact. This question transposes to the context of mainstream cinema, a turn that cultural theorist Giuliana Bruno has located in fine art practices as a move away from the optic toward a more haptic materiality, one that is engaged with surfaces rather than images as the material substance of visual culture.[20] Instead of making a purely decorative cinema,[21] Dolan's sensitivity to the sensorial appeal of surfaces involves subjecting style to emotion. How, then, do affect and style combine in Dolan's cinema? At times, the manifest emotionalism of his domestic dramas—the dominant melodramatic mode of *J'ai tué ma mère*, *Mommy*, and *Juste la fin du monde*—is accentuated by the jarring stylistic juxtapositions and visual clichés that over-score the severity of the drama with overtly brash design. The fixed poses of high fashion when combined with the rhythmic montage of music video provide an affective release from dramatic tension for character *and* viewer, in particular the euphoric party scenes, which operate as fashionable set pieces and points at which style is used to break out of the imposed structures of the melodrama and the characters' self-imposed interiority. Commenting on *Mommy*, a suburban narrative "bathed in affect," Bill Marshall argues that Dolan's surface fetishism complements the extreme emotional states of mind of the dysfunctional mother and son in relation to the alternative spatial and temporal modes of belonging suggested by the film.[22] This "proliferation of surfaces," Marshall also explains, "whose playfulness, plurality and expressiveness challenge imposed categories of 'normality,'"[23] began with *Laurence Anyways*, a film that deploys vintage styling as part of its affective mode.

To ask the question of a film's fashionable appeal, conveyed as much through tone as through costume, implies a shift in focus from attention to individual looks toward a more complex investigation of vintage style in terms of historical layering. Film theorist Emiliano Morreale has defined vintage cinema as an interdisciplinary relationship between screen and design, between cinema and artistic and commercial practices such as fashion photography and advertising.[24] By focusing more on design than history, unlike the period or costume drama, vintage is essentially an aesthetic space rather than a temporal marker; it implies reading history through the lens of style, through attention to mood and sensibility as much as to costume or dress. In *Laurence Anyways* the handling of time, memory and style is complex: the film's temporal structure traces a decade-long relationship to the point of exhaustion. Fred's early promise to Laurence on learning of his desire to transition ("we'll do it together") sets up the impossibility of the couple's trajectory, an adventure followed through to its bitter end as they last meet awkwardly in 1999, only to accept reluctantly that they no longer connect.

Alongside the stylized performances of the actors, stop-start rhythms and radical mood changes are key to understanding the film's visual patterning. The narrative flow is broken up by an abrupt editing style that ruptures the smooth progress of the relationship. This uneven tone, partly a result of the capacious final cut, is important to understanding the film's address. Dolan stages affective metaphors that function as artistic installations that punctuate the story and melodramatically over-score what the dialogue foregrounds in more subtle ways. In *Les Amours*, in one of Francis's daydream fantasies, he pictures Nicolas showered in marshmallows, a stylistic borrowing from Gregg Araki's *Mysterious Skin* (2004). Similarly, when Laurence enters Fred's life again through writing via a code embedded in her poetry, Fred is literally drenched by a torrential shower that shatters her illusion of happiness and masquerade of domesticity. These visual flourishes are part of Dolan's larger design to reconfigure the codes and clichés of romantic love in non-hegemonic ways. Such moments of spectacular excess are intentionally shallow; the pop imagery effectively translates mood by literalizing emotion.

Laurence Anyways samples the vulgarly kitsch, including the dry ice and lip gloss of 1980s music video, with the savagely sophisticated. From a cultural perspective, this eclecticism situates Dolan as part of a post-digital mindset that indiscriminately "channels" past sartorial styles. He developed the film's aesthetic by copying fashion magazines of the 1980s and 90s (hence the historical blurring of two decades) in which the costume designs fold into one another rather than providing accurate versions of past styles. For example, there is little attempt to convey a credible social setting outside the choreographed orchestration of extras, and the trans milieu is highly codified and theatrically staged through the lens of performance. Passers-by are singled out to make an ethical point about the judgment of others as in the opening sequence, which shows reactions made by anonymous onlookers to the public display of the trans body. Later, students are shot reacting to Laurence who demonstrates her personal courage by parading in slow motion down the corridor in a camp tribute to catwalk glamour. The faces show a range of aversion, curiosity, admiration, and envy. The film mixes sequences shot as moving fashion editorials—for example, the shots of the couple in torment following Laurence's disclosure—with more neutral images that mark anonymous others out as ordinary, normal, and unfashionable, which in turn conflates the different, queer, and marginal with the high fashion look.

Some critics have perceived Dolan's rejection of realist social dynamics as a form of narcissistic elitism.[25] In my view, this position misinterprets the mode of his cinema and its transparent investment in the codes of popular genres (romance and melodrama) and subcultural forms (camp and drag) more than in the (straight) art-house tradition of social realism. If we embrace the film's anti-naturalistic flourishes, taking *Laurence Anyways* as a queer fashion film of sorts, how does that affect how we configure the filmmaker beyond the residual category of the indie auteur? Instead of critiquing Dolan's versatility as a sign of total control or individual narcissism, one might associate it more readily with the aesthetic strategies of today's branded fashion designers and the citational mood board or mixing board approach of the creative director. Beyond fashion, thinking of Dolan's approach to narrative through pop is also instructive because it focuses attention on the film's rhythms, temporal structure, and investment in excess (both the pretty and the garish), a feature developed subsequently with the shocking images of teen violence in the video for French band Indochine's single "College Boy" in 2013, which concludes with an art installation staging the crucifixion of a gay teenager.

Combining sound with vision, music videos have always promoted fashionable styles as much as music. Fashion photographers such as Jean-Baptiste Mondino and Jean-Paul Goude are earlier examples of 1980s "postmodern video-auteurs,"[26] who transformed the music video into a "minor art form" in the words of film critic Serge Daney, who was an early adopter, and influential in

promoting the distinct codes of a form rooted in fragmentation and instantane-
ity.[27] While the spectacular "Fade to Grey" ball sequence in *Laurence Anyways*
visualizes energy and excess through speed and movement, Dolan is also known
for his use of slow motion. When Fred and Laurence take flight to an island,
multicolored CGI clothes slowly rain down on them. Color is also used elsewhere to express Fred's liberation from domesticity. Brash red lipstick revives
her former edginess, expressed through wild dyed red hair, which is used earlier
in the film as part of the chaotic clashing motifs in the restaurant confrontation scene. In a mode reminiscent of Rainer Werner Fassbinder's disruptive
aesthetics from the 1970s, the decor is more than the setting for the couple's
divergence: it graphically acts it out. Laurence's appearance oscillates between
the natural and the spectacular, instances of which include posed editorial-style
shots on a ferry and the campy blue tailored suit with pussy-bow blouse in an
interview with a journalist—a drag-inspired look that nods to the expressionis-
tic angular shapes routinely worn by icons of Hollywood glamour such as Bette
Davis and Joan Crawford.[28] From an ideological perspective, Dolan's trans costuming problematically borders on drag, which is compounded by the casting
of a cisgender actor in the title role, a strategy which despite underscoring the
constructed artifice of gender performance also potentially reifies and re-natu-
ralizes binary difference through the narrative vehicle of transgender. However,
Dolan's drag-coded styling does also illustrate what film theorist Stella Bruzzi
analyzes as an approach to costuming that tends to disrupt, or act independently
of, the film's narrative framework.[29] For her first appearance in public, Laurence wears harsh, unflattering make-up and boxy, geometric shapes, a look that
foregrounds the bravery and confrontation of the act rather than any realistic
desire to pass.

This graphic austerity is later echoed in the scenes that recount Fred's
"confinement" at Trois-Rivières, where she is trapped in an angular, modernist house the bleached decor of which encases a woman drained of life. Fred's
earlier vitality is showcased in the ball sequence, which stops time and serves
little narrative function but stages the character's desire for release. The setting does not imitate the original Visage clip from 1981, which contained
mostly static shots direct to camera, but it draws on the video for another song
played diegetically in the car wash sequences: Kim Carnes' 1981 hit "Bette
Davis Eyes," which features the androgynous singer performing at a costume
ball. Theorist of popular music Simon Frith has argued that one function of
pop music is its static quality, its ability to stop time.[30] The elliptical format
of the clip enables Dolan to juxtapose diegetic reality (Fred's self-confident
arrival at the ball as she strides through the admiring crowd wearing a luminous Yves Saint Laurent couture cape) with her own subjective fantasy (the
spectacular, slow motion tracking forward movement as she floats through the
crowd articulates her release from the confrontational outburst in the café).

The self-contained scene works as an escape mechanism into an idealized parallel reality: into the world of fashion. Dolan draws on the full battery of pop clichés—from elliptical jump cuts to oblique close-ups—going heavy on the dry ice and wind machines. The shots alternate between Fred's glamorous revolve and her cocky procession through the crowd before dissolving to an exterior shot of Laurence seated alone on a bus. Just like the camp icon Dalida's version of "Bang Bang," which is played on a loop in *Les Amours*, the ball sequence encapsulates Dolan's idiosyncratic blend of narrative, music, and styling within a film that explores the formal tension between surface brilliance (fashion and the look) and thematic depth (identity and the body).

HOME IS WHERE IT HURTS: COSTUME AND CLASS

In the narrative context of *Laurence Anyways*, the ball scene works as a fantasy escape mechanism for Fred to enter a seductive dream world, to leap from the domesticity of the home onto the public stage of style. The focus on the judgmental stares from the assembled guests, who range from the chic to the freaky (including the fleeting presence of the director), also points to the cultural exclusivity of taste that frames the film's contrived vision of an urban creative milieu. By contrast, the intentionally failed taste and vulgar fashions of Dolan's lower middle-class suburban or provincial mothers raise other more complex questions of age, femininity, class, and regional identity in relation to the handling of costume design. Dolan's creative cultivation of lowbrow styling, one that is intentionally tasteless, might be a case of "naïve camp," in Sontag's understanding, of a form of "seriousness that fails."[31] However, it also finds more high-brow parallels in designer fashion, in the contemporaneous trend for re-aestheticized "ugly" styles associated with designer Demna Gvasalia's creations for the labels Vetements and Balenciaga, and elsewhere in the "new baroque" sensibility noted by curator Judith Clark in her radical reassessment of the creativity of the vulgar in fashion history for the 2016 Barbican exhibition in London, *The Vulgar: Fashion Redefined*. Rather than simply denoting outlandish garments, the "new baroque" designs are based on the assumption that "a desire for excess is the norm. They improvise with the leftovers of other styles: they are testing new ground, without the compromise of established taste."[32]

A desire for excess is the norm: this idea also describes Dolan's practice of costuming and stylization. The early stages of *J'ai tué ma mère* contrast the gaudy decor and dowdy style of Hubert's mother (Anne Dorval)—ornate furnishings, mannequin trinkets, and a leopard print coat—with the modernity of boyfriend Antonin's (François Arnaud) mother, Hélène (Patricia Tulasne), who is youthfully dressed and sexually liberated. The later image of suburban housewives dressed as hyperbolic tributes to soap opera divas is extended

through the brassy look of Diane 'Die' Després (Dorval) in *Mommy*, whose
character and location (a struggling widow in lower middle-class suburbia)
are represented through clothing and setting in the camerawork of the film's
opening shots: in the lingering close-up of a pair of boxer shorts drying on
the washing line, followed by a pan shot of her tight studded jeans, costume
is again revealed as the entry key to characterization. However, these looks are
plain compared to the extravagant designs for Martine (Nathalie Baye), the
mother in *Juste la fin du monde*, the first shots of whom focus on her bejew-
eled fingers and varnished nails as she busily prepares for the return, after an
absence of twelve years, of her gay son, Louis (Gaspard Ulliel), a celebrated
writer, who returns home to announce his imminent death, and whom she
describes stereotypically enough as loving fashion. The artificiality of her look
(a dark fitted suit, chunky gold necklace, black wig, and blue eye shadow) is
criticized by her volatile daughter Suzanne (Léa Seydoux) for resembling a
"tranny." The script therefore acknowledges the contribution of style to the
film's operative mode—its melodramatic sensibility—by integrating costume
and decor as features of the dramatic performances as much as the production
designs. The transphobic slur also serves to acknowledge the more intertextual
drag styles of some of Dolan's mothers, whose looks, in true serial pop fashion,
tend to resemble one another. But Baye's costume is not just a superficial gag;
it also makes an emotional point: Martine is over-dressed for the reunion lunch
and her look is out of context and embarrassing. Failed aspirations and social
immobility form part of the theme of affective disconnection and spatial dislocation, which is articulated through the linguistic patterns—the disjointed
phrasing and abrupt rhythms—of the source text, Jean-Luc Lagarce's original
1999 stage play. The moving scene, in which Martine tries in vain to communicate with Louis, ends with their prolonged embrace, the son clutching his
mother's suit jacket for comfort.

The expressive codes of melodrama have often been linked to the performances of screen stars.[33] Dolan cast five of French cinema's most famous faces
and bankable names, three of whom, like the director, have secured lucrative
contracts to model for fashion brands: Marion Cotillard for Christian Dior,
Léa Seydoux for Louis Vuitton and Prada, and Gaspard Ulliel for Chanel. In
"Signs of melodrama," Christine Gledhill argues that the link between screen
melodrama and stardom involves a process of personalization; the formal role
of the star "as a composite structure" is "to manage the tension between melodrama's emblematic, non-psychological personae and its drive to realize in
personal terms social and ethical forces."[34] Dolan conjoins melodrama with
stardom by setting virtually the entire film in a domestic *huis clos* and framing it
through a series of intense close-ups to maximize the emotional intensity of the
series of exchanges between Louis and each family member. Gledhill further
explains that melodramatic excess "exists in paradoxical relation to the form's

commitment to the real world."[35] Excess, then, has been read as a mode of critique, a symptom of the ideological contradictions that are channeled through the visual, through formal features such as set and costume. The opening montage sequence alternates between Louis's taxi ride from the airport—elegantly orchestrated by director of photography André Turpin in a series of pseudo-documentary tracking shots of local inhabitants, ghosts from the past who are shot from Louis's perspective—and the domestic images of his mother at work. As elsewhere in Dolan's cinema, the ambiguous gazes of strangers oppose antagonistically the successful creative urban exile—the queer artist in this instance—against the faces and activities of ordinary local folk.[36] The foreboding non-diegetic pop song ironically undercuts Martine's careful preparations for the family meal—"home is not a harbor, home is where it hurts," warns the singer Camille.

The exaggeration and exposure that characterize the subsequent scenes also form part of the film's intentionally melodramatic mode and its emotional translation through costume and decor. The opening montage ends to the chime of a cuckoo clock, a kitsch design feature that reoccurs in disruptive fashion at the film's end in a spectacularly over-determined metaphor in which the bird flies out of the clock only to flounder and drop to the floor. This supremely kitsch expression of fake emotion ironically deflates the tension by literalizing the exhaustion of the domestic drama, the tense build-up to the protagonist's failure to disclose his illness and his expulsion from the family cell. The kitsch object effectively lays bare the poignant denouement as a sentimental artifice. Sontag included this type of deployment of camp as a distancing device in her taxonomy, describing how it "refuses both the harmonies of traditional seriousness, and the risks of fully identifying with extreme states of feeling."[37] Moreover, in a commentary on Sontag's notes, literary critic Terry Castle links repressed memories of home, of domestic confinement and childhood disappointment (like the urbane Louis's unglamorous rural origins) as a psychic context for understanding camp styling. Drawing on Sontag's own disavowed feelings of being misplaced, Castle argues that camp

> mediates . . . between childhood outrage and a more sophisticated "adult" self. From one angle, camp objects summon up the detested paraphernalia of the *past*—they are emblems of that world of ugliness, dishonesty, and emotional bathos one prides oneself on having escaped or transcended.[38]

Castle thus specifically links the attachment to the ugly to affective states like shame and suffering. She could also be summarizing the action in Dolan's film. The theatrical framing device that precedes the opening credit sequence shows Louis's plane journey while he recounts in voice-over his decision to return home after a prolonged absence. This subjective frame conditions the perspective of the subsequent melodrama, of scenes that could well be read as the character's own fearful imagining of what is to follow or the writer's traumatic fantasy of the immediate future shot through the ambivalent lens of past suffering. We do not learn exactly why Louis severed contact with his family; only Antoine's wife, Catherine (Marion Cotillard) intuits the real reason for his visit. In one scene, she discovers Louis alone in the garage surrounded by his former belongings, haunted by the discarded paraphernalia of his past. It is precisely the affective sincerity of these dramatic scenes that is punctured by the kitsch design and phony emotion of the final moments of the film.

How critical, ironic, or distanced this type of stylistic maneuver is in Dolan's cinema more broadly is unclear, and the purposeful inclusion of "unfashionable" music tracks by the likes of Dido and Moby in his films would seem to indicate a more immediate understanding of pop simply as popular and mainstream—"vulgar" in the sense of vernacular. The accessible appeal of Dolan's cinema (not to mention the relative global box office success of a film like *Mommy*) is therefore a way of countering the elitist pretensions of the auteur and market positioning of indie "world" cinema. Dolan achieves this through style and content, through genre and location, and by examining questions of aesthetic value and taste, which are germane to both pop music and fashion culture.

Dolan's popular appeal through style indicates how hierarchies of taste are still important to thinking about contemporary practices of film costuming. Social questions of class, milieu, and distinction haven't entirely been subsumed by the eclectic *self*-expression associated with contemporary designer fashions and popular street styles. Recent hyperbolic talk of the end of the fashion system suggests the cultivation of excess to be a new industry norm. Dolan's signature style—both personal and cinematic, cultivated through a public and commercial profile that straddles indie cinema and fashion branding—makes creative use of excess (both melodrama and camp) to shape and visualize narrative through the practice of costume design.

As I have argued, Dolan takes fashion seriously as an integral part of the visual elaboration of his storytelling. But rather than view his cinema as superficial or modish, I have attempted to recuperate its mobilization of pop style and decorative styling as a lens through which to consider his narratives of romance, desire, longing, and transformation. The signature flourishes of excess that characterize Dolan's aesthetic are certainly heady (and evidently off-putting for some critics and audiences—*Juste la fin du monde* was, indeed, booed following its presentation in competition at Cannes in 2016) and they signal an inscription within a queer melodramatic tradition; this despite his own vocal disliking of the LGBTQ minority label. In my view, criticisms of Dolan's cinema as formally elitist or socially condescending miss the point precisely because they overlook the *mode* of his films—how they work as authorial covers of popular genres such as the queer romance, melodrama, or fashion film, and also how they use style—especially costume and production design—as a key point of entry into dramatic narrative.

NOTES

1. Sontag's final note reads: "The ultimate Camp statement: it's good *because* it's awful." Susan Sontag, "Notes on 'Camp,'" in *Against Interpretation* (London: Vintage, 1994), p. 292.
2. Pamela Church Gibson, "Film costume," in John Hill and Pamela Church Gibson (eds), *Film Studies: Critical Approaches* (Oxford: Oxford University Press, 2000), p. 35.
3. Peter Wollen, *Raiding the Icebox: Reflections on Twentieth-Century Culture* (London: Verso, 1993), p. 161.
4. Sontag, *Against Interpretation*, p. 287.
5. Xavier Dolan quoted in Luke Seomore, "Why Xavier Dolan's mesmerising new drama is a must-watch," *Another Magazine*, February 27, 2017. Available at <http://www.anothermag.com/design-living/9579/why-xavier-dolans-mesmerising-new-drama-is-a-must-watch> (accessed June 1, 2017).
6. Xavier Dolan, "Xavier Dolan: 'Tous mes films parlent d'un amour impossible,'" interview by Jean-Marc Lalanne, *Les Inrockuptibles*, July 18, 2012. Available at <https://www.lesinrocks.com/2012/07/18/cinema/xavier-dolan-tous-mes-films-parlent-dun-amour-impossible-11279693/> (accessed August 29, 2018).
7. Patricia Garcia, "Meet Xavier Dolan, the indie director behind Adele's 'Hello' music video," *Vogue*, October 27, 2015. Available at <https://www.vogue.com/article/xavier-dolan-adele-hello-video?verso=true> (accessed August 29, 2018).
8. Georg Simmel, "The problem of style," *Theory, Culture and Society*, 8/63, 1991, pp. 64, 65.
9. Sontag, "On style," in *Against Interpretation*, p. 19.
10. Fredric Jameson, "Postmodernism and consumer society," in Hal Foster (ed.), *The Anti-Aesthetic: Essays on Postmodern Culture* (Seattle: Bay Press, 1983), pp. 111–25.
11. Guillaume Narduzzi, "Xavier Dolan: ses déclarations les plus décoiffantes," *Le Figaro*, last updated September 20, 2016. Available at <http://www.lefigaro.fr/cinema/2016/09/20/03002-20160920ARTFIG00286-xavier-dolan-ses-plus-retentissantes-declarations.php> (accessed August 28, 2018).
12. Jean-Philippe Tessé, "Aller plus haut," *Cahiers du Cinéma*, 680, July–August 2012, p. 42. My translation.
13. Richard Brody, "An auteur is not a brand," *New Yorker*, July 10, 2014. Available at <https://www.newyorker.com/culture/richard-brody/an-auteur-is-not-a-brand> (accessed August 29, 2018).
14. Stéphane Delorme, "Xavier Dolan, X/Y," *Cahiers du Cinéma*, 678, May 2012, p. 36.
15. For example, the reviewer for *Sight & Sound* opened his article on *Laurence Anyways* thus:

> Xavier Dolan's third feature finds the 23-year old Québécois filmmaker giving ever-freer rein to his ambition. Dolan's prodigiously talented directorial debut *J'ai tué ma mère* caused a sensation at its premiere in Cannes in 2009, when the director had just turned twenty; and Dolan showed no strain in following it up, with *Heartbeats* ready for unveiling at the next year's festival.

Samuel Wigley, "Laurence Anyways," review of *Laurence Anyways* directed by Xavier Dolan, *Sight & Sound*, 22/12, 2012, p. 95.

16. "Ils ont réuni un vieux metteur en scène qui fait un jeune film avec un jeune metteur en scène qui fait un film ancien." Jean-Luc Godard quoted in Pierre de Gasquet, "Xavier Dolan Le dandy enragé," *Les Echos Week-end*, September 23, 2016. Available at <https://www.lesechos.fr/23/09/2016/LesEchosWeekEnd/00046-013-ECWE_xavier-dolan-le-dandy-enrage.htm> (accessed August 29, 2018). My translation.

17. Stéphane Delorme and Jean-Philippe Tessé, "Titanic: entretien avec Xavier Dolan," *Cahiers du Cinéma*, 680, 2012, pp. 42–4.

18. Dolan's current notoriety extends beyond cinema: in the second season of the French TV sitcom, *Dix pour cent/Call My Agent* (France 2, 2017), the character of a megalomaniac wunderkind filmmaker, who terrorizes Isabelle Adjani, is allegedly based on the Dolan persona. Marine Chassagnon, "'Dix pour cent' s'est inspiré dans la saison 2 de Xavier Dolan pour créer un cinéaste insupportable," *HuffPost*, Edition FR, last updated April 26, 2017, 04:54 CEST. Available at <https://www.huffingtonpost.fr/2017/04/25/dix-pour-cent-sest-inspire-de-xavier-dolan-pour-creer-un-cine_a_22035263/> (accessed August 29, 2018).

19. Seemore, "Why Xavier Dolan's mesmerising new drama is a must-watch."

20. Giuliana Bruno, *Surface: Matters of Aesthetics, Materiality, and Media* (Chicago: University of Chicago Press, 2014), pp. 3–5.

21. The dismissal of the decorative is something Rosalind Galt has traced as a denigration of the pretty. Galt locates a "discomfort with a style of heightened aesthetics that is too decorative, too sensorially pleasurable to be high art, and yet too composed and 'arty' to be efficient entertainment." Rosalind Galt, *Pretty: Film and the Decorative Image* (New York: Columbia University Press, 2011), p. 12.

22. Bill Marshall, "Spaces and times of Québec in two films by Xavier Dolan," *Nottingham French Studies*, 55/2, 2016, p. 201.

23. Bill Marshall quoted in Kester Dyer, Andrée Lafontaine, and Fulvia Massimi (eds), "Interview with Bill Marshall," *Synoptique*, 4/2, 2016, p. 113.

24. Emiliano Morreale, "Le cinéma vintage," trans. Lili Hinstin, *Cahiers du Cinéma*, 673, 2011, pp. 16–19.

25. See Alexandre Fontaine Rousseau, "Culte de la personnalité: le cinéma de Xavier Dolan," *24 images*, 173, September 2015, pp. 11–13.

26. Richard Dienst, *Still Life in Real Time: Theory After Television* (Durham, NC: Duke University Press, 1994), p. 84.

27. See Serge Daney, *Le Salaire du zappeur* (Paris: P.O.L, 1993), pp. 103–5 and *Ciné-Journal 1981–1986* (Paris: Cahiers du Cinéma, 1986), pp. 299–300. On the larger relationship between music video and fashion film, see Nick Rees-Roberts, *Fashion Film: Art and Advertising in the Digital Age* (London: Bloomsbury, 2018), pp. 32–5.

28. On the broader relationship between fashion and transgender in *Laurence Anyways*, see Katrina Sark, "The language of fashion and (trans)gender in Dolan's *Laurence Anyways*," *Synoptique*, 4/2, 2016, pp. 127–34.

29. See Stella Bruzzi, *Undressing Cinema: Clothing and Identity at the Movies* (Abingdon: Routledge, 1997).

30. See Simon Frith, "Towards an aesthetic of popular music," in *Taking Popular Music Seriously* (Aldershot: Ashgate, 2007), pp. 257–74.

31. Sontag, *Against Interpretation*, p. 283.

32. Judith Clark, "The new baroque," in Jane Alison and Sinéad McCarthy (eds), *The Vulgar: Fashion Redefined* (London: Barbican/Koenig Books, 2016), p. 166.

33. See, for example, Thomas Elsaesser, "Tales of sound and fury: observations on the family melodrama," in Christine Gledhill (ed.), *Home Is Where The Heart Is: Studies in Melodrama and the Woman's Film* (London: British Film Institute, 1987), pp. 43–69.

34. Christine Gledhill, "Signs of melodrama," in *Stardom: Industry of Desire*, ed. Christine Gledhill (Abingdon: Routledge, 1991), p. 214.
35. Ibid. p. 213.
36. The complexity of the gazes in Dolan's cinema is analyzed in Corey Kai Nelson Schultz, "The sensation of the look: the gazes in *Laurence Anyways*," *Film Philosophy*, 22/1, February 2018, pp. 1–20.
37. Sontag, *Against Interpretation*, p. 287.
38. Terry Castle, "Some notes on 'Notes on Camp,'" in Barbara Ching and Jennifer A. Wagner-Lawlor (eds), *The Scandal of Susan Sontag* (New York: Columbia University Press, 2009), p. 28.

Bibliography

Ahmed, Sara, *The Promise of Happiness* (Durham, NC: Duke University Press, 2010).

Ahmed, Sara, "Melancholic universalism," *Feminist Killjoys*, December 15, 2015, <https://feministkilljoys.com/2015/12/15/melancholic-universalism/> (accessed March 24, 2018).

Andrew, Dudley, "An atlas of world cinema," *Framework*, 45/2, Fall 2004, pp. 9–23.

Armbrecht, Thomas J. D., "'On se baigne jamais deux fois dans le même fleuve': l'ontologie trans- de *Laurence Anyways*," *L'Esprit Créateur*, 53/1, Spring 2013, pp. 31–44.

Babuscio, Jack, "The cinema of camp (AKA camp and the gay sensibility)," in Fabio Cleto (ed.), *Camp: Queer Aesthetics and the Performing Subject* (Edinburgh: Edinburgh University Press, 1999), pp. 117–35.

Bailey, Benjamin, "Multilingual forms of talk and identity work," in Peter Auer and Li Wei (eds), *Handbook of Multilingualism and Multilingual Communication* (Berlin: de Gruyter, 2009), pp. 341–69.

Barker, Jennifer M., *The Tactile Eye: Touch and the Cinematic Experience* (Berkeley: University of California Press, 2009).

Baronnet, Brigitte, "Nathalie Baye et son look dans Juste la fin du monde: 'C'est Xavier Dolan le patron!,'" *Allociné*, September 25, 2016, <http://www.allocine.fr/article/fichearticle_gen_carticle=18656162.html>.

Barnett, Emily, "'J'ai tué ma mère': plongée dans la violence d'une relation mère-fils," *Les Inrockuptibles*, July 10, 2009, <https://www.lesinrocks.com/cinema/films-a-l-affiche/jai-tue-ma-mere/> (accessed July 14, 2018).

Bazin, André, *What Is Cinema?*, vol. 1. trans. and ed. Hugh Gray (Berkeley: University of California Press, 2005), pp. 53–75.

Berlant, Lauren, *Cruel Optimism* (Durham, NC: Duke University Press, 2011).

Besse, Caroline, "Anne Dorval et Suzanne Clément—actrices-muses de Xavier Dolan. Elles l'inspirent, il les met en valeur," *Télérama*, May 23, 2014, <http://www.telerama.fr/festival-de-cannes/2014/anne-dorval-et-suzanne-clement-actrices-muses-de-xavier-dolan,112857.php>.

Betz, Mark, *Beyond the Subtitle: Remapping European Art Cinema* (Minneapolis: University of Minnesota Press, 2009).

Biswas, Moinak, "The couple and their spaces: *Hurano Sur* as melodrama now," in Ravi Vasudevan (ed.), *Making Meaning in Indian Cinema* (New Delhi: Oxford University Press, 2000), pp. 122–42.

Blondeau, Romain, "Teaching film studies in India: curricula and crises," *Journal of the Moving Image*, II, December 2012, pp. 13–19.

Blondeau, Romain, "Xavier Dolan: 'Je fais des films pour me venger,'" *Les Inrockuptibles*, October 1, 2014, <https://www.lesinrocks.com/2014/10/01/cinema/xavier-dolan-fais-films-venger-11520012/> (accessed March 17, 2018).

Bombarda, Olivier, "La fièvre insolente," *Bande à part*, September 21, 2016, <http://www.bande-a-part.fr/cinema/critique/juste-la-fin-du-monde-de-xavier-dolan-magazine-de-cinema/> (accessed July 20, 2018).

Bordwell, David and Kristin Thompson, *Film Art: An Introduction*, 9th edn (New York: McGraw-Hill, 2010).

Bouchard, Chantal, *La langue et le nombril: histoire d'une obsession québécoise*, Collection Nouvelles études québécoises (Montréal: Fides, 1998).

Bouchard, Chantal, *Obsessed With Language: A Sociolinguistic History of Quebec*, trans. Luise von Flotow (Toronto: Guernica, 2009).

Bouchard, Chantal, *Méchante langue: la légitimité linguistique du français parlé au Québec* (Montréal: Les Presses de l'Université de Montréal, 2012), Kindle.

Bouchard, Michel Marc, "Le théâtre au cinéma ou le dramaturge devient scénariste!," in Carla Fratta (ed.), *Littérature et cinéma au Québec (1995–2005)* (Bologna: Pendragon, 2008).

Bouchard, Michel Marc, *Tom at the Farm*, trans. Linda Gaboriau (Vancouver: Talonbooks, 2013).

Bourdieu, Pierre, *Distinction: A Social Critique of the Judgment of Taste*, trans. Richard Nice (Cambridge, MA: Harvard University Press, 1984).

Bourdieu, Pierre, *Outline of a Theory of Practice*, trans. Richard Nice (Cambridge: Cambridge University Press, 2012).

Boym, Svetlana, *The Future of Nostalgia* (New York: Basic Books, 2008).

Brady, Emily and Arto Haapala, "Melancholy as an aesthetic emotion," *Contemporary Aesthetics*, I, 2003, <https://contempaesthetics.org/newvolume/pages/article.php?articleID=214> (accessed March 24, 2018).

Brody, Richard. "An auteur is not a brand," *New Yorker*, July 10, 2014, <https://www.newyorker.com/culture/richard-brody/an-auteur-is-not-a-brand> (accessed August 29, 2018).

Browne, Michael P., *Closet Space: Geographies of Metaphor from the Body to the Globe* (London: Routledge, 2000).

Bruno, Giuliana, *Surface: Matters of Aesthetics, Materiality, and Media* (Chicago: University of Chicago Press, 2014).

Bruzzi, Stella, *Undressing Cinema: Clothing and Identity at the Movies* (Abingdon: Routledge, 1997).

Buchanan, Kyle, "Xavier Dolan on *Mommy*, art, and his Harry Potter tattoo," *Vulture*, January 21, 2015, <http://www.vulture.com/2015/01/xavier-dolan-mommy-interview.html> (accessed March 24, 2018).

Butler, Judith, *Gender Trouble* (New York: Routledge, 1990).

Butler, Judith, *Excitable Speech: A Politics of the Performative* (New York: Routledge, 1997).

Cahir, Linda Costanzo, *Literature into Film: Theory and Practical Approaches* (Jefferson, NC: McFarland, 2006).

Castle, Terry, "Some notes on 'Notes on Camp,'" in Barbara Ching and Jennifer A. Wagner-Lawlor (eds), *The Scandal of Susan Sontag* (New York: Columbia University Press, 2009), pp. 21–31.

Chahine, Joumane, "Mommy," *Film Comment*, 51/1, January–February 2015, pp. 63–5.

Chambers, Samuel A. and Michael O'Rourke, "Jacques Rancière on the shores of queer theory," in Samuel A. Chambers and Michael O'Rourke (eds), "Jacques Rancière on the shores of queer theory," *Borderlands*, 8/2, 2009, pp. 1–19.

Chassagnon, Marine, "'Dix pour cent' s'est inspiré dans la saison 2 de Xavier Dolan pour créer un cinéaste insupportable," *HuffPost*, Edition FR, updated April 26, 2017, 04:54 CEST, <https://www.huffingtonpost.fr/2017/04/25/dix-pour-cent-sest-inspire-de-xavier-dolan-pour-creer-un-cine_a_22035263/> (accessed August 29, 2018).

Chastain, Jessica, "Xavier Dolan," *Interview*, January 12, 2015.

Chaudhuri, Shohini, "Color design in the cinema of Wong Kar-wai," in Martha P. Nochimson (ed.), *A Companion to Wong Kar-wai* (Chichester: Wiley-Blackwell, 2016), pp. 153–81.

Chihon, Michel, *Le Son au cinéma* (Paris: Édition de l'Étoile, 1985).

Ciment, Michel, "Cannes 2014, 67ᵉ edition," *Positif*, 641/642, July/August 2014, pp. 68–70.

Clark, Judith, "The new baroque," in Jane Alison and Sinéad McCarthy (eds), *The Vulgar: Fashion Redefined* (London: Barbican/Koenig Books, 2016), p. 166.

Clémence, Allard, "Xavier Dolan: le talent de mettre en lumière les femmes," *Tribune citoyenne*, May 18, 2016, <https://latribunecitoyenne.wordpress.com/2016/05/18/xavier-dolan-le-talent-de-mettre-en-lumiere-les-femmes/> (accessed March 12, 2018).

Cleto, Fabio (ed.), *Camp: Queer Aesthetics and the Performing Subject* (Edinburgh: Edinburgh University Press, 1999).

Corrigan, Timothy, "The commerce of auteurism," in Virginia Wright Wexman (ed.), *Film and Authorship* (New Brunswick, NJ: Rutgers University Press, 2003), pp. 96–11.

Cvetkovich, Ann, *An Archive of Feelings: Trauma, Sexuality, and Lesbian Public Cultures* (Durham, NC: Duke University Press, 2003).

D'Aoust, Jason, "The queer voices of Xavier Dolan's *Mommy*," *European Journal of American Studies*, 11/3, 2017, pp. 1–17, <https://doi.org/10.4000/ejas.11755>.

Daney, Serge, *Ciné Journal 1981–1986* (Paris: Cahiers du Cinéma, 1986).

Dass, Manishita, "The cloud-capped star: Ritwik Ghatak on the horizon of global art cinema," in Rosalind Galt and Karl Schoonover (eds), *Global Art Cinema: New Theories and Histories* (Oxford: Oxford University Press, 2010), pp. 238–51.

Debruge, Peter, "Cannes film review: 'It's Only the End of the World,'" *Variety*, May 18, 2016, <https://variety.com/2016/film/festivals/its-only-the-end-of-the-world-review-xavier-dolan-1201777980/> (accessed June 24, 2018).

Deleuze, Gilles, *Cinema 1: The Movement–Image*, trans. Hugh Tomlinson and Barbara Habberjam (Minneapolis: University of Minnesota Press, 1986).

Delorme, Stéphane, "Xavier Dolan, X/Y," *Cahiers du Cinéma*, 678, May 2012, pp. 36–7.

Delorme, Stéphane and Jean-Philippe Tessé, "Titanic: entretien avec Xavier Dolan," *Cahiers du Cinéma*, 680, July–August 2012, pp. 42–4.

Del Río, Elena, *Deleuze and the Cinemas of Performance: Powers of Affection* (Edinburgh: Edinburgh University Press, 2008).

Dennison, Stephanie and Song Hwee Lim (eds), *Remapping World Cinema: Identity, Culture and Politics in Film* (London: Wallflower Press, 2006).

Dienst, Richard, *Still Life in Real Time: Theory After Television* (Durham, NC: Duke University Press, 1994).

Dolan, Xavier, "Cannes 2012: Canadian director Xavier Dolan on *Laurence Anyways* (Q&A)," interview by Etan Vlessing, *Hollywood Reporter*, May 18, 2012, <https://www.hollywoodreporter.com/news/cannes-festival-xavier-dolan-qa-326081>.

Dolan, Xavier, "Xavier Dolan: 'Tous mes films parlent d'un amour impossible,'" interview by Jean-Marc Lalanne, *Les Inrockuptibles*, July 18, 2012, <https://www.

lesinrocks.com/2012/07/18/cinema/xavier-dolan-tous-mes-films-parlent-dun-amour-impossible-11279693/> (accessed August 29, 2018).

Dolan, Xavier, "Interview: Xavier Dolan," interview by Emma Myers, *Film Comment*, June 24, 2013, <https://www.filmcomment.com/blog/interview-xavier-dolan/> (accessed July 26, 2017).

Dolan, Xavier, "Director Xavier Dolan on *Laurence Anyways* and the ghetto of queer cinema," interview by Tyler Coates, *Flavorwire* (blog), June 27, 2013, <http://flavorwire.com/400845/flavorwire-interview-director-xavier-dolan-on-laurence-anyways-and-the-ghetto-of-queer-cinema> (accessed February 27, 2016).

Dolan, Xavier, interviewed by Marie-France Bazzo, *Bazzo.tv*. Télé-Québec, September 27, 2012, quoted in Valérie Mandia, "Le septième art hors des frontières nationales: le pouvoir de la langue et de l'imaginaire culturel dans les films du cinéaste québécois Xavier Dolan," *Francophonies d'Amérique*, 37, Spring 2014, pp. 105–32.

Dolan, Xavier, "*Mommy* director Xavier Dolan doesn't want you to label his films," interview by Eric Eidelstein, *IndieWire*, January 19, 2015, <https://www.indiewire.com/2015/01/mommy-director-xavier-dolan-doesnt-want-you-to-label-his-films-2-66142/> (accessed March 10, 2018).

Dolan, Xavier, "Meet Xavier Dolan, the indie director behind Adele's 'Hello' music video," interview by Patricia Garcia, *Vogue*, October 27, 2015 01:55 EST <https://www.vogue.com/article/xavier-dolan-adele-hello-video?verso=true> (accessed August 29, 2018).

Dolan, Xavier, "Why Xavier Dolan's mesmerising new drama is a must-watch," interview by Luke Seomore, *Another Magazine*, February 27, 2017, <http://www.anothermag.com/design-living/9579/why-xavier-dolans-mesmerising-new-drama-is-a-must-watch> (accessed June 1, 2017).

Dolan, Xavier, "Xavier Dolan: 'I've never experienced love as something calm and tender,'" interview by Sophie Monks Kaufman, *Little White Lies*, <https://lwlies.com/interviews/xavier-dolan-mommy/> (accessed November 16, 2017).

Ducharme, André, "L'étrange histoire de Xavier Dolan," *L'Actualité*, July 3, 2010, <https://lactualite.com/culture/2010/07/03/letrange-histoire-de-xavier-dolan/>.

Dundjerovic, Aleksandar, "Appendix: interview with Robert Lepage," in *The Cinema of Robert Lepage: The Poetics of Memory* (London: Wallflower Press, 2003), pp. 147–57.

Dyer, Kester, Andrée Lafontaine, and Fulvia Massimi (eds.), "Locating the intimate within the global: Xavier Dolan, queer nations and Québec cinema," Special issue, *Synoptique*, 4/2, Winter 2016.

Dyer, Richard, *Heavenly Bodies: Film Stars and Society* (Basingstoke: Macmillan, 1986).

Edelman, Lee, "The future is kid stuff: queer theory, disidentification, and the death drive," *Narrative*, 6/1, January 1998, pp. 18–30.

Elsaesser, Thomas, "Tales of sound and fury: observations on the family melodrama," in Christine Gledhill (ed.), *Home is Where the Heart Is: Studies in Melodrama and the Woman's Film* (London: British Film Institute, 1987), pp. 43–69.

Elsaesser, Thomas, *European Cinema: Face to Face with Hollywood* (Amsterdam: Amsterdam University Press, 2005).

Espineira, Karine, *Médiacultures: la transidentité en télévision. Une recherche menée sur un corpus à l'INA (1946–2010)*, Collection Logiques Sociales, Série Sociologie du genre (Paris: Éditions L'Harmattan, 2015).

Estève, Michel, *Un Cinéma humaniste* (Paris: Septième Art, 2007).

Evangelista, Matthew, *Gender, Nationalism, and War: Conflict on the Movie Screen* (Cambridge: Cambridge University Press, 2011).

Faradji, Helen, "Les cinéastes cinéphiles," *24 images*, 152, June–July 2011, pp. 23–5.

Ferreira, Romain, "*Tom à la ferme*," *La Kinopithèque* (blog), May 24, 2014, <http://www.
    kinopitheque.net/tom-a-la-ferme/> (accessed September 10, 2018).
Fisher, Dominique, "*Vic + Flo ont vu un ours* de Denis Côté: histoire des femmes cruelles ou
    esthétique de la cruauté?," *Québec Studies*, 60, 2015, pp. 67–82.
Fontaine Rousseau, Antoine, "Culte de la personnalité: le cinéma de Xavier Dolan,"
    Images, 173, September 2015, <https://www.erudit.org/fr/revues/images/2015-n173-
    images02054/78552ac.pdf>.
Fortin, Andrée, *Imaginaire de l'espace dans le cinéma québécois* (Sainte-Foy: Presses de
    l'Université Laval, 2015).
Foucault, Michel, "The stage of philosophy: a conversation between Michel Foucault and
    Moriaki Watanabe," April 22, 1978, trans. Rosa Eidelpes and Kevin Kennedy, Scenes of
    Knowledge, *New York Magazine of Contemporary Art and Theory*, 1/5.
Foucault, Michel, "The eye of power," trans. Colin Gordon, in *Power/Knowledge: Selected
    Interviews and Other Writings 1972–1977*, ed. Colin Gordon, trans. Colin Gordon, Leo
    Marshall, John Mepham, and Kate Soper (New York: Pantheon Books, 1980), pp. 146–65.
Fradet, Pierre-Alexandre, "Le parler québécois, du Roi Soleil à Xavier Dolan," *Positif*, 674,
    April 2017, pp. 69–72.
Freeman, Elizabeth, "Packing history, count(er)ing generations," *New Literary History*, 31/4,
    2000, pp. 727–44.
Freud, Sigmund, *The Uncanny*, trans. David McClintock (New York: Penguin Books, 2003).
Frith, Simon, "Towards and aesthetic of popular music," in *Taking Popular Music Seriously*,
    Ashgate Contemporary Thinkers on Critical Musicology (Aldershot: Ashgate, 2007),
    pp. 257–74.
Galt, Rosalind, *Pretty: Film and the Decorative Image* (New York: Columbia University Press, 2011).
Gararanga, Joseph, "Code-switching as a conversational strategy," in Peter Auer and Wei Li
    (eds), *Handbook of Multilingualism and Multilingual Communication* (Berlin: Mouton de
    Gruyter, 2007), pp. 279–313.
Gardies, André, "Le narrateur sonne toujours deux fois," in André Gaudrault and Thierry
    Groensteen (eds), *La transécriture: pour une théorie de l'adaptation* (Québec: Nota bene,
    1999), pp. 65–80.
Gaudreault, André, *Du littéraire au filmique: système du récit* (Paris: Méridiens-Klincksieck, 1988).
Gaudreault, André and Philippe Marion, "Un art de l'emprunt: les sources intermédiales de
    l'adaptation," in Carla Tratta (ed.), *Littérature et cinéma au Québec (1995–2005)* (Bologna:
    Pendragon, 2008), pp. 13–30.
Gendron, Nicolas, "J'avais envie de montrer une figure maternelle héroïque," *Ciné-Bulles*,
    32/3, Summer 2014, pp. 4–9.
Genette, Gérard, *Palimpsestes: la littérature au second degré* (Paris: Seuil, 1982).
Gerstner, David A. and Janet Staiger (eds), *Authorship and Film* (New York: Routledge, 2003).
Ghaziani, Amin, "Post-gay collective identity construction," *Social Problems*, 58/1, February
    2011, pp. 99–125.
Gibson, Pamela Church, "Film costume," in John Hill and Pamela Gibson Church (eds),
    Film Studies: Critical Approaches (Oxford: Oxford University Press, 2000), pp. 34–40.
Gledhill, Christine, "Signs of melodrama," in *Stardom: Industry of Desire*, ed. Christine
    Gledhill (Abingdon: Routledge, 1991), pp. 207–27.
Gledhill, Christine, Introduction to *Gender Meets Genre in Postwar Cinemas*, ed. Christine
    Gledhill (Chicago: University of Chicago Press, 2002), pp. 1–14.
Godard, Jean-Luc quoted in Pierre de Gasquet, "Xavier Dolan le dandy enragé," *Les
    Echos Week-end*, September 23, 2016, <https://www.lesechos.fr/23/09/2016/
    LesEchosWeekEnd/00046-013-ECWE_xavier-dolan-le-dandy-enrage.htm> (accessed
    August 29, 2018).

Godbout, Jacques, "Entre l'Académie et l'Écurie," *Liberté*, 16/3, May–June 1974, pp. 16–33.

Green, Mary Jean, *Women and Narrative Identity: Rewriting the Quebec National Text* (Montréal: McGill-Queen's University Press, 2001).

Grugeau, Gérard, "Xavier Dolan: l'accélérateur d'intensité," *24 images*, 165, December 2013, pp. 40–3.

Guichard, Louis, "L'urgence, son moteur," *Télérama*, 3353, April 19, 2014.

Guichard, Louis, "'Mommy' Xavier Dolan," *Télérama*, 3378, October 11, 2014.

Gunning, Tom, *D. W. Griffith and the Origins of American Narrative Film: The Early Years at Biograph* (Urbana: University of Illinois Press, 1994).

Halberstam, Judith, *In a Queer Time and Place: Transgender Bodies, Subcultural Lives* (New York: New York University Press, 2005).

Halberstam, Judith, "Theorizing queer temporalities: a roundtable discussion," *GLQ*, 13/2–3, 2007, pp. 177–95.

Halberstam, Judith, *The Queer Art of Failure* (Durham, NC: Duke University Press, 2011).

Handler, Richard, *Nationalism and the Politics of Culture in Quebec* (Madison: University of Wisconsin Press, 1988).

Harris, Malcolm, *Kids These Days: Human Capital and the Making of Millennials* (New York: Little, Brown, 2017).

Hediger, Vinzenz, "What do we know when we know where something is? World cinema and the question of spatial ordering," *Screening the Past*, 21, October 2013, <http://www.screeningthepast.com/2013/10/what-do-we-know-when-we-know-where-something-is-world-cinema-and-the-question-of-spatial-ordering/> (accessed March 2, 2017).

Hill, Logan, "*Enfant terrible* Xavier Dolan is a director who really wants to act," *Vulture*, February 25, 2011, <http://www.vulture.com/2011/02/enfant_terrible_xavier_dolan_i.html> (accessed March 24, 2018).

Holmes, Su and Sean Redmond, *Framing Celebrity: New Directions in Celebrity Culture* (New York: Routledge, 2012).

Hurley, Erin, *National Performance: Representing Québec from Expo 67 to Céline Dion* (Toronto: University of Toronto Press, 2011), Kindle.

Hutcheon, Linda, *A Theory of Adaptation* (London: Routledge, 2006).

Jameson, Fredric, "Postmodernism and Consumer Society," in Hal Foster (ed.), *The Anti-Aesthetic: Essays on Postmodern Culture* (Seattle: Bay Press, 1983), pp. 111–25.

Jasmin, Claude, "Pour en finir avec le bon parler français!," *Claude Jasmin, écrivain—Point comme net*, August 28, 2001, <http://www.claudejasmin.com/wordpress/2001/08/28/pour-en-finir-avec-le-bon-parler-francais/> (accessed June 12, 2016).

Johnson, Colin R., Brian J. Gilley, and Mary L. Gray, "Introduction," in Mary L. Gray, Colin R. Johnson, and Brian J. Gilley (eds), *Queering the Countryside: New Frontiers in Queer Studies* (New York: New York University Press, 2016), pp. 1–23.

Judell, Brandon, "Mommy's boy: Xavier Dolan explains why women are like gay men," *HuffPost*, February 20, 2015, <https://www.huffingtonpost.com/brandon-judell/mommys-boy-xavier-dolan-e_b_6590548.html> (accessed July 10, 2018).

Kael, Pauline, "Raising Kane," *New Yorker*, February 20, 1971.

Kiang, Jessica, "Cannes review: Xavier Dolan's shrill, shrieking drama 'It's Only the End of the World,'" *Playlist*, May 18, 2016, <https://theplaylist.net/cannes-review-xavier-dolans-end-world-lea-seydoux-marion-cotillard-vincent-cassel-20160518/> (accessed June 24, 2018).

Knegt, Peter, "Xavier Dolan gets respect," *Film Quarterly*, 68/2, 2014, pp. 31–6.

Laforest, Daniel, "La banlieue dans l'imaginaire québécois. Problèmes originels et avenir critique," *Temps zéro*, 6, April 2013, <http://tempszero.contemporain.info/document945> (accessed February 27, 2016).

Lagarce, Jean-Luc, *Juste la fin du monde* (Québec: Hamacs, 2007).

Lamoureux, Diane, *L'Amère patrie: féminisme et nationalisme* (Montréal: Éditions Remue-ménage, 2001).

Lanz, Michelle and Cameron Kell, "Xavier Dolan talks about his Oedipal drama, 'Mommy,'" *Frame*, January 22, 2013, <http://www.scpr.org/programs/the-frame/2015/01/22/41203/xavier-dolan-talks-about-his-oedipal-drama-mommy/> (accessed March 24, 2018).

Laverdière, Gabriel, "L'esthétique rock queer, de C.R.A.Z.Y. à Xavier Dolan," *Nouvelles Vues*, 16, Spring-Summer 2015, <http://www.nouvellesvues.ulaval.ca/no-16-printemps-ete-2015-musique-rock-et-cinema-dirige-par-j-p-sirois-trahan-et-e-fillion/articles/lesthetique-rock-queer-de-crazy-a-xavier-dolan-par-gabriel-laverdiere/> (accessed February 27, 2016).

Lawson, Richard, "Xavier Dolan's *It's Only the End of the World* is the most disappointing film at Cannes," *Vanity Fair*, May 19, 2016, <https://www.vanityfair.com/hollywood/2016/05/xavier-dolan-its-only-the-end-of-the-world-review> (accessed June 24, 2018).

Lepastier, Joachim, "*Mommy* de Xavier Dolan: en fusion," *Cahiers du Cinéma*, 704, October 2014, pp. 6–9.

Létourneau, Jocelyn, *Que veulent vraiment les Québécois?* (Montréal: Boréal, 2006).

Létourneau, Jocelyn, "Le Québec, la révolution silencieuse," *Québec Studies*, 56, Winter 2013, pp. 97–111.

Loiselle, André, "*Look* like a worker and *act* like a worker: stereotypical representations of the working class in Quebec fiction feature films," in Malek Khouri and Darrell Varga (eds), *Working On Screen: Representations of the Working Class in Canadian Fiction Feature Films* (Toronto: University of Toronto Press, 2006), pp. 207–34.

Love, Heather, *Feeling Backward: Loss and the Politics of Queer History* (Cambridge: Harvard University Press, 2007).

McBride, Joseph, *Frank Capra: The Catastrophe of Success* (New York: Simon & Schuster, 1992).

McDermott, Patrick D., "The soundtrack to 'Mommy' is a music snob's worst nightmare," *Fader*, January 30, 2015, <http://www.the fader.com/2015/01/30/xavier-dolan-mommy> (accessed March 24, 2014).

Maddison, Stephen, "All about women: Pedro Almodóvar and the heterosocial dynamic," *Textual Practice*, 14/2, 2000, pp. 265–84.

Maddison, Stephen, *Fags, Hags and Queer Sisters: Gender Dissent and Heterosocial Bonds in Gay Culture* (New York: St. Martin's Press, 2000).

Magnier, Laure and Matthieu Amaré, "Xavier Dolan et le cinéma français: amour imaginaire?," *Café Babel*, December 6, 2011, <http://www.cafebabel.fr/culture/article/xavier-dolan-et-le-cinema-francais-amour-imaginaire.html> (accessed March 24, 2018).

Major, Ginette, *Le Cinéma québécois à la recherche d'un public: bilan d'une décennie 1970–1980* (Montréal: Presses de l'Université de Montréal, 1982).

Mandia, Valérie, "Le septième art hors des frontières nationales: le pouvoir de la langue et de l'imaginaire culturel dans les films du cinéaste québécois Xavier Dolan," *Francophonies d'Amérique*, 37, 2014, pp. 105–32.

Marks, Laura U., *Touch: Sensuous Theory and Multisensory Media* (Minneapolis: University of Minnesota Press, 2002).

Marshall, Bill, *Quebec National Cinema* (Montréal: McGill-Queen's University Press, 2001).

Marshall, Bill, "Interview with Bill Marshall," by Kester Dyer, Andrée Lafontaine, and Fulvia Massimi, Special issue, *Synoptique*, 4/2, Winter 2016, pp. 111–20, <http://synoptique.hybrid.concordia.ca/index.php/main/article/view/127/139> (accessed February 25, 2016).

Marshall, Bill, "Spaces and times of Québec in two films by Xavier Dolan," *Nottingham French Studies*, 55/2, 2016, pp. 189–208.

Martin, Adrian, *Mise-en-Scène and Film Style: From Classical Hollywood to New Media Art* (Basingstoke: Palgrave Macmillan, 2014).

Massimi, Fulvia, "'A boy's best friend is his mother': Quebec's matriarchy and queer nationalism in the cinema of Xavier Dolan," Special issue, *Synoptique*, 4/2, Winter 2016, pp. 8–31.

Mayhew, Susan, *A Dictionary of Geography*, 4th edn (Oxford: Oxford University Press, 2009).

Medhurst, Andy, "That special thrill: *Brief Encounter*, homosexuality and authorship," *Screen*, 32/2, July 1991, pp. 197–208.

Médioni, Gilles, "Xavier Dolan, le (ciné)fils prodige," *L'Express*, 3229, September 30, 2014.

Memmi, Albert, "Are the French Canadians colonized?," in *Dominated Man: Notes towards a Portrait*, trans. Jane Brooks (Boston: Beacon, 1969), pp. 72–83. [Published in French, Paris: Gallimard, 1968].

Mercier, Noémi, "Xavier Dolan: 'Tout est possible,'" *L'Actualité*, September 15, 2017, <https://lactualite.com/culture/2017/09/15/xavier-dolan-tout-est-possible/>.

Moifightclub, "VTOD: Dharam Paaji's *Sitamgar* > Xavier Dolan's *Mommy*," *F.I.G.H.T C.L.U.B.* (blog), October 24, 2014, <https://moifightclub.com/2014/10/24/votd-dharam-paajis-sitamgar-xavier-dolans-mommy/> (accessed August 8, 2017).

Mokkil, Navaneetha, "Queer encounters: film festivals and the sensual circuits of European cinema in India," *Studies in European Cinema*, 15/1, 2018, pp. 85–100.

Moran, Claire, *Staging the Artist: Performance and the Self-Portrait from Realism to Expressionism* (New York: Routledge, 2017).

Morrealle, Emiliano, "Le cinema vintage," trans. Lili Hinstin, *Cahiers du Cinéma*, 673, December 2011, pp. 16–19.

Murgue, Hermance, "Clip d'Indochine: Françoise Laborde (CSA) pour une interdiction aux moins de 16 ou 18 ans," *L'Express*, May 2, 2013, <https://www.lexpress.fr/actualite/medias /clip-d-indochine-francoise-laborde-csa-pour-une-interdiction-aux-moins-de-16-ou-18-ans_1245833.html> (accessed November 19, 2018).

Nadeau, Chantal, "*Barbaras en Québec*: variations on identity," in Kay Armatage, Kass Banning, Brenda Longfellow, and Janine Marchessault (eds), *Gendering the Nation: Canadian Women's Cinema* (Toronto: University of Toronto Press, 1999), pp. 197–211.

Natter, Wolfgang and John Paul Jones, "Signposts toward a poststructuralist geography," in John Paul Jones, Wolfgang Natter, and Theodore R. Schatzki (eds), *Postmodern Contentions: Epochs, Politics, Space* (New York: Guilford Press, 1993), pp. 165–203.

Nayman, Adam, "Imaginary love: Xavier Dolan's *Mommy*," *Cinema Scope*, 60, Fall 2014, pp. 46–9.

Nicoll, Allardyce, "Film reality: the cinema and the theatre," in Albert Cardullo(ed.), *State and Screen: Adaptation Theory From 1916 to 2000* (New York: Continuum, 2012), pp. 73–90.

Pidduck, Julianne, "The time of *The Hours*: queer melodrama and the dilemma of marriage," *Camera Obscura*, 28/1, Spring 2013, pp. 37–67.

Pidduck, Julianne, "The 'Affaire Jutra' and the figure of the child," *Jump Cut: A Review of Contemporary Media*, 58, Winter 2017–18.

Poirier, Christian, "Le cinéma québécois et la question identitaire. La confrontation entre les récits de l'empêchement de l'enchantement," *Recherches sociologiques*, 45/1, 2004, pp. 11–38.

Probyn, Elspeth, *Outside Belongings* (London: Routledge, 1996).

Probyn, Elspeth, "Bloody metaphors and other allegories of the ordinary," in Caren Kaplan, Norma Alarcón, and Minoo Moallem (eds), *Between Woman and Nation: Nationalisms, Transnational Feminisms, and the State* (Durham, NC: Duke University Press, 1999), pp. 47–62.

Protat, Zoé, "L'Amour fou: *Mommy* de Xavier Dolan," *Ciné-Bulles*, 32/3, Summer 2014, pp. 10–11.

Provencher, Denis M., *Queer Maghrebi French: Language, Temporalities, Transfiliations* (Liverpool: Liverpool University Press, 2017).

Quirot, Nicole, "Michel Tremblay: l'hymne au *joual*." *Bibliobs*, March 8, 2012, <https://bibliobs.nouvelobs.com/theatre/20120301.OBS2697/michel-tremblay-l-hymne-au-*joual*.html>.

Rachit, "A gripping tale about how far a mother would go for her son," *YKA: Youth Ki Awaaz* (blog), 2016, <https://www.youthkiawaaz.com/2016/05/comedy-drama-mommy-xavier-dolan/> (accessed September 27, 2017).

Radhakrishnan, Ratheesh, "Kim Ki Duk's Promise, Zanussi's Betrayal: film festival, world cinema and the subject of the region," *Inter-Asia Cultural Studies*, 17/2, 2016, pp. 206–22.

Rajadhyaksha, Ashish, "Why film narratives exist," *Inter-Asia Cultural Studies*, 14/1, 2013, pp. 67–75.

Rancière, Jacques, "It's up to you to invent the rest," interview by Stéphane Delorme and Dork Zabunyan, in Emiliano Battista (ed. and trans.), *Dissenting Words: Interviews with Jacques Rancière* (London: Bloomsbury, 2017), pp. 285–304.

Rees-Roberts, Nick, *Fashion Film: Art and Advertising in the Digital Age* (London: Bloomsbury, 2018).

Robert, Lucie, "L'impossible parole de femmes," in Gilbert David and Pierre Lavoie (eds), *Le monde de Michel Tremblay Tome II: Romans et récits*, 2nd edn (Carnières: Éditions Lansman, 2005), pp. 177–94.

Rooney, David, "Tom at the Farm: Venice review," *Hollywood Reporter*, September 2, 2013, <https://www.hollywoodreporter.com/review/tom-at-farm-venice-review-619296> (accessed July 6, 2018).

Rosello, Mireille, *France and the Maghreb: Performative Encounters* (Gainesville: University of Florida Press, 2005).

Rothberg, Michael, *Multidirectional Memory: Remembering the Holocaust in the Age of Decolonization* (Stanford, CA: Stanford University Press, 2009).

Rousseau, Alexandre Fontaine, "Culte de la personnalité: le cinéma de Xavier Dolan," *24 images*, 173, September 2015, pp. 11–13.

Roux, Annelise, "'Juste la fin du monde': l'impossible Annonce faite à Martine," *La République du cinéma*, September 20, 2016, <http://larepubliqueducinema.com/juste-la-fin-du-monde-limpossible-annonce-faite-martine/> (accessed March 15, 2018).

Rouyer, Philippe and Yann Tobin, "Entretien avec Xavier Dolan: 'Je me pose des questions sur chaque plan,'" *Positif*, 644, October 2014, pp. 17–22.

Saint-Martin, Lori, *Le nom de la mère: mères, filles et écriture dans la littérature québécoise au féminin* (Montréal: Éditions Nota bene, 1999).

Sarkar, Mela, "'Ousqu'on chill à soir?' Pratiques multilingues comme stratégies identitaires dans la communauté hip hop montréalais," Supplement, *Diversité urbaine*, Fall 2008, pp. 27–44.

Sarris, Andrew, "Notes on the auteur theory in 1962," *Film Culture*, 27, Winter 1962–3, pp. 1–8.

Sarris, Andrew, *The American Cinema: Directors and Directions 1929–1968* (New York: Stanford Dutton, 1968).

Schehr, Lawrence R., *Parts of an Andrology: On Representations of Men's Bodies* (Sanford, CA: Stanford University Press, 1997).

Schneider, Vanessa, "L'exception Dolan," *M Le Magazine du Monde*, May 28, 2016.

Schultz, Corey Kai Nelson, "The sensation of the look: the gazes in *Laurence Anyways*," *Film Philosophy* 22/1, February 2018, pp. 1–20.

Schwartzwald, Robert, "Fear of federasty: Québec's inverted fictions," in Hortense J. Spillers (ed.), *Comparative American Identities: Race, Sex and Nationality in the Modern Text* (New York: Routledge, 1991), pp. 175–95.

Schwartzwald, Robert, "'Symbolic' homosexuality, 'false feminine' and the problematics of identity in Québec," in Michael Warner (ed.), *Fear of a Queer Planet* (Minneapolis: University of Minnesota Press, 1993), pp. 264–99.

Schwartzwald, Robert, "Explorations of suburban non-space in Stéphane Lafleur's *Continental*," *Québec Studies*, 48, Fall 2009/Winter 2010, pp. 25–34.

Sedgwick, Eve Kosofsky, *Tendencies* (London: Routledge, 1994).

Sellier, Geneviève, *Masculine Singular: French New Wave Cinema*, trans. Kristin Ross (Durham, NC: Duke University Press, 2008).

Simmel, Georg, "The problem of style," *Theory, Culture and Society*, 8/63, 1991, pp. 63–71.

Singer, Leigh, "Ten great modern films shot in Academy ratio," *British Film Institute*, updated August 10, 2017, <http://www.bfi.org.uk/news-opinion/news-bfi/lists/10-great-modern-films-shot-43-academy-ratio> (accessed October 2, 2017).

Sirois-Trahan, Jean-Pierre, "La mouvée et son dehors: renouveau du cinéma québécois," *Cahiers du Cinéma*, 660, October 2010, pp. 76–8.

Sirois-Trahan, Jean-Pierre, "Table ronde: le renouveau du cinéma d'auteur québécois," *24 images*, 152, June–July 2011, pp. 14–22.

Sirois-Trahan, Jean-Pierre, "Table ronde sur le renouveau du cinéma québécois," *Nouvelles Vues*, 12, Spring-Summer 2011, pp. 1–37, <http://www.nouvellesvues.ulaval.ca/le-renouveau-dirige-par-jean-pierre-sirois-trahan/table-ronde-sur-le-renouveau-du-cinema-dauteur-quebecois-avec-martin-bilodeau-philippe-gajan-marcel-jean-germain-lacasse-sylvain-lavallee-marie-claude-loiselle-et-jean-pierre-sirois-trahan-organisee-par-bruno-dequen/>.

Smart, Patricia, *Écrire dans la maison du père: l'émergence du féminine dans la tradition littéraire du Québec* (Montréal: XYZ éditeur, 2003).

Smith Paul Julian, "Almodóvar's self-fashioning: the economics and aesthetics of deconstructive autobiography," in Marvin D'Lugo and Kathleen M. Vernon (eds), *A Companion to Pedro Almodóvar* (Cambridge: Blackwell Publishing, 2013), pp. 21–38.

Sobchack, Vivian, *The Address of the Eye: A Phenomenology of Film Experience* (Princeton, NJ: Princeton University Press, 1992).

Sontag, Susan, "Notes on 'Camp,'" in *Against Interpretation and Other Essays* (New York: Octagon Books, 1978), pp. 272–89.

Sontag, Susan, "Notes on 'Camp,'" in *Against Interpretation* (London: Vintage, 1994), pp. 275–92.

Staiger, Janet, "Authorship studies and Gus Van Sant," *Film Criticism*, 29/1, Fall 2004, pp. 1–22.

Stam, Robert, *Literature and Film: A Guide to the Theory and Practice of Film Adaptation* (Malden: Blackwell, 2005).

Stam, Robert, *Literature Through Film: Realism, Magic, and the Art of Adaptation* (Malden: Blackwell, 2005).

Stein, Joel, "The me me me generation," *Time Magazine*, May 20, 2013.

Stockton, Kathryn Bond, *The Queer Child, or Growing Sideways in the Twentieth Century*, Series Q (Durham, NC: Duke University Press, 2009).

Taylor, Diane, *Performance* (Durham, NC: Duke University Press, 2016).

Taylor, Kate, "'Psychologically scarred' millennials are killing countless industries from napkins to Applebee's—here are the businesses they like the least," *Business Insider*, October 31, 2017, <https://www.businessinsider.com/millennials-are-killing-list-2017-8> (accessed October 31, 2018).

Tétu, Martin, "L'assistance aux films québécois sous la bare des 10%," *Optique culture*, no. 1, Institut de la statistique du Québec, Observatoire de la culture et des communications du Québec, February 2011, <http://www.stat.gouv.qc.ca/observatoire>.

Todorov, Tzvetan, "The categories of literary narrative," trans. Joseph Kestner, *Papers on Language and Literature*, 16, 1980, pp. 3–36.

Tremblay-Daviault, Christiane, *Un cinéma orphelin: structures mentales et sociales du cinéma québécois (1942–1953)* (Montréal: Éditions Québec/Amérique, 1981).

Trépanier-Jobin, Gabrielle, "Le Cinéma québécois: un succès réel ou imaginé?," *Nouvelles Vues*, 9, Autumn 2008, <http://www.nouvellesvues.ulaval.ca/fileadmin/nouvelles_vues/fichiers/Numero9/TrepanierNVCQ9.pdf>.

Tessé, Jean-Philippe, "Aller plus haut," *Cahiers du Cinéma*, 680, July–August 2012, pp. 40–2.

Vacante, Jeffery, "Writing the history of sexuality and 'national' history in Quebec," *Journal of Canadian Studies*, 39/2, 2005, pp. 31–55.

Vacante, Jeffery, "Liberal nationalism and the challenge of masculinity studies in Quebec," *Left History*, 11/2, 2006, pp. 96–117.

Valck, Marijke de, *Film Festivals: From European Geopolitics to Global Cinephilia* (Amsterdam: Amsterdam University Press, 2007).

Vaughan, Hannah, "Filming fracture in Xavier Dolan's *J'ai tué ma mère*," Special issue, *Québec Studies*, Winter 2013, pp. 107–15.

Viviani, Christian, "Mai en cinéma: morose mois de mai," *Positif*, 641/642, July/August 2014, pp. 134–37.

Waugh, Thomas, *The Romance of Transgression in Canada: Queering Sexualities, Nations, Cinemas* (Montréal: McGill-Queen's University Press, 2006).

Weiner, Joshua J. and Damon Young (eds), "Introduction: queer bonds," Special issue, *GLQ*, 17/2–3, 2011, pp. 223–41.

Weinmann, Heinz, *Du Canada au Québec: Généalogie d'une histoire* (Montréal: Éditions de l'Hexagone, 1987).

Weinmann, Heinz, *Cinéma de l'imaginaire québécois: De La Petite Aurore à Jésus de Montréal* (Montréal: Éditions de l'Hexagone, 1990).

Weissberg, Jay, "I Killed My Mother," *Variety*, May 18, 2009, <http://variety.com/2009/film/markets-festivals/i-killed-my-mother-1200474797/>.

Wigley, Samuel, "Laurence Anyways," review of *Laurence Anyways*, directed by Xavier Dolan, *Sight & Sound*, 22/1, 2012, p. 95.

Willmore, Alison, "The 25-year-old filmmaker who's the king of Cannes," *Buzzfeed*, May 22, 2014, <https://www.buzzfeed.com/alisonwillmore/the-25-year-old-filmmaker-whos-the-king-of-cannes> (accessed March 24, 2018).

Wilson, Carl, *Céline Dion's Let's Talk About Love: A Journey to the End of Taste* (33 1/3) (London: Continuum, 2007).

Withenshaw, Anne Marie, "Les femmes de Dolan," *HuffPost*, Edition QC, February 7, 2012, <https://quebec.huffingtonpost.ca/anne-marie-withenshaw/xavier-dolan-lawrence-anyways_b_1237021.html>.

Wittmann, Henri, "Le *joual*, c'est-tu un créole?," *La Linguistique*, 9/2, 1973, pp. 83–93.

Wollen, Peter, *Signs and Meaning in the Cinema* (London: Secker & Warburg/British Film Institute, 1969).

Wollen, Peter, *Raiding the Icebox: Reflections on Twentieth-Century Culture* (London: Verso, 1993).

Index